Meinde Pfullbarke
September 2018

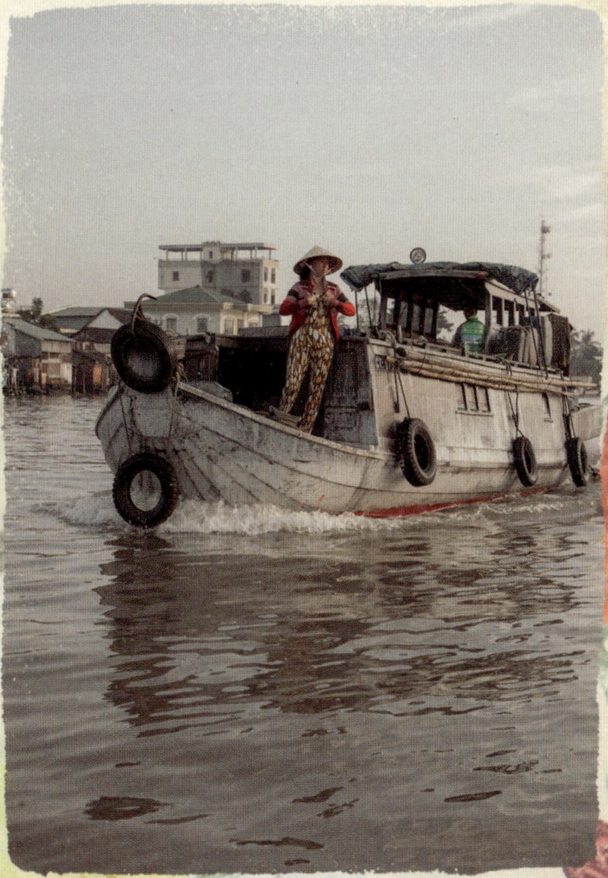

PROVENCE TO PONDICHERRY

TESSA KIROS

Photography by Manos Chatzikonstantis
Styling by Michail Touros

quadrille

CONTENTS

French threads 6

PROVENCE 11

GUADELOUPE 55

VIETNAM 93

PONDICHERRY 143

LA RÉUNION 199

NORMANDY 243

Index 284

FRENCH THREADS

On a journey to Paris, I watched a family travelling with a beautiful collection of baskets. The mother was dark and freckled. I wondered where they were from, and so I asked them: The baskets – Laos. And the family – she was born in Martinique, to a father from Guadeloupe and a Parisian mother, and grew up in Paris, where she met her husband – pure French. And here they were – bringing home baskets and other treasures from around the world.

Paris and other parts of France are now such an assemblage – a fascinating mix. The airport in Paris is a bustling commotion. Around me there are women with madras cotton cloths on their heads and knotted foulards, travelling to their homeland for the summer. Entire extended families upping and downing, from the métropole that they now call home to other départements scattered around the world. Some are carrying breadfruits back from Guadeloupe, palm hearts from La Réunion, and green mangoes and other parcels of speciality. It is incredible to see – a tapestry so richly intertwined from so many traditions and cultures around the world. Stitched together with French threads.

In the 1600s France began forming trading companies, establishing overseas colonies to compete with Spain, Portugal, the United Provinces (Holland) and Britain. Other than financial gain and imperial prestige, spreading Catholicism as well as the French language and culture were among the objectives. Trade routes to the Far East and the Americas were established, and new and exotic foods were brought back to Europe by the shipload.

Potatoes, tomatoes, fresh peppers and maize were among the first and exciting discoveries from the New World. Spices such as cloves, nutmeg and pepper had been arriving overland from the East for awhile, and were already customary in European cuisine. But it was the challenge to find more economical routes to the spice trade of the East that motivated the great seafarers.

Not all trade was in unusual ingredients. The new territories also provided land to cultivate products like tobacco, wheat and sugar, which were in increasing demand in Europe. As settlements flourished, produce from Europe travelled to the colonies and a market for European goods grew. Immigrants brought back familiar foods with them and introduced their own flavours, and so began the weaving of one cuisine into another – a blending of spices, methods and tastes that quietly settled into the culture at each end of the voyage.

Later, with the breaking up of France's colonial Empire, several of the colonies were lost to war or independence. Others were incorporated into France as overseas departments – these départements and territoires d'outre-mer remaining today as part of the French Union.

My own journey began in Provence, with my appreciation of the fabrics, colours and patterns. I thought about my first trip to India and the details and designs of the cottons there. How one inspires and connects to another. How a loaf of bread in France can become an everyday essential in a country half a world away. I had been dreaming of the sun of Provence and the mist of Normandy, located respectively on the shores of the Mediterranean and the Atlantic Ocean. These two places, among others, provided continental France with access to travel the world. I had listened to stories about fascinating faraway places, where French governors had been deposited and where fragrant fruits and wonderful people mingled with the scents of cinnamon and ginger.

I wanted to go to some of these places where French explorers had established colonies. Dragging hessian sacks and wooden tea crates filled with fine porcelain across oceans, to settle their families and display their wares far off in tropical temperatures under whirring ceiling fans in vanilla and rum ambiences. I wanted to discover the foods and flavours and how these had been mixed with different traditions and new lands.

Traces of the French zest for adventure are today sprinkled across the world map. The places I am instinctively drawn to, with their lyrical names and evocative images, are all reached by water. An obvious consequence of the seafaring nature of colonialism, this has also given these places a cuisine laden with ingredients from the sea. It is lovely to see how iridescent fish, mussels and crayfish can be common to all these places but arrive at the table as ambassadors to their nation. Flambéed in rum, simmered in tomatoes and spices, steeped in saffron or a splash of coconut cream – the result is a dish true to its homeland, and yet undeniably tied to another nation.

This is a collection of recipes from my travels to some of these places.

INTRODUCTION

PROVENCE *PROVENÇA* *PROUVENCO*	*SOUTHERN FRANCE*
MOST SEEN ACTIVITY: BOULES	*CAPITAL: MARSEILLE*
PROVENÇAL-OCCITAN DIALECT	*SEA: MEDITERRANEAN*
PRODUCES: OLIVES, OLIVE OIL, LAVENDER, HERBS, PASTIS, PEPPERS, HONEY, ALMONDS, NOUGAT, BLACK TRUFFLES	*MISTRAL WIND*

PROVENCE

** SCATTER
2 TABLESPOONS
SOFT GOAT'S CHEESE
WITH HERBES DE
PROVENCE, TOP WITH
HEAPED TEASPOON OF
LAVENDER HONEY
& A GOOD GRIND
OF BLACK PEPPER*

PROVENCE

HERE IS WHERE MY JOURNEY BEGAN,

THE PLACE THAT DREW MY THOUGHTS OF LONG SEA VOYAGES

AND TRADING WITH FOREIGN LANDS TOGETHER.

I am lucky that I live near enough to Provence to be able to drive there on a whim for an almond croissant, or bouillabaisse. And come home then, with baskets of treasures, resources and tales of aïoli.

Provincia Romana – the first Roman province outside Italy – became Provence. It has been a part of France since 1481, but still retains its own very strong cultural identity and dialect, particularly noticeable in the smaller villages. Its capital Marseille, a main town and port, was, along with Toulon, a major gateway for the French empire to North Africa and the Orient, for the exchange of exotic spices and produce.

There are lemons and oranges in Menton, the first town I arrive in. I stop in Nice for socca from the market in the old town. It's well worth the traffic: they are crisp, paper-thin and well seasoned. The cook scuffs off pieces from her huge pan and settles them into a paper cone for me, scattering enough finely ground pepper over to make the chest burn. "Eat it here and now," she says to me a couple of times. She even breaks off from serving her next customer to tell me again, that I must eat it while it is still warm.

Further on there are grilled peppers with anchoïade and tapenade. Fresh goat's cheese salad and beautiful, more mature goat's cheese to sample that leave a tingling in the mouth for a while after the last bite. There are salted as well as sweet chard tarts and stuffed mini vegetables on display.

Everywhere, people are drinking pastis. Flocking to Saint-Tropez for Tarte Tropezienne – a soft brioche-type pastry filled with crème, gleaming from its eggwash and crowned with sugar crystals. I love the very small ones that immediately vanish in the mouth. In Grasse there are large fougasses with orange flower water, and further on calissons – sweets made of candied fruit and almonds. There are nuts, nougats, sorbets and glaces of every flavour.

• •

I don't know how they organized this, but you could pick on any occasion, blindfolded, any number of dishes from the Provençal repertoire and they would all work well together. It's the same with the fabrics. Initially they may seem mismatched, but you can heap any amount of them together, and it all just works. The colourful tians and ratatouilles piled into ceramic dishes and laid out on the fabrics. They look just right. Maybe it's to do with the combinations in the landscape – the stones and water. And that light. Other than having such a hand in the prime materials, it also manages to age the backdrop and furniture perfectly.

It was a good thing, then, that the inhabitants of the rugged scrub and open landscape were able to shuffle their land and produce the wonders they did. The olives stacked up on pissaladières, the oils mashed with garlic – pounded and whipped into glistening sauces. Wild herbs gathered from all round and scattered year long into roasts and vegetables. Small things that turn a meal from the ordinary into a masterpiece.

If you write down the dishes of Provence onto bits of paper, mix them up, pick one, then a couple more – then mingle the whole lot together – you will see. How you can slide one into another, swap one for the other. The colours, the fabrics, the food. Seamless. Nothing is out of place. Quite extraordinary. Chapeau!

· ·

On I drive, through endless miles of nothing and beauty. It is not easy to approach a cuisine from the outside. To feel the heartbeat of a nation's cooking. But as an outsider you can always observe.

We always knew. I had always read of these Provençal images: the closed shutters, sun shining through the leaves of the plane trees and their shadows that fell onto surfaces. The sounds of cicadas and pastis glasses scattered on bar tops. Life flowing from one calm day into another…

It is hard to fault anything really. It is overwhelming how understated everything is. It is as though they sat and discussed things here, thought everything through thoroughly. The olive trees. Faded buildings blending in with pale trees that flank the streets and boules squares. Different markets every day. Anchovies, herbs, figs, brocante – colours and furniture I want to drag home with me. Inspiration and beauty every single day.

· ·

I had my second lemon tart of the day, leaving France on my way home. As I was walking to my car a young man asked me: "Vous êtes d'ici? Vous connaissez le romarin?" (If only he knew how much I love rosemary!). The chef had sent him out to collect it, so I helped him search amongst the wild shrubs and flowers growing near the sea. His face lit up when we found it and he dashed off, with an armful of the blossoming herb.

I left then, my hands perfumed with rosemary, happy to have made a small culinary contribution to France.

PROVENCE

MOULES AU PISTOU

Here mussels are cooked with a little tomato and then served with a splash of pistou, the garlicky basil purée characteristic of Provence. The pistou is best made fresh, but if you are making it ahead, make sure you serve it at room temperature. You will need nice wide serving bowls and a couple of empty bowls on the table for the mussel shells.
Serve with long halves of toasted baguette.

Serves 2

1.2kg (2½lb) mussels
2 tablespoons olive oil
1 garlic clove, peeled
185ml (¾ cup) tomato passata
60ml (¼ cup) white wine
a few stems of parsley
salt and freshly ground black pepper

For the pistou
1 garlic clove, roughly chopped
a handful basil leaves
2 tablespoons olive oil

De-beard the mussels, then scrub them with a brush under cold running water, discarding any that are open and don't close when tapped sharply on the kitchen counter.

Heat the olive oil and garlic together in a small saucepan and, when the garlic starts to smell good, add the tomato and a grind or two of black pepper. Cover and simmer for about 5 minutes, then remove from the heat and keep warm.

To make the pistou, put the garlic and basil in a blender or food processor. Pulse, adding the oil gradually. Season with a grinding of pepper and just a dash of salt (the mussels will be salty).

Heat a large, wide pan over a high heat and tip in the cleaned mussels. Add the wine and parsley, cover and cook until the mussels open up. Remove from the heat and discard any that have not opened. Holding the mussels back with a slotted spoon, pour about 125ml (½ cup) of the cooking liquid into a bowl. (You won't need the rest here.)

Add the tomato sauce with the saved liquid to the mussel pot. Return to the heat for a minute or so, turning through gently with a large spoon, to mingle the flavours.

Spoon into wide bowls and dollop a generous tablespoon or so of pistou over each. Before eating, mix the pistou through the mussels and tomato sauce.

PASTIS

This makes a good-sized aperitif, rather than a single swig. Pour 25ml (5 teaspoons) pastis into a long glass and add about 100ml (3½fl oz) cold water, followed by 4 or 5 ice cubes.

HERBES DE PROVENCE

You can add any other fresh herbs to this mixture – tarragon or oregano, for example. It is lovely to have a jar of this in your kitchen, to add layers of flavour to any dish. It stores well, providing the herbs are all thoroughly dried.

Makes about ¾ cup

2 tablespoons thyme leaves
3 tablespoons marjoram
3 tablespoons savory
2 teaspoons chopped rosemary
1 teaspoon chopped sage

Put the herbs on a tray lined with paper towels and leave to dry completely.

Crumble up the dried herbs and mix together well. Put into an airtight jar and store in a dark, cool spot.

PAN BAGNAT

A lovely lunch, that actually improves if you leave it sitting for a while. I make the filling and then leave it to mingle in the fridge for a while before heaping it between the bread. You can then leave it again to dampen, or wrap it to eat later. You can adjust the filling, adding other ingredients if you like.

Serves 4

1 baguette
For the filling
½ red onion, peeled and sliced
1 garlic clove, peeled and finely chopped
200g (7oz) large cherry tomatoes, each cut into 4
2 tablespoons capers in vinegar, drained
12 pitted green olives, halved
4 large anchovy fillets in oil, drained, chopped
100g (½ cup) tuna in oil, drained
20–30g (1 oz) celery, sliced
a couple of radishes, sliced
4 tablespoons olive oil
sea salt and freshly ground black pepper
Tabasco green jalapeno pepper sauce or other
  chilli sauce, to taste

Put all the filling ingredients, except the Tabasco, in a bowl with a few grinds of pepper and a little salt (allow for the anchovies). Mix well, then taste and adjust the seasoning. Cover and leave for at least a couple of hours in the fridge.

Cut the baguette into 4 lengths and split each in half. Lightly press in the filling and shake in some Tabasco or other chilli sauce. Put the baguette tops on and squash together. Eat now or later.

TAPENADE

This is delicious and versatile; it comes in many different versions – from smooth to quite chunky. You can vary the quantities in the ingredients, adding and adjusting to suit your tastes. Les Filles du Pâtissier, a charming restaurant in Saint-Rémy, make a lovely one with almonds. Tapenade is delicious spread on toasted baguette and served with an apéritif. Or serve as a starter, with chunks of fresh vegetables – chicory, fennel, radishes – and boiled eggs and goat's cheese.

Make sure that you like the flavour of the olives from the start, and that they are not too salty and intense as this will make the result here.

Makes about 1 cup

½ garlic clove
½ teaspoon finely grated lemon zest
3 thyme sprigs, leaves stripped
3 anchovy fillets in oil (10g), drained and broken up
1 heaped tablespoon capers in vinegar, drained
150g (1½ cups) pitted black olives
2 tablespoons olive oil, plus extra if needed
1 teaspoon lemon juice
1 tablespoon chopped parsley
freshly ground black pepper

Pulp the garlic in a pestle and mortar, or mash to a paste on a chopping board. Pound in the lemon zest, then the thyme leaves.

Put the anchovies and capers into a blender and pulse briefly. Add the olives and pulse with 1 tablespoon of the oil until combined but the olives still have some texture. Add the garlic and lemon zest mix, the lemon juice, parsley, some black pepper and the remaining tablespoon of olive oil.

Pulse again briefly to combine, so that it comes together. Spoon into a bowl for serving, stirring in a little more olive oil if you think it's needed. (If your olives are very intense, add a little more lemon juice.)

Store covered in the fridge. It's also good the next day, when the flavours have mingled.

PISTOUNADE

This is like a tapenade, and lovely spread onto bread. It is also delicious served with grilled fish, or stirred through pasta or boiled potatoes, or even into a salad. You will need 200g (2 cups) pitted green olives and a large handful of basil. Put three-quarters of the olives into a blender. Add 1 crushed garlic clove, 1 tablespoon capers in vinegar (drained), 3 tablespoons olive oil and half the basil. Pulse to small bits. Add the rest of the olives and basil and pulse briefly, leaving some small pieces. Season with black pepper to taste and more olive oil of you think it is needed.

PISSALADIÈRE

I cook the onions without any salt, as I love the contrast of almost sweet onions and a sudden rush of salty anchovy and olive. This is also very good with some crushed tomato (or slices) added to the base before the anchovies and olives (which should be top quality). If your anchovy fillets are large, then halve the number and slice each in half lengthways.

Serves 4–6

For the dough
1 sachet (7g/1½ teaspoons) dried yeast
a pinch of sugar
150ml (⅔ cup) tepid water
250g (2 cups) plain (all-purpose) flour
2 pinches of salt
1 tablespoon olive oil

For the topping
about 7 tablespoons olive oil
4 large onions (800g/1¾lb), thinly sliced
1 tablespoon thyme leaves, stripped from their stalks
about 24 (not too large) anchovy fillets in oil, drained
about 18 whole pitted black olives
freshly ground black pepper

In a wide bowl, dissolve the yeast and sugar in the water, then whisk in a handful of the flour. Cover with a cloth and leave for 30 minutes or so until it froths up.

Add the rest of the flour, the salt and olive oil. Transfer the dough to the work surface and knead well. Scatter a little flour into the bottom of the bowl and return the dough to it. Make a slash on the top of the dough and cover the bowl with a clean cloth. Leave for 1½ hours, or until doubled in size.

For the topping, heat 4 tablespoons olive oil in a large frying pan over a low-medium heat. Add the onions and thyme leaves and sauté gently for about 20 minutes to soften. Remove from the heat.

Drizzle 1 tablespoon olive oil into a shallow baking sheet, about 33 x 28cm (13 x 11in), and spread it with your hands to cover the base. Gently knead the dough down in the bowl, then stretch it out into a rough rectangle and transfer to the baking sheet. Using both palms, ease the dough towards the corners of the tray.

Spread the sautéed onions evenly over the dough, almost to the edges, pressing them into the dough so they adhere a little.

Arrange the anchovies in a criss-cross pattern and place an olive in the centre of each diamond. Drizzle a couple of tablespoons more oil evenly over top and give a good grinding of pepper.

Leave to rise for 30 minutes or so while you heat the oven to 200°C/400°F/Gas 6.

Bake for about 30 minutes, until the base is cooked all over (check the middle) and the top is golden here and there with a slight charring in places, taking care not to overcook it as it will dry out. Cut into pieces and eat while still warm.

TARTE À LA TOMATE

This simple summer tart relies on beautiful, ripe tomatoes – there is not much else to hide behind here. I like to serve it plain with a salad on the side and some goat's cheese.

Serves 4–6

125g (4½oz) chilled unsalted butter, diced
125g (1 cup) plain (all-purpose) flour,
 plus extra for dusting
about 2½ tablespoons iced water
650g (1lb 7oz) ripe tomatoes,
 sliced 4–5mm (¼in) thick
a few thyme sprigs, leaves stripped
coarse salt, such as Camargue

Rub the butter into the flour in a bowl with your fingertips to give a coarse sandy texture. Scatter in a couple of pinches of salt and add enough iced water to bring the dough together into a rough ball with your hands.

Scatter a little flour over the work surface, turn the dough out and spread it with your hands or roll with a rolling pin to a rough rectangular shape. Fold it over on itself as for a letter, and roll it out again. Repeat 4 or 5 times more (no need to chill it between rolls). Wrap in plastic wrap and chill for at least 30 minutes.

Lightly flour a 24cm (9½in) springform cake tin and preheat the oven to 190°C/375°/Gas 5. Place a baking sheet, wide enough to fit the springform tin, on the middle shelf.

Roll out the pastry on a lightly floured surface, not pressing too much, to a circle slightly larger than the base of the tin, about 28cm (11in) in diameter. Carefully lift it into the tin, taking it up the sides by 6cm (2½in) before folding it over to create a 2–3cm (¾–1¼in) high border.

Lay the tomato slices across the pastry as though you were dealing a pack of cards on a gaming table – spread them out to where they fall, overlapping and with no spaces (or you can arrange them in overlapping concentric circles, starting from the middle). Scatter the thyme leaves over the tomatoes, sprinkle with salt and a little pepper, if you like, and set it on the baking sheet in the oven.

Bake for 45–50 minutes, until the pastry is golden and the tomatoes are tinged with colour here and there. Turn the oven up to 200°C/400°F/Gas 6 and bake for a further 10 minutes, or until the tomatoes are deeper in colour and thinly charred in places. There will probably still be a little liquid on top of the tomatoes, which is fine.

Remove the tart on its baking sheet from the oven and set the tin on a rack, so that any liquid will fall into the sheet. Remove the outer ring from the tart case as soon as it is cool enough to handle.

Serve slightly cooled or at room temperature, with an extra sprinkling of salt for the crunch and, if you like, a drizzle of olive oil.

BOUILLABAISSE

A true bouillabaisse from Marseille includes rascasse (rockfish) from the surrounding waters, but it seems that everyone has their own particular favourite way of making and serving the dish. For the broth you will need fish bones and small whole fish, then two or three different types of fillets for serving, along with some shellfish.

The dish can be served all together in a big bowl, or the broth separately with croûtons, and the fish on a platter, with bowls of rouille and/or aïoli on the side for spreading onto the toasted bread. If you love garlic, serve a couple of extra cloves on the side to stab your fork into and rub on the toasted bread. The only real protocol is to use very fresh fish and to serve the dish hot, on the day you make it. It will need something light, such as a salad, to accompany it.

Serves 4

For the rouille
1 small red (bell) pepper
2 ripe tomatoes, 80g (3oz) each, halved lengthways
4 garlic cloves, unpeeled
1 thick slice of white bread (about 20g/¾oz), crusts removed and torn
a pinch each of saffron threads and paprika
2 pinches of cayenne
75ml (⅓ cup) light olive oil
salt and freshly ground pepper

For the broth
2 litres (8 cups) water
600g (1¼lb) fish bones and heads, and small soupfish, cleaned
60g (⅔ cup) celery, cut into 2 or 3 pieces
1 onion, unpeeled, halved
60g (¼) leek, cut into 2–3 pieces
a small bundle of parsley
a small bundle of thyme
a couple of fennel fronds
2 bay leaves
2 garlic cloves, peeled
1 tablespoon olive oil
2 teaspoons coarse salt
a few black peppercorns

For the base
4 tablespoons olive oil
40g (scant 1 cup) leek, roughly chopped
100g (¾ cup) shallots, chopped
8 prawn (shrimp) heads (from the prawns used later)
60ml (¼ cup) pastis
125ml (½ cup) white wine
400g (14oz) very ripe tomatoes, peeled and chopped (or use tinned)
1 tablespoon tomato purée
2 good pinches of saffron threads
a pinch of chilli powder

For the fish
½ fennel bulb
4 small potatoes, peeled and sliced into 8mm (⅜ in) rounds
40g (⅓ cup) celery, thickly sliced
40g (⅓ cup) leek, thickly sliced
300g (10½oz) each of 3 different fish fillets, such as gurnard, cod, John Dory, sea bass, monkfish, snapper or mullet, each cut into 4 serving pieces
8 large prawns (shrimp), peeled and cleaned, tails left on
16 mussels, scrubbed, de-bearded and rinsed
1 tablespoon chopped parsley

To serve
about 16 slices of baguette (cut slightly on the diagonal)
olive oil, for drizzling
aïoli (page 29)

PROVENCE

To make the rouille, preheat the oven to 220°C/425°F/Gas 8. Line a small dish with foil and put the pepper, tomato halves, cut side up, and the garlic cloves on the foil. Scatter very little salt over the tomatoes and garlic. Roast until deep golden and charred here and there, turning the pepper over a couple of times so it darkens on all sides. Make sure the juices from the tomatoes have dried out.

Remove and cool, then put the tomatoes into a blender. Squeeze the garlic cloves out of their skins into the blender. Remove the skin and seeds from the pepper and put the flesh into the blender, shaking away the liquid first. Add the bread and pulse until completely smooth, then tip in the saffron, paprika and cayenne. Blend to thicken.

Now add the olive oil a little at a time, blending until all the olive oil is incorporated and you have quite a thick purée. Season with salt and pepper, pulsing to combine. Taste and add extra cayenne or paprika if you think it needs it. If making ahead of time, store in the fridge but bring it to room temperature for serving.

To make the broth, put all the ingredients in a stockpot and bring to a gentle boil. Simmer over a low heat, uncovered, for 30 minutes, skimming the surface when necessary. Strain, gently pressing down on the solids in the sieve with a wooden spoon to extract as much flavour as possible. Discard the solids and set aside 1 litre (1 quart) of the broth; save the rest for another dish.

To make the base, heat the oil in a large, wide (this is important) pan. Add the leek, shallot and prawn heads and sauté for about 10 minutes, until the shallots are soft and starting to turn golden, and the prawn heads are deeply coloured. Add the pastis, let it simmer a little, then add the wine and cook until it has almost all reduced, then remove the prawn heads and discard. Add the tomatoes, tomato purée, saffron, chilli powder and a little salt, and simmer for about 10 minutes. Add 250ml (1 cup) of the reserved fish broth and cook for a minute or two. Blend until completely smooth and return the purée to the pan. Stir in the remaining reserved broth and bring to the boil.

Cut the fennel vertically into 8 wedges, keeping them joined at the base. Add the fennel, potato, celery and leek to the pan and simmer, covered, for 7–8 minutes. Increase the heat, add the fish fillets and cook rapidly, uncovered, for 3–4 minutes. Add the prawns, cook until they change colour before finally adding the mussels, plunging them down in the broth with a slotted spoon. When they have all opened (discard those which won't), scatter the parsley over and keep hot without cooking further.

Meanwhile, have the oven preheated to 180°C/350°F/Gas 4. Line a baking sheet with baking paper and spread the baguette slices on it. Drizzle a little olive oil over the slices and a small scattering of salt. Toast in the oven until golden, turning them over to brown evenly, then remove.

To serve, put the rouille into a bowl and the aïoli in a separate bowl – or you can give each person small individual bowls of each. Put the baguette slices in a basket. Into each of 4 warmed, deep soup bowls, put a fillet of each type of fish, 3 or 4 potato slices, 2 fennel wedges, 4 mussels and a couple of prawns. Ladle in some of the hot broth. Give a small scattering of black pepper and salt over the fish and potatoes.

Everyone can choose how they eat this; maybe a dab of aïoli over a potato and fish; a dollop of rouille on a baguette slice floated on top. Any way, it is a lovely adventure.

BRANDADE DE MORUE

I love the rich simplicity of this creamy, garlicky salt cod and mashed potato dish, which makes a good starter or light main course. I like to serve it with a green side salad dressed with lemon and olive oil. Some brandade can be eaten with a spoon; some can be spread onto crisp baguette slices.

Salt cod needs to be soaked in cold water for at least 24 hours, changing the water a few times. You can vary the proportions of salt cod to potato. I find these amounts here a nice balance. If you prefer a less strong taste of garlic – boil the whole peeled cloves together with the potatoes for the last 10 minutes of their cooking time, then mash them together with the potatoes.

Serves 8

1 salt cod fillet (about 700g/1½lb), soaked
5 garlic cloves, peeled
200ml (scant 1 cup) cream
1 teaspoon thyme leaves
750g (26oz) potatoes, peeled
4 tablespoons olive oil
1–2 tablespoons breadcrumbs
1 baguette, sliced thinly (about 5 slices per person)
about 1 tablespoon unsalted butter, for frying
Camargue or other crunchy sea salt
freshly ground black pepper

Soak the salt cod fillet in cold water for at least 24 hours, changing the water 2 or 3 times. Drain and remove the skin. Bring a saucepan of water to the boil. Add the cod fillet, bring back to the boil, then lower the heat and simmer gently for 10–15 minutes, until the fish is tender and flakes easily. Remove from the heat and let it stand for 5 minutes. Drain and set aside to cool a little.

While the cod is cooking, crush the garlic in a mortar, then put into a small saucepan with the cream and thyme leaves. Bring to the boil, lower the heat and simmer for a few minutes. Remove from the heat and set aside.

Meanwhile, in another saucepan, boil the potatoes in unsalted water until tender. Drain, put into a wide bowl and mash until smooth.

Break up the warm cod with your hands, flaking it over the potato. Check meticulously for bones and discard as you go. Squash the cod flakes together with your fingers to get some smaller bits and some flakes. Add the olive oil.

Bring the infused cream back to the boil and pour over the cod. Add a generous grinding of black pepper and beat well with a wooden spoon. Taste for seasoning. Depending on your salt cod, you may need to add a touch of salt. Beat in a little more olive oil if you'd like a softer texture.

Preheat the grill (broiler) to high. Spoon the brandade between 8 shallow gratin dishes, about 12cm (4¾in) diameter (or use smaller individual moulds and dollop higher). Spread out a little with the back of a spoon (not too flat or smooth) and scatter over the breadcrumbs. Stand the dishes on an oven tray and place under the grill to gratinée until the top is flecked with golden brown.

Melt a little butter in a frying pan, add a small sprinkling of salt and pepper, then fry the baguette slices on both sides until pale golden and crisp. Serve with the hot brandade.

PROVENCE

AÏOLI

Aïoli is traditionally served on Fridays in Provence. The name refers to the finished dish as well as the sauce. It is best made fresh just before serving and the ingredients have to be top. You can add any vegetables that you like to this lovely platter, or other seafood to take it to a grander aïoli, though I like the simplicity of using just salt cod. I use half olive oil and half vegetable oil in the aïoli as the flavour can be too strong if you use all olive oil.

Serves 4

1 small cauliflower (400g/14oz), cut into florets
4 medium potatoes (each about 140g/5oz), peeled
8 small carrots, peeled
2 small turnips, peeled
4 artichokes, trimmed, with some stalk left on
2 large handfuls green beans, trimmed
about 800g (1¾lb) thick salt cod fillet, soaked for up to 48 hours in several changes of water
4 eggs

For the aïoli
3 medium garlic cloves, peeled
2 egg yolks
125ml (½ cup) olive oil (not too overpowering)
125ml (½ cup) sunflower oil
2 tablespoons lemon juice
salt and freshly ground black pepper

To serve
Camargue or other crunchy sea salt
olive oil

To prepare the aïoli, crush the garlic to a paste using a pestle in a mortar. Whip the egg yolks in a bowl until creamy. Add the garlic, whisking it in well. Start to whisk in the oils, a few drops at a time to begin with, until the mixture starts to thicken, then in a thin stream, until the oils are used up and the aïoli is thick and creamy. Whisk in the lemon juice. Add salt and pepper to taste.

Bring a wide pot of salted water to the boil and cook the cauliflower, potatoes, carrots, turnips, artichokes and beans separately until just tender. Drain and put into separate bowls. When cool enough to handle, halve the artichokes and remove the choke.

Drain the salt cod. Bring a pot of water to the boil and add the cod. Bring back to a gentle simmer and cook for about 10–15 minutes, depending on thickness. Remove from the heat, let sit for 5 minutes, then drain and gently lift the fillet onto a board. Remove the skin and cut into chunky pieces for serving, removing all bones.

Meanwhile, add the eggs to a small pan of water and bring to the boil. Cook for 2½–3 minutes from when it boils; they should be slightly soft inside but still hold their shape. Drain and peel.

To serve, place a piece of cod on each plate with a whole egg, a heap of each vegetable and a ramekin of shiny aïoli on the side. Scrunch some salt flakes over the vegetables (and even over the salt cod if it needs it). Add a grind of black pepper, and even a little olive oil if you like.

LOUP DE MER AU FENOUIL ET PASTIS

This is very quick and easy to make. You can use another whole fish if you prefer, but sea bass is very much appreciated for its fine flavour, and is a very typical sight over wood fires with fennel stalks. In this recipe, it is oven-baked.

Serves 2

4 tablespoons olive oil
1 large fennel bulb (about 500g/18oz), trimmed and fronds reserved
1 sea bass (500–600g/18–21oz), cleaned
3 garlic cloves, peeled
a small bundle of parsley, with stalks
70g (¾ cup) whole pitted black olives
20g (4 tablespoons) butter
3–4 tablespoons pastis
Camargue or other crunchy sea salt and freshly ground black pepper

Preheat the oven to 200°C/ 400°F/Gas 6. Drizzle half the olive oil over the base of a roasting tin about 22 x 30cm (8 x 12in). Halve the fennel and slice into wedges about 7mm (¼in) thick, keeping each wedge attached at its base.

Salt and pepper the fish, inside and out. Put one of the garlic cloves inside with the parsley and a couple of small fennel fronds. Settle it into the middle of the dish, then arrange the fennel wedges around it in a single layer.

Salt and pepper the fennel. Add the olives to the dish with the remaining garlic cloves, then drizzle the remaining oil over the top of everything.

Bake for about 30 minutes, until golden. Add the butter in small blobs here and there over the vegetables and a little over the fish. Drizzle the pastis over the fish and fennel and put back into the oven for another 5 minutes or so.

Remove the bass to a serving platter, arranging the fennel and olives around the edge. Scatter a handful of fennel fronds over the fish, then add a grind of pepper and some grains of good salt. Fillet the bass to serve, spooning some pan juices over each serving.

POULET À L'AIL

This is far more subtle than the amount of garlic suggests, as the whole bulbs soften beautifully as they cook alongside the chicken. It's good served with a vegetable tian and some plain sautéed Swiss chard. The garlic cloves from the leftover whole roasted bulb can be mashed onto baguette.

Serves 4–5

2 tablespoons olive oil
60g (2oz) butter
1 chicken (about 1.2kg/2¾lb)
a few spring onion (scallion) green tops
a handful thyme sprigs
2 fairly thick lemon slices
3 whole heads of garlic
3 tablespoons Cognac, or eau de vie
sea salt and freshly ground black pepper

Preheat the oven to 200°C/400°F/Gas 6. Drizzle the olive oil into a roasting tin, about 22 x 30cm (8 x 12in).

Rub a little of the butter over the chicken and sprinkle salt and pepper inside and out. Put the spring onion tops, some of the thyme sprigs, the lemon slices and a little more of the butter into the cavity. Put the chicken in the tin breast side down.

Separate one of the garlic bulbs into single cloves, leaving their skins on, and scatter them around the chicken. Halve the other 2 garlic bulbs horizontally and put them cut side up around the chicken. Break the remaining butter into chunks and put over the chicken and garlic, and here and there in the dish. Put the rest of the thyme in amongst the garlic.

Roast in the hot oven for 30–40 minutes, until the chicken has taken on a good golden colour. Turn it over to breast side up and baste the garlic with some of the juices. Close the garlic heads, putting the top halves onto the bottoms. Drizzle the Cognac over the chicken and garlic and add about 125ml (½ cup) water to the dish.

Lower the oven setting to 190°C/375°F/Gas 5 and roast for a further 40 minutes, basting a couple of times, until the skin is golden crisp, and there is a nice amount of buttery juice in the dish.

Remove from the oven and pour the sauce into a small pan; there should be about 125ml (½ cup). Add a little water to top up if necessary. Remove 2 halves of garlic bulb and squeeze the flesh out of their skins into the juices in the pan. Press with a fork or purée to give a thick but smoothish sauce, and heat through.

Cut the chicken into serving pieces using poultry scissors. Serve with a couple of the whole garlic cloves in their skins on the side, and the warm garlic sauce spooned over the top.

POULET AU POIVRON, FENOUIL ET OLIVES

This is the kind of thing I could eat once a week. I ate it at a rôtisserie: chicken dripping onto a tray of colourful vegetables. Here, I have roasted it all in one dish. You can add any vegetables you like. If you don't have any herbes de Provence, just chop up a mixture of fresh herbs.

Serves 4–5

1 large red (bell) pepper, halved and deseeded
1 fennel bulb (about 500g/18oz), trimmed
500g (18oz) small potatoes, peeled
1 large red onion
6 garlic cloves (unpeeled)
7 tablespoons olive oil
about 2 tablespoons herbes de Provence (page 17)
1 chicken (about 1.2kg/2¾lb)
100g (1 cup) pitted black olives
sea salt and freshly ground black pepper

Preheat the oven to 200°C/400°F/Gas 6. Cut the pepper into chunks. Halve the fennel and cut each half into 6 fairly thin wedges. Halve the onion, then cut each half into wedges (slightly thicker than the fennel), keeping them attached at the base. Cut the potatoes into roughly 3cm (1¼in) chunks.

Drizzle 5 tablespoons of olive oil into a large baking dish (I use a round one, 34cm/13½in in diameter). Add the pepper, fennel, potatoes, onion, 4 garlic cloves, a good scattering of herbes de Provence and some salt and pepper. Turn through well.

Drizzle the remaining 2 tablespoons of olive oil over the chicken and rub it into the skin. Salt and pepper the chicken inside and out, and give a good scattering of the herbes as well, also inside the cavity. Put the 2 garlic cloves inside the cavity. Make a hollow in the vegetables in the centre of the dish and place the chicken, breast side down, in the hollow, so it is touching the base of the dish. Roast for 45 minutes, until the chicken is golden and the vegetables are looking good.

Turn the chicken over, add the olives to the vegetables and turn them through. Continue roasting until the chicken is deep golden and the vegetables look lovely, up to 45 minutes longer. You can baste the chicken with some of the juices in the last part of cooking. There should be a nice amount of not-too-watery sauce in the bottom of the dish to serve with the chicken, and the vegetables should be deeply roasty looking.

Remove from the oven and let it sit for 10 minutes before cutting up the chicken into serving pieces. Nice served with baguette for the juices – you can even make small baguette sandwiches with a few of the vegetables and olives and juices and just snack on them as you go.

LAPIN AU THYM, AIL ET LARDONS

This straightforward and down-to-earth rabbit dish could also be made using skinless chicken, cooked for a shorter time. The flavour of the thyme is important here, so use wild, deeply perfumed thyme if you can. This is good served with a macaroni gratin.

Serves 4–6

4 tablespoons olive oil
1 rabbit (about 1.5kg/3¼lb), cut into 8 pieces
8 garlic cloves, unpeeled
2 thick slices (150g/5oz) porc salée or lardons
2 good handfuls thyme sprigs, plus extra to serve
375ml (1½ cups) white wine
sea salt and freshly ground black pepper

Heat the oil in a large non-stick pan into which the rabbit pieces will fit in a single layer. Brown the rabbit pieces, turning them over with tongs until they are deep golden on all sides. Season with salt and pepper.

With a small sharp knife, cut a small slit in each garlic clove so the flavour can seep out. Cut each pork slice into large, irregular pieces about 4–5cm (1½–2in). Add the garlic and pork to the rabbit along with the thyme sprigs, and sauté for a few minutes.

Now add the wine and let it bubble over a high heat for 5 minutes or so, then cover, lower the heat and simmer for about 1 hour, turning the rabbit over 2 or 3 times during cooking. The liquid will reduce considerably while cooking, so add more water (roughly 125ml/½ cup) as and when it is needed. The sauce should be deep golden, nicely thickened and still quite abundant.

Check that the meat is tender by poking a fork in near the bones. It should feel very tender with no resistance to the fork; cook a little longer if necessary. Serve warm with the sauce spooned over and a heap of thyme on top.

MACARONI AU GRATIN

This is a lovely accompaniment to a main course, such as the rabbit. Preheat the oven to 200°C/400°F/Gas 6. Rub the base and sides of a 22 x 30cm (8 x 12in) oval gratin dish (or a few smaller ones) with a little butter. Bring a pot of well-salted water to the boil, add 250g (9oz) short, thin macaroni and cook until just tender.

Meanwhile, heat 250ml (1 cup) cream in a small saucepan with a peeled garlic clove, and a good grind of black pepper. Grate about 80g (¾ cup) Gruyère.

As soon as the macaroni is ready, drain and tip into your gratin dish. Pour on the cream (a few shavings of truffle mixed in here is wonderful). Add about two-thirds of the Gruyère and mix through, then level out the mixture.

Dot about 1 tablespoon butter over the surface and sprinkle with the rest of the cheese and 1 tablespoon of dry breadcrumbs. Bake on a high shelf in the oven for about 20 minutes until bubbling and a little golden on top here and there.

BLETTES AU GRATIN

This Swiss chard dish accompanies meat or fish very well. Try to use younger chard so you don't have to discard too many tough stalks. You can also use another green here if you like.

Serves 6

1.5kg (3¼lb) Swiss chard, trimmed of tough stalks (about 1.2kg/2¾lb trimmed weight)
250ml (1 cup) cream
1 garlic clove, peeled and halved
20g (4 teaspoons) butter
4 tablespoons finely grated Gruyère
sea salt and freshly ground black pepper

Rinse the chard well, drain in a colander, then chop well. Bring a pot of salted water to the boil and add the chard. Bring back to the boil and cook for a few minutes until tender. Drain in a colander, pressing out all excess water.

Heat the cream in a small saucepan with one of the garlic halves, a little salt and a few grinds of black pepper to a simmer, then take off the heat and set aside to infuse.

Preheat the oven to 190°C/ 375°F/Gas 5. Rub the base and sides of a 22 x 30cm (8 x 12in) baking dish with the cut side of the other garlic half, then rub with some of the butter too. Tip in the chard, distributing it evenly, and then pour the cream in, rocking the dish to spread it evenly.

Grind a little more pepper over, and dot the rest of the butter here and there. Bake for 20 minutes, until it is bubbly. Scatter the cheese over the top, then bake until golden and crisp in places, about 10 minutes. Serve hot, in rough squares.

TIAN DE LÉGUMES

The tomatoes here must be lovely and ripe, as they give the dish moisture and flavour. If you prefer you can use a single herb, such as fresh thyme, in place of the herbes de Provence.

Serves 6–8

1 small, long aubergine (eggplant) (about 400g/14oz), trimmed
2 large courgettes (zucchini) (400g/14oz in total)
a bunch of spring onions (scallions) (200g/7oz)
5 ripe tomatoes (500g/18oz in total)
185ml (¾ cup) olive oil
3 garlic cloves, peeled and chopped
2 tablespoons herbes de Provence (page 17)
crunchy sea salt and freshly ground black pepper

Preheat the oven to 200°C/ 400°F/Gas 6. Slice the aubergine in half lengthways, then cut into 5mm (¼in) half-moon slices. Slice the courgettes on the diagonal to the same thickness. Thinly slice the spring onions. Slice the tomatoes into rounds.

Drizzle 3 tablespoons of the olive oil into a 36cm (14in) round ovenproof dish and put into the oven for a few minutes to heat up. Mix the rest of the oil with the garlic and herbes de Provence.

Layer the aubergines slices in the hot dish. Sprinkle with a little salt, some pepper and about 2 tablespoons of the herb oil. Layer the onions, courgettes and finally the tomatoes on top, seasoning and drizzling each layer with herb oil.

Pour in about 185ml (¾ cup) water around the edges and bake for about 1¼ hours until softened and golden. Turn the oven off and leave the dish inside to settle. Lovely just warm (also the next day) with bread, or next to a main course.

RESTAURANT
OUVERT

COIFFEUR

CAFE

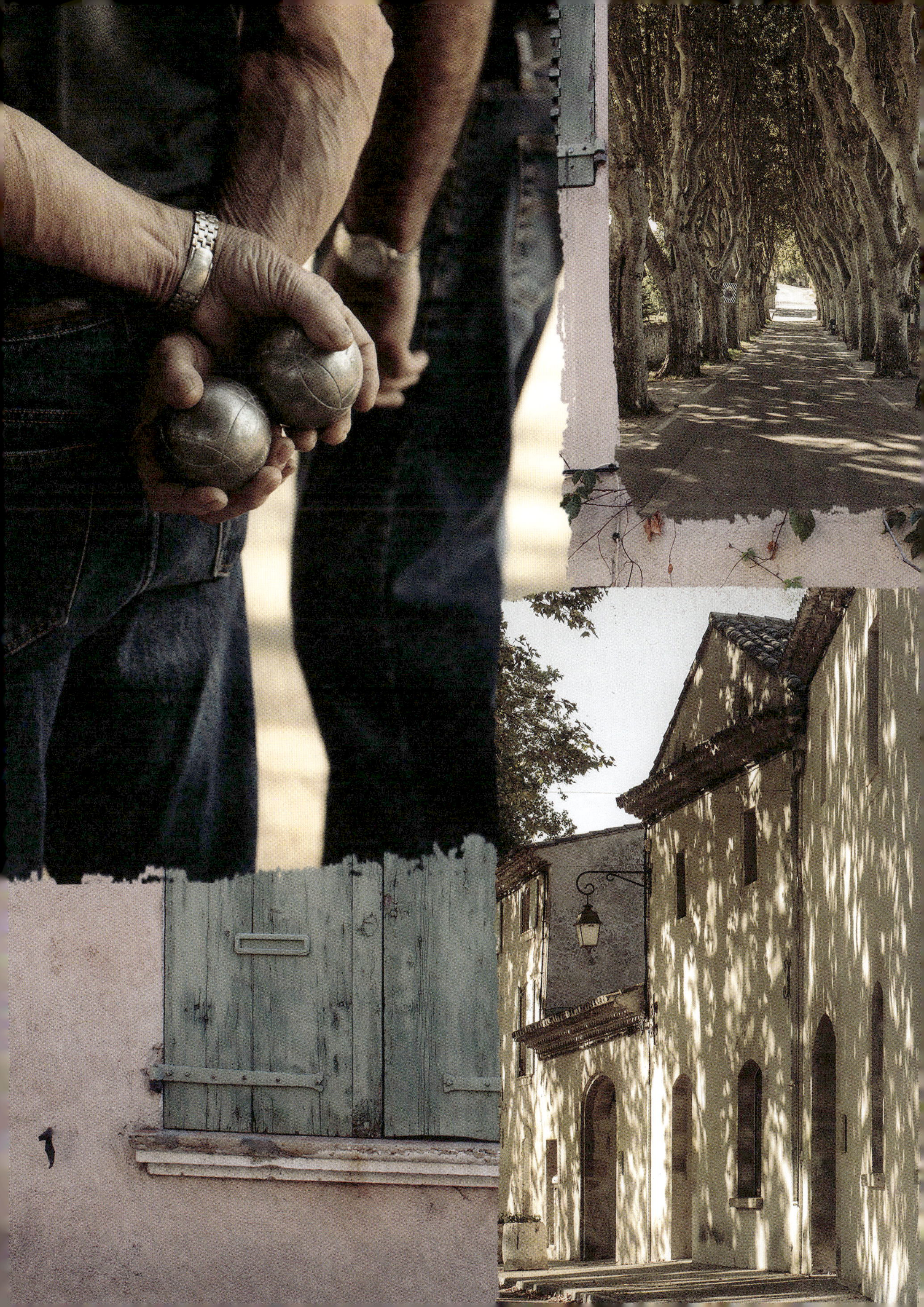

GIGOT D'AGNEAU AUX ANCHOIS

I have such a lovely memory of eating this deep in the countryside one sunny day, under a huge tree that provided shade for the masses... It is good served with a potato gratin or a vegetable tian. Braised artichokes are also very good served either as a starter to this or on the side.

Serves 6

6 garlic cloves, finely chopped
6 anchovy fillets in oil, drained and chopped
2 tablespoons chopped rosemary
1 tablespoon thyme leaves
6 tablespoons olive oil
1 small leg of lamb (about 1.2kg/2¾lb)
20 large cherry tomatoes (600g/21oz in total), 10 halved and 10 left whole
185ml (¾ cup) white wine
sea salt and freshly ground black pepper

Preheat the oven to 200°C/400°F/Gas 6. In a small bowl, mix the garlic, anchovies, rosemary and thyme leaves with 2 tablespoons of the oil. Drizzle 3 tablespoons of the oil into the base of a not too large roasting tin that will fit the lamb and tomatoes.

Make 3 incisions, about 2cm (¾in) deep, on each side of the lamb. Stuff the herb mixture into the incisions and rub all over the lamb. Rub the surface with a little salt (not too much as the anchovies are salty) and a generous grinding of pepper, then put the lamb in the baking dish, presentation side down.

Surround the lamb with the tomatoes. Lightly sprinkle them with salt and pepper and drizzle with the last tablespoon of oil. Roast for 30–40 minutes until the lamb is golden and the tomatoes are starting to look gooey.

Turn the lamb over, move the tomatoes around if necessary and check that nothing is burning. Add 125ml (½ cup) of the wine, turn the oven down to 180°C/350°F/Gas 4 and roast for a further 30 minutes.

Add the remaining wine to ensure that the sauce around the lamb is jammy and tomatoes are not blackening and roast for a final 10–15 minutes. The cooking time will depend on how well done you want the lamb, and on the size of the leg of lamb – I like this dish with the meat cooked through, and with a jammy, gooey sauce.

Remove from the oven and leave to rest for 10 minutes. Transfer the lamb and tomatoes to a platter and serve warm.

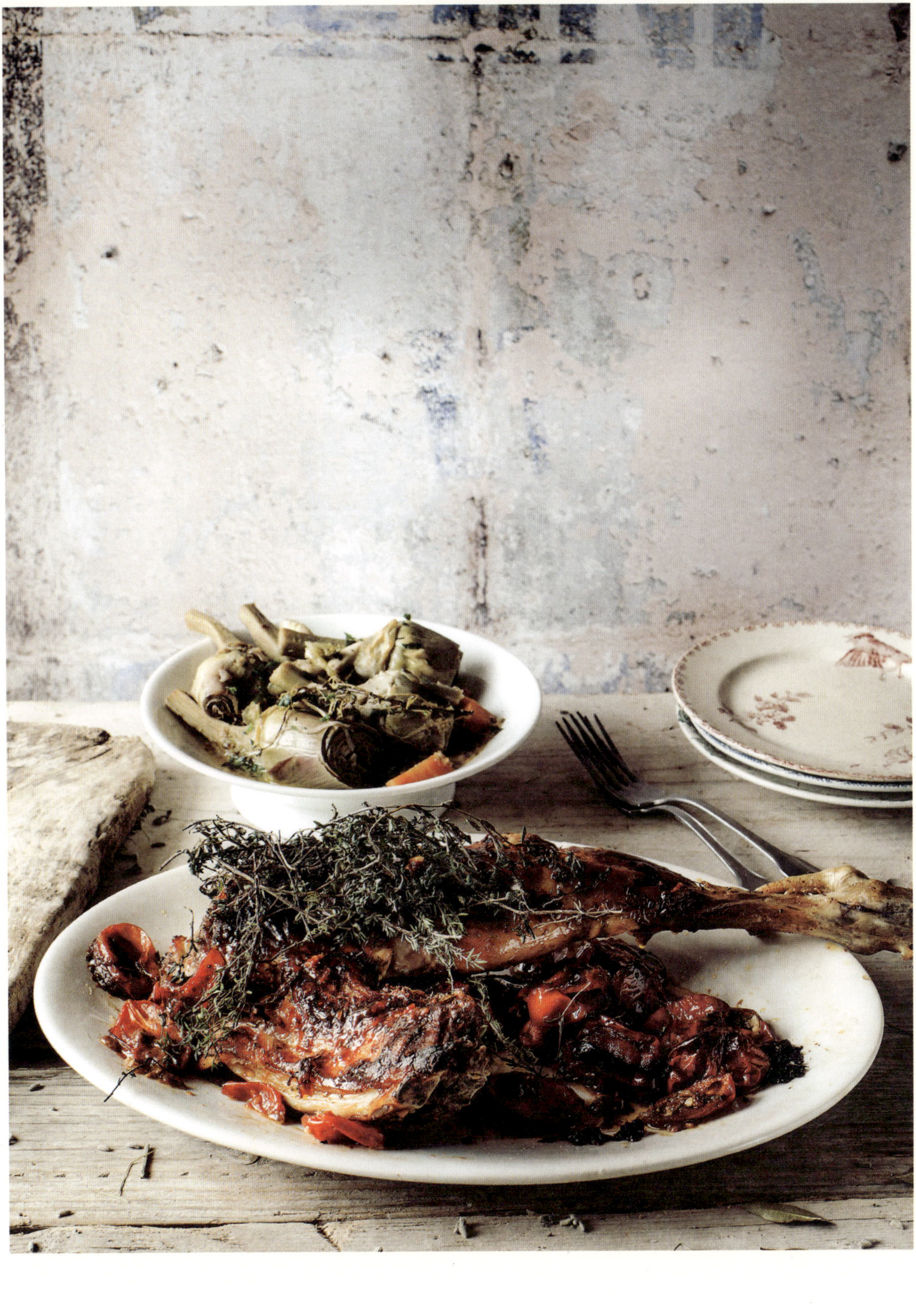

ARTICHAUTS À LA BARIGOULE

These small artichokes are lovely served as a starter, perhaps before a lamb dish, or with one. If you can only find large artichokes, use just five and cut each in half to serve. They need to have their chokes scraped out and may need to be cooked for longer.

Serves 5

1½ lemons
10 small artichokes, with at least 6cm (2⅜in) stem
6 tablespoons olive oil
1 onion, chopped
50g (2oz) porc salée, cut into 2 or 3 big chunks, or lardons
4 garlic cloves, chopped
120g (4oz) carrots, peeled and sliced
125ml (½ cup) white wine
1 bay leaf
a small handful thyme sprigs
about 100g (3½oz) inner butterhead lettuce leaves
1 tablespoon chopped parsley
Camargue or other crunchy sea salt and freshly ground black pepper

Cut the whole lemon in half, squeeze the juice from both halves into a bowl of cold water and set aside, saving the halves. Strip away the outer leaves from the artichokes, to get to the tender inner part. Cut off all but 2–3cm (¾–1¼in) of stem and pare off the dark green outer skin to reveal the paler inner stalk. Pare the removed stems in the same way, then place these stem pieces in the lemon water. Slice off the top third of each artichoke. With a spoon, scoop out the hairy choke, if there is one. As you finish each artichoke, rub it all over with the saved lemon halves and drop into the lemon water.

Heat the oil in a wide, heavy-based pan. Add the onion and pork and sauté gently until lightly golden. Add the garlic and sauté for a minute before adding the carrots and wine. Let bubble up for 5 minutes or so until much has evaporated, then add the drained whole artichokes and stem pieces.

Tie the bay leaf and thyme sprigs together with string and add to the pan. Season the artichokes well, pour in 185ml (¾ cup) water and squeeze in the juice from the remaining lemon half. Bring to the boil, cover, lower the heat and simmer for about 20 minutes until the artichokes are quite tender to a fork, turning once or twice during cooking.

Take off the heat and transfer the artichokes, pork pieces, herb bundle and carrots to a plate, leaving the stems, onions and sauce in the pan. Add about 125ml (½ cup) water to the pan and purée with a hand-held blender until smooth.

Return everything to the pan. Place the lettuce leaves on top, leaving small leaves whole and tearing larger ones in half. Simmer for another 5 minutes or until the lettuce has wilted, mixing it through the sauce and adding a little water if too thick.

Taste for seasoning. Remove from the heat, sprinkle over the parsley, cover with the lid and let cool a little before serving warm, with some crunchy salt and a grind of pepper over the top.

DAUBE DE BOEUF

This rather wintry dish is easy to make, as once the meat has browned it all bakes for about 3 hours, giving a beautiful result. The orange rind here gives a truly wonderful flavour and scent, but is very good to eat too. I love this with potato gratin, or with boiled potatoes that have a little mustard turned through them. You could also marinate the meat in the wine for a few hours, or even overnight.

Serves 4–5

5 tablespoons olive oil
1kg (2¼lb) beef (blade or rump), trimmed of most of its fat and cut into 5–6cm (2–2¼in) cubes
2 scant tablespoons flour
1 onion, chopped
3 garlic cloves, chopped
2 tablespoons Cognac
750ml (3 cups) good red wine
4 or 5 shallots, peeled and left whole
3 carrots, cut into 4cm (1½in) chunks
125g (½ cup) chopped tomatoes
a handful thyme sprigs
a small bundle of parsley sprigs
2 bay leaves
1 long pared strip of orange rind
sea salt and freshly ground black pepper

Preheat the oven to 160°C/325°F/Gas 2½. Heat 3 tablespoons of the oil in a large non-stick frying pan. In a bowl or colander, toss the beef in the flour to lightly coat. Add the beef to the hot oil and fry until the undersides are deep golden before shifting and turning until golden all over.

Season with salt and pepper, then push to one side and add the remaining oil to the pan. Add the onion and sauté for a couple of minutes. Stir through the meat and continue sautéeing until the onion has softened and turned golden. Add the garlic and sauté for a minute more. Now add the Cognac and simmer to evaporate. Add a third of the wine and simmer for a couple of minutes to collect all the flavours.

Transfer the contents of the pan to a casserole dish with a tight-fitting lid. Add the shallots and carrots with the rest of the wine and the tomatoes. Tie together the thyme, parsley and bay leaves with kitchen string and settle the bundle amongst the meat. Add the orange strip and gently stir to mix, checking that nothing is sticking out of the liquid too much.

Cover and bake in the oven for about 3 hours, until the meat is very tender and the sauce is deep coloured and thick, giving it a couple of stirs as it cooks and adding 250ml (1 cup) water halfway through, stirring and scraping the sides of the dish.

Leave to stand, covered with the lid, for at least 10 minutes before serving.

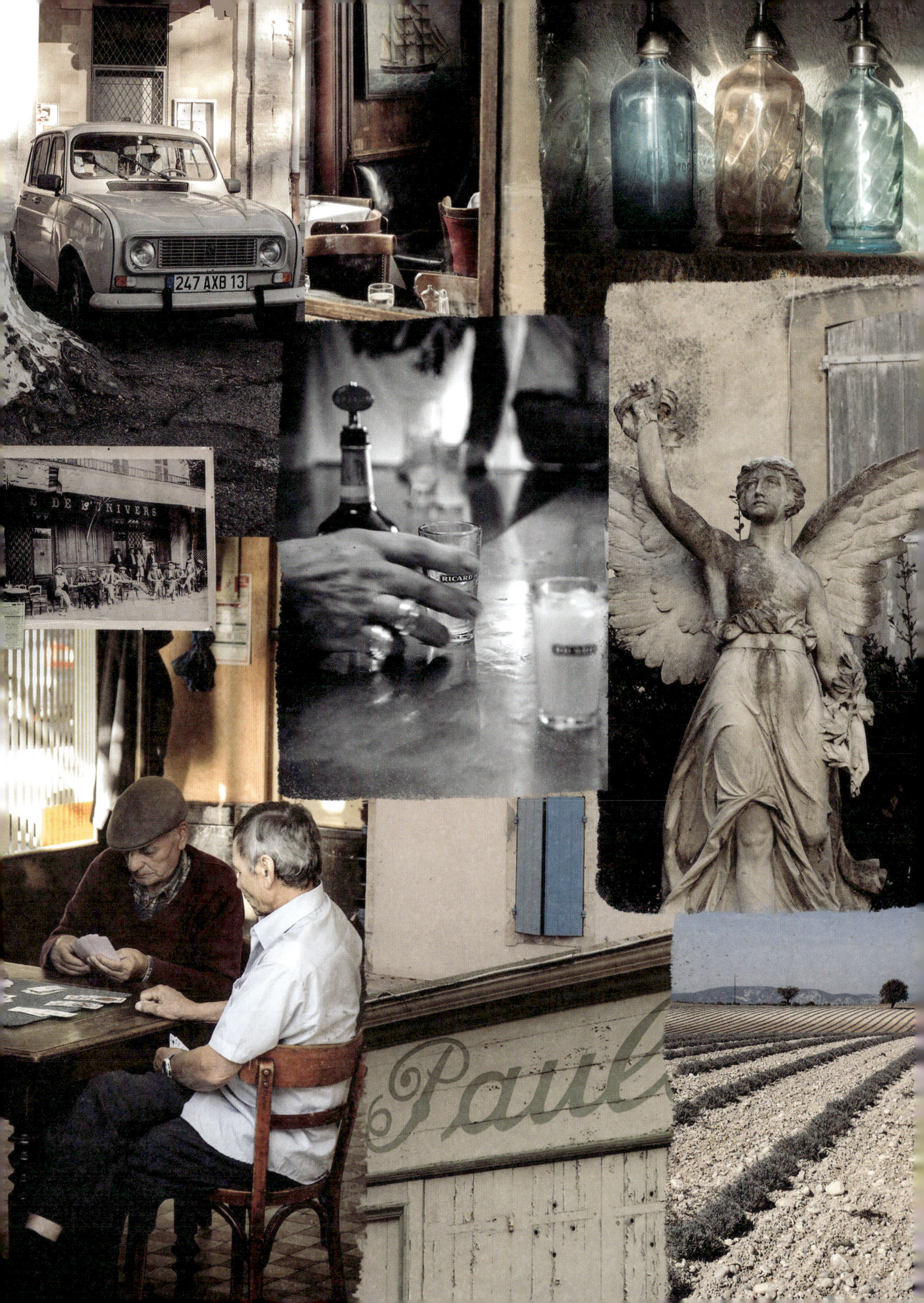
247 AXB 13
RICARD
Paul

GRATIN DE POMMES DE TERRE

This is beautiful with dishes such as daube of beef (or, actually, with anything!). I like to cook it until the cream has been almost completely absorbed by the potatoes, resulting in a soft, fluffy golden pile. You can also cook this in individual baking dishes, which look good. This gratin is lovely with a few shavings of black truffle scattered between the layers...

Serves 6

1 garlic clove, peeled and halved
50g (2oz) butter
250ml (1 cup) cream
250ml (1 cup) milk
about 1.3kg (3lb) potatoes
    (5 or 6 large potatoes)
a few thyme sprigs, leaves stripped
sea salt and freshly ground black pepper

Preheat the oven to 200°C/ 400°F/Gas 6. Rub one of the garlic halves over the base and sides of a baking dish, 22 x 30cm (8 x 12in), then rub some of the butter over.

Put the cream, milk and remaining garlic half into a small saucepan, with a couple of good pinches of salt and grinds of pepper. Bring to the boil, lower the heat and simmer for a minute or two, stirring so it doesn't boil over. Take off the heat and set aside to mingle the flavours.

Peel the potatoes, rinse, then slice into 2mm (⅛in) rounds. Arrange about a quarter in a slightly overlapping layer in the prepared dish. Scatter evenly with a little salt and some thyme leaves. Add a second layer of potato rounds. Pour in half of the cream mixture, discarding the garlic. Scatter with a little salt, some pepper and more thyme. Put a third layer of potatoes in, some salt and thyme leaves, then a fourth layer of potato. Pour in the rest of the cream, scatter lightly with salt and a dusting of pepper. Dot the rest of the butter here and there over the top.

Cover the dish with foil and bake for 40 minutes until bubbling. Lower the oven setting to 180°C/ 350°F/Gas 4, remove the foil and bake for another 30–40 minutes, or until the cream has been absorbed and there are golden patches here and there on the top. Leave to cool and settle a little before serving warm, in squares.

ENTRECÔTE À L'ANCHOÏADE

Anchoïade is a wonderful thing: intense and lovely, so add as much as you want to the top of the steaks. You will have more than enough sauce here for a couple of steaks, so keep any left over in the fridge to serve on grilled bread, or with vegetables such as endive, cauliflower and fennel, or stirred into boiled potatoes. You can add more oil and blend it to a smoother sauce, as many choose to do. I love this served with a Swiss chard gratin and frites. Bring the steaks out of the fridge an hour or two before cooking so they come to room temperature.

Serves 2

2 tablespoons unsalted butter
2 entrecôte steaks (each about 220g/8oz and 1.5cm/⅝in thick)
2 tablespoons Cognac
Camargue or other crunchy sea salt and freshly ground black pepper

For the anchoïade
about 3 tablespoons olive oil
12 anchovy fillets in oil, drained and chopped
2 plump garlic cloves, finely chopped
2 tablespoons chopped parsley
1 teaspoon thyme leaves
2 teaspoons good red wine vinegar

To make the anchoïade, heat a tablespoon of the oil in a small non-stick frying pan. Add the anchovies and mash them to pulpy bits as they sizzle. Add the garlic and sauté for a minute or so.

Stir through the parsley and thyme, and lastly add the vinegar, letting it cook until nearly all evaporated, scraping the sides of the pan with a wooden spoon. Set aside to cool, then transfer to a bowl and gradually stir in a couple more tablespoons of olive oil, mixing well to make a thick sauce.

Heat a heavy-based non-stick frying pan. Add a scant tablespoon of the butter and, when hot and sizzling, add the steaks. Cook over a high heat until the undersides have a good golden crust. Turn them over and do the same to the other side, then add the remaining butter to the pan. Sprinkle just a very few salt flakes over the meat (the anchovies will provide plenty of salt).

When the meat is cooked to your liking, add the Cognac. Standing well back, you can put a lighted match to it if you like and flambé off the alcohol, otherwise just let it cook out.

Remove the steaks to warm plates and spoon some of the pan juices over them. Dollop some anchoïade over each steak, add a good grind of black pepper and serve at once.

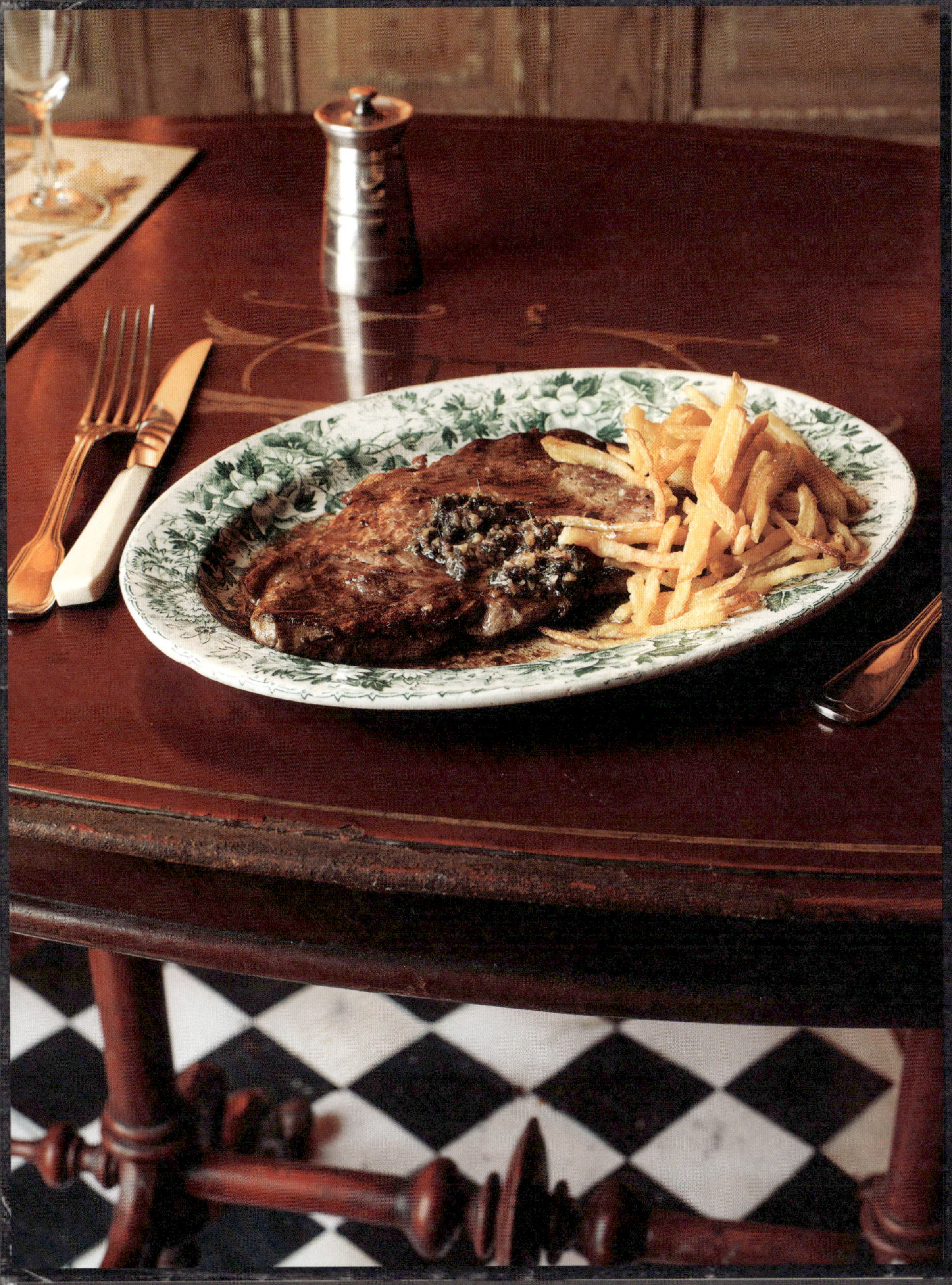

TARTE AU CITRON

This is my friend Luigi's lemon tart. He used to make it many years ago when he lived and worked in a hotel in Mougins. Actually, he told me even Picasso came along to eat the tart (he liked it warm). I love a lemon tart that is generous on the lemon, like this one.

Makes 1 x 22cm (8in) tart

For the pastry
200g (1½ cups) plain (all-purpose) flour, plus extra for dusting
a pinch of salt
80g (3oz) chilled unsalted butter, cut into small cubes, plus extra for greasing
80g (3oz) sugar
1 egg yolk
3–4 tablespoons chilled water

For the filling
4 eggs
150g (¾ cup) sugar
finely grated zest of 1 lemon
65g (2¼oz) unsalted butter, melted and cooled
150ml (⅔ cup) lemon juice (3 or 4 lemons)

For the pastry, put the flour, salt and butter into a bowl. Using your fingertips, rub the butter into the flour until it resembles coarse crumbs, then add the sugar and mix to combine. Add the egg yolk mixed with 1 tablespoon of the water and knead lightly and quickly until smooth, adding as much of the remaining water as you need, to bring it together into a dough. Wrap in plastic wrap and refrigerate for at least 30 minutes.

Preheat the oven to 180°C/ 350°F/Gas 4. Lightly butter a 22cm (8in) tart tin or springform cake tin. Roll out the pastry on a lightly floured surface to a circle about 28cm (11in) in diameter, large enough to line the base and sides of the tin. (Roll out a few biscuits with any leftover pastry.)

Using the rolling pin to lift it, lower the pastry into the tin. Level the sides with a small sharp knife to about 3.5cm (1⅜in) high, and press firmly against the sides of the tin so they adhere. Prick the base of the pastry with a fork in a few places and line the pastry with baking parchment, bringing it up and over the sides to completely cover the pastry. Fill with baking beans, pressing them into the corners.

Bake for about 15 minutes until the edges of the pastry are firm. Remove the baking parchment and beans and bake for another 10 minutes or so, until the pastry base is pale golden. Reduce the oven temperature to 160°C/ 325°F/Gas 2½.

Meanwhile, make the filling. Whip the eggs and sugar together in a wide bowl until quite thick and pale. Whisk in the lemon zest, then scrape in the butter. Add the lemon juice, whisking to combine. Pour into the pastry shell (if using a springform tin, stand it on a baking sheet).

Bake for about 20 minutes, until the filling is just golden around the edges and set but still a little wobbly in the middle. Rotate a couple of times.

Remove from the oven and leave to cool, then slide onto a serving plate. Serve in slices, plain or with a dusting of icing (powdered) sugar and a blob of thick cream.

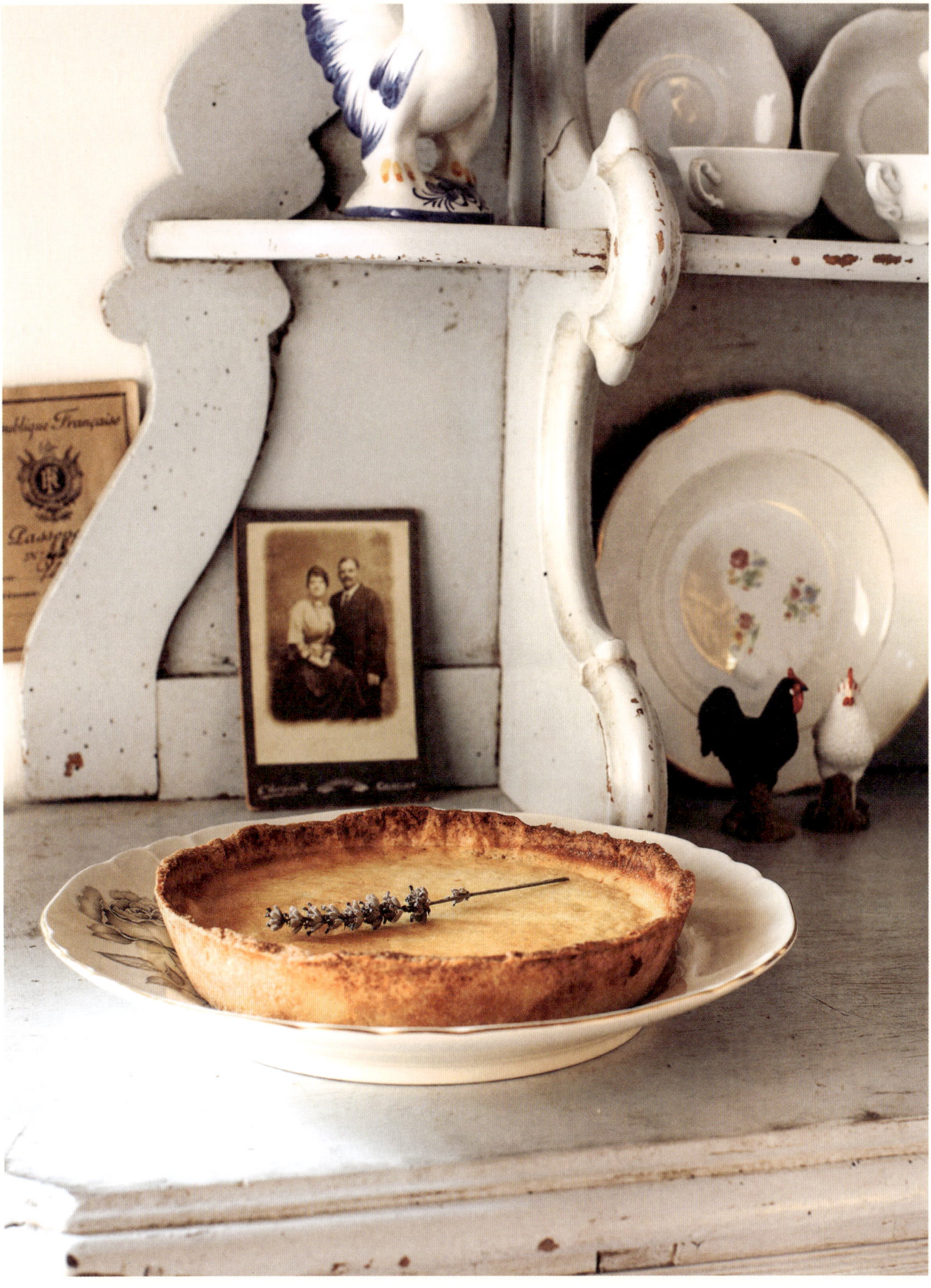

CRÈME GLACE NOUGAT, CRÈME CHANTILLY

This is a lovely finish to a meal with a fresh raspberry coulis and crème Chantilly. Using ready-made nougat makes it quick and easy to prepare.

Serves 5

For the ice cream
3 whole eggs
60g (2¼oz) sugar
250ml (1 cup) cream
250ml (1 cup) milk
100g (3½oz) classic, firm nougat, chopped

For the coulis
125g (1 cup) raspberries
2 scant tablespoons sugar
2 teaspoons crème de cassis

For the crème Chantilly
185ml (¾ cup) whipping cream
¼–½ teaspoon vanilla extract, to taste
2 teaspoons sugar

To make the ice cream, whisk the eggs and sugar together in a bowl until thick and pale. Heat the cream and milk together in a saucepan, then gradually whisk into the egg mixture. Pour back into the pan and cook over a low heat, stirring continuously until it thickens slightly. Remove from the heat and let it cool completely, then chill in the fridge, whisking every now and then.

Stir in about half of the nougat, pour into an ice cream machine and churn according to the manufacturer's instructions. When just about solid, add the rest of the nougat and churn to incorporate. Scrape out into a freezer container (If you don't have an ice cream machine, pour into a shallow dish and put in the freezer. When it is just frozen, after about 1 hour, whisk vigorously with a fork to break up the ice crystals. Return the tray to the freezer and repeat this process twice, stirring through the last of the nougat after the last whisking. Leave to freeze completely before transferring to a sealable tub for keeping.)

To make the coulis, put the raspberries, sugar and cassis into a saucepan and simmer for a couple of minutes. Purée with 2 tablespoons of water, strain through a sieve and leave to cool.

When ready to serve, whisk the cream, vanilla and sugar in a bowl until thick and pillowy.

Serve a scoop of ice cream in each bowl, with a splash of raspberry coulis and a dollop of crème Chantilly on top.

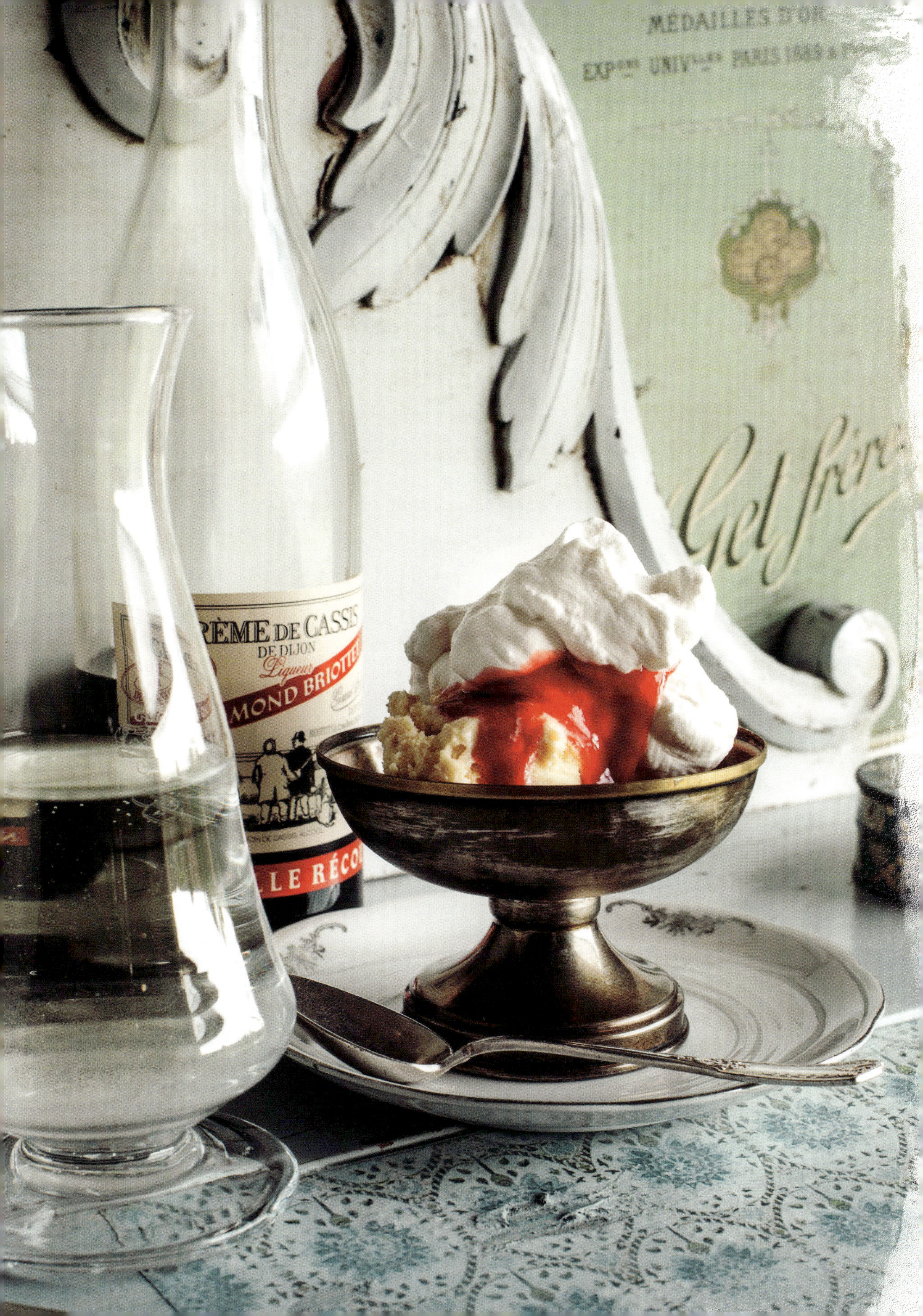
MÉDAILLES D'OR
DE DIJON
Liqueur

SACRISTAINS

True, these fantastic sweet pastry twists are not so easy to make, but worth the effort. Or you can just go to Jean-Marie's Boulangerie Bergèse in Saint Rémy de Provence and buy one or two for breakfast or teatime. His sacristains are incredible, the best I've had.

Makes 14

For the pastry
250g (2 cups) plain (all-purpose) flour, plus extra for dusting
1 level teaspoon salt
40g (scant 3 tablespoons) chilled unsalted butter, diced, plus a chilled 250g (9oz) block
125ml (½ cup) chilled water
125g (1½ cups) flaked almonds
icing (powdered) sugar, for dusting

For the glace royale
250g (1¾ cups) icing (powdered) sugar
1 teaspoon lemon juice
1 egg white

For the frangipane
250ml (1 cup) milk
½ vanilla pod, split lengthways
1 egg yolk
65g (⅓ cup) sugar
10g (¼oz) plain (all-purpose) flour
25g (¼ cup) cornflour (cornstarch)
75g (⅔ cup) unblanched almonds, ground to a powder
50g (heaped ⅓ cup) icing (powdered) sugar

To make the pastry, put the flour and salt in a heap on the work surface and add the diced butter. Rub the butter into the flour using your fingertips until it resembles fine breadcrumbs. Add the water and work into the flour to give a uniform dough. Add a few drops more water if it seems too dry. Wrap in plastic wrap and leave to rest for an hour in the fridge, or overnight.

On a floured surface, roll out the dough to a square. Take the block of butter out of the fridge and work it a little with the rolling pin so it softens and can bend. Shape it into a rectangular block big enough to cover one half of the pastry square, leaving a small border. Place over one half of the pastry and fold the uncovered side over to enclose the butter completely.

Roll out the pastry to a rectangle. Fold one short side into the centre and cover this with the other short side, as you would fold a letter. Fold this in half over itself, wrap in plastic wrap and chill in the fridge for 20 minutes or so to rest the dough and to prevent the butter from becoming too soft.

Take the pastry from the fridge and place on the work surface with the fold towards you. Roll out again into a rectangle, fold like a letter once again (just a single letter fold this time), wrap and chill, then repeat this process once more. You can either roll it out now, or store in the fridge for later, or the freezer for future use.

To make the glace royale, whip the ingredients together using an electric mixer for about 10 minutes, until you have a thick, brilliant white cream that is quite stiff.

To make the frangipane, heat the milk with the vanilla pod in a medium, heavy-based saucepan. Whisk the egg yolk in a bowl to give it a bit of volume, then add the sugar, flour and cornflour and whisk until smooth and pale. Whisk in a few

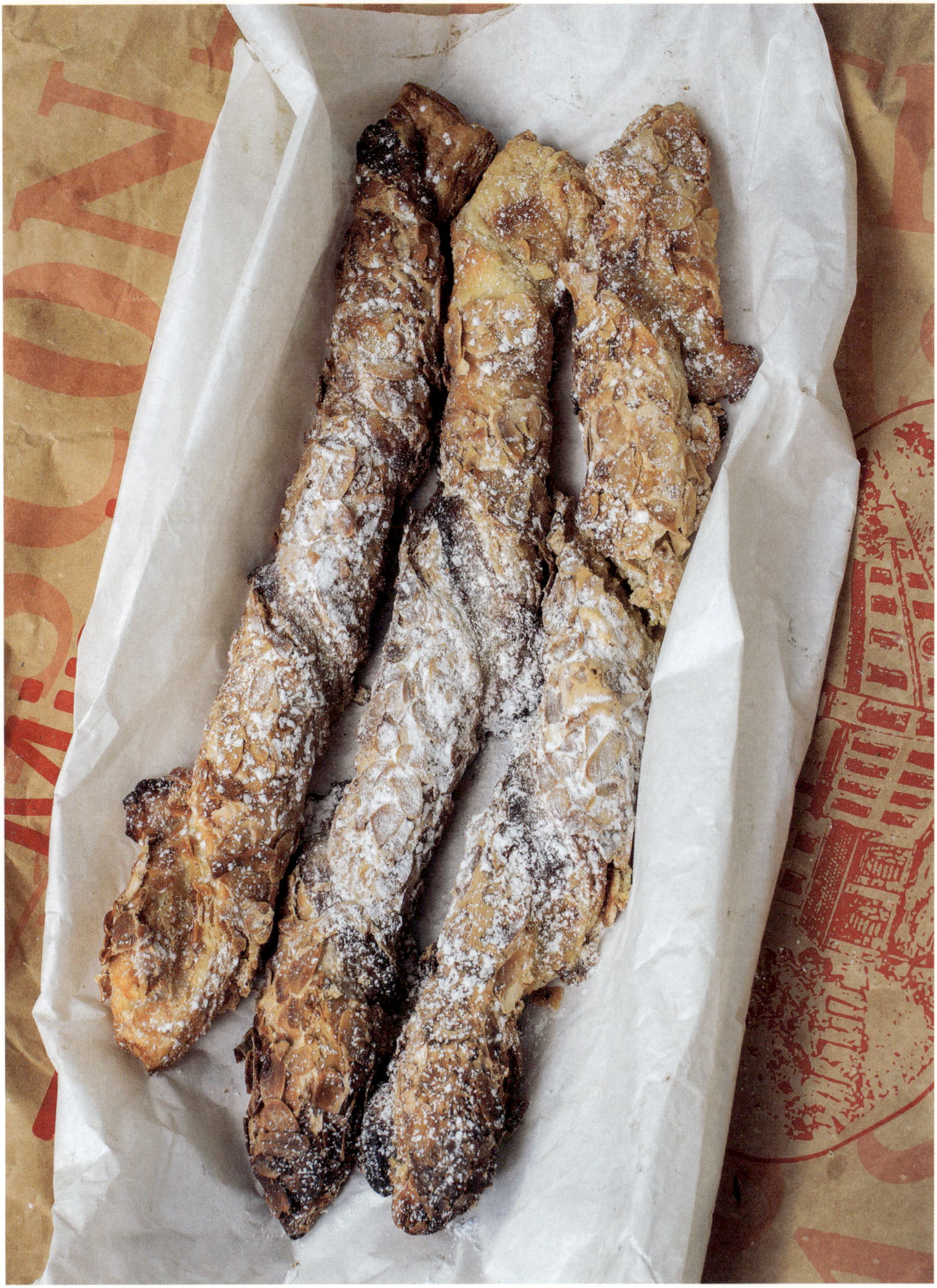

drops of the warm milk, then gradually whisk in the rest. Pour back into the pan and place over a very low heat. Whisk continuously until smooth and thickened. Take off the heat and leave to cool, whisking now and then and ensuring that there are no lumps. Remove the vanilla pod (rinse and dry, then tuck it into a jar of sugar to make vanilla sugar). Fold through the ground almonds and icing sugar.

To make the sacristains, preheat the oven to 180°C/350°F/Gas 4 and line a couple of large baking sheets with baking parchment. On a lightly floured surface, roll out the pastry to a large rectangle, 28 x 56cm (11 x 22in), and about 4mm (⅛in) thick. Using a spatula, spread a thin (1mm/¹⁄₁₆in), even layer of glace royale over the pastry, right to the edges and taking care not to drag or tear the pastry. Scatter the flaked almonds evenly over the whole surface, spreading out with your palms and pressing them down to ensure that they stick as much as possible.

Using a sharp knife, cut the pastry into 14 strips, 4cm (1½in) wide and 28cm (11in) long. Now the unusual part: flip them all over so that the glace royale and almonds are face down on your work surface. Some almonds will fall off but don't worry. Fit a piping bag with a 1cm (⅜in) nozzle and fill with the frangipane mixture. Pipe a line of it down the middle of each pastry strip, leaving 1cm (⅜in) or so clear at both ends.

Now fold a small triangle on the top end of a pastry strip using your left hand, and the same fold at the bottom of the strip with your right hand and then twist, with both hands in opposite directions; the pastry will start to roll on itself. You will produce a long spiral of pastry with the frangipane in the middle and nuts outside (collecting many of the fallen almonds as you twist). Take care not to flatten the spiral nor squash the frangipane out. Repeat with all the pastry strips, placing them 2–3cm (¾–1¼in) apart on the prepared baking sheets as you finish them.

Bake for about 20 minutes, until golden here and there and the pastry is crisp. Some parts may be crustier than others but that is fine. Remove from the oven and leave on the baking sheets to cool completely. Dust here and there with a little icing sugar and eat, ideally as soon as possible, although they will keep in an airtight container for up to 48 hours.

PROVENCE

Restauration
Copie
d'Ancien
Meubles
tous
Styles

MT 134022

GUADELOUPE GWAH-DE-LOOP GWADLOUP	PART OF A CLUSTER OF ISLANDS IN THE CARIBBEAN
FRENCH WEST INDIES LES ANTILLES FRANÇAISES SUGAR ISLAND	SHAPE: BUTTERFLY FOOD: CREOLE
PRODUCES: BANANAS, PINEAPPLES, SUGAR, RUM, COFFEE, FLOWERS, COCONUTS	
DISTANCE FROM PARIS: ABOUT 7000 KILOMETRES	OVERSEAS DEPARTMENT & REGION OF FRANCE

GUADELOUPE

*DON'T FORGET
MOSQUITO CREAM*

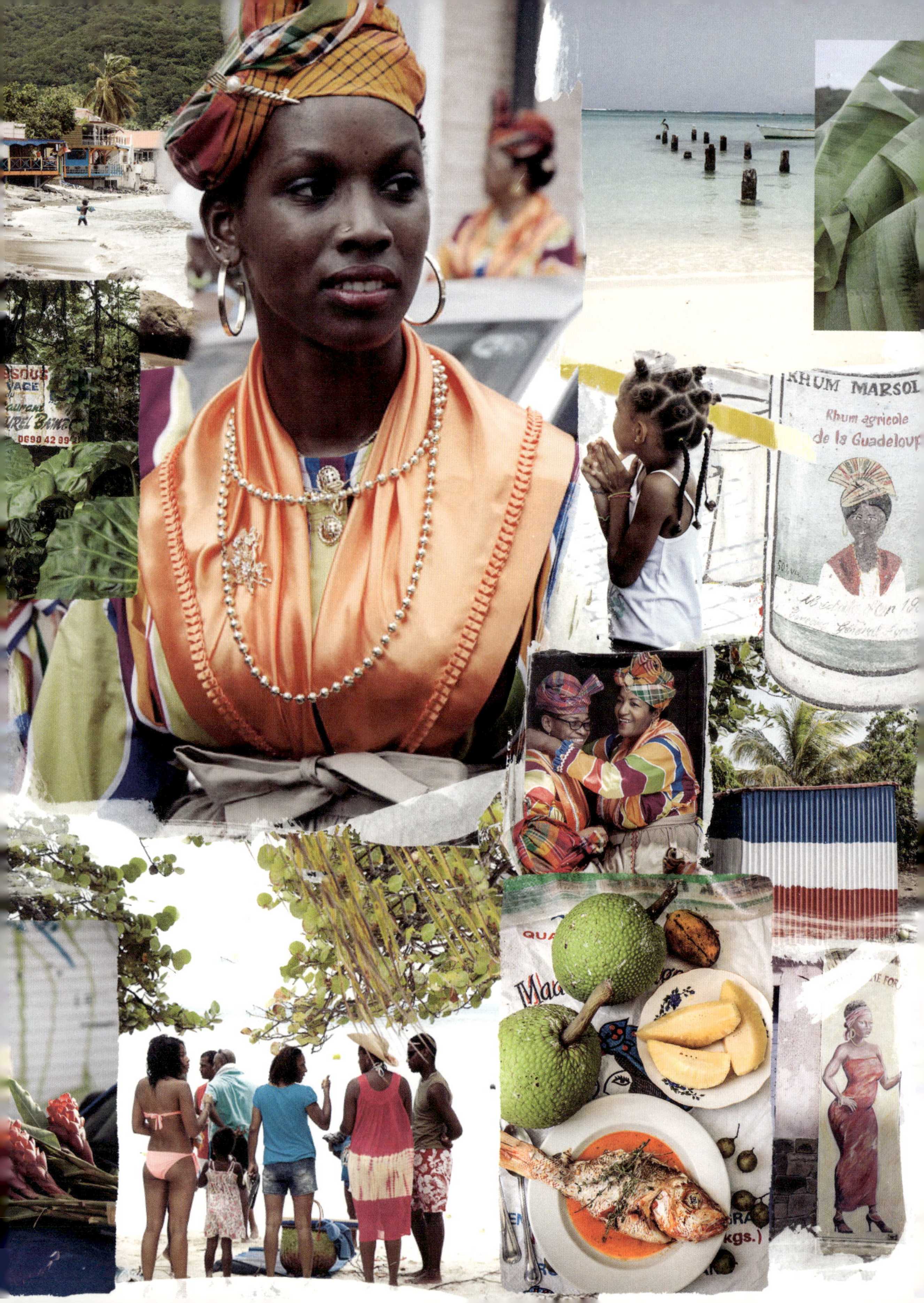
RHUM MARSOL
Rhum agricole
de la Guadeloup

GUADELOUPE

I LOVE THIS WORD – GUADELOUPE – THE TUMBLE OF CONSONANTS AND VOWELS.

And the sound of the exotic pineapple: 'a bouteille' and the tartes au coco that I had read about. French flavours and an island paradise rolled into one. Boudins, daubes, ratatouilles – at first glance dishes directly from the kitchens of France, but closer up there are local ingredients and sunshine mingling in the marinades.

Columbus was the first European to arrive in Guadeloupe in 1493, on a quest for fresh water. He called the group of islands Santa Maria de Guadalupe de Extremadura after a painting of the Virgin Mary in a monastery in Spain. But with Spain's main colonial ambitions focused elsewhere, the archipelago served chiefly as a trading port and warehouse for provisions.

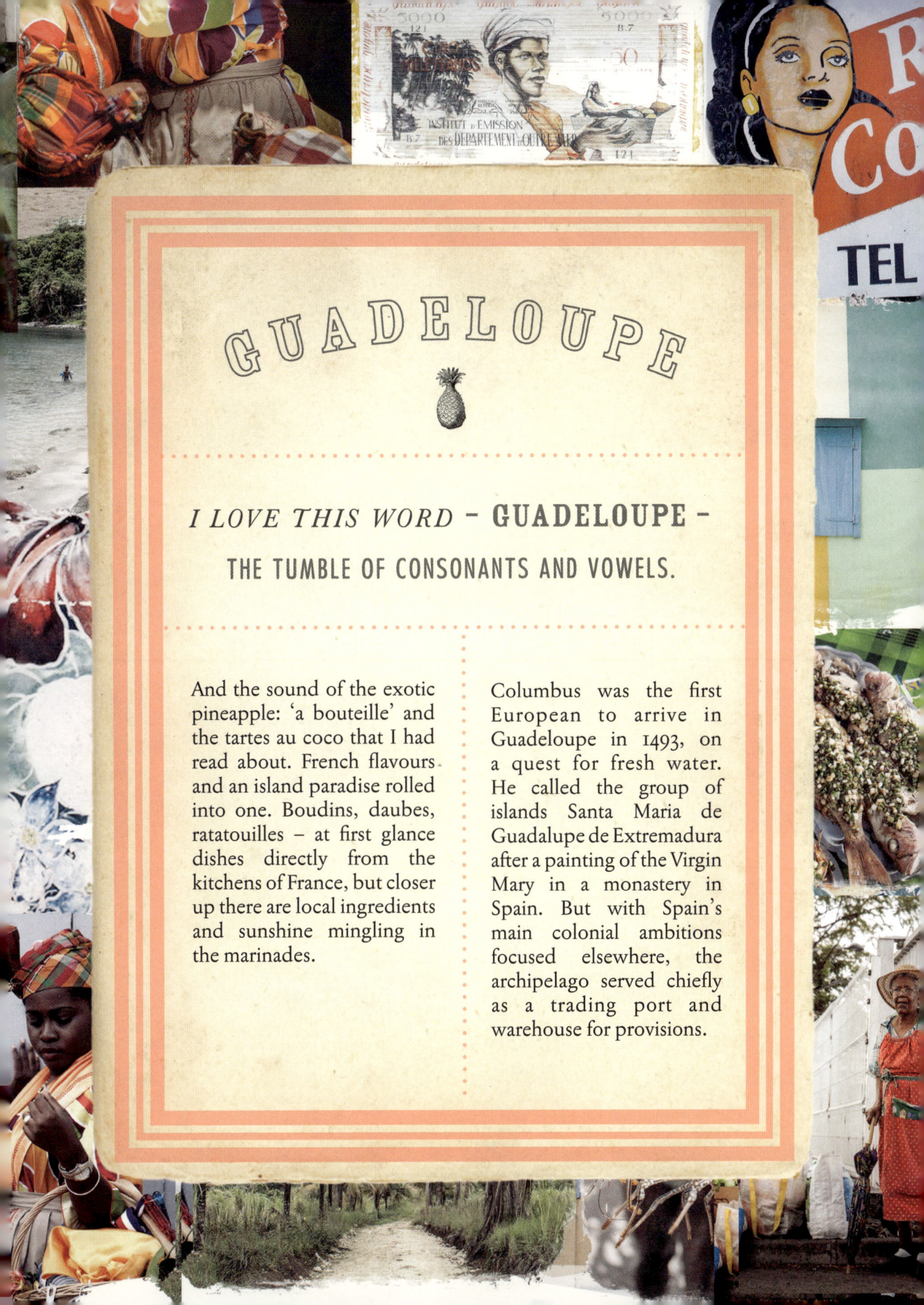

There was no real European settlement until 1635, when French explorers were sent to cultivate tobacco, leading to the island's annexation to the kingdom of France some years later. Slaves from Africa had been brought in to work the tobacco fields and, in time, most of the island's population was of African origin. Sugar had also become a lucrative export crop. When slavery was finally abolished, labour from French territories in India was introduced, with many arriving from Pondicherry. The island is now a diverse mix made up of the descendants of Africans, Indians, colonials and indigenous people. All these influences make up the distinctive cuisine of Guadeloupe today.

The sun burns down. The mosquitoes are relentless; there is nowhere to hide. Rain tumbles suddenly from the sky with no warning. We are darting to find shelter. At the chemist, the lady (who has never met me before), tells me to come back the next day so she can give me a recipe book to help with my research. And the sun drops so very suddenly out of sight to its setting point that I am wondering how it all happened.

The fruit is abundant here: guava, mango, papaya and lychees. Coconuts everywhere, and red and green piments to spice up all the dishes. Plantain and breadfruit are among avocados, limes and regal pineapples – with deep scents of bois d'Inde and cinnamon, and the smell of salt cod forcing its way into the mix. The shops and sea-front market spill onto powdery shores lined with palm trees.

GUADELOUPE

I am staring out at the Caribbean waters. Everyone has come out onto this white sand and brought much of their homes with them.

They have come with their tables and are setting up card games under the shade of the sea-grape trees. Some are setting their lunch tables out on the beach. Tablecloths and chairs. Pots carried from their houses. People are lighting barbecues. I ask if the food is just for them, or if they are selling. It's just for them: pâté en pot, boudin noir, poulet grille, baguette. Callaloo, lambis and soupe des habitants. Showered with creole sauce and fine rums.

Others have set up shop. La Doyenne is shouting out her sorbet specials for the day. She gives me a couple of tastes of the exotic fruits, calling out ingredients and scooping energetically from her beautiful wooden sorbet bucket. There are men here and there with transistor radios. A few playing boules. Some are braiding hair in doorways. And waiting in orderly lines to buy chichis after a late swim. Everywhere – there is the lively chatter of Creole. No matter where you go, people love and embrace the cuisine that is theirs.

Inland, the landscape unfolds into plains, then fields and fields of sugarcane. Through forests, mangroves, waterfalls and rich, colourful layers of flowers and trees, banana and coffee plantations, it rolls up towards the volcanic foothills.

In the main town, on a road leading off from the church, there are hundreds of women. Creole cooks – all of them stunning with beautiful shoes and smiles. They are carrying baskets of food and offerings to Saint-Laurent for La Fête des Cuisinieres…

The bells chime 10 am and the procession starts to move forward. I have never seen anything like this. Checked headscarves and layers of fabric and aprons, petticoats and gold jewels. It is as though a fantasy boat has washed this all up onto the shores. A treasure chest that has ended up here this morning in Rue d'Ennery. All ready for the church, they have come from far and wide. From rum distilleries and sugar plantations, carrying sugarcane. Cocoa, acras and bonbons. Some of the women are not here – they are preparing food at home or in their restaurants, busy chopping chives and shelling peas.

I join the many women who fill the church with their beauty and pride. We are singing to their history and tradition, with the calm spirit and disposition they seem to be blessed with here.

MOULES FRITES À FRUIT À PAIN

You need to time the fries and mussels to be ready at the same time, so have everything prepared before you start to cook. Here, as in other Guadeloupe dishes, milder chillies are used in the cooking process and a hot, fresh chunk of chilli is added to the finished plate, at the discretion of the individual diner.

Serves 3

1.5kg (3¼lb) mussels
2 tablespoons sunflower oil
50g (2oz/about 4) mild, sweet chillies, sliced
¼ spring onion (scallion), including some green, sliced
1 tablespoon chopped chives
2 garlic cloves, chopped
a few thyme sprigs, leaves stripped
2 tablespoons chopped parsley
juice of 1 lime
freshly ground black pepper

For the breadfruit fries
1 small, not too ripe breadfruit
sunflower oil, for deep-frying
sea salt

To serve
2 small hot chillies, halved
lime wedges

De-beard the mussels and scrub them under cold running water. Give each one a sharp tap on the work surface and discard any that stay open. Keep them in a bowl of cold water until you are ready to cook (but not too long in advance).

Quarter the breadfruit, then carefully peel it and cut away the core and spongy inner part. Cut into slices about 1cm (⅜in) thick, then cut the slices into chunks. Boil the chunks in a pot of boiling water for about 10 minutes until tender. Drain.

Have a wide bowl lined with paper towels ready to absorb the excess oil. Pour enough oil for deep-frying into a large, deep pan to fill it by two-thirds. Heat to just below smoking. Working in two batches, drop the breadfruit into the oil and deep-fry, regulating the temperature so it doesn't burn and turning often until pale gold and crisp.

While they are frying, cook the mussels. Put the oil into a large saucepan. Add the chillies, spring onions and chives and sauté for a few minutes. Add the garlic, thyme and parsley. When it smells good, drain the mussels and add to the pan. Put the lid on and cook over a high heat until all the mussels open up. Pour in the lime juice, give a good grinding of black pepper (no salt) and turn through with a spoon or put the lid on and rock the pan to distribute the flavours.

Using a slotted spoon, remove the fries to the lined bowl and scatter well with salt, shaking the bowl to distribute the salt and get rid of excess oil. Divide the mussels with sauce between 3 large, wide bowls. Rest a chilli half in the broth of each bowl. Serve the breadfruit fries on the side, with lime wedges for squeezing.

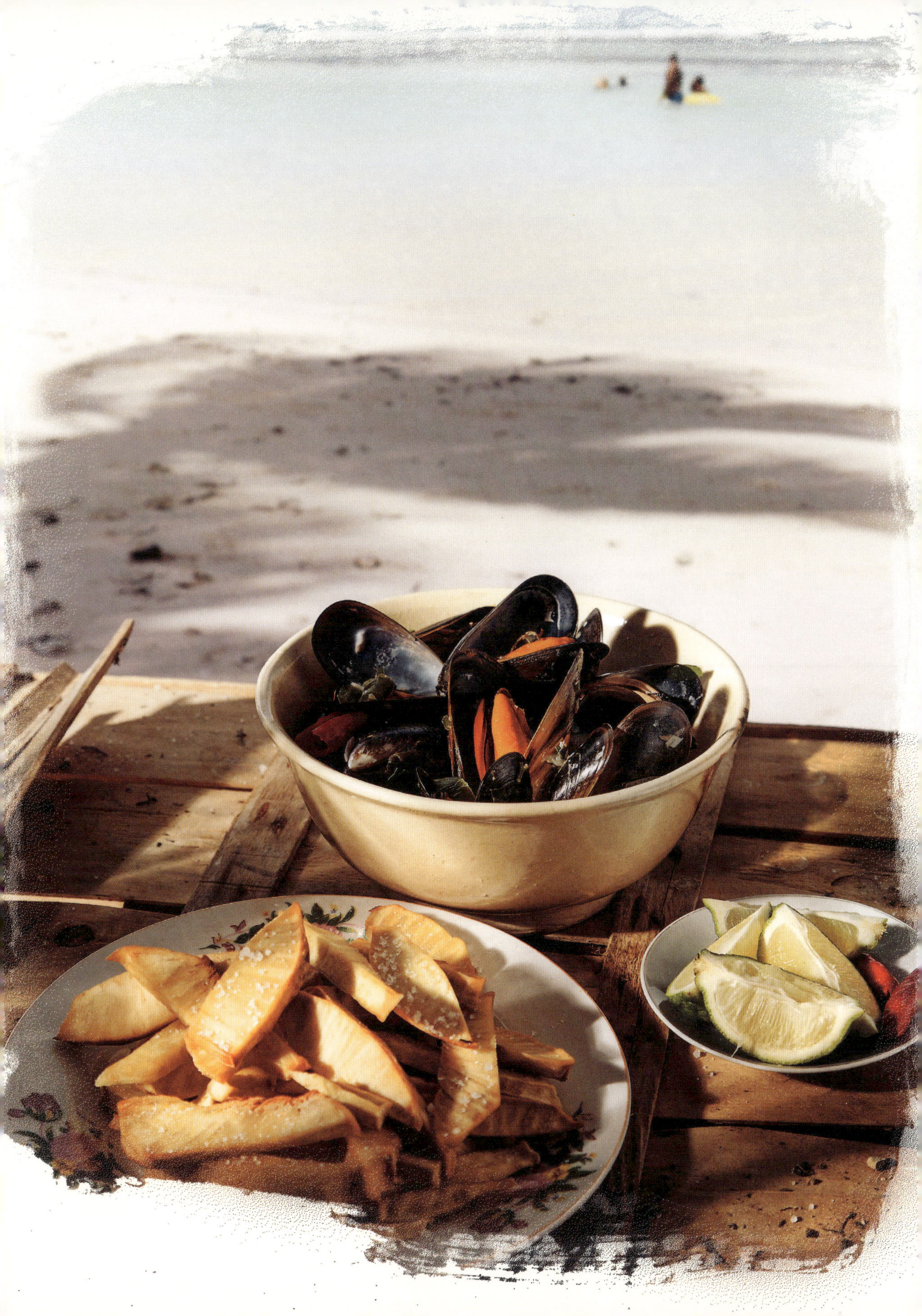

ACRAS DE MORUE

These salt cod fritters are a very typical hors d'oeuvre in Guadeloupe, made with a variety of single ingredients, so as well as salt cod, you might come across prawn, pumpkin or aubergine acras, or the delicate acras de pisquette – transparent tiny fish considered quite a delicacy.

In Guadeloupe, salt cod is sold in many of the fruit and vegetable shops. It needs to be soaked in cold water for a day or two, with a couple of changes of water, to get rid of the salt, but you could also buy ready-soaked cod if you can find it.

Serves 5–6

about 200g (7oz) salt cod fillet, soaked for up to 48 hours in several changes of water (250g/9oz soaked weight), drained
50g (2oz) spring onions (scallions), including some green, chopped
2 garlic cloves, chopped
2 tablespoons chopped chives
2 tablespoons chopped parsley
40g (heaped ¼ cup) red or green mild, sweet chillies, chopped
a few thyme sprigs, leaves stripped
a pinch of hot chilli powder
1 teaspoon dried yeast
200g (1½ cups) plain (all-purpose) flour
250ml (1 cup) chilled sparkling or soda water
sunflower oil, for shallow-frying
freshly ground black pepper

To serve
lime quarters
sea salt

Bring a saucepan of water to the boil and add the drained salt cod. Lower the heat and simmer for 8–10 minutes, skimming the surface as needed. Remove from the heat and let it stand for 10 minutes, then drain, skin and flake the still warm cod into a bowl, removing all bones.

Add the spring onion, garlic, chives, parsley, chillies and thyme leaves to the bowl. Add the chilli powder and a good grinding of black pepper, mix well and leave to cool.

Meanwhile, dissolve the yeast in a large bowl with 2 tablespoons or so of warm water. Add the flour, then the sparkling water, mixing it through until smooth. Add to the cod mixture, turn it through well and leave, without disturbing, for 50–60 minutes to puff up.

Heat 3–4cm (1¼–1½in) depth of oil in a large, wide pan. Working in batches so you don't overcrowd the pan, drop spoonfuls of the batter directly into the hot oil, using a second spoon scrape it off the first, turning each fritter over with a slotted spoon almost immediately when in the oil, so they puff better. Fry until golden on all sides, then remove with a slotted spoon to a plate lined with paper towels.

Serve hot, with a squeeze of lime juice and a scattering of salt.

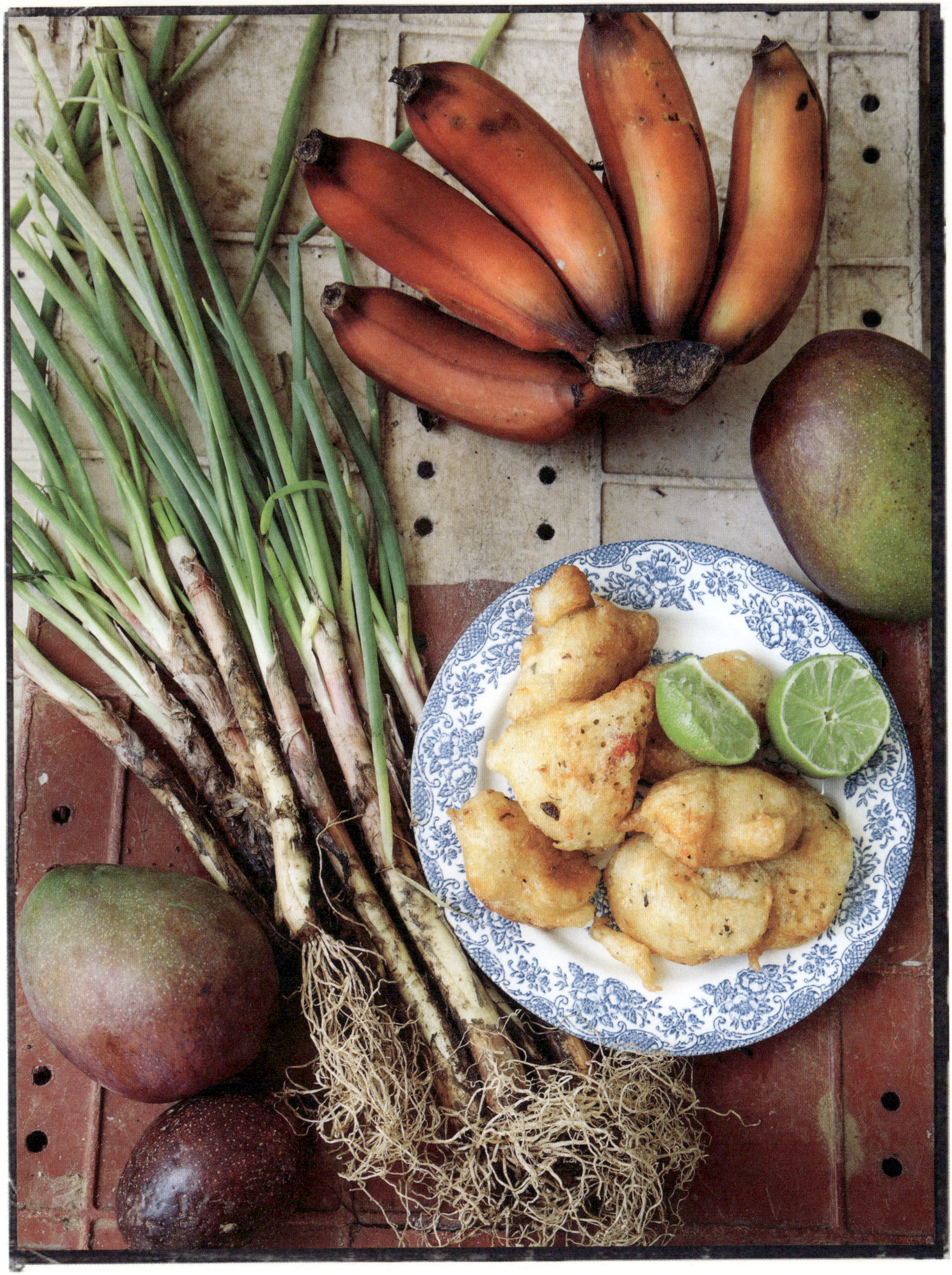

LANGOUSTE FLAMBÉE AU VIEUX RHUM

A familiar sight in Guadeloupe, langoustes are small lobsters that don't have the claw meat, are less expensive but should be treated as lobsters. They are also often grilled and served with the popular sauce chien (Creole sauce). The cooking time will depend on the size of the langoustes you have, so judge accordingly. You may need more than one per person if they are small.

Serves 2

2 langouste (also known as spiny lobster or seawater crayfish)
about 100g (3½oz) butter
4 tablespoons aged rum
sea salt and freshly ground black pepper

Using a cleaver or large chef's knife, cut the langoustes in half from head to tail. Clean out the intestinal tracts (or ask your fishmonger to prepare them for you). Rinse and pat dry with paper towels.

Melt the butter in a small saucepan while the barbecue heats up. When the barbecue is good and hot, scatter the langoustes with a little salt and pepper and grill flesh side down, until there are some deep golden crusty parts here and there. Turn over and cook the shell side; the flesh should be white all the way through.

Transfer the langoustes flesh side up to an oven dish in which they fit in a single layer, and sit the dish directly on the barbecue rack over the fire. Pour the warm butter over, sprinkle with the rum and, standing back, set it alight using a taper or long match. Shake the dish a little to move things around until the flames burn out and the sauce has simmered and reduced a bit. Serve at once.

TI'PUNCH

Many people say not to waste an old rum in a cocktail, but I like a bit of colour to the rum and have been using a not-too-old one for ti'punches. They can be made to measure, and often a sugar syrup is made up and served on the side with some cut up limes and everyone does their own thing. You may decide to use more or less sugar or rum.

For an individual serving, scatter a heaped teaspoon of cane sugar into a lovely not-too-big glass. Squeeze in the juice of ¼ lime and drop the lime shell into the glass, squashing it with a teaspoon. Splash with rum (5 tablespoons or as much as you like) and stir to dissolve. Ice is optional.

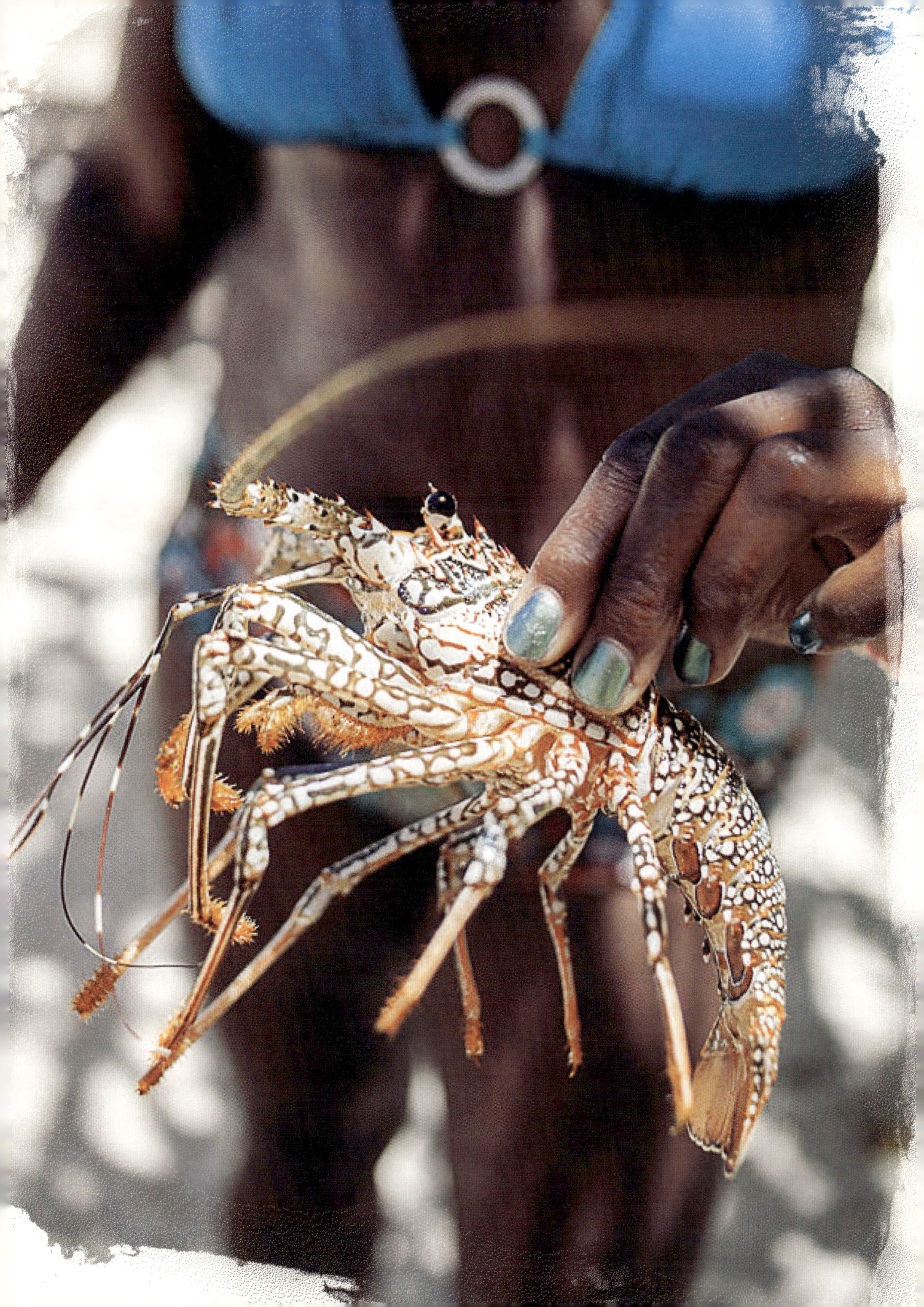

MADAME CLOTILDE'S COURT-BOUILLON DE POISSON

I made this with Madame Clotilde – a truly wonderful cook who let me into her kitchen to watch her cooking one morning. This is one of the few dishes she serves in her restaurant each day. She likes to soak her chillies and garlic in cold water before chopping. Serve with red beans, rice and boiled breadfruit chunks. Beurre rouge is an infusion of pebbly annatto seeds in oil that adds the rusty red tinge to this bouillon. You can make your own or you could add an extra couple of tomatoes at the start.

Serves 2

2 red snapper (each about 500g/18oz)
2 tablespoons sunflower oil
1 small onion, peeled and halved
1 ripe tomato, peeled
1 heaped tablespoon chopped chives
20g (¾ oz/about 2) mild, sweet chillies, deseeded and chopped
3 garlic cloves, peeled
a few thyme sprigs, leaves stripped
2 tablespoons chopped parsley
3 cloves
2 tablespoons beurre rouge (page 76)
juice of 1½ limes
sea salt and freshly ground black pepper

To serve
1 small fat hot chilli, halved and deseeded
lime wedges

Clean the fish well, gut and scale, then cut away all fins and spines (or ask your fishmonger to do this). You can cut in half if your fish are big. Put in a bowl of salted cold water while you prepare the rest.

Put a large, wide saucepan over a medium-high heat, add the oil and slice the onion and tomato into thin slivers directly into the pan. Add the chives and chopped chillies. Grate the garlic into the pan on the coarse side of a grater. Sauté briefly, then add the thyme and parsley.

Add the cloves and a good sprinkling of salt and pepper. When it has a good colour and the tomatoes have melted, add 500ml (2 cups) water and the beurre rouge, and bring to a simmer.

Drain the fish and add to the pan, then splash in the lime juice. The liquid should be just covering the fish; add a little extra water if necessary. Put the lid on and simmer gently for about 15 minutes, until the fish is cooked but not falling apart. Taste for seasoning.

Carefully remove the fish to deep plates, taking care not to loosen any bones. Spoon some of the broth around it. Or, if you prefer, you can fillet the fish first.

Serve with a hot chilli half in each bowl and lime wedges.

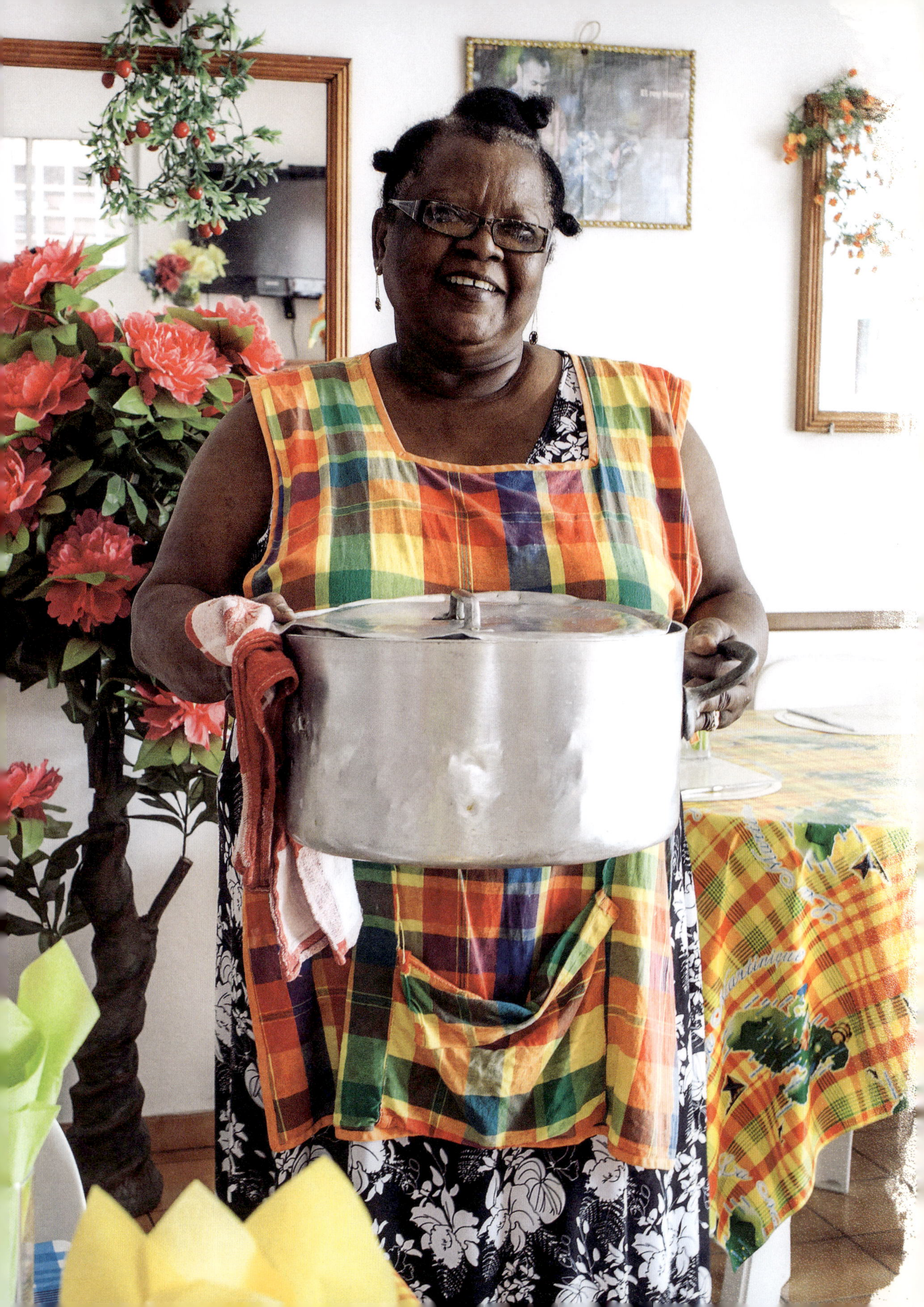

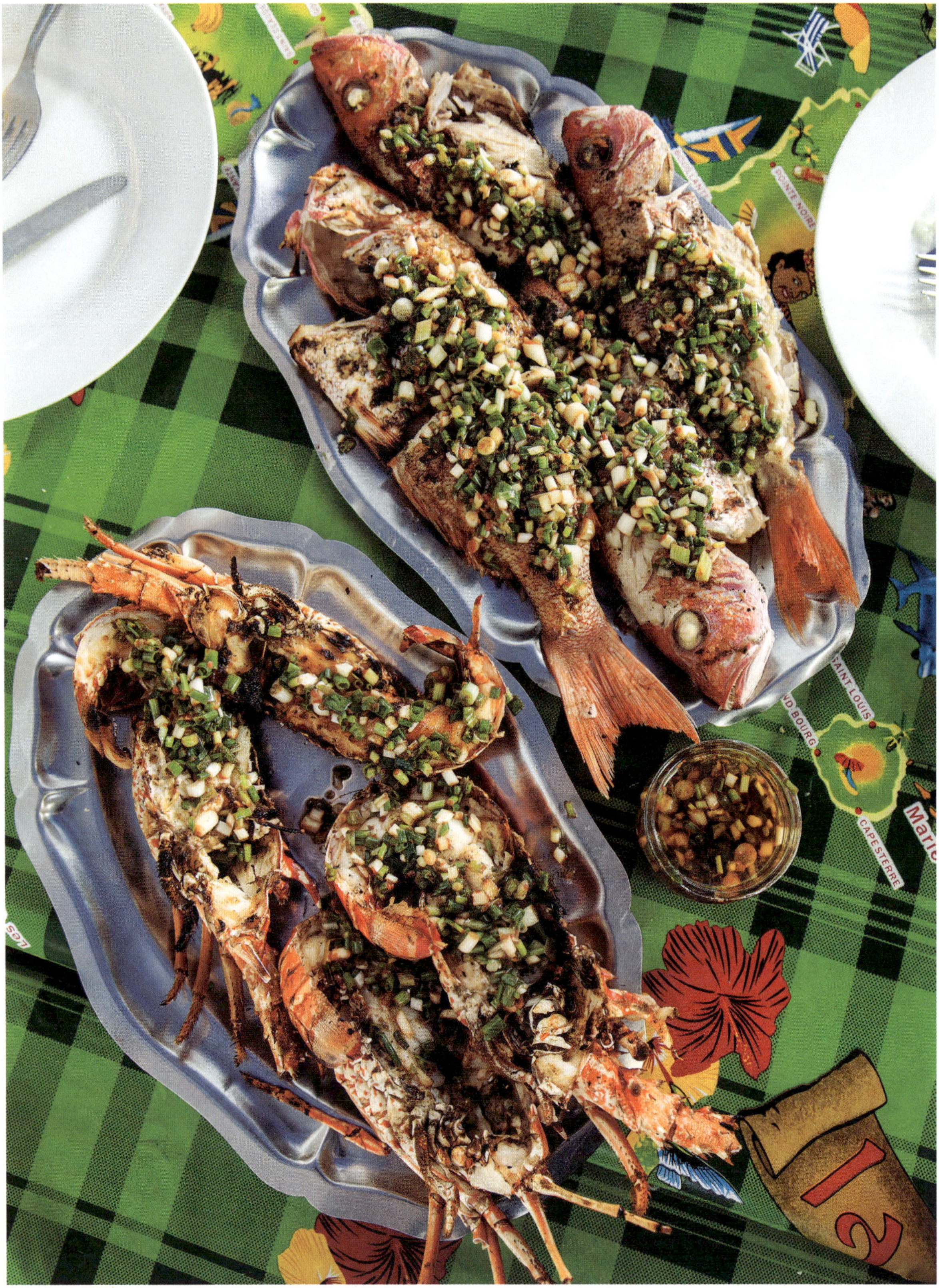
POINTE NOIRE
SAINT-LOUIS
CAPESTERRE

POISSON GRILLÉ ET SAUCE CRÉOLE

This is on every menu: grilled fish (or langouste) served with sauce créole (or chien). I ate this version on the beach in St François and loved it. Use any fish that is good for grilling whole on the barbecue, and allow for a couple of hours of marinating time.

Serves 2

2 red snapper or other fish (each about 500g/18oz)
juice of 2 limes
2 garlic cloves, coarsely grated
1 mild, sweet chilli, (about 20g/¾oz) deseeded and chopped
1 tablespoon chopped chives
a small bunch of thyme, leaves stripped
1 tablespoon oil
1 chunk of hot chilli
sea salt and freshly ground black pepper

For the sauce créole
2 tablespoons oil
1 large spring onion (scallion), about 50g (2oz) white and green parts chopped separately
1 mild, sweet chilli, deseeded and chopped
2 garlic cloves, coarsely grated
1 tomato, peeled and coarsely grated
a bundle of thyme sprigs, leaves stripped
juice of 1 lime

To serve
1 tablespoon chopped chives
1 lime, quartered
2 chunks of hot chilli

Clean and gut the fish, if necessary, but leave the scales on if possible (to stop the fish sticking on the barbecue). Snip off the fins and spines. Wipe away any loose scales with paper towels. Cut 2 or 3 slashes on either side of each fish and season both sides and the insides with salt and pepper.

In a small bowl, mix together the lime juice, garlic, chilli, chives, thyme and oil. Add the hot chilli and leave to infuse for half a minute, or longer for more heat. Remove and reserve the chilli. Put the fish in a dish and slather all over with the marinade. Cover with plastic wrap and leave for about 2 hours, turning once or twice.

Meanwhile, heat up the barbecue. To make the sauce créole, heat the oil in a pan and sauté the white spring onion with the chilli, until pale golden. Add the garlic and sauté until fragrant. Add the tomato and thyme leaves. Season with salt and pepper and simmer for 5 minutes or so.

Purée the sauce using a hand-held blender, then add the lime juice and simmer for a few more minutes. Taste and adjust the seasonings as necessary. Swirl the reserved hot chilli in for half a minute, then taste; swirl it for longer if you want more heat. Keep warm.

When the barbecue is ready, put the fish into a grilling rack and cook close to the hot coals (about 10cm/4in away) until the undersides are deep golden. Turn and barbecue until the other side is deep golden, the flesh is cooked through and the skin crisp.

Carefully transfer the fish to a serving plate and scatter over the spring onion greens and chives. Serve with the sauce créole, lime wedges and the extra hot chilli to swirl through the sauce for more heat if you like.

BLAFF DE POISSON

Blaff is a tasty broth, good with any fish, even prawns or crayfish. Serve with a chunk of hot chilli that can seep into the abundant broth on the plate and you can just lift it out if too hot or smother it about with your spoon if you want more heat. I loved this in Guadaloupe.

Serves 2

1 red snapper, about 550g (19oz)
juice of 1 lime
1 garlic clove, roughly chopped
2 wild taros, each 150g (5oz), peeled and thickly sliced
2 small, firm young bananas
1 hot red chilli, halved and deseeded
sea salt

For the bouillon
a few black peppercorns
3 cloves
40g (1½oz) mild, sweet chillies, halved and deseeded
1 white onion, peeled
a grating of nutmeg
1 small spring onion (scallion), including some green
a small bundle of parsley
a small bundle of chives
a small bundle of thyme
a couple of bois d'Inde (allspice) leaves
1 garlic clove, roughly chopped
juice of 1 lime

Clean the fish, gut and scale it, then cut away the fins and spines. Rinse and wipe it dry with paper towels. Slash in a couple of places with a sharp knife and put in a large shallow dish with the lime juice, a little salt and the garlic. Leave to marinate for an hour or so.

To prepare the bouillon, pour 1 litre (1 quart) water into a wide, low-sided pan. Salt well and add the peppercorns, cloves, chillies and whole onion. Grate in some nutmeg. Make a bouquet garni by tying together with string the spring onion, parsley, chives, thyme and the allspice leaves, and drop into the pan. Toss in the garlic, bring to the boil and simmer for 5–6 minutes.

Remove the fish from its marinade and add to the bouillon. Spoon some broth over it, put the lid on and simmer very gently (so the fish can steam rather than stew) for about 12 minutes, then carefully transfer the fish to a serving dish and keep warm.

While the fish is cooking, cook the taro slices in a saucepan of simmering unsalted water for about 10 minutes until just softened; drain.

Meanwhile, add the lime juice to the bouillon and take the pan off the heat. Using a slotted spoon, take out and discard the bouquet garni and vegetables. Taste the broth and adjust the seasoning. Add the taro to the broth and leave for 10 minutes or so to absorb the flavours.

Peel the bananas, then drop into the hot broth for a few minutes. Serve with a good amount of broth around the snapper, with the taro slices and bananas. Put a piece of the fresh hot chilli onto each serving.

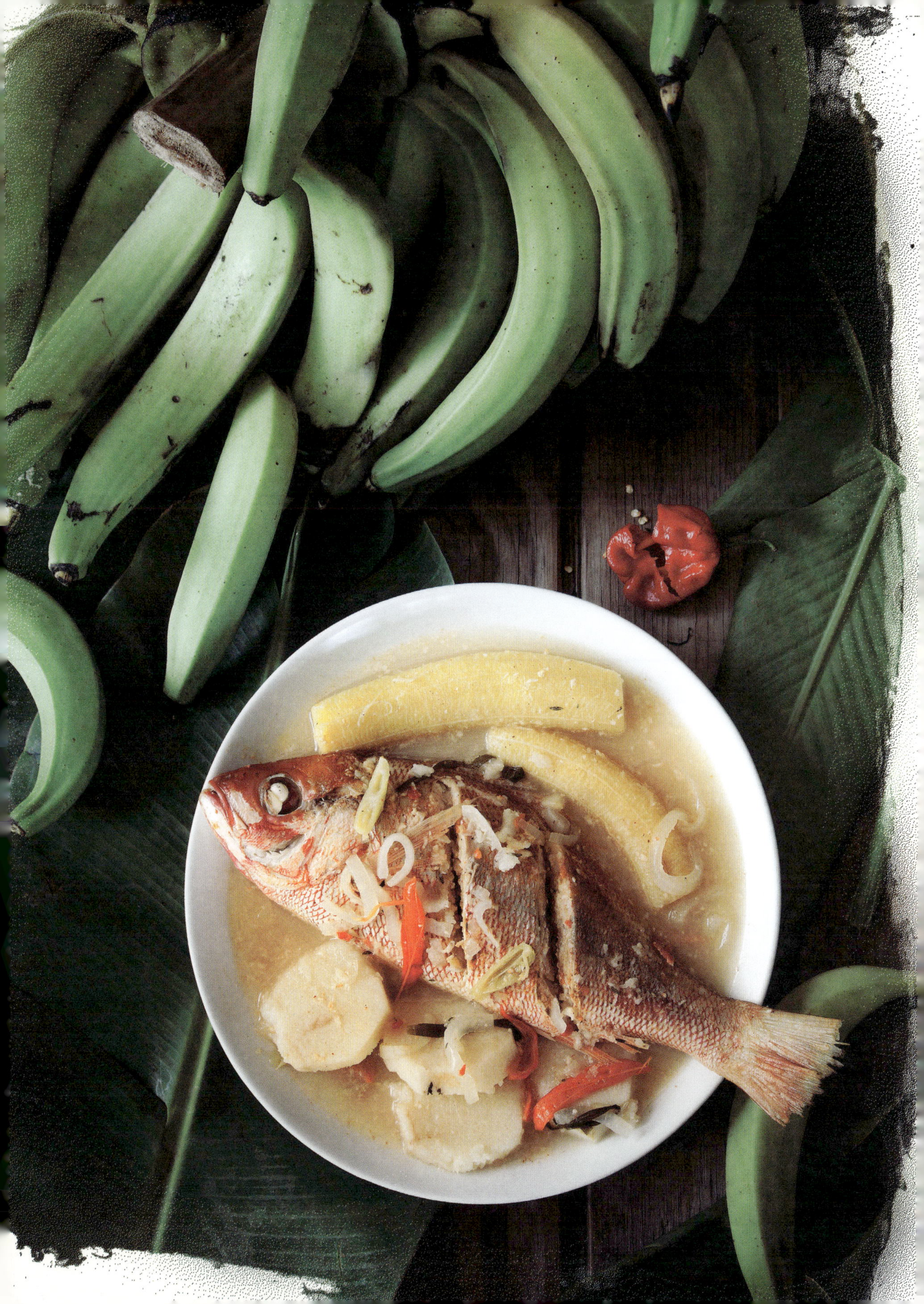

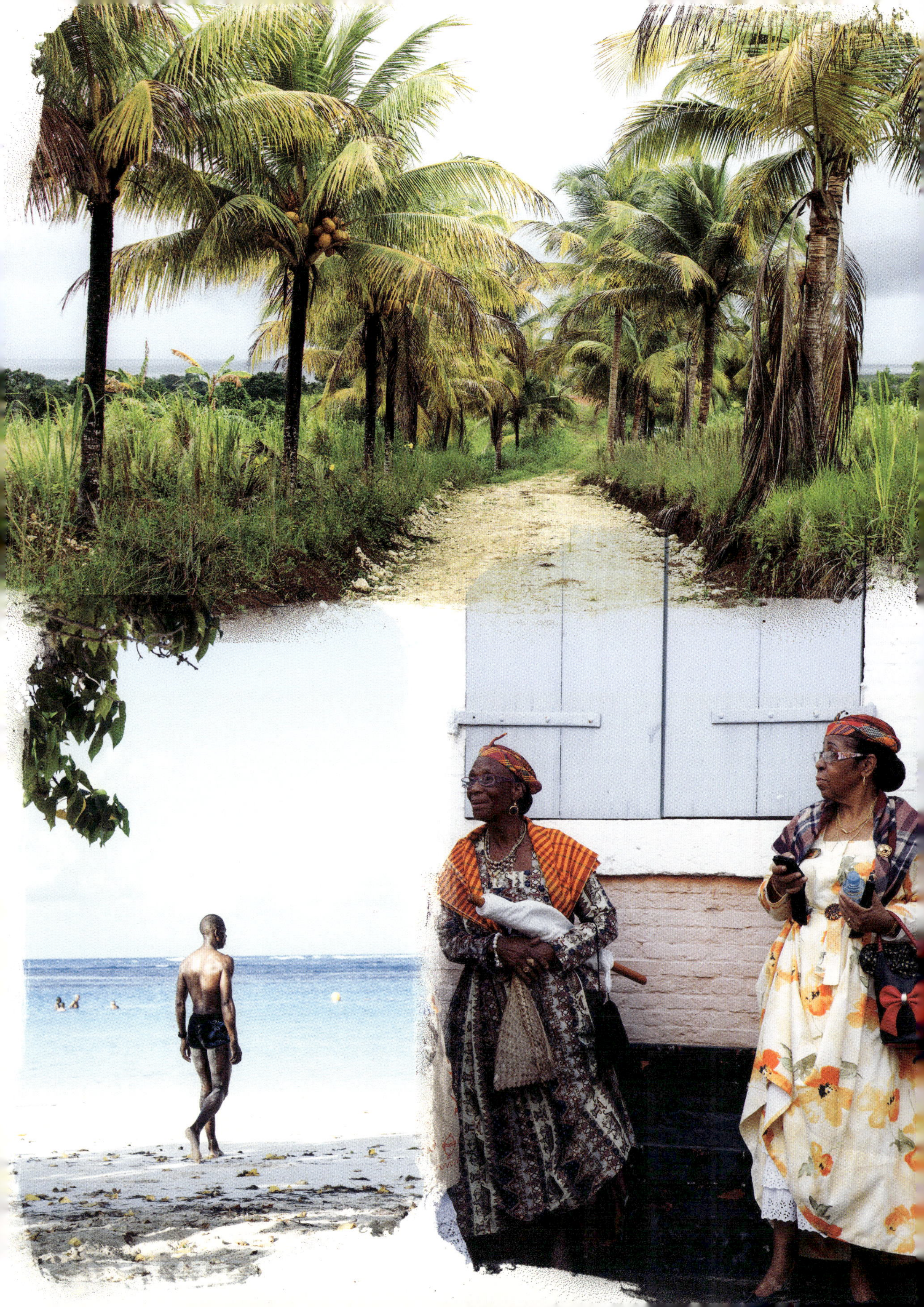

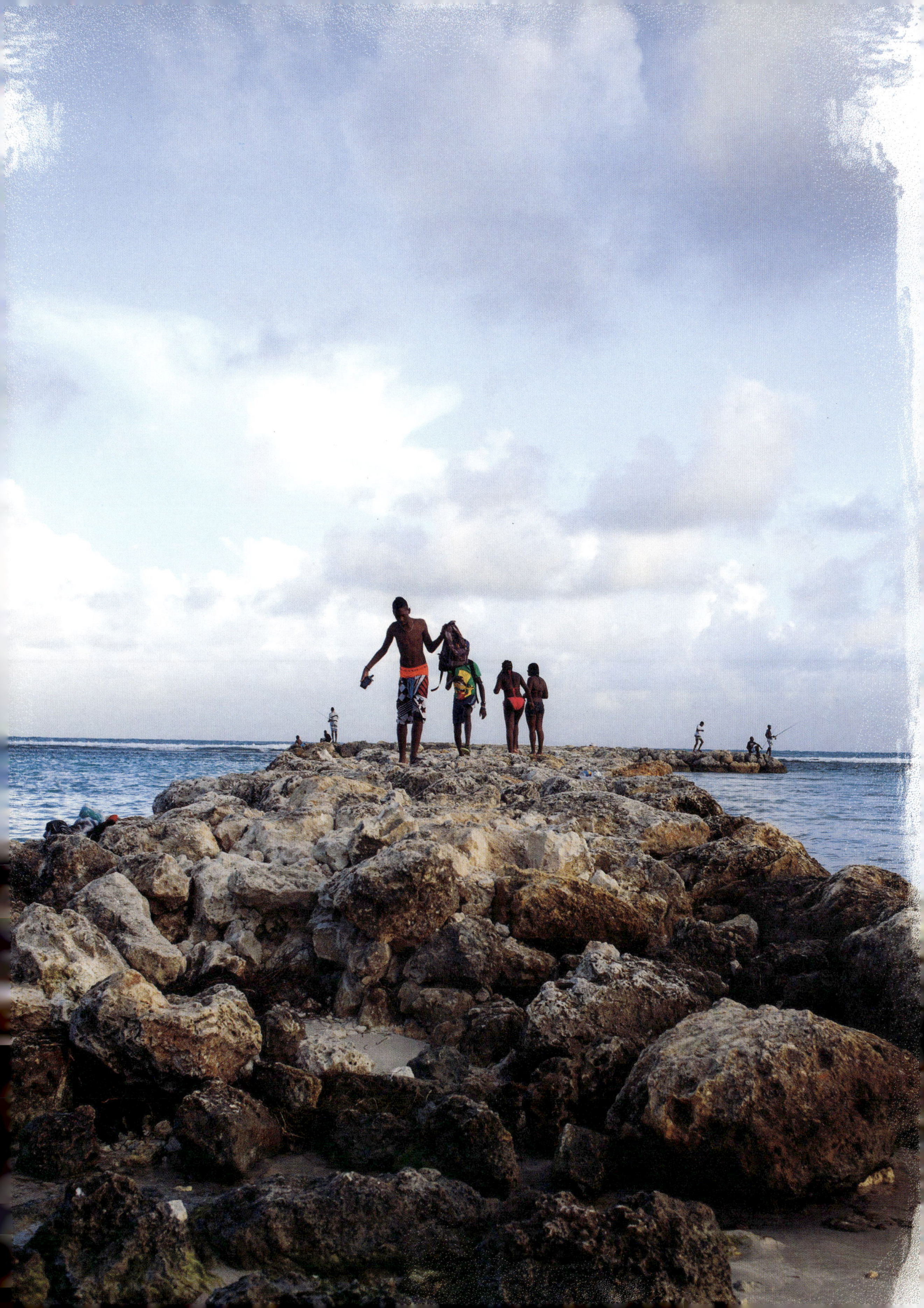

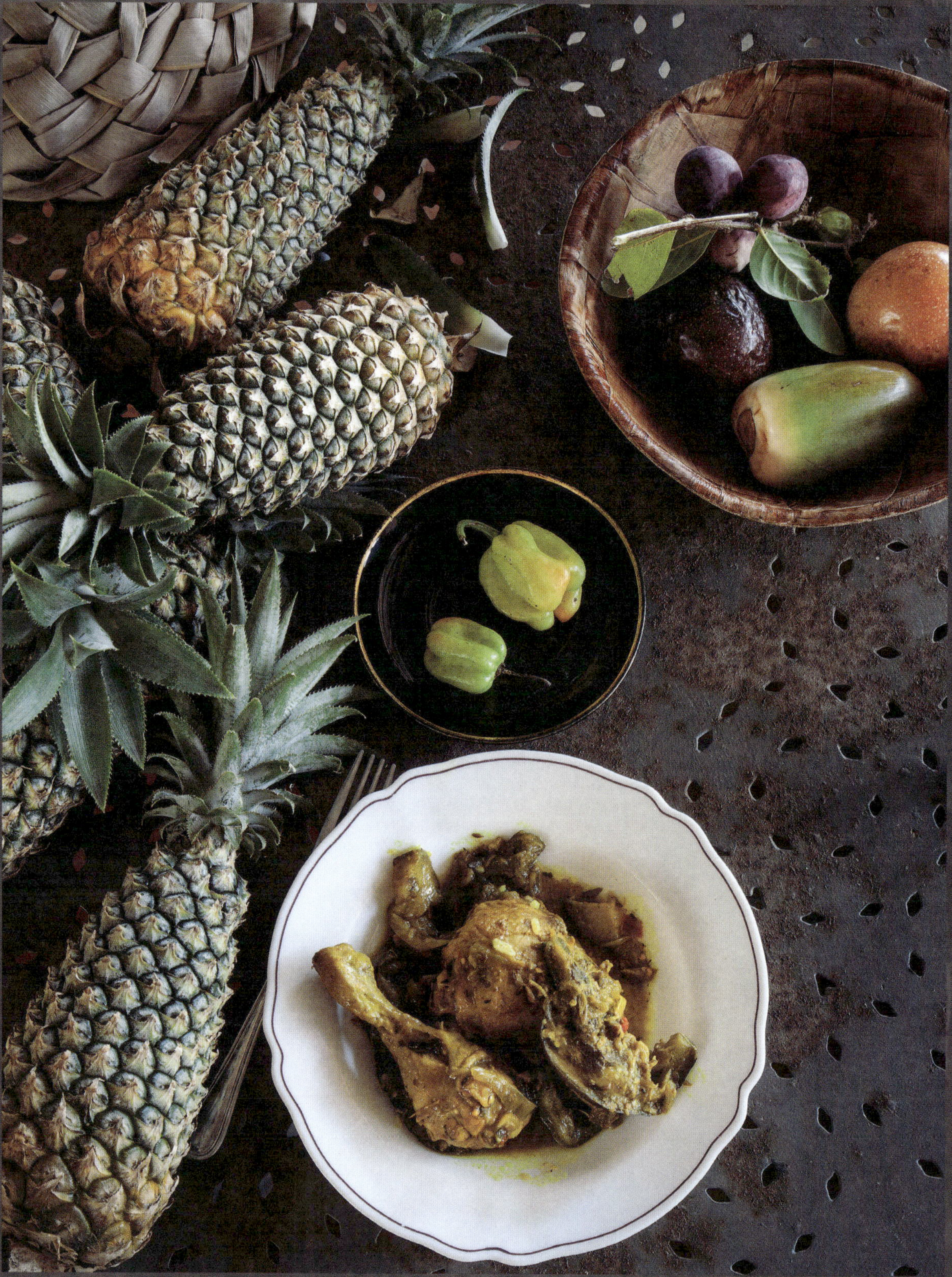

COLOMBO DE POULET

Deep-flavoured and delicious, this is one of Guadeloupe's national dishes. Also sometimes made with pork, fish or goat, it is very special and typical of Creole cuisine. The origins stem from Indian soil, brought over in colonial times with the workers.

Colombo powder is the French West Indies' version of masala mix and, like grains à roussir, is readily available in Guadeloupe. Sometimes potatoes and other vegetables are cooked in with the dish. It's good served with white rice.

Serves 4

1 chicken, cut into 8 pieces
juice of 1½ limes
3 garlic cloves, peeled
1½ medium onions, peeled
a few sprigs of thyme, leaves stripped
3 tablespoons chopped parsley
1 small hot dried chilli, deseeded
2 sweet chillies, deseeded and sliced
4 tablespoons sunflower oil
1 tablespoon grains à roussir (see next page)
3 cloves
3 tablespoons colombo powder (see next page)
625ml (2½ cups) water
1 small aubergine (eggplant), about 350g (12oz)
sea salt and freshly ground black pepper
2 small hot, green chillies, halved and deseeded, to serve

Put the chicken pieces into a dish and splash over the juice of the half lime. Coarsely grate in one of the garlic cloves, and slice the onion half into thin slivers directly into the dish. Add the thyme leaves and 2 tablespoons of the parsley. Crumble in the hot dried chilli, the sliced chillies and 1 tablespoon of the oil. Season with salt and pepper, turn the chicken pieces to coat well, and set aside for a couple of hours to marinate.

Halve the remaining onion and cut into thin wedges. Heat the remaining 3 tablespoons of oil in a large, wide pan (that will take the chicken in a single layer. Add the onion, grains à roussir and cloves. Grate in the remaining 2 garlic cloves. Sauté over a medium heat until golden.

Add the chicken pieces in a single layer, then add the marinade. Stir the colombo powder into the water and pour this into the pan. Bring to the boil, then lower the heat, cover and simmer for about 15 minutes.

Quarter the aubergine lengthways, then cut into thin wedges (less than 1cm/⅜in). Add to the pan, making sure they are immersed. Simmer, covered, for another 40 minutes or so, until the chicken is cooked through; there should be plenty of sauce.

Towards the end of the cooking time, add the rest of the parsley. Just before serving, add the remaining lime juice. Give it another couple of minutes of heat, then serve hot with half a green chilli in each serving, for mingling into the sauce if you want extra heat.

GRAINS À ROUSSIR

Makes 5 tablespoons

4 tablespoons cumin seeds
2 teaspoons fenugreek seeds
1 teaspoon yellow mustard seeds

Mix everything together and store in an airtight container.

COLOMBO POWDER

Makes about 1 cup

3 tablespoons uncooked white rice
3 tablespoons coriander seeds
2½ tablespoons cumin seeds
1 tablespoon yellow mustard seeds
1 tablespoon fenugreek seeds
½ tablespoon fennel seeds
½ tablespoon black peppercorns
4 cloves
1 teaspoon chilli powder
2 tablespoons ground turmeric

Toast the rice in a dry frying pan over a medium heat until lightly golden, 4–5 minutes, stirring often to prevent burning. Spread on a tray and leave to cool completely.

In a spice grinder or small food processor, grind the rice with all the seeds, peppercorns and cloves to a powder. Add the chilli and turmeric and mix until well blended. Store in an airtight container.

BEURRE ROUGE

Makes 5 tablespoons

1 tablespoon annatto seeds
4 tablespoons sunflower oil
1 teaspoon paprika
1 tablespoon melted butter

Put the annatto seeds and sunflower oil in a small saucepan and bring slowly to the boil. Let it bubble for 10–15 seconds, then take off the heat. Leave until cold, then strain; the seeds can be kept and used once or twice more.

In a small bowl, stir 2 tablespoons of the infused oil with the paprika. Stir in the melted butter then put in the fridge until the butter thickens. Stir to a paste then incorporate 1 tablespoon of the remaining infused oil.

The beurre rouge will keep in a covered container in the fridge for 2–3 weeks.

RAGOÛT DE PORC, YAM ET POIS D'ANGOLE

This is a very typical Guadeloupe dish, often served with pumpkin gratin, and with pigeon peas for Christmas. Dried pigeon peas (also called gungo peas) will need overnight soaking, while fresh ones, if you can find them, can be cooked straight from the pod until tender. You can use chickpeas or black-eyed peas instead.

Serves 4–5

1kg (2¼lb) pork shoulder, excess fat trimmed off, cut into 5cm (2in) chunks
5 tablespoons sunflower oil
juice of 2 limes
2 bay leaves
a good pinch of chilli powder
a good grating of nutmeg
1 onion, chopped
2 spring onions (scallions), including green part, chopped
2 mild, sweet chillies, about 40g (1½oz), deseeded and chopped
4 garlic cloves, chopped
3 or 4 cloves
2 tablespoons chopped parsley
a small bundle of chives, chopped
a small bundle of thyme, leaves stripped
600g (1¼lb) yam or sweet potato
sea salt and freshly ground black pepper
fresh deseeded red chillies, to serve

Put the pork in a bowl with 2 tablespoons of the oil, the lime juice, bay leaves, chilli powder and nutmeg. Mix to coat, cover and leave to marinate for a couple of hours.

Heat the remaining oil in a large, wide non-stick frying pan over a high heat. Shake the pork from the marinade, patting dry with paper towels, and reserving the marinade. Fry, turning the pieces of pork with tongs, until very deep golden brown on all sides.

Season with salt and pepper, then add the onion, spring onions and chillies to one side of the pan. Sauté until a little golden, shifting the meat to the side to make space as necessary. Add the garlic, cloves, parsley, chives and thyme leaves. Sauté for another minute, then add 500ml (2 cups) water to the reserved marinade and pour all of this over the meat. Bring to a simmer, cover and cook until tender, about 50 minutes, turning once or twice.

Meanwhile, peel the yam and cut into long, thick chunks. Keep in a bowl of cold water until needed, then drain and add to the pan (after the 50 minute simmer) with a light sprinkle of salt. Turn through, burying the pieces in the liquid and adding another 250ml (1 cup) or so of water. Cover and continue cooking for another 20–30 minutes or until the yam is tender, turning a couple of times. Taste for seasoning, and make sure there is a good amount of sauce, adding extra water if needed.

Take off the heat and leave to stand with the lid on for 15 minutes or so for the flavours to settle. Serve with a piece of fresh chilli drifting in the sauce for extra heat, and pigeon peas on the side.

POIS D'ANGOLE

A little coconut cream added towards the end of cooking is lovely also. Any leftover peas can be added to rice the next day.

Serves 6 or more

500g (18oz) dried pigeon peas (gungo peas), soaked overnight in cold water
3 tablespoons oil
1 onion, chopped
2 garlic cloves, chopped
50g (2oz) chunk or slice of salt pork or lardons
a bouquet garni (1 bay leaf, 1 allspice leaf and a small bundle each of parsley, chives and thyme, tied together with string)
sea salt freshly ground black pepper
To serve
3 red chillies, halved and deseeded
lime quarters

Drain the peas and rinse in a colander.

Heat the oil in a large saucepan and add the onion and garlic. Sauté until golden, then add the peas, salt pork and about 1.5 litres (1⅔ quarts) water. Add a grinding of pepper and the bouquet garni.

Bring to the boil, skim the surface of scum, then lower the heat, partly cover and simmer for about an hour until the peas are starting to turn tender, then season with salt and add more water if necessary. Continue cooking for another 30 minutes, or until the beans are soft and tender, and much of the water has been absorbed.

Taste and adjust the seasoning. Serve warm, with a chilli half for each serving and lime for squeezing over.

RIZ ET HARICOTS ROUGE

'Rice and beans' is often served in Guadeloupe to soak up the many sauced dishes they have. This is the most typical dish, although rice is also mixed with chickpeas, pigeon peas, lentils or dumplings, or eaten plain.

Serves 6

200g (7oz) red beans, soaked overnight in cold water
a bouquet garni (a few each celery tops, spring onion (scallion) tops, chives, parsley stalks and thyme sprigs, tied together with string)
3 cloves
1 onion, peeled
2 garlic cloves, peeled
a piece of salt pork or small ham hock
350g (scant 2 cups) medium-grain rice
sea salt and freshly ground black pepper

Drain the beans and rinse in a colander. Tip into a wide pan, cover with about 1.5 litres (1⅔ quarts) water and bring to the boil; skim the surface. Add the bouquet garni, cloves, onion, garlic, salt pork or ham hock and a good grind of black pepper. Bring to the boil, lower the heat and partly cover with a lid. Simmer until the beans are tender, 1¼–1½ hours, seasoning with salt after an hour.

Add about 250ml (1 cup) water and bring back to the boil. Remove and discard the onion and bouquet garni. Stir in the rice and bring back to the boil. Lower the heat and simmer, covered, until the liquid has been absorbed, 10–15 minutes.

Fluff up with a fork, put the lid back on and place on a simmer mat over the lowest possible heat until all the moisture has been absorbed and the rice and beans are quite dry.

JOELLE'S SOUPE DES HABITANTS

"Throw in any amount of vegetables," says Joelle, "and let them melt down to a creamy texture to feed many." She likes to include breadfruit, so add some if you can get it and a handful of sugar peas at the end. The salt pork or beef is important here, to add depth of flavour. In Guadeloupe, fresh bunches of assorted vegetables are sold tied together with string ready to put into a pot. The variety of greens in Guadeloupe also gives this its special flavour, but use a mixture of what you can get.

Serves 6–8

2 tablespoons oil
200g (7oz) salt beef or pork, cubed
80g (3oz) spring onions (scallions), including some green, chopped
100g (3½oz) onions, chopped
200g (7oz) leeks, trimmed and sliced
a handful chives, chopped
80g (3oz) mild, sweet chillies, deseeded and chopped
2 garlic cloves, chopped
450g (1lb) sweet potato
300g (10½oz) turnips
180g (6½oz) taro
240g (8½oz) yam
400g (14oz) pumpkin (unpeeled weight), peeled and cubed
240g (8½oz) carrots, chopped
80g (3oz) celery, chopped
300g (10½oz) greens, such as Swiss chard or spinach, rinsed and chopped
a good grating of nutmeg
a bouquet garni, made from a small bundle of parsley, 1 bay leaf, 1 allspice leaf and a few thyme sprigs, tied together with string
a handful sugar snap peas
sea salt and freshly ground black pepper

Heat the oil in a large saucepan and add the salt beef or pork. Sauté until golden then add the spring onion, onions, leeks, chives and chillies. Sauté until the vegetables are slightly coloured, then stir in the garlic.

Peel and chunk the sweet potato, turnips, taro and yam and add to the pan along with the pumpkin, carrots, celery and greens. Add about 1.25 litres (1⅓ quarts) water and bring to the boil. Season with some salt and pepper (but bear in mind the salt beef or pork) and nutmeg, and add the bouquet garni.

Lower the heat, put the lid on and simmer for about 50 minutes until creamy and some of the vegetables have melted, with others still in chunks, adding the sugar peas after 30–35 minutes. Stir now and then to check that nothing is sticking on the bottom. Taste for seasoning and serve warm.

GUADELOUPE

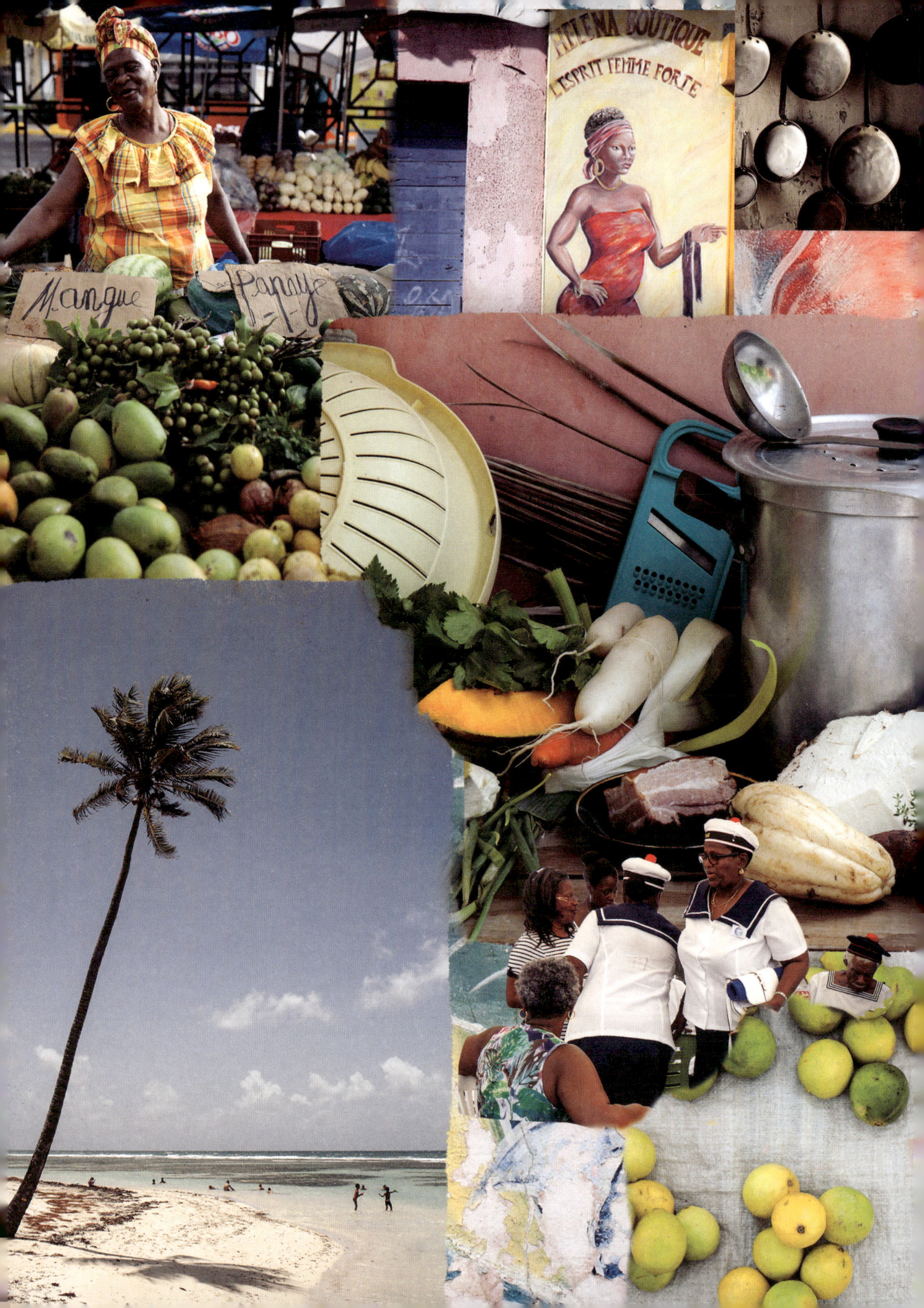
Mangue
Papaye
HELENA BOUTIQUE
L'ESPRIT FEMME FORTE

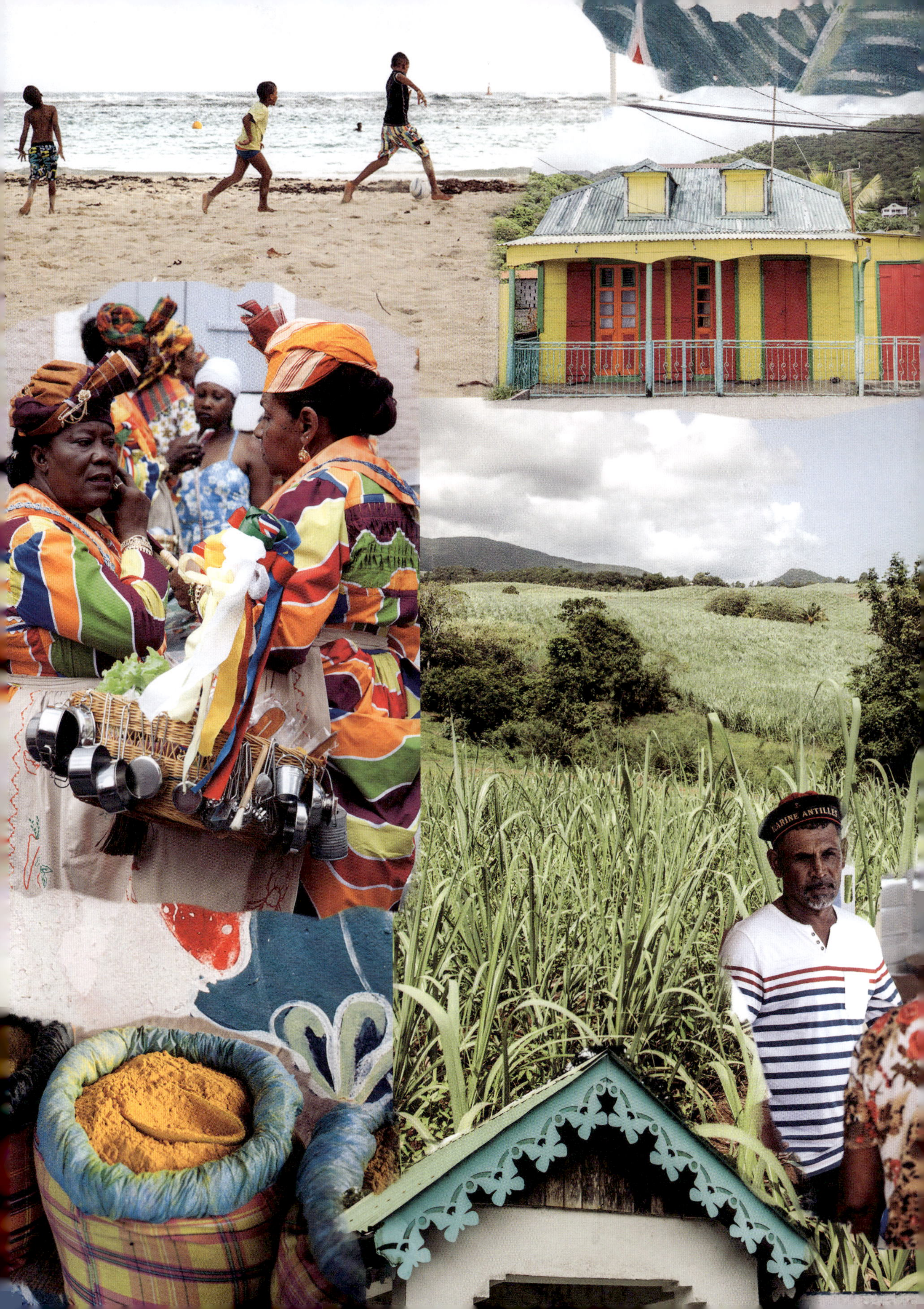
ARINE ANTILLES

RATATOUILLE CRÉOLE

This is a wonderful accompaniment to any roast or grilled main course. It is also lovely served warm on its own, with baguette. This recipe is similar to the Provençal version, but using pumpkin, cucumber and chayote rather than courgette. Olive oil is brought in from France, though not widely used in Guadeloupe. It is important that the aubergine takes on a deep golden colour at the start, so it is well cooked and has a good flavour in the finished dish.

Serves 6–8

1 aubergine (eggplant) (about 500g/18oz)
1 large red (bell) pepper (about 350g/12oz)
1 large cucumber (about 450g/1lb), scrubbed
6 tablespoons olive oil
1 celery stalk, sliced
2 spring onions (scallions) (100g/3½oz total weight), green and white parts, chopped
500g (18oz) pumpkin flesh, cut into chunks
½ chayote (about 200g/7oz), peeled and cut into chunks
2 mild, sweet chillies, deseeded and chopped
3 garlic cloves, chopped
a small bundle of chives, chopped
3 ripe tomatoes (300g/10½oz total weight), peeled and cut into chunks
a good pinch of chilli powder
2 bay leaves
a small handful thyme, leaves stripped
2 tablespoons chopped parsley
sea salt and freshly ground black pepper

Cut the top off the aubergine, halve lengthways and cut into half-moon slices, about 5mm (¼in) thick, then cut these into 4cm (1½in) chunks.

Halve the red pepper, remove the seeds and cut into chunks. Halve the cucumber lengthways, scoop out the seeds using a pointed teaspoon and discard (or eat) and slice (with skin on) into discs about 2cm (¾in) thick.

Heat most of the oil a large, wide non-stick frying pan (big enough to fit all the vegetables in a single layer) and add the aubergine. Sauté, turning the pieces with tongs, until deep golden all over, sprinkling with a little salt.

Add the red pepper, celery, spring onions, pumpkin, chayote, cucumber, chillies, garlic and chives to the pan and sauté until they too have taken on a bit of colour, stirring from time to time. Add the tomatoes and chilli powder and stir through, seasoning well with salt and pepper. Add the bay and thyme leaves.

Lower the heat and cook, uncovered, for about 45 minutes, or until all the vegetables are soft, stirring from time to time but taking care not to mush things up. If it seems dry towards the end of cooking, and the vegetables are not all cooked, add a little water and continue cooking. Stir the parsley gently through 10 minutes or so toward the end of cooking.

Take off the heat and leave the dish to settle a little, covered, before serving.

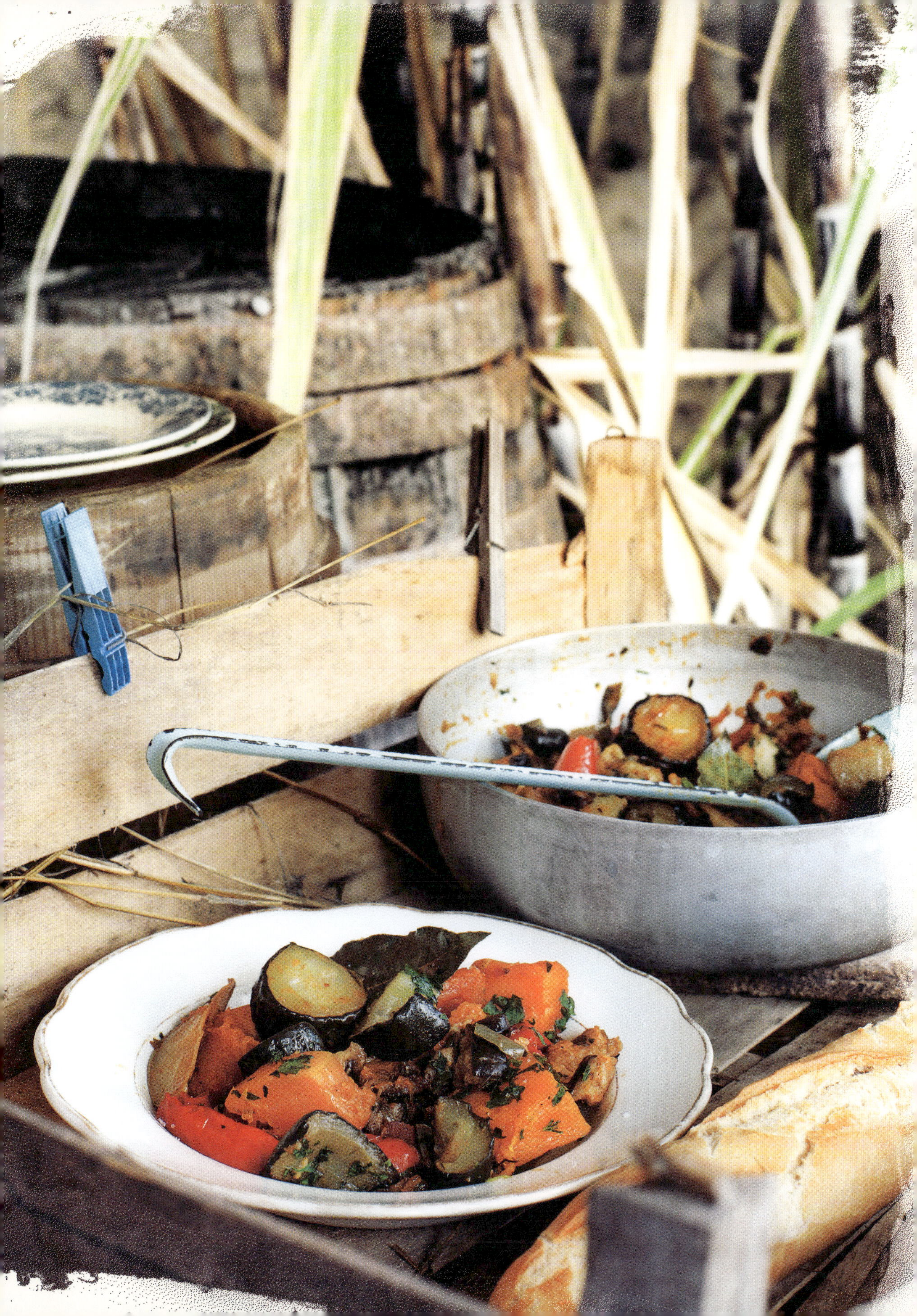

SORBET À LA NOIX DE COCO

This coconut sorbet is sold everywhere along the beaches, from beautiful ancient-looking wooden barrels containing crushed ice mixed with salt to keep the sorbet frozen. I love its beautiful simplicity, but you can add a few drops of almond extract, some lemon zest or grated nutmeg if you like. Made with fresh grated coconut and water, this version has a pure flavour. You can also use tinned coconut milk, which gives a creamier texture and makes the sorbet easier to scoop from frozen.

Serves 6

1 fresh coconut
80g (3oz) raw cane sugar (pale golden)

Break open the coconut, reserving the water (you should get about 185ml/¾ cup). Extract the flesh from the husk and break into pieces (you should have 300–350g/10½–12oz). Using a vegetable peeler or paring knife, peel away the brown outer skin (the odd brown fleck is lovely in the finished sorbet).

Coarsely grate the coconut flesh or whizz to small pieces in a food processor.

Top up the coconut water to 625ml (2½ cups) with water, and heat in a saucepan. Add the flesh and simmer for a few minutes. Remove from the heat and blend a little, using a hand-held blender (it won't be completely puréed). Leave to cool, stirring from time to time.

Strain into a jug through a fairly fine sieve, pressing down firmly with a wooden spoon to extract as much of the liquid and flavour as possible. Add a wooden spoonful of the bits to the liquid and stir in the sugar. Pour back into the saucepan and simmer gently over a low heat, stirring until the sugar dissolves. Remove from the heat and cool completely, then chill.

Churn in an ice cream machine according to the manufacturer's instructions. Alternatively, pour into a shallow container, cover, and put in the freezer. After an hour or so when it starts to freeze, remove from the freezer and beat briskly with a whisk or electric beaters to break up the crystals, and return the container to the freezer. Whisk again after another couple of hours then, when it is nearly firm, whisk one last time. Return to the freezer to set completely.

Remove from the freezer a little before serving, to soften slightly and make it easier to scoop.

GUADELOUPE

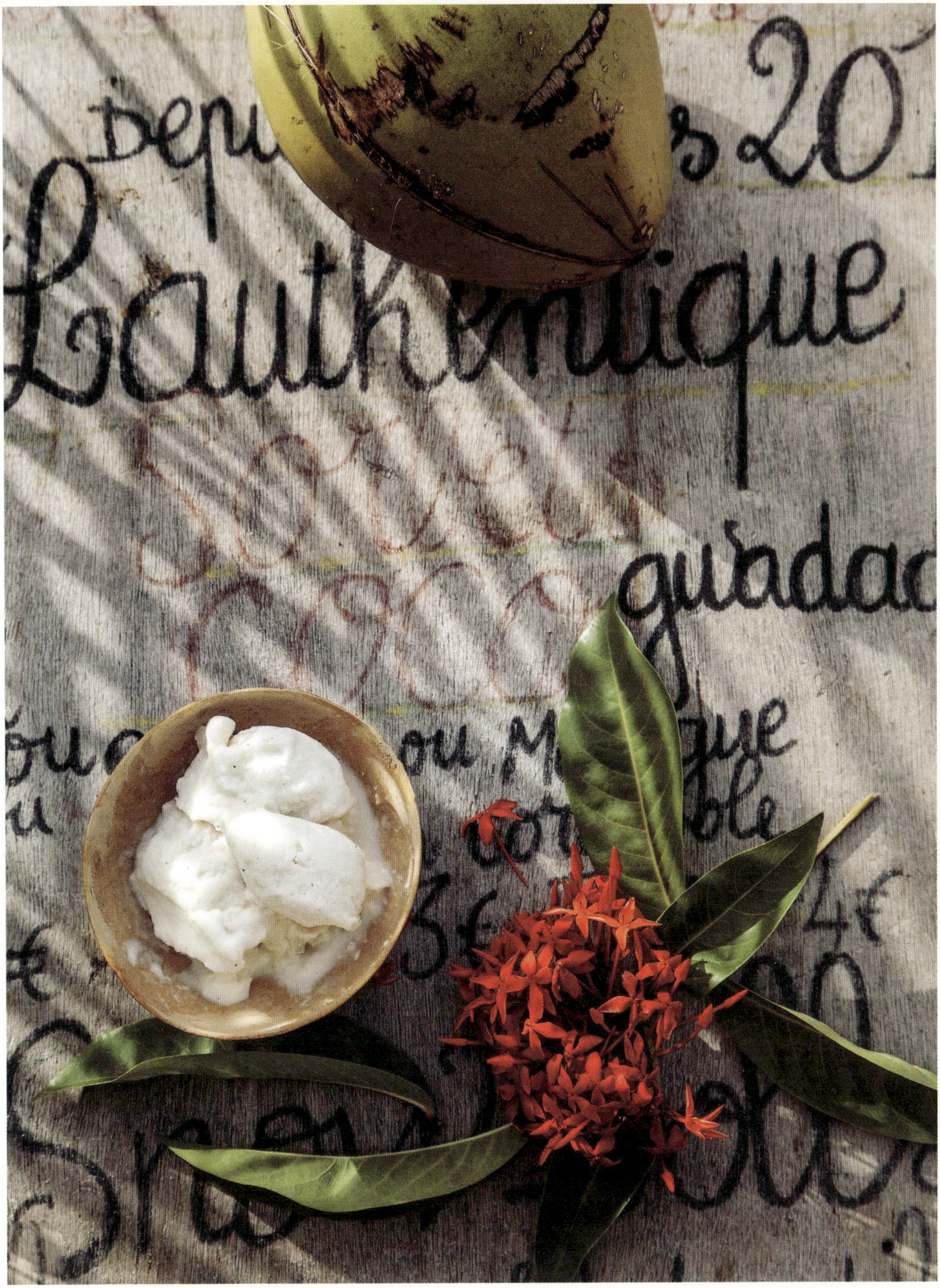

TARTE À LA NOIX DE COCO

I ate many different versions of coconut tart in Guadeloupe, and this is the one I liked best. It's quite simple – freshly grated coconut turned through a little cream and cane sugar and baked in a flaky pastry case. I like it best served still slightly warm, with a dollop of thick cream on the side to gather the stray coconut. It's fragile to cut when warm, especially the first slice, but is also very good cold the next day, when it has settled a bit. The pastry needs fridge time, so allow for that or make the day before.

Makes 1 x 26cm (10in) tart

For the flaky pastry
125g (4½oz) chilled unsalted butter, cut into small cubes, plus extra for greasing
125g (1 cup) plain (all-purpose) flour
2 tablespoons chilled water
salt

For the filling
275g (10oz) fresh coconut flesh (1 small coconut)
100g (½ cup) raw light brown cane sugar
1 egg
3 tablespoons cream
2 tablespoons coconut water (from the coconut)

For the pastry, put the butter, flour and a pinch of salt into a bowl and rub together with your fingertips until coarse crumbs. Add the water and mix just until it comes roughly together.

Roll out on a lightly floured surface to a neat rectangle about 20 x 30cm (8 x 12in). Fold one short side into the centre and cover this with the other short side, as you would fold a letter. Fold it all in half (to create more layers in the pastry) then wrap in plastic wrap and refrigerate for 30 minutes.

Roll out the pastry and repeat the folds once more. It is now ready to use, or can be kept in the fridge for a couple of days, or frozen.

Preheat the oven to 190°C/375°F/Gas 5 and lightly grease a 26cm (10in) tart tin, 3cm (1¼in) deep. Roll out the pastry on a lightly floured surface to a 30cm (12in) circle. Using the rolling pin to lift it, lower the pastry into the tin, easing the sides down and pressing them gently against the sides of the tin with the edges of your hands, so they adhere. Neaten the edges; the sides should be about 3cm (1¼in) high.

Line with baking parchment, fill with baking beans and bake for about 15 minutes until pale golden. Remove the beans and parchment and prick the pastry base with a fork in 4 or 5 places. Lower the oven setting to 180°C/350°F/Gas 4 and return the pastry case to the oven for another 10–15 minutes, until the base is pale golden and dry.

Meanwhile, for the filling, coarsely grate the coconut into a bowl, sprinkle in the sugar and stir to mix. Set aside.

Lightly whisk the egg in a bowl, then whisk in the cream and coconut water. Pour over the sugary coconut and mix well, using your hands to combine it well. Spread the coconut filling evenly into the tart case (if using a springform tin, stand the tin on a baking sheet).

Bake the tart in the oven for 20 minutes or so, until there are golden flecks here and there over the top. Serve warm in slices, or leave to cool.

TARTE AU CHOCOLAT ET PASSION

Jeanne, one of the many great cooks I met in Guadeloupe, gave me this recipe, which is deliciously interesting. The pastry case is fully baked before the chocolate and passionfruit filling is poured in and the tart needs at least 4 hours in the fridge to set. Serve plain, or with some whipped cream if you like.

Makes 1 x 26cm (10in) tart

For the pâte sablée
250g (2 cups) plain (all-purpose) flour
50g (heaped ⅓ cup) icing (powdered) sugar
180g (6⅓oz) chilled unsalted butter, cut into small cubes, plus extra for greasing
1 egg, lightly beaten
salt

For the filling
200ml (7fl oz) cream
6–8 passionfruit
200g (7oz) good-quality dark chocolate, chopped into small pieces

To make the pastry, put the flour, icing sugar and 2 good pinches of salt in a bowl. Add the butter and rub together with your fingertips until the mixture has the texture of damp sand. Add the egg and incorporate it gently to make a soft pastry. Wrap in plastic wrap and refrigerate for a few hours.

Preheat the oven to 180°C/350°F/Gas 4 and put a baking sheet on the middle shelf.

Lightly grease a 26cm (10in) unfluted tart tin or springform cake tin. Roll out the pastry on a lightly floured surface to a 30cm (12in) circle. This is a fragile pastry, so add a little more flour as needed and don't press too hard with your rolling pin.

With the help of your rolling pin, lift the pastry and lower it in the tin. Press the edges gently against the sides of the tin, so they adhere. Neaten the edges; the sides should be about 3.5cm (1⅜in) high.

Line with baking parchment, fill with baking beans and place on the tray in the oven. Bake for 20 minutes until the visible pastry is golden. Remove the beans and parchment and prick the bottom of the pastry in 4 or 5 places with a fork. Bake for another 15–20 minutes, or until the pastry is golden and the base is completely cooked. Remove from the oven and leave to cool.

Meanwhile, make the filling. Halve the passion fruit and scoop out the pulp (you should have about 130g/4½oz). Heat the cream in a small pan to just below simmering, then add the passionfruit pulp and stir through. Take off the heat and leave to infuse for 5 minutes.

Add the chocolate to the warm passionfruit cream and stir with a wooden spoon until it is completely melted. Leave to cool until it begins to thicken, but not so long that the chocolate starts to harden.

Scrape the chocolate filling into the pastry case. Place uncovered in the fridge for at least 4 hours to set. The filling should retain its lovely sheen. Use a thin, sharp knife to cut into slices.

BANANES FLAMBÉES AU RHUM

This is everywhere in Guadeloupe. I never thought it was my type of dessert, but now that I love rum so much, I really like this.

Serves 3

185ml (¾ cup) whipping cream
3 or 4 drops of almond extract
20g (1½ tablespoons) butter
3 bananas, peeled and halved lengthways
40g (1½oz) raw cane sugar
juice of 1 orange
3 tablespoons aged rum

Whip the cream with the almond extract in a bowl to a nicely firm but pillowy consistency. Cover and chill.

Melt the butter in a wide non-stick frying pan and, when sizzling, add the banana halves in a single layer. Cook until golden on the underside, then turn them carefully and scatter the sugar onto the base of the pan as best as you can manage.

Once the sugar starts to caramelize, shake the pan a bit to distribute the sugar, then add the orange juice (don't let the caramel turn too dark or burn). Let it all bubble up and reduce a bit, then add the rum. Using a taper or long match, stand well back and set the rum alight.

As soon as the flames have subsided, serve onto plates with a dollop of whipped cream and a drizzle of the pan juices.

COCONUT CARAMELS

Take care you don't burn yourself (or the caramel) while making these. I enjoyed many simple snacks like this in Guadeloupe, sold from small stalls that line the beach.

Makes a good amount

1 coconut
350g (1¾ cups) raw cane sugar
a few drops of vanilla extract
2 tablespoons runny honey
100ml (3½fl oz) coconut milk
40g (3 tablespoons) butter

Line a baking sheet with baking parchment. Break open the coconut, reserving the water (you should get about 185ml/¾ cup; drink the rest if you have more, it is so good for you). Extract the flesh from the husk and break into pieces. You will need about 300g (10½oz). Using a vegetable peeler or paring knife, peel away the brown outer skin. Slice into fine strips, 1–2 mm (1/16in) thick.

Put the sugar in a heavy-based wide pan with the coconut water and the vanilla extract. Put over a fairly high heat and stir until the sugar has melted and started to turn golden.

Add the remaining ingredients and stir through quickly. Add the coconut slices (the caramel will bubble up) and, without stirring, cook until the caramel is deep golden, about 30 minutes. Brush down any sugar crystals that form on the sides with a brush dipped in water. Take care not to overcook. Remove from the heat and leave for 20 seconds, then scrape out onto the prepared sheet. It needs a bit of height, so don't spread it out too much. Cool, then chop into good-sized pieces.

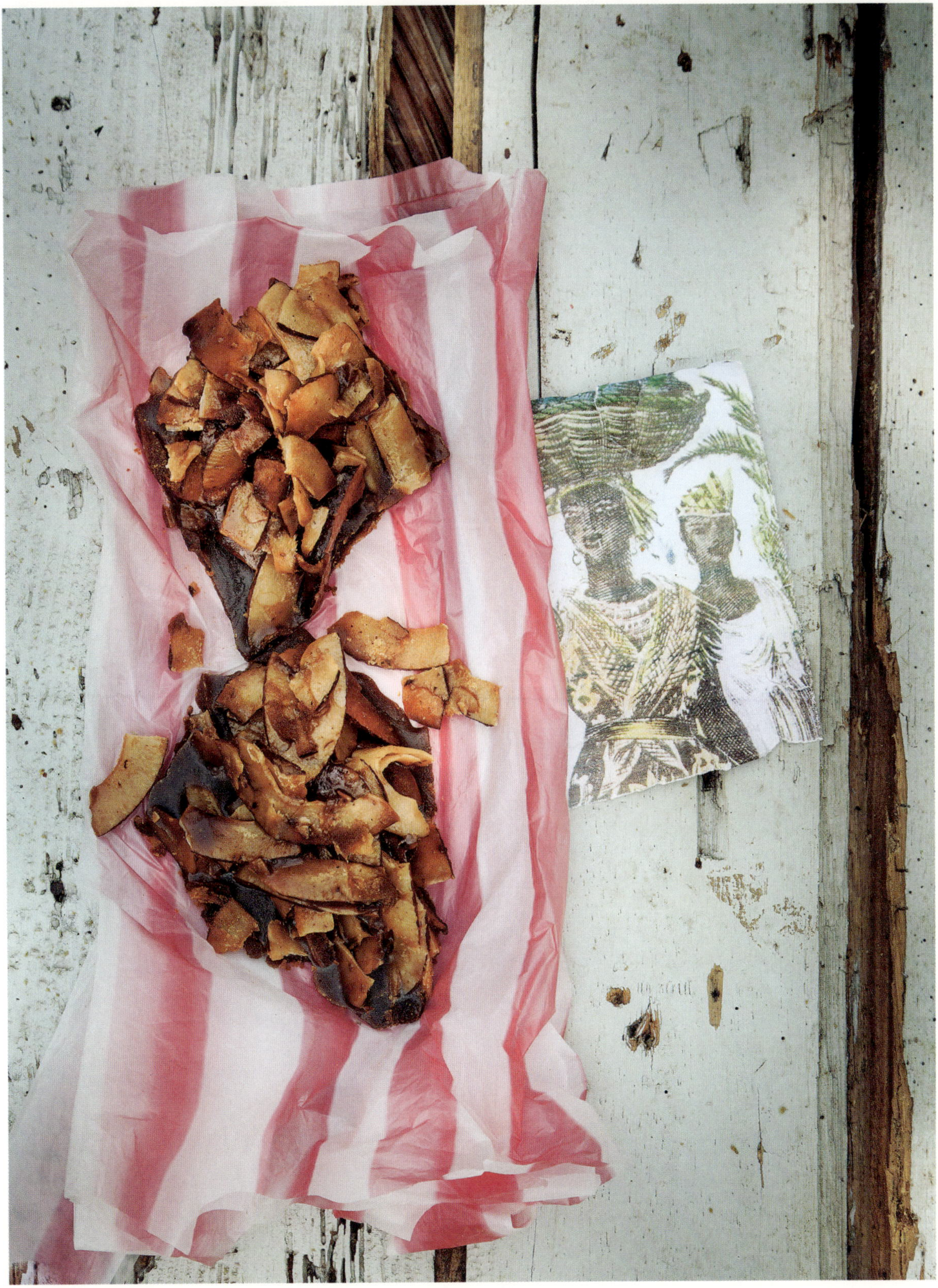

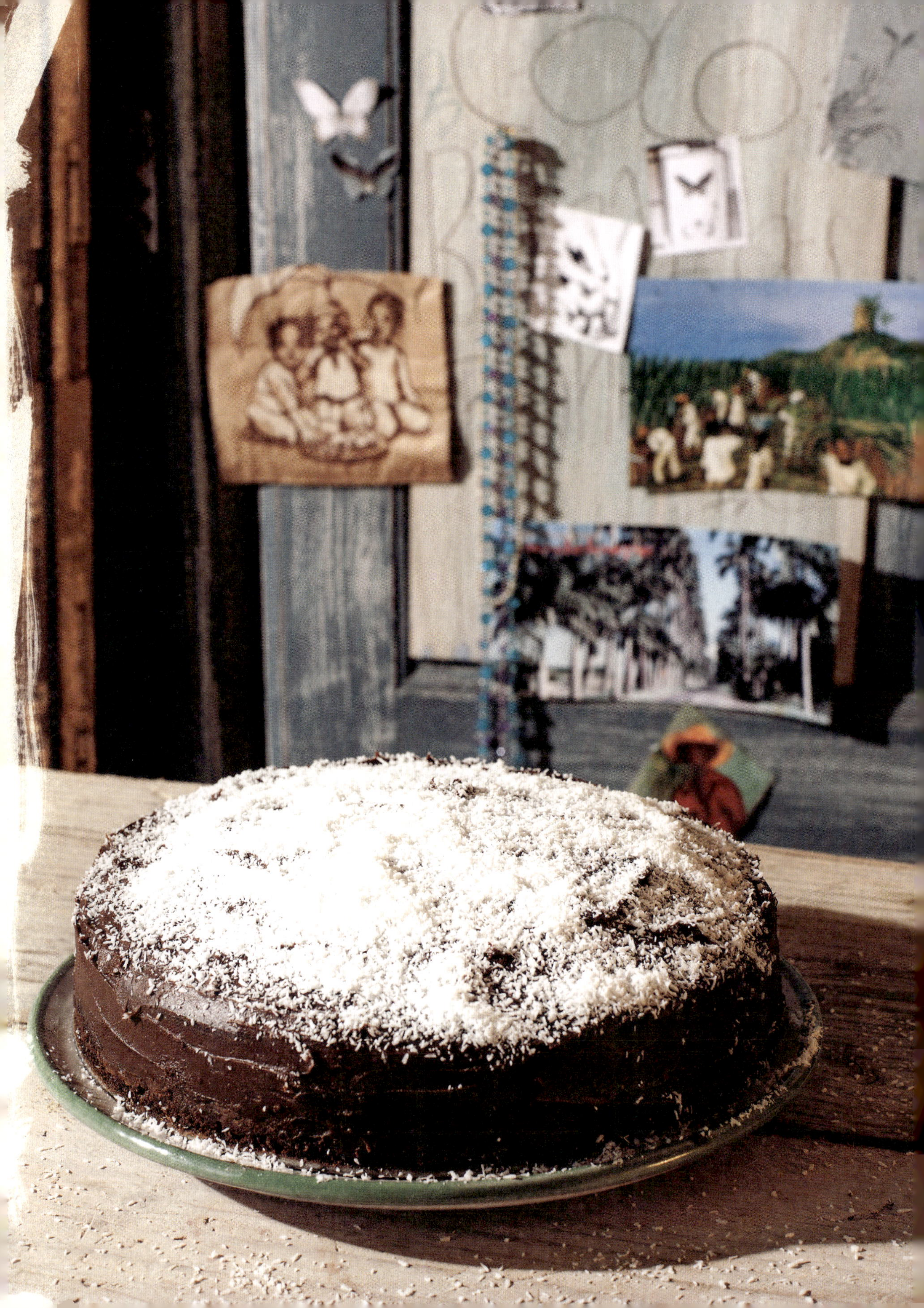

PLANTATION CHOCOLATE CAKE

I tasted many lovely cakes in Guadeloupe and one on a chocolate plantation, which you could tell was made with cocoa butter and the chocolate logs for grating that you find there. I also saw several other inspiring, tall chocolate cakes ready-cut into pieces for buying to eat on the beach or take home.

250g (9oz) unsalted butter, softened
300g (2¼ cups) self-raising flour
100g (1 cup) unsweetened cocoa powder
2 teaspoons baking powder
½ teaspoon salt
300g (1½ cups) sugar
300ml (1¼ cups) milk
2 teaspoons vanilla extract
125ml (½ cup) cream
3 eggs

For the icing (frosting)
60g (2¼oz) dark chocolate
50g (2oz) unsalted butter
½ teaspoon vanilla extract
40g (1½oz) icing (powdered) sugar
1 tablespoon hot water from the kettle
3 heaped tablespoons desiccated (shredded) coconut

Preheat the oven to 160°C/325°F/Gas 2½. Grease a 26cm (10in) springform cake tin with a little of the butter. Sprinkle in a little of the flour and swirl the tin around to lightly coat the base and sides.

Sift the flour, cocoa powder, baking powder and salt into a large bowl. Stir in the sugar and add the butter, milk and vanilla. Using electric beaters, mix everything together on a low speed until nicely blended. Scrape down the sides with a rubber spatula, then add the cream, mixing to combine. Add the eggs one a time, mixing well after each.

Scrape the mixture into the prepared tin and bake for about 1 hour 10 minutes rotating once, until the centre is set and a skewer comes out slightly damp still from the middle. Set aside in the tin to cool completely, then remove from the tin.

For the icing, put the chocolate, butter and vanilla in a heatproof bowl set over a pan of barely simmering water (making sure the base of the bowl isn't touching the water) and stir until melted with a wooden spoon. Remove the bowl from the pan, then sift in the icing sugar and stir in the water. It will seem a bit thin, but it will thicken as it cools.

When the icing has thickened enough, use a spatula to spread it over the top and sides of the cake. Scatter over the coconut.

VIETNAM
VIET NAM

LOCATION: EASTERN
INDOCHINA PENINSULA

INDOCHINE
COCHINCHINE
FRANÇAISE

SHAPE: DRAGON

CAPITAL: HANOI

HAT: NON LA
CONICAL, BAMBOO
& PALM LEAVES –
FROM HUE
IT OFTEN HAS A
SMALL POEM OR
DRAWINGS SLID
BETWEEN THE
LEAVES, THAT CAN
BE SEEN WHEN THE
HAT IS HELD UP TO
THE LIGHT

A NATIONAL
DRESS:
AO DAI

NATIONAL
FLOWER: LOTUS

VIETNAM

IN HANOI IT IS UNLUCKY TO BUY DUCK IN THE FIRST FEW DAYS OF THE LUNAR MONTH

PRODUCES: RICE, COFFEE, TEA, FISH SAUCE, DRAGON FRUIT, LYCHEE, ROSE APPLES, BLACK PEPPER, MUNG BEANS

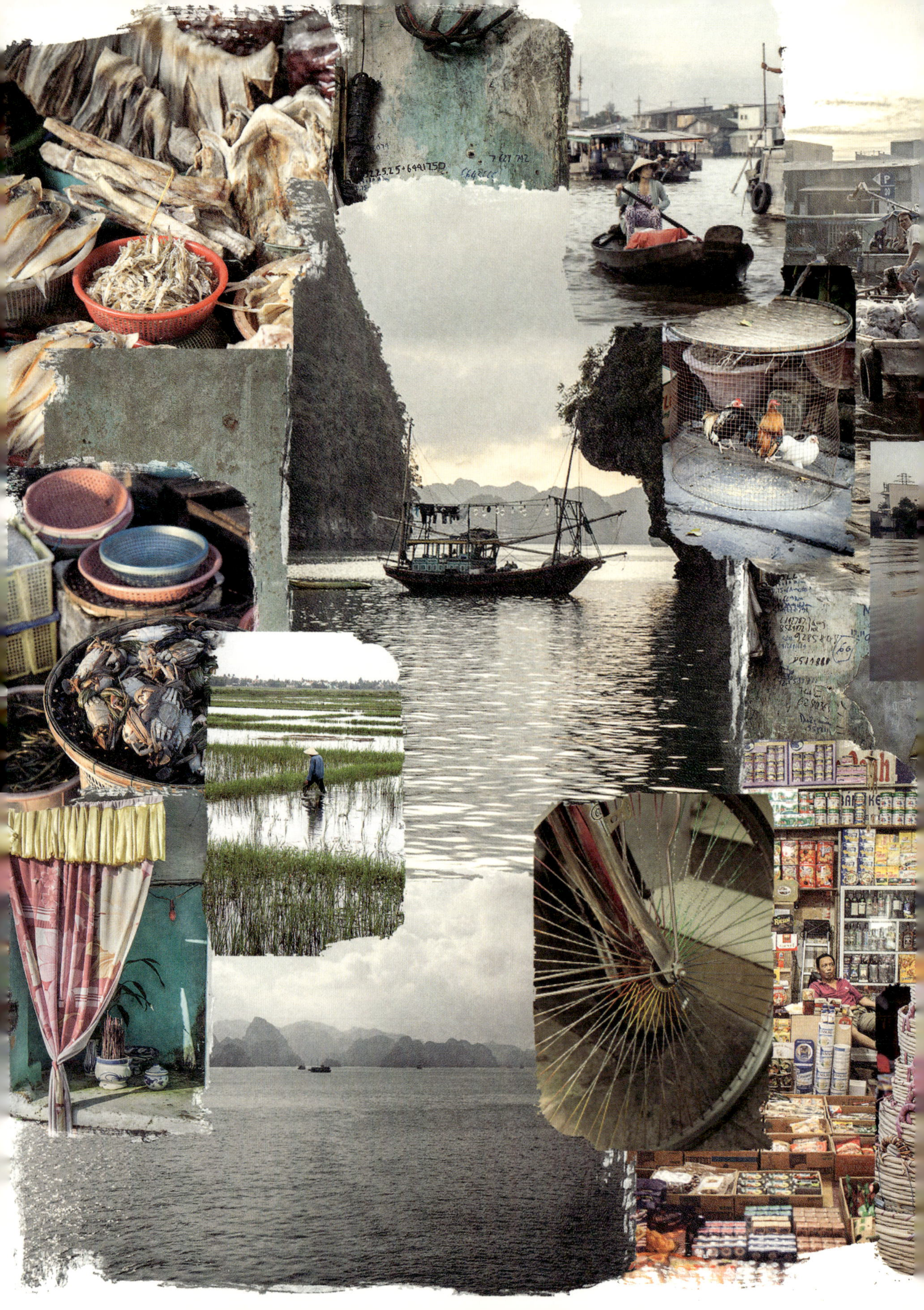

VIETNAM

LONG AGO, BEFORE ANYONE APPEARED ON EARTH, THERE WAS A COUPLE. **THE MAN WAS A DRAGON, LAC LONG QUAN AND THE WOMAN A PHOENIX, AU CO, WHO LAID A LARGE EGG. INSIDE WERE 100 SMALL BOYS AND GIRLS. WHEN THE EGG HATCHED 50 WENT TO THE MOUNTAINS AND 50 TO THE COAST,** *AND LEGEND HOLDS THAT THIS BECAME THE VIETNAMESE POPULATION.*

I had always dreamed of travelling the length of Vietnam. Stopping for warm bowls of mango layered broth and sipping lotus tea in delicate patterned cups. Watching kites over the South China Sea and eating baguette with pâté and crème caramel with coconut.

The first thing I notice under the Hanoi sky – pale, like freshly spun silk, are the lovely ao dai the ladies are wearing. Then come the motorbikes – thousands of them, and drivers wearing checked and floral colourful masks. I am taking in the small details everywhere on this sensory rollercoaster, trying to just hang on and fall into step with the others crossing the road. A dance of individuals with everyone moving as one mass, together. Seen from above it must appear as a brilliant choreography of bikes and people moving around each other.

This initially chaotic-seeming place is at the same time like a beautiful and unassuming theatre. The colours – random as they are – seem on one hand as though those in charge had, with great ceremony, debated the possibilities over tea. And on the other, that they had just been splashed here and there, so as to look unstyled. It seems though, that the bottom line of the brief was to please the viewer. And pleased I am. Inspired from the word go and scooping things up from every angle. The small plastic chairs contrasting fantastically with the ageing walls. The tangle of streets that make up the fairy-tale old quarter. Roads called by the name of the thing they are selling so you can work out what's what – so cleverly and compactly together that it makes me want to applaud.

....

French influence on Vietnamese cuisine is surprisingly strong. Baguettes are a staple, and pâté and terrines common components of a banh mi. Coffee has been popular ever since the French established coffee plantations in the highlands.

The earliest French presence in Vietnam came in 1620, when Jesuits arrived with a mission to convert the inhabitants to Christianity. By 1680 the importance of the country strategically and economically was clear, and the French East India Company came from Pondicherry in India and opened a warehouse. The signing of the Treaty of Versailles in 1787 gave France exclusive trading rights.

Vietnam became part of the French Empire in 1886 with France extending its control to include Laos and Cambodia. In 1887 the federation of French Indochina was formally established, with Hanoi as the capital, lasting until France gave up all claim on former territories in Indochina in 1954.

In Vietnam the French set up mining in the north. They planted rubber, pepper, coffee and tea plantations. They brought tiles and textiles, railway tracks and western architecture, their language and education system. They have come and gone and left a certain style behind. An old fading elegance drifting out from slim shopfronts. A thin blue stripe running down a trouser leg. Small things that the French are so good at. Certain combinations and telling details that show they have been.

I spoke with a young Vietnamese man, and in his beautifully thick French-accented English, he explained that he didn't speak a word of French. But that his English teacher was from Paris. What a mix of things going on here. It is remarkable what you can end up learning from others. This ability that people have to absorb things, turn it through themselves, then give it out again.

A man will do what he loves – turn to what he knows. And so it seems, the Vietnamese are comfortable amongst Chinese lacquered dishes and ducks, tea ceremonies and coffee bars. Industrious and forward-looking, they have absorbed their often turbulent history, along with the savoir-faire of other nations. They have graciously collected the pearls of the past and woven them into the present. It is lucky that they are such skilled weavers.

The result is a true masterpiece. A glorious patchwork of French elegance and ice cream. Small ox-blood coloured chairs and a many layered cuisine that manages to tumble five elements of sweet, salty, sour, bitter and spicy into every meal – in a collage of crunch and silky smooth. With so many different tasting leaves and such harmony.

Here from the kitchen on a junk in Halong Bay, I can see the night. We are preparing dinner in by far the best kitchen I have ever been in. The back door removed and just an open space out to the inky waters. Sometimes there are many lights, but at moments we drift away and it is just deep black out there. I wonder if a dragon might reach in and swallow me whole like an amuse-bouche, along with the daikon and carrot flowers that chef is carving.

There are crabs in a bucket. Turmeric, limes and chillies. A forest of leaves and herbs lying in hand-woven baskets ready to be mingled into our meal. The crabs will be steamed. The squid is ready for frying. The rice is cooked. Outside there are small lights now. And there it is:
The Yin of the waters
The Yang of the mountains.

ESSENTIAL FLAVOURINGS

Different layers of flavours and textures are an important part of Vietnamese cuisine. Vast mixtures of leaves, such as lettuce, shredded morning glory stems, sprouts, coriander, water mint, basil, perilla... all give a very fresh and unique taste to Vietnamese dishes along with other finishing notes.

NUOC CHAM

This basic Vietnamese dressing is great as a dipping sauce or dressing for almost anything. You can alter it to suit your personal taste – a bit more sugar, or chilli, as you like. Let it mingle for half an hour or so before serving, but remove the garlic if you will be keeping it for much longer in the fridge.

Makes about 185ml (¾ cup)

2 tablespoons fish sauce
3 tablespoons lime juice
1 tablespoon rice vinegar
2 tablespoons water
3 teaspoons brown sugar
¼ teaspoon deseeded finely chopped red chilli
1 small piece of peeled ginger
½ peeled garlic clove

Mix everything together and leave to mingle for half an hour or so before use. It will keep in a covered container in the fridge for a few days.

ROASTED CRUSHED PEANUTS

These keep well and are handy to add a pleasing layer of crisp and crunch to many dishes or salads.

Makes about 1½ cups

250g (9oz) raw unsalted peanuts

In a dry frying pan over moderate heat, dry-roast the peanuts, stirring frequently, until the skins start to dry and crack, 6–8 minutes. Transfer to a plastic food bag and rub them together through the bag to dislodge the skins.

Discard the skins, roughly chop the nuts and dry-roast again so some surfaces are golden. When cooled, store in an airtight container for up to a few weeks.

FRIED SHALLOTS

These are great to scatter over any number of dishes, giving a sweet delicious crunch. In Vietnam, there is a special peeler for slicing shallots into very thin slices of about 2mm (1/16in), but you can slice them very finely with a knife or mandoline. Ready-fried crispy shallots and other goodies are conveniently available at Vietnamese markets.

Makes about 1½ cups

250g (9oz) red Asian shallots
about 750ml (3 cups) vegetable oil

Peel the shallots then slice very thinly. Heat the oil in a wok over a medium heat and add half the shallots; they will be quite crowded, but this is fine. Keep the temperature low enough for there to just be small bubbles, and stir the shallots regularly, more often when they start to colour after about 10 minutes. When the colour changes to deeper golden immediately fish them out, using a wire scoop, onto a tray lined with paper towels.

Spread them out, adding a new layer of paper towels to ensure that all the oil is drained off. Repeat with the remaining shallots. When completely cool, transfer to an airtight container, where they will keep for a few weeks.

SESAME SALT

For an extra little bit of salt and crunch, scatter on just before serving.

Makes about 4 tablespoons

3 tablespoons lightly toasted white sesame seeds
3 teaspoons coarse salt

Pound the sesame seeds and salt together in a mortar (in two batches if easier) until crushed medium-fine. It keeps well in an airtight jar.

CARROT AND DAIKON PICKLE

This is fairly straightforward and an essential component to several dishes – you can add some green papaya, or celery if you like. I like the vegetables cut flat, so just chipped away with a good knife into thin slices, but you can also make thin batons if you prefer. Amounts are approximate and it's fine to add more or less of an ingredient.

Makes about 500ml (2 cups)

1 carrot (about 170g/6oz), peeled
170g (6oz) peeled daikon/white radish
125ml (½ cup) rice vinegar
2 tablespoons sugar
1 teaspoon salt
½ small red chilli, deseeded and sliced
a piece of peeled ginger
½ peeled garlic clove
freshly ground black pepper

Using a large sharp knife, chip away at the carrot and daikon, a little on the diagonal, to get thin flat slivers, turning the carrot and daikon as you slice. Put in a bowl and cover with the rest of the ingredients and some grinds of black pepper. Turn through. When it has sunk a bit turn through again.

Put a small plate or saucer upside down on top of the vegetables to weigh them down and keep them immersed. Leave for a couple of hours before serving, or longer if you like (up to a week in the fridge). To serve, take out a handful, shake away the dressing and put into a bowl.

LIME, SALT AND PEPPER DIPPING SAUCE

I loved this in Vietnam, served in separate little heaps. A heap of salt. A heap of finely crushed pepper. And then some lime quarters (which never seemed to be enough), or halved kumquats (or calamansi) and sliced chillies on the side to mix together for your own serving, and to suit your taste.

Makes 1 serving

¼ teaspoon salt
¼ teaspoon finely ground black pepper
1 small lime, quartered
1 small red chilli, deseeded and sliced

In a small, shallow bowl, make separate small heaps of the salt and the pepper. Serve the lime wedges and chillies alongside.

Squeeze as much lime juice as you like into the salt and pepper bowl. Using chopsticks, mix as much salt and pepper as you want into the juice. Add chilli slices at the last moment for their heat to seep into the sauce. You can add more, or remove them if it's too hot.

The sauce can be made in advance, but the pepper should be added at the very last minute, as it colours the sauce.

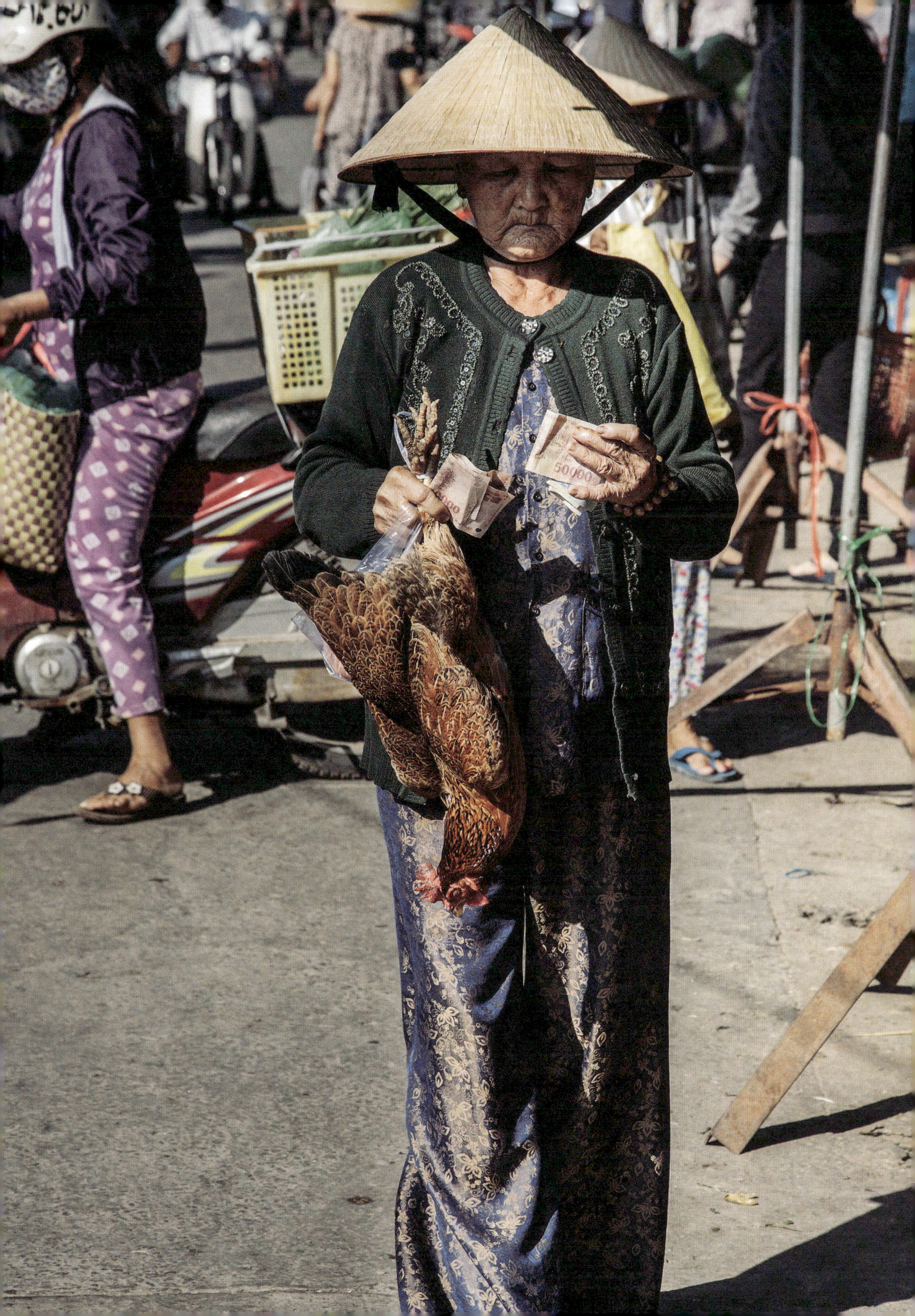
50000

MUSSELS WITH CHILLI, LIME, LEMONGRASS AND COCONUT

This must be served hot with some baguette. Have a couple of large bowls on the side for the shells.

Serves 3

1.5kg (3¼lb) mussels
1 tablespoon vegetable oil
2 spring onions (scallions), including green, finely sliced lengthways
2 lemongrass stalks, 1 (inner part only) chopped, the other cut into 3 lengths
2 garlic cloves, chopped
2 small red chillies, chopped
1 heaped teaspoon brown sugar
1 scant tablespoon fish sauce
juice of ½ lime, plus extra for serving
125ml (½ cup) coconut cream
a small handful coriander (cilantro) sprigs, leaves and stalks separated
freshly ground black pepper

De-beard the mussels then scrub them with a brush under cold running water, discarding any that are open and do not close when given a sharp tap on the work surface.

Heat the oil in a large wok and sauté the spring onions quickly over a high heat. Add all the lemongrass, the garlic and chillies and sauté briefly. Stir in the sugar, fish sauce and lime juice, then add the coconut cream and let it bubble up for a minute.

Heat a large saucepan and add the mussels and coriander stalks. Put the lid on tightly and steam over a high heat for a couple of minutes until the shells have opened. Leaving the juices in the pan, transfer the mussels to the coconut sauce.

Strain about 125ml (½ cup) of the cooking juices through a fine sieve, over the mussels. Heat quickly, turning the mussels through so the flavours can mingle. Squeeze in extra lime juice to taste.

Add the coriander leaves with some pepper. Serve at once in large individual bowls.

CHANH MUOI

This is a quick version of the lengthier preserved lemon (or plum) drink and lovely to serve in the heat for its sweet, sour and salty combination. You can make it with still water, though I love fizzy.

Halve 1 large juicy lime, cut a thinnish slice from one half and put aside. Scatter 3–4 teaspoons light brown sugar into the bottom of a glass and squeeze the lime juice over. Scatter in ¼ teaspoon salt and add a handful of crushed ice. Top up with about 185ml (¾ cup) chilled fizzy water and mix through with a long spoon. Add the lime slice and serve.

FRIED SQUID WITH LIME SALT AND PEPPER

Crisp food is always appreciated; it adds such a good texture to a meal. I love this way of serving fried squid with lime, salt and pepper dipping sauce on the side. Use small, tender squid here, or calamari if you like. If you have a splatter guard, have it handy here.

Serves 2 (or more)

500g (18oz) small squid
1 garlic clove, peeled
a piece of ginger, the same size as the garlic, peeled
1 tablespoon fish sauce
1 teaspoon ground turmeric
½ teaspoon sugar
a large pinch of freshly ground black pepper
1 egg, whisked
about 5 tablespoons each of rice flour and wheat flour, combined
vegetable oil, for deep-frying

To serve
coriander (cilantro) leaves
2 quantities lime, salt and pepper dipping sauce (page 100)

Remove and discard the head from the squid, keeping the tentacles. Slice the squid and clean and rinse, removing the quill. Pat dry with paper towel then cut into 2–3cm (¾–1¼in) chunks.

Pound the garlic and ginger to a paste with a pestle and mortar. Put in a bowl with the fish sauce, turmeric, sugar and pepper, and stir the egg through. Add the squid and stir with chopsticks to coat well. Cover the bowl with plastic wrap and set aside to marinate for an hour or so.

Put both flours into a bowl, mixing well to combine. Heat enough oil in a large wok to deep-fry the squid. Using your hands or a slotted spoon, lift out a few pieces of squid at a time from the marinade, shake lightly and toss into the flour, turning through to coat each piece thoroughly. Move them to a clean plate and coat the rest of the squid like this.

Carefully drop the pieces into the hot oil (in 2 or 3 batches to avoid overcrowding the pan) and deep-fry until golden and crisp on all sides. Remove to a plate lined with paper towels. Serve hot, scattered with a few coriander leaves and very little salt. Serve the dipping sauce on the side.

PHO BO

Some say that pho comes from the French feu, as in pot-au-feu, but others that it refers to a local word for noodle. I love this simple Hanoi version, which is often served for breakfast. You can use fresh pho noodles if available.

Serves 4 generously

For the broth
1kg (2¼lb) beef bones, with some meat on
a chunk (about 7cm/2¾in) of fresh unpeeled ginger
120g (4¼oz) red Asian shallots, unpeeled
800g (1¾lb) beef brisket, with some fat
5 star anise
2 sticks of cassia bark
2 Vietnamese cardamom pods
2 teaspoons Vietnamese peppercorns
1 teaspoon sugar
4 tablespoons fish sauce
1 tablespoon salt

To serve
400g (14oz) dried flat pho noodles
½ small white onion, thinly sliced
300g (10½oz) rump or sirloin steak, sliced 2mm (⅛in) thick
4 spring onions (scallions), sliced into long strips
a couple of handfuls coriander (cilantro) leaves
a couple of handfuls Vietnamese mint leaves
2 limes, quartered
a few small red chillies, sliced
smooth chilli sauce, to serve

For the broth, put the bones into a stockpot and cover with water. Bring to the boil, simmer for 5 minutes, then pour off the water. Rinse the bones, return to the pot, cover with 4 litres (4 quarts) water and bring to a boil. Skim, then cover and simmer gently for 2 hours. Heat a griddle pan or barbecue and cook the ginger and shallots until golden charred on all sides.

Add the shallots, ginger and remaining broth ingredients to the pot. Simmer, covered, skimming occasionally, for about 2½ hours, until the meat is very tender when you poke it with a chopstick. Take off the heat and leave to cool, then skim off the layer of fat. Remove the brisket and wrap in plastic wrap until needed.

Strain the broth through a fine sieve. You should have about 2 litres (2 quarts); top up with water if necessary. Put into a pan and bring to a simmer. Check the seasoning. Slice the brisket thinly, or into small pieces (leaving some fat on if you like).

To serve, cook the noodles in boiling water until tender. Meanwhile, bring about 375ml (1½ cups) broth to the boil in a small separate saucepan. Have 4 large, deep warmed bowls ready. Cut the steak into 4cm (1½in) pieces. Drain the noodles and divide between the bowls. Add some brisket to each and divide the onion slices between them.

Drop half the steak slices into the boiling broth, swish them around for 10 seconds or so and, as soon as they change colour, scoop them out and divide between two of the bowls. Quickly cook the rest of the steak and divide between the other two bowls. Add a big ladleful of hot broth to each bowl.

Top each with a heap of spring onions and a small handful of coriander and mint leaves. Serve with the limes, chillies and chilli sauce on the side. To eat, squeeze in some lime juice and float a few chillies in the broth to release their heat.

VIETNAM

Khuếch âm iPhone - 6 điểm
MÃ - TÍCH ĐIỂM
Thời gian: từ ngày 17/3/2014 đến ngày 25/5/2014
0902.213.267 – 38.236.651
có thể kết thúc sớm hơn nếu số lượng quà tặng đã hết)

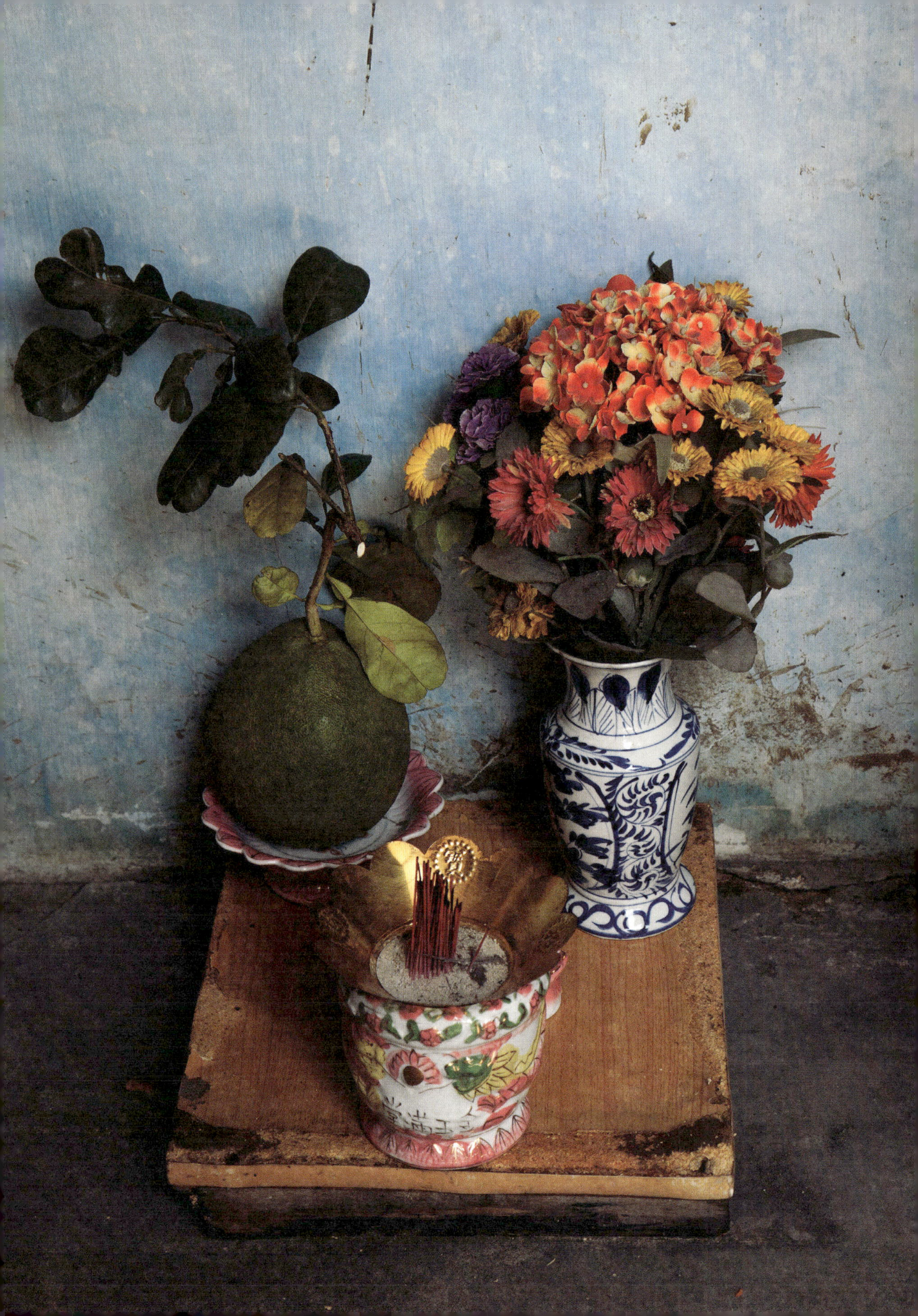

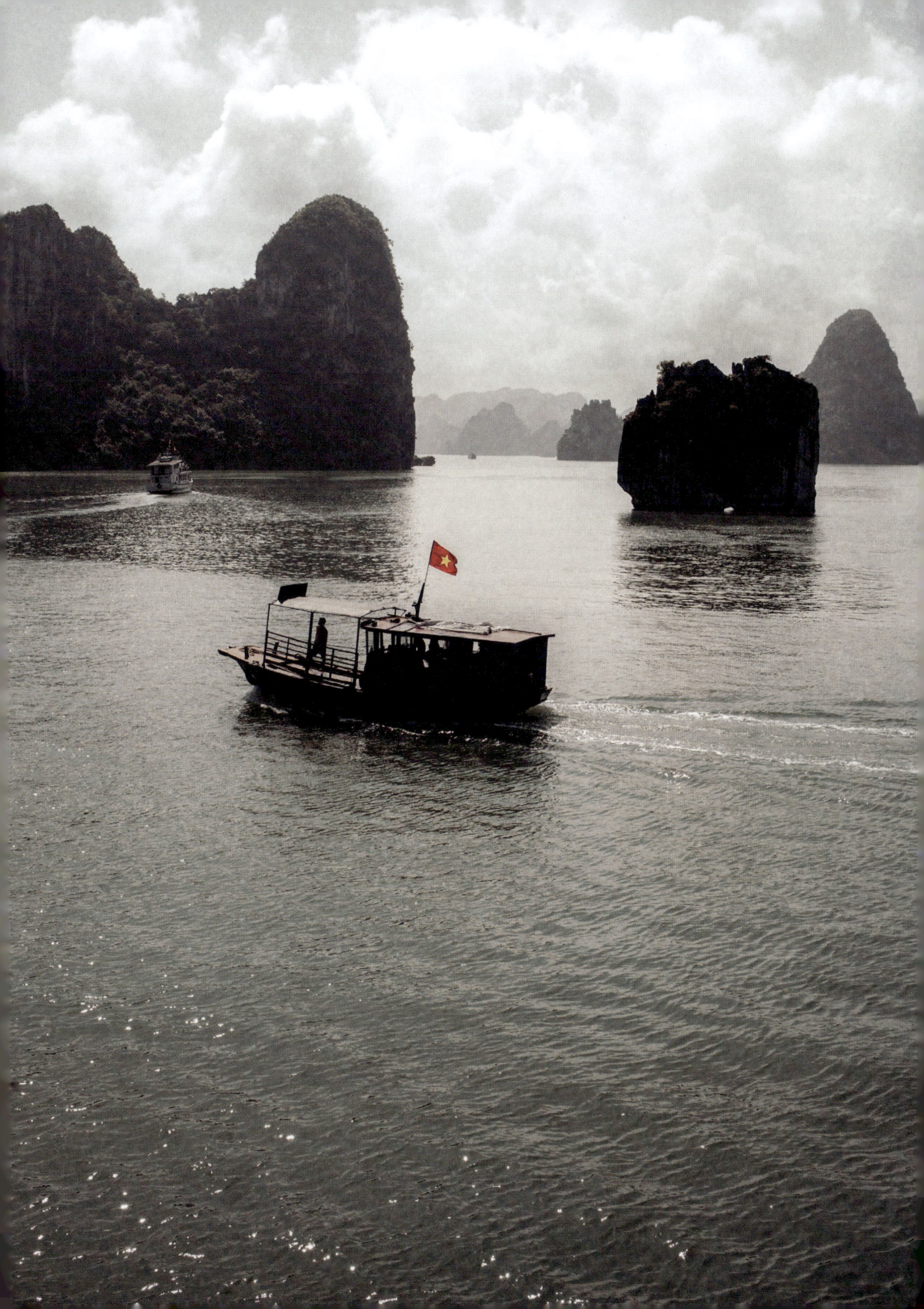

BUN BO

It is nice to have all these separate bowls of bits and pieces, so everyone can add more or less of something to their bowls of broth if they want. You can also serve some carrot and daikon pickle (page 100) on the side here along with the other accompaniments.

Serves 5

400g (14oz) sirloin steak, sliced 2mm (⅛in) thick and into 5cm (2in) pieces
200g (7oz) dried rice vermicelli noodles
2 teaspoons vegetable oil
300g (10½oz) bean sprouts
1½ tablespoons soy sauce
a couple of handfuls mixed leaves, such as torn lettuce, morning glory, watercress, Thai basil, perilla
a couple of handfuls coriander (cilantro) leaves
a couple of handfuls Vietnamese mint

For the broth
about 2kg (4½lb) beef bones
5cm (2in) piece of ginger, peeled and sliced
2 star anise
1 small onion, peeled

For the marinade
1 lemongrass stalk, inner part chopped
2 garlic cloves, chopped
1 teaspoon chopped ginger
2 tablespoons fish sauce
¼ teaspoon chopped red chilli
3 teaspoons light brown sugar
¼ teaspoon freshly ground black pepper

To serve
roasted crushed peanuts (page 98)
fried shallots (page 99)
about 10 kumquats (or calamansi), halved
sliced red chillies
smooth chilli sauce

For the broth, put all the ingredients into a stockpot with 4 litres (4 quarts) water and simmer, partly covered, for 3 hours. Strain through a colander, then strain through a sieve lined with muslin. You will need about 625ml (2½ cups) hot broth, so save the remaining for future use (it freezes well).

Mix all the marinade ingredients together in a bowl. Add the steak pieces and turn through to coat. Leave for 30–45 minutes.

Cook the noodles in boiling water until tender. Drain in a colander and rinse with warm water.

Heat half the oil in a wok and add the bean sprouts. Stir-fry until slightly wilted, then add the soy sauce. Let it bubble up, then tip the contents of the wok into a bowl. Wipe out the wok with paper towels then add the remaining oil. When hot, add the beef and stir-fry quickly over a high heat to sear it. Don't over-cook or the meat will toughen. Remove from the heat.

To serve, put a small handful of lettuce and other leaves into each of 5 large, wide bowls. Divide the noodles between the bowls. Ladle about 125ml (½ cup) hot broth into each, then divide the bean sprouts between the bowls. Put a pile of beef pieces on top and drizzle in any juice from the wok. Add some coriander and mint leaves, then top with a heaped tablespoon each of crushed peanuts and fried shallots. Serve at once, with the kumquats and chillies, and chilli sauce and extra herbs in bowls on the side for diners to add as they wish.

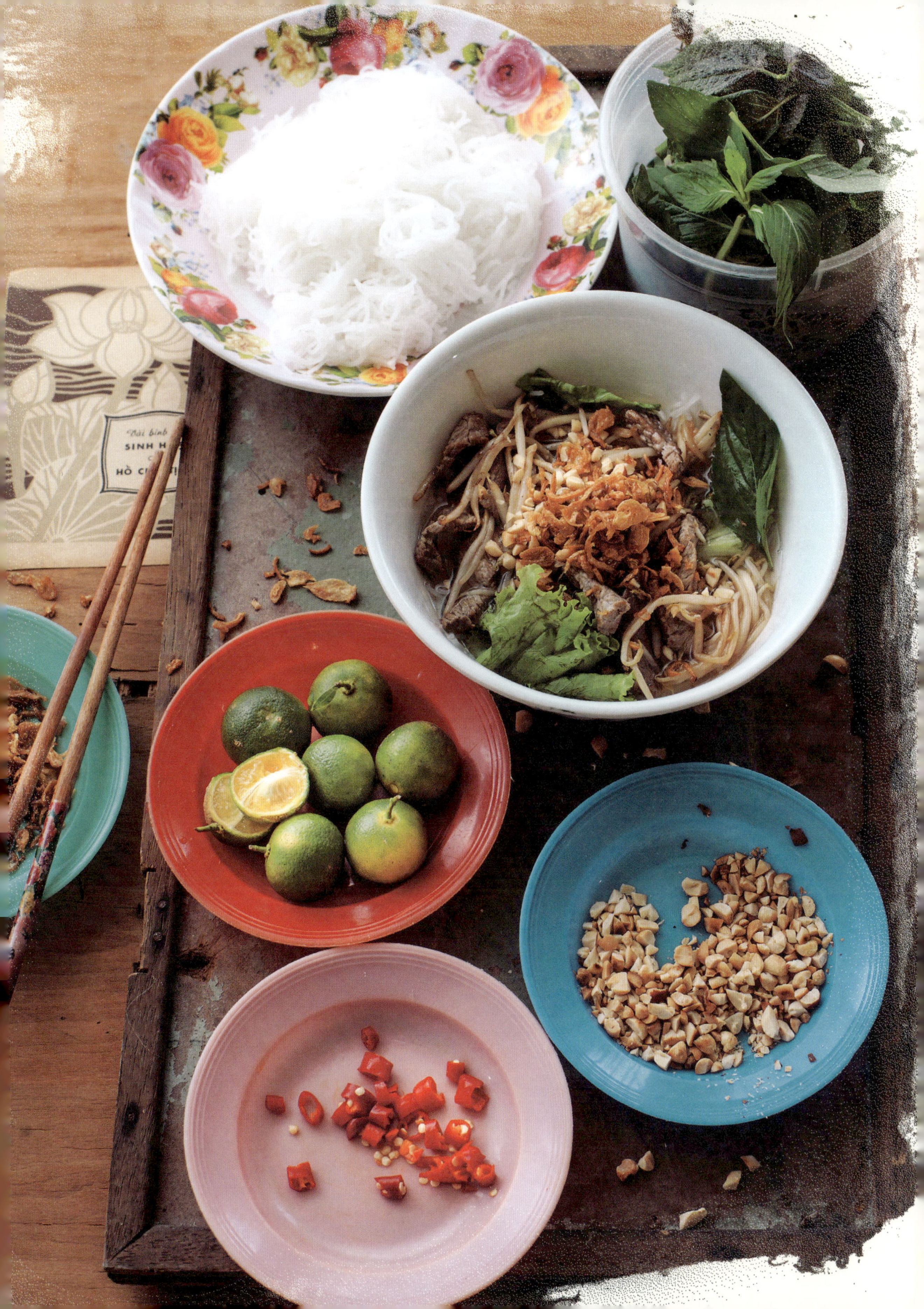

BUN CHA

Here is another dish with noodles I loved in Hanoi, from a lovely lady, Thuy Do. Scrunch up the lettuce and herbs with one hand, pressing them down into your broth with your chopsticks in the other hand and eat them once they have softened a little.

Serves 4

vegetable oil, for deep-frying
1 quantity spring rolls (page 112), uncooked
200g (7oz) dried rice vermicelli noodles
3–4 handfuls mixed leaves and herbs, such as coriander (cilantro), mint, perilla, shredded morning glory, basil, lettuce, mustard leaf
2 small red chillies, sliced or chopped
4 garlic cloves, chopped

For the pork patties
500g (18oz) minced (ground) pork
2 tablespoons fish sauce
1 tablespoon light brown sugar
2 tablespoons pounded inner lemongrass stalks
80g (3oz) Asian shallots, pulsed finely in blender
¼ teaspoon freshly ground black pepper
about 8 betel leaves, stalks removed, rinsed

For the pork belly
1 tablespoon light brown sugar
2 tablespoons fish sauce
½ teaspoon each of salt and ground black pepper
600g (21oz) rindless pork belly, cut into 6 slices (7–8mm/¼in thick)

For the broth
5 tablespoons fish sauce
2 tablespoons sugar
30g (1oz) carrot, peeled and sliced into thin rounds
50g (2oz) green papaya or kohlrabi, sliced into thin rounds
juice of 1 lime
2 tablespoons rice vinegar

In a bowl, mix together all the ingredients for the pork patties (except the betel leaves). Form into 16 balls, flatten slightly and wrap half of them in betel leaves. Place seam down, on a plate, cover with plastic wrap and refrigerate for an hour or so.

For the pork belly, combine the sugar, fish sauce, salt and pepper in a dish. Add the pork slices and turn to coat. Cover and leave for about an hour, turning the slices over once or twice with a fork.

For the broth, heat 400ml (1¾ cups) water, the fish sauce and sugar in a pan, stirring until the sugar dissolves. Add the carrot and papaya and simmer for a minute or so. Remove from the heat and stir in the lime juice and rice vinegar. Keep warm.

Heat up a griddle pan or barbecue. Add the patties and pork and cook until deep golden; take care not to overcook. Halve the pork slices.

Meanwhile, heat the oil in a wok and deep-fry the spring rolls until golden. Remove to a plate lined with paper towels to drain. Cut each into 3 pieces. Cook the noodles in boiling water until tender, then drain and rinse with warm water.

Put everything on the table in bowls: the spring rolls, herbs, sliced chillies, chopped garlic and half the broth, including some carrot and papaya. Divide the remaining broth, with carrot and papaya, between 4 bowls and add some noodles. Add some patties and pieces of pork belly. Serve hot, for everyone to do their own thing.

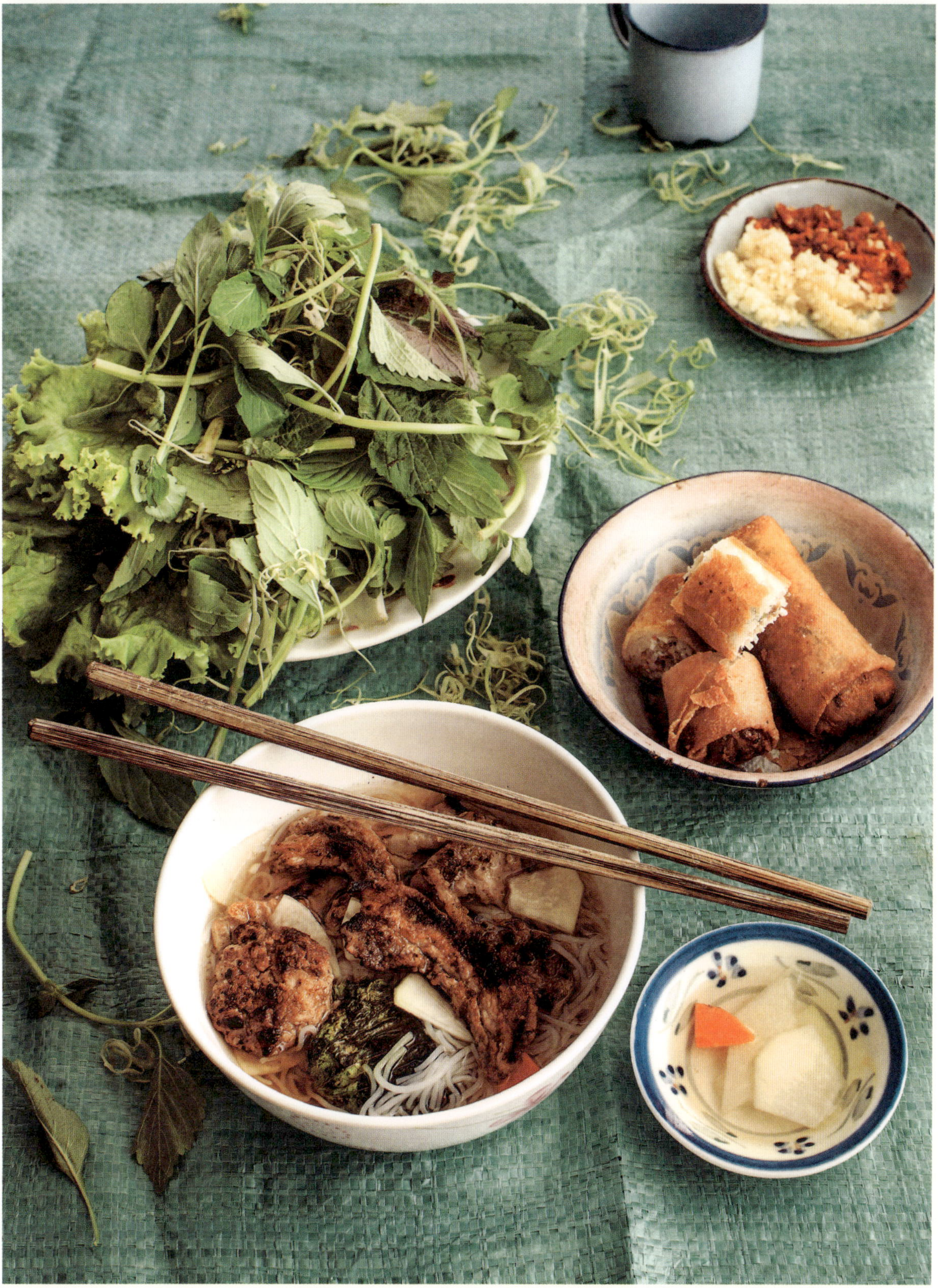

CRISPY SPRING ROLLS

Put a little salt into the oil as it helps it to splash less, says Quang, the excellent chef I made these with. They are served with bun cha, but are also lovely eaten on their own as a starter, with dipping sauce and some lettuce leaves.

Makes 8

15g (¾ cup) dried Chinese mushrooms
170g (6oz) minced (ground) pork
30g (½ cup) dried rice vermicelli noodles, cooked, drained and snipped into 1cm (⅜in) lengths
50g (2oz) carrot, peeled, shredded
50g (2oz) kohlrabi or green papaya, shredded
50g (2oz) spring onion (scallion), white and green part, chopped
1 teaspoon fish sauce
½ teaspoon light brown sugar
1 egg, separated
freshly ground black pepper

To assemble and serve
8 rice paper wrappers (about 22cm/9in diameter)
vegetable or peanut oil, for deep-frying
2 handfuls tender lettuce leaves
2 handfuls coriander (cilantro) leaves
2 handfuls mint leaves
1 quantity nuoc cham (page 98, but omitting the ginger and whole garlic, and adding 1 chopped garlic clove)

Soak the mushrooms in hot water until softened, then drain and chop into small pieces.

Put the mushrooms in a bowl and add the pork, vermicelli, carrot, kohlrabi, spring onion, fish sauce, sugar and some ground black pepper. Mix well. Lightly whisk the egg yolk and turn it through well to combine; reserve the white.

Put a dry cloth on the work surface and have a shallow dish of tepid water beside it. Dip a rice paper wrapper in the water for a few seconds until softened. Give it a gentle shake to get rid of excess water then lay it out on the cloth. Take an eighth (about 2 tablespoons) of the pork filling and make a narrow row about 3cm (1¼ in) in from one edge of the wrapper, leaving a border of 2cm (¾in) along each side.

Fold the bottom of the wrapper up over the filling, tucking it under firmly. Fold the 2 sides of the wrapper over the ends of the filling so it is completely covered, and continue the folds up the length of the wrapper so it is now the same width as the filling all the way along. Continue rolling, compactly but not tightly. Press the filling along gently with your hands so it is evenly distributed as you roll.

Mix a little water into the egg white and dampen the end lip of the wrapper so it seals the roll well. Put on a plate while you roll the rest. Refrigerate, covered with plastic wrap, until ready to cook.

Heat enough oil in a large wok to to fry the spring rolls and turn them to colour well. In two batches, deep-fry them over a fairly high heat for a few minutes, turning once or twice until evenly golden. Remove and drain on paper towels.

To eat, cut each spring roll into 2 or 3 pieces, wrap in lettuce with some coriander and mint leaves scrunched up and the dipping sauce on the side.

CHARGRILLED MARINATED QUAIL

I like to serve these gently chargrilled quail as I ate them in Hanoi – with slices of jicama and mint on the side, and French fries with salt and vanilla sugar. With lime, salt and pepper dipping sauce, it is truly lovely.

You can use a couple of poussins or a small whole chicken – butterflied as described below – in place of the quails. You will need to allow time for them to marinate. The number it serves will depend on the size of the quails and whether you will be serving them as part of a larger meal.

Serves 2–4

4 quail

For the marinade
1 tablespoon fish sauce
2 tablespoons rice wine
1 tablespoon rice vinegar
1 tablespoon soy sauce
2 tablespoons oyster sauce
1 teaspoon finely chopped garlic
1 teaspoon finely grated ginger
1 small red chilli, finely chopped
½ teaspoon freshly ground pepper
½ teaspoon five-spice powder
1 tablespoon light brown sugar

To serve
sea salt
vanilla icing (powdered) sugar
a few slices of freshly peeled jicama
a handful mint sprigs
lime, salt and pepper dipping sauce (page 100)
freshly cooked fries

Cut through the backbones of the quail and butterfly by flattening them as much as possible. In a dish large enough to take the quail in one layer, mix together all the ingredients for the marinade. Add the quail, turning them over a couple of times to coat well on both sides.

Cover and leave to marinate for 3–4 hours in a cool place. (Put them in the fridge if the weather is very hot and take them out an hour before grilling.)

Heat up the chargrill. Add the quail, skin side up to start with, and not too close to the heat. Grill until cooked through and golden, then turn and cook on the other side until a little charred on the skin, basting the quail with the marinade as they cook. Check often as they can burn easily.

Cook the fries and drain on paper towel to absorb the excess oil. Scatter with just a little salt and some vanilla (or plain) sugar. Put the jicama on a plate and top with the mint sprigs.

Serve the quail accompanied by the jicama and mint, the fries and the dipping sauce. Best eaten with your fingers!

VANILLA SUGAR

Put about 125g (¾ cup) icing (powdered) sugar into a jar that has a tight-fitting lid. Split a vanilla pod lengthways in half and bury it in the icing sugar. The vanilla will permeate the sugar. Leave for at least a week before using; it will keep indefinitely in a sealed jar.

CRISPY DUCK WITH CLEMENTINES AND KUMQUATS

The duck is brushed with spices and a cornflour wash then left in the fridge for 48 hours to dry the skin completely, so you need to allow for that time. I use clementines here, as they are seedless, but you can use mandarins or small oranges instead.

Serves 3–4

1 duck (about 1.5kg/3¼lb), trimmed of excess fat
1 tablespoon Sichuan peppercorns
1 tablespoon black peppercorns
1 star anise
2 cloves
1½ tablespoons coarse salt
½ teaspoon Chinese five-spice powder
4 tablespoons cornflour (cornstarch)
300ml (1¼ cups) clementine juice (from 7–8 fruit, 4 halves saved)
1 tablespoon soy sauce
1 teaspoon sesame oil
5cm (2in) piece of ginger, peeled, lightly bruised and cut into 3 or 4 pieces
2 spring onions (scallions), halved and lightly smashed
1 lemongrass stalk, trimmed and cut into 3 pieces
6 clementines (3 halved, 3 whole)
2 handfuls (about 200g/7oz) kumquats
3 tablespoons Chinese rice wine

Cut off the end section of the duck wings. Prick the skin of the duck all over with a sharp-tined fork to allow the fat to escape on roasting.

In a dry frying pan over a medium heat, toast all the peppercorns, the star anise, cloves and salt until fragrant, stirring and shaking the pan to prevent them burning. Tip onto a plate and leave to cool, then transfer to a spice grinder with the five-spice powder and process to a fine powder.

Put the cornflour, 3 tablespoons of clementine juice, the soy sauce and sesame oil in a small bowl and stir until smooth. Set aside 2 tablespoons in a covered bowl. Brush the rest all over the skin of the duck, then rub the spice mix inside and over the surface of the duck, massaging it in well and finishing with a brush to give an even coverage.

Put the duck in a flameproof baking dish or tin, breast up, and refrigerate uncovered for 48 hours, until the skin and its coating are completely dry.

Preheat the oven to 200°C/ 400°F/Gas 6. Stuff the ginger, spring onions, lemongrass and 4 saved clementine halves into the duck cavity. Roast for 45 minutes, then pour off all the fat from the dish. Place the whole and halved clementines and the kumquats around the duck. Return to the oven and roast for another 45 minutes, until the duck is dark brown and crispy. Spoon some pan juices over the clementines, but not over the duck, which must be kept dry.

Lift the duck onto a board and the fruit to a platter. Put the dish over a medium-high heat and add the rice wine. As it bubbles, scrape the bits from the bottom of the pan. Stir in the reserved cornflour mixture. Add the remaining clementine juice, stir and simmer for 5–10 minutes until glossy.

Cut the duck in half through the backbone, then cut into serving portions. Serve with the hot sauce and clementines and kumquats on the side.

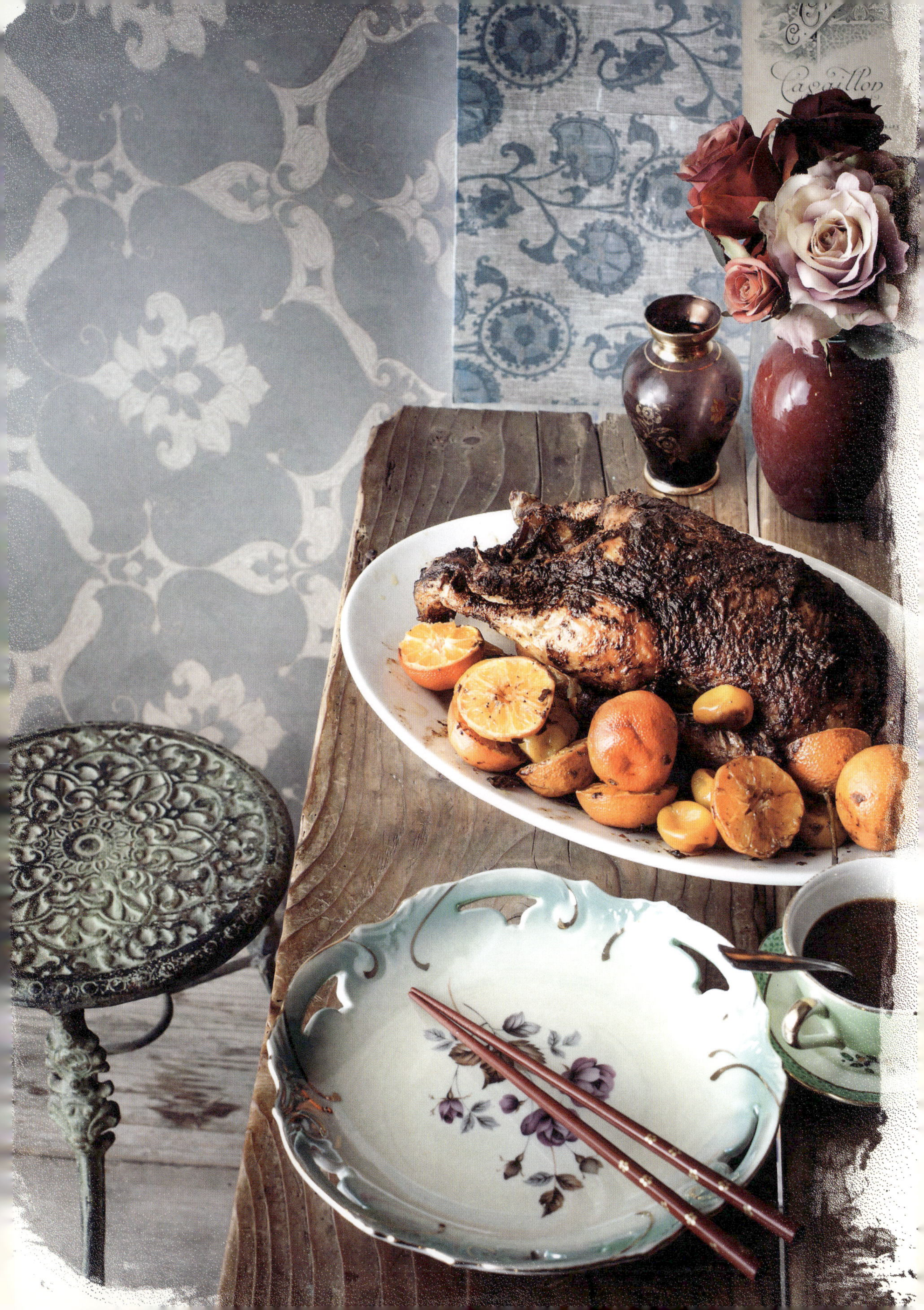
Cavaillon

MORNING GLORY AND BEEF SALAD

In Vietnam they have a special, simple gadget for shredding morning glory stems into thin curls in an instant. There are also skilled ladies early in the mornings at markets shredding them with a knife, and you can tell that they have been doing this for years. Shred the stems lengthways as finely as you can. You can substitute other salad leaves here if you like.

Serves 4

For the beef
2 garlic cloves, coarsely chopped
2cm (¾in) nugget of ginger, peeled and coarsely chopped
2 lemongrass stalks, inner parts trimmed and coarsely chopped
¼ teaspoon freshly ground black pepper
1 teaspoon fish sauce
1 tablespoon lime juice
1½ tablespoons light brown sugar
400g (14oz) piece of lean beef, cut into 4mm (⅛in) slices, then cut into 5cm (2in) pieces
about ½ tablespoon vegetable oil

For the dressing
3 tablespoons lime juice
1 tablespoon rice vinegar
2 tablespoons fish sauce
3 teaspoons light brown sugar
1 small red chilli, deseeded and finely chopped

For the salad
4 handfuls morning glory stems, shredded
a handful coriander (cilantro) leaves
a handful mint leaves
1 cucumber, peeled, sliced on diagonal then shredded
2 large spring onions (scallions), shredded

For the garnish
sesame salt (page 99)
roasted crushed peanuts (page 98)
fried shallots (page 99)

For the beef, pound the garlic, ginger and lemongrass together with a pestle and mortar to a coarse paste. Add the pepper, fish sauce, lime juice and sugar. Slather the paste all over the beef pieces and leave to marinate for about an hour.

For the dressing, mix all the ingredients together in a bowl, stirring until the sugar dissolves. Cover and set aside.

For the salad, assemble all the leaves and cucumber on serving plates. Top with the spring onions. Drizzle about 1 tablespoon of dressing over each, and turn through to combine.

Heat a large wok until very hot then drizzle in the oil. When hot, fry the beef in two batches, searing quickly on both sides so it remains soft and is a little golden here and there. Add any leftover marinade to the pan, cooking quickly, shifting the meat around the sides of the pan to collect any golden bits.

Divide the meat between the plates. Top each with a sprinkle of sesame salt, then at least a tablespoon each of crushed peanuts and fried shallots. Serve with the rest of the dressing on the table.

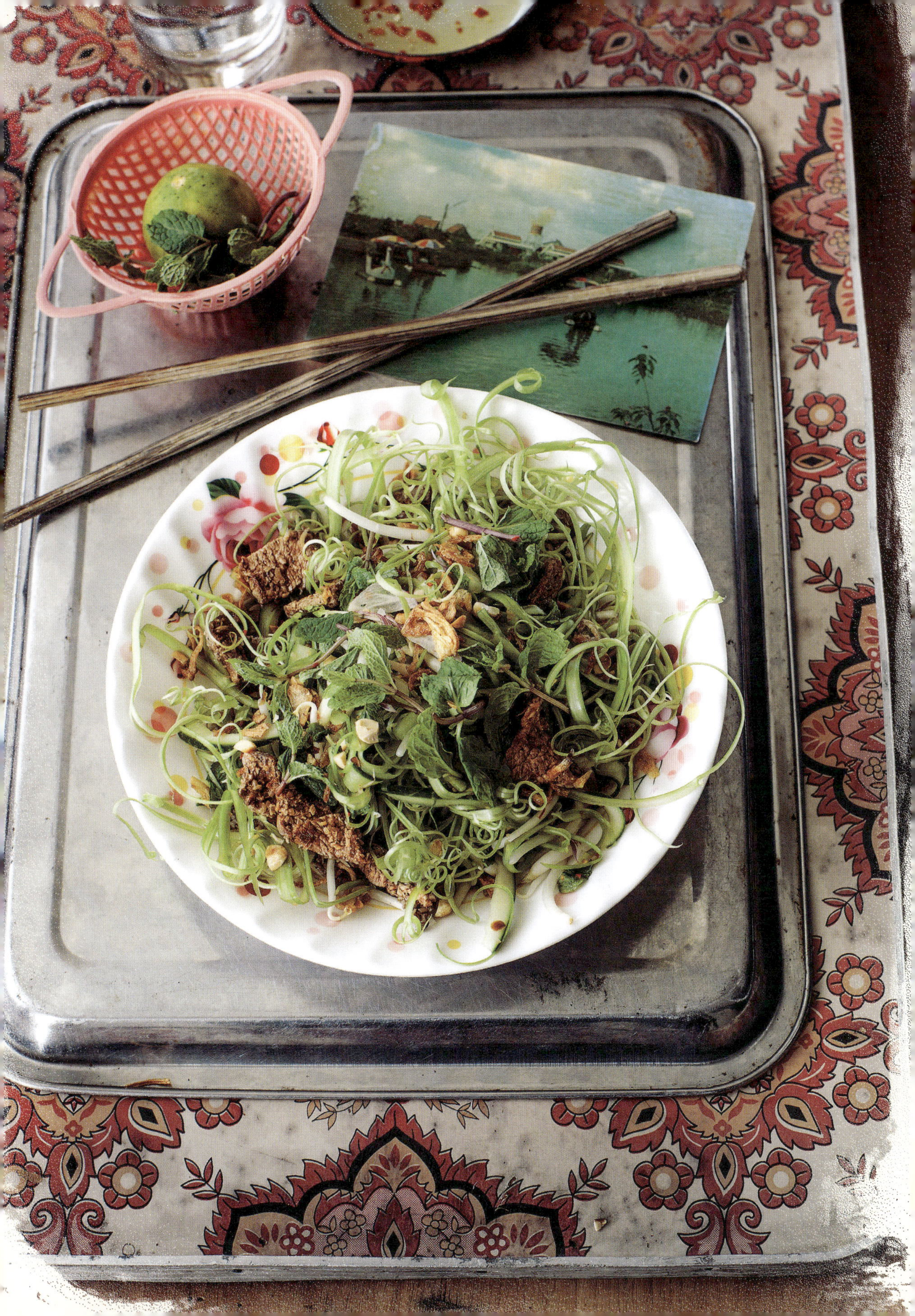

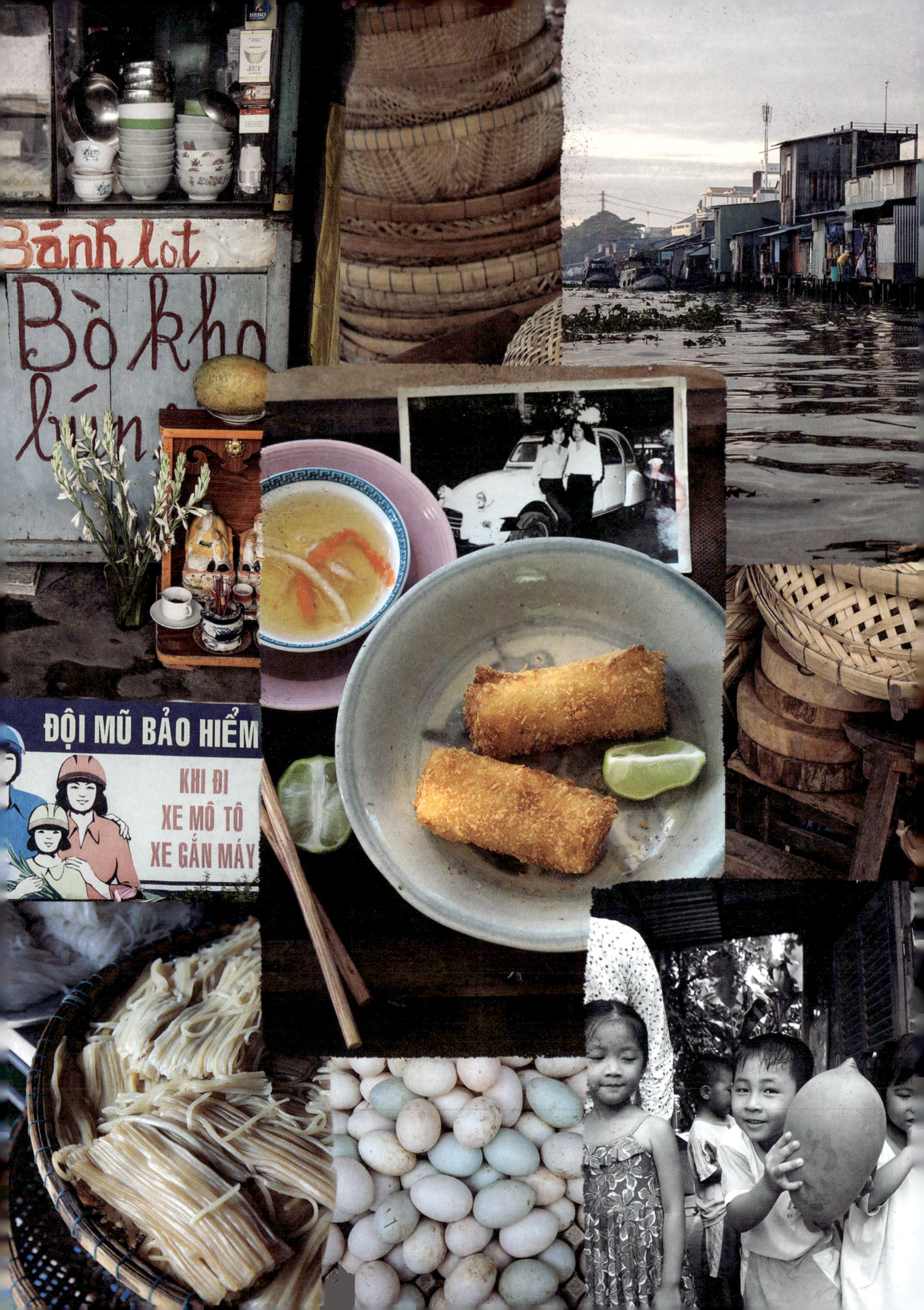
Bánh lot
Bò kho
bún
ĐỘI MŨ BẢO HIỂM
KHI ĐI
XE MÔ TÔ
XE GẮN MÁY

HiẾN 37

65
TRAN PHU

147

ĐƯỜNG SẮT VIỆT NAM

BO SOT VANG

This Vietnamese version of beef (bo) in red wine (vang) is easy to make. I ate it cooked with carrots, potatoes and served with noodles, which I found a lovely mix of French and Vietnamese. The beef needs to marinate in the wine for a couple of hours (or longer if you prefer). Vietnamese peppercorns have an incredible flavour – try and get these if you can for this dish and for general cooking. I like a smooth chilli sauce splashed over to serve.

Serves 5

800g (1¾lb) lean beef (rump or sirloin), cut into 5–6cm (2–2½in) chunks
375ml (1½ cups) red wine
4 tablespoons fish sauce
1 tablespoon soy sauce
¼ teaspoon chopped red chilli
3 garlic cloves, chopped
2 teaspoons finely chopped ginger
3 red Asian shallots, peeled
2 teaspoons sugar
10cm (4in) stick of cassia bark
3 star anise
1 teaspoon Vietnamese black peppercorns
1 teaspoon Sichuan peppercorns
3 tablespoons soya bean oil
4 tablespoons chopped tomatoes
350g (12oz) carrots, peeled and cut into chunks
500g (18oz) potatoes, peeled and cut into chunks
250g (9oz) flat (about 5mm/2in) dried rice noodles

To serve
2 or 3 spring onions (scallions), white and green part, sliced lengthways
a handful coriander (cilantro) leaves

Put the beef into a bowl and add the wine, fish sauce, soy sauce, chilli, garlic and ginger, whole shallots, sugar and cassia. Tie up the star anise and both peppercorns in a small piece of muslin and add to the bowl. Cover and leave to marinate for a couple of hours or longer.

Remove the meat from the marinade with a slotted spoon; keep the marinade. Heat the oil in a large pan. Brown the meat on all sides in batches. Return all the meat to the pan. Add the tomatoes, stir through, then add the marinade with the spice bag. Add 500ml (2 cups) water, bring to the boil, then lower the heat and simmer, covered, for about 1½ hours, or until the meat is tender when poked with a chopstick.

Add the carrot and potato chunks and turn them through the liquid. Stir in another 500ml (2 cups) water and simmer, uncovered, for 30 minutes or so, until everything is very tender. There should be a nice amount of sauce, but not too liquid, to serve with the noodles, so add a bit more water towards the end if you think it needs it. Remove from the heat and leave to stand with the lid on for 15 minutes or so before serving.

Bring a large pan of water to the boil. Cook the noodles until tender, then drain in a colander and rinse with warm water.

Serve the noodles with the beef and a generous amount of the sauce. Scatter liberally with spring onions and coriander to turn through while you are eating.

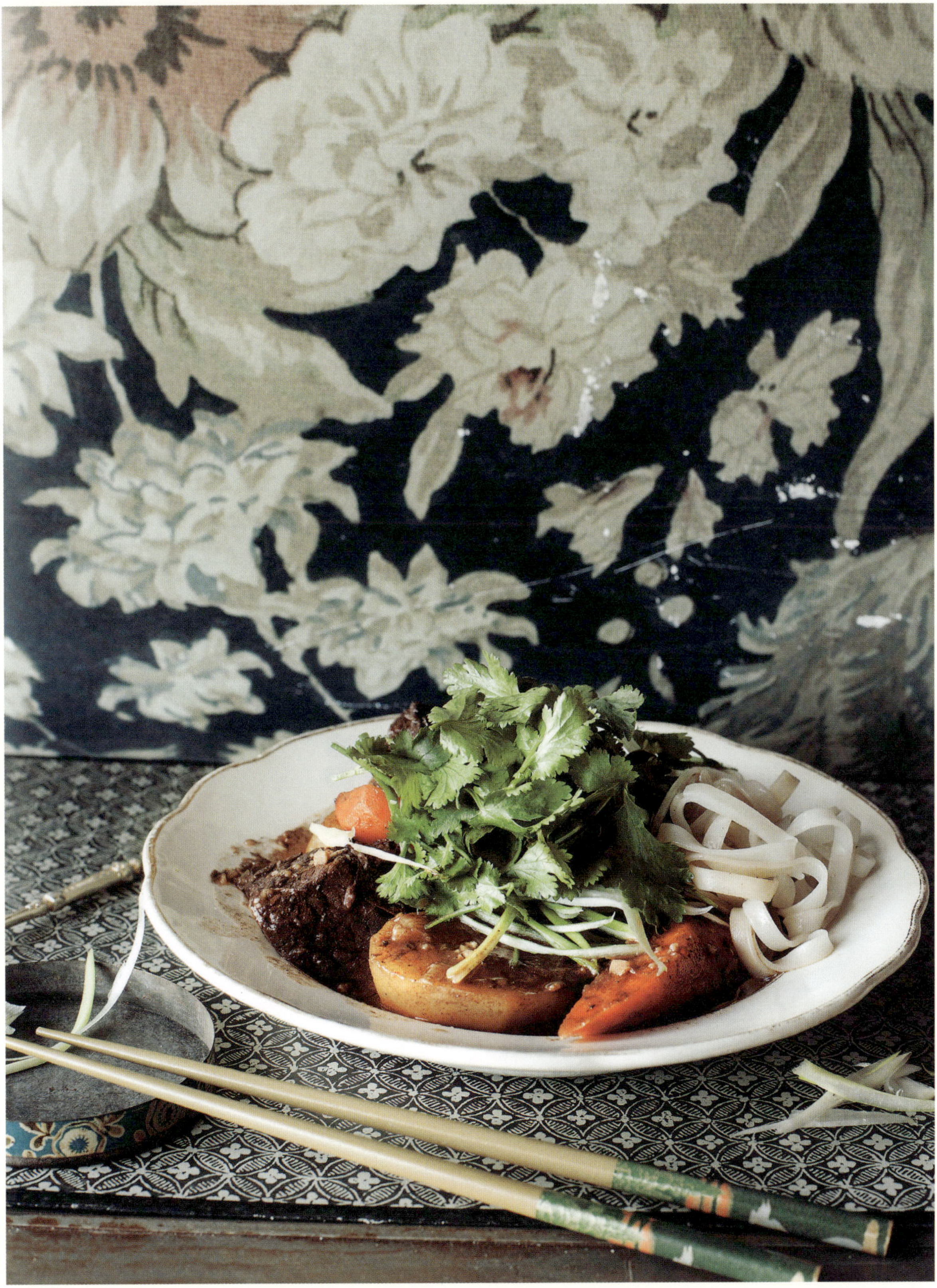

BO BIT TET

This is a beauty. In Hanoi and to the south I saw whole roads specializing in steak frites. Here I pan-fry the steaks, but you can also char-grill them. You have to be well organized to get this all on the table at the same time but it is worth it. Make sure you have all the pans ready and the plates warm.

Serves 2

2 entrecôte or sirloin steaks (with a little fat), each about 200g (7oz)
vegetable oil, for deep-frying
500g (18oz) potatoes, peeled and cut into fries
2 eggs
salt and freshly ground black pepper

For the marinade
2 lemongrass stalks, trimmed and cut into big chunks
2 small spring onions (scallions), trimmed, each cut into 3 long pieces
2 heaped teaspoons brown sugar
1 garlic clove, peeled and squashed
1 red chilli, halved and deseeded
1 tablespoon fish sauce
1 tablespoon soy sauce
1 tablespoon lime juice
¼ teaspoon coarsely crushed black pepper

To serve
red chillies, deseeded and finely sliced
a large handful coriander (cilantro) leaves
lime quarters

Put all the marinade ingredients into a bowl, and mix well to combine. Add the steaks and turn them over once or twice to coat both sides. Leave to marinate for 20–30 minutes, turning them a couple of times.

Heat the oil for deep-frying in a pan and, when hot, add the potatoes. Fry until golden and crisp. Using a wire scoop, remove the fries to a wide bowl lined with paper towels to absorb excess oil. Scatter them with just a little salt.

Meanwhile, heat a non-stick frying pan over a high heat until very hot. Add about 2 teaspoons oil to the pan, swirl it around and, when hot, add the steaks. Sizzle until deep gold on both sides. Using tongs to hold them, fry on their sides too, so the fat takes on some colour. Add the spring onions from the marinade to the pan towards the end and cook quickly. Pour in any marinade, cooking briefly, then take off the heat. Leave the steaks to rest in the pan for 5 minutes or so.

While the steaks are resting, heat a little oil in a small frying pan. Swizzle it around to cover the bottom, then break in the eggs. Cook for a minute or so, then cover with a lid and cook just until the tops turn opaque, but still with soft yolks. Sprinkle with a tiny bit of salt.

Serve the steaks drizzled with some sauce, topped with an egg and a little pepper. Add the fries to the plate and scatter with the slices of red chilli and the coriander leaves. Serve with lime wedges.

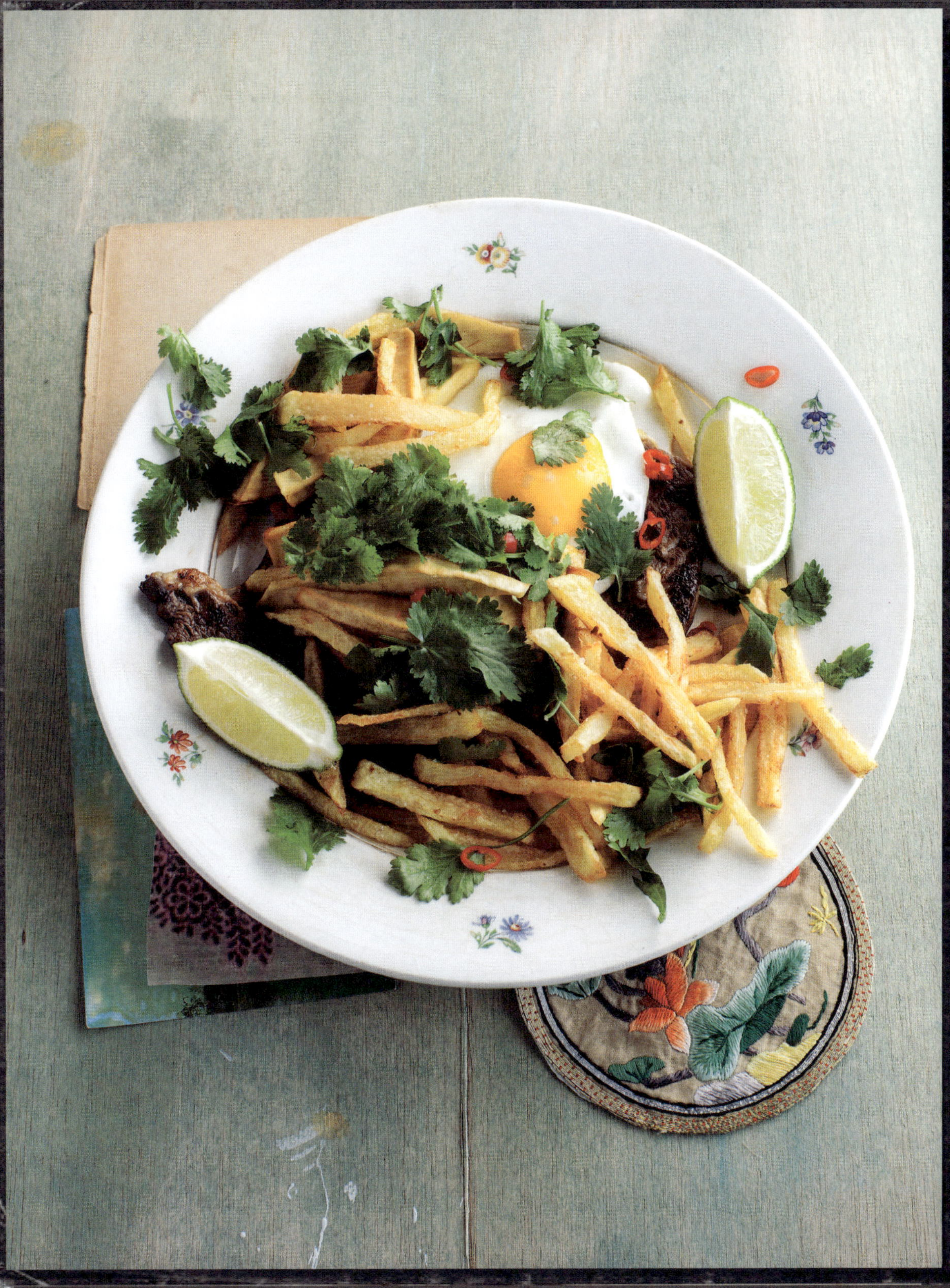

THUONG'S SPRING ONION OMELETTE

They say if you marry a woman from Hue it is like winning a lottery ticket. Thuong, a lovely housewife from Hue, made this for us one evening. She told me she used two duck eggs and one chicken egg. This omelette is lovely warm in a baguette.

Makes 1

1 teaspoon vegetable oil
40g (1½oz) minced (ground) pork
1 teaspoon fish sauce
½ teaspoon sugar
a pinch of chilli powder
3 eggs (duck or chicken)
1 small ripe tomato (about 80g/3oz), skinned, deseeded and excess water squeezed out, cut into small cubes
2 tablespoons finely chopped spring onions (scallions), white and green
sea salt and freshly ground black pepper

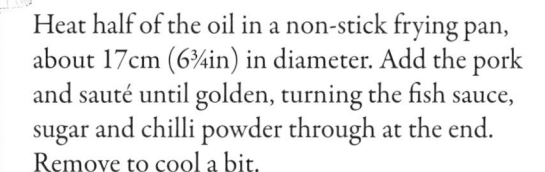

Heat half of the oil in a non-stick frying pan, about 17cm (6¾in) in diameter. Add the pork and sauté until golden, turning the fish sauce, sugar and chilli powder through at the end. Remove to cool a bit.

In a bowl, gently whisk the eggs with a few grinds of black pepper. Scrape in the pork, the tomatoes and spring onions and whisk gently to incorporate well.

Wipe out the frying pan, then add the rest of the oil and put over a medium-high heat. When hot, pour in the egg mixture and let it sizzle. Lift the cooked edges with a wooden spoon to allow some egg to slide underneath. Reduce the heat to low, cover the pan and cook for a little longer – until the eggs are still very soft but not too runny on top... just a little. Serve with a little salt and pepper over.

VIETNAM

CHICKEN LIVER AND PORK PÂTÉ

Actually, this is very similar to the pâté served with cornichons in France, but in Vietnam they serve it with daikon and carrot pickles. It's easy to make and can be eaten cold or warm – slipped under a hot grill in a small dish and served with sticky rice or baguette it is lovely.

Makes 1 small pâté

200g (7oz) chicken livers
150g (5½oz) pork liver
1–2 tablespoons plain (all-purpose) flour
1½ tablespoons butter or pork fat
100g (¾ cup) shallots, chopped
100g (3½oz) rindless pork belly, chopped
2 garlic cloves, chopped
1 lemongrass stalk, cut into 4 or 5 lengths
3 teaspoons fish sauce
½–¾ teaspoon Chinese five-spice powder
a couple of pinches of chilli powder
about 5 tablespoons melted butter, cooled
salt and freshly ground black pepper

Cut the chicken and pork liver into small pieces, trimming them where necessary as you go. Toss with the flour to coat.

Heat the butter in a large, non-stick frying pan over a medium heat and fry the shallots until soft, 4–5 minutes. Add the livers, pork belly, garlic and lemongrass and stir-fry over a high heat until all the liver has changed colour, about 5 minutes.

Add the fish sauce, five-spice powder, chilli powder, a good grinding of pepper and a little salt. Pour in 375ml (1½ cups) water and bring to the boil. Simmer over a low heat, uncovered, until roughly three-quarters of the liquid has evaporated, about 15 minutes.

Using a slotted spoon, transfer the livers and pork belly to a food processor or blender and whizz until finely puréed, adding as much of the cooking liquid as necessary for a soft consistency. Taste for seasoning.

Line a loaf tin, 22 x 10cm (9 x 4in) and 5cm (2in) deep, with plastic wrap so it hangs over the sides. Pack the mixture into the tin, smooth the top with a spatula and cover the surface with the melted butter. Leave to cool, then bring the plastic wrap over to cover, store in the fridge and eat within 3 days.

WARM PÂTÉ WITH STICKY RICE

When warm and just-made, the soft pâté drips down into the rice, and is delicious. Soak about 150g (5½oz) sticky (glutinous) rice for a few hours in cold water. Drain and rinse. Add it to a pan with a couple of pinches of salt, a pandan leaf tied in a knot and 500ml (2 cups) cold water. Cover, bring to the boil and simmer for about 15 minutes until the water has all been absorbed and the rice is a sticky, tender mass, stirring often to make sure it is not catching. Discard the pandan leaf. If the pâté is not just-made and still warm, heat through under the grill (broiler) in a flat gratin dish. Serve a good couple of dollops of rice on each plate with a heaped tablespoon of warm pâté over each, and a sprinkle of sesame salt (page 99).

BAGUETTE

Probably the most French, and beautiful thing that was left behind, these are just about everywhere in Vietnam. I made them with a wonderful baker, Loi, and once I had seen the technique, I found it very easy. These have a little rice flour added into the wheat flour.

These baguettes can be frozen once baked.

Makes 6

450g (3½ cups) strong white bread flour, plus extra for dusting
50g (⅓ cup) rice flour
½ teaspoon baking powder
1 sachet (7g/1½ teaspoons) dried yeast
1 teaspoon salt
½ teaspoon sugar
300ml (1¼ cups) tepid water
butter, for greasing

Mix all the ingredients (except the butter) together in a bowl, adding a little more water or bread flour if needed to give a soft dough. Knead on a lightly floured surface for 4–5 minutes. Leave the dough in a ball on the work surface, with the bowl covering it, for 1½–2 hours, until risen to double its size.

Brush 2 baguette racks with butter or line 2 baking sheets with baking parchment and brush with butter.

Divide the dough into 6 equal portions roughly 130g (4½oz) each. Punch down each ball of dough with your palms, shaping them as much as you can into an even oval of roughly 20cm (8in) length. Then roll up the third nearest you over itself and punch down flat with your palms. Roll up the next third over itself upward and punch down flat. Then roll the last third so you have a long skinny roll, but don't punch this flat. Crimp the edges where they meet all the way along to seal.

Roll out gently to about 22cm (9in) in length, barely pressing with your palms and maintaining a fat middle tapering to the ends. (This technique is very simple when you have tried it a few times.) Sit the shaped loaves on the prepared sheets with the seam line upright. Cover loosely with a cloth, making troughs and leave to rise until puffed up well, 45–60 minutes.

Preheat the oven to 200°C/ 400°F/Gas 6 and put a dish of water in the bottom. Using a very sharp knife or a razor blade, make a shallow slash down the length of each baguette over the crimped join, stopping about 3cm (1¼in) from each end. Using a sprayer, spray water evenly over the baguettes and bake until golden, about 15 minutes.

Slide the sheet a little out of the oven and lightly spray the baguettes again with a mist of water. Return to the oven for another few minutes and remove when golden and crusty (but not too much, as overbaking will make them hard).

Lift the baguettes onto a wire rack to cool a little before serving.

ánh Mì Paté

BÁNH

DÂN VIỆT N

LE PEUPLE VIETNA

BULLETIN RELATIF AUX FAITS PRÉHISTORIQUES,
ARCHÉOLOGIQUES, HISTORIQUES, ETHNOGRAPHIQUES,

BANH MI

This is delicious. So many things are piled into baguettes in Vietnam. I saw saucisson, terrine, pâté, grilled pork slices, other cold cuts, mayonnaise, pickles, coriander, spring onions, chilli – all heaped into a baguette, and it just works. Put whatever you like inside, but make sure you always include some warm sauce for adding flavour and keeping the baguette moist.

Makes 6

6 baguettes (page 126)
about 12 thin slices of warm stove-top garlic and spice pork (page 131) with sauce
½ quantity of chicken liver and pork pâté (page 125)
smooth chilli sauce
6–8 tablespoons mayonnaise
6 or more skewers of warm barbecued lemongrass pork (page 130)
6 warm pork patties (page 110)
1 lime
a couple of small cucumbers, unpeeled, in long chunky batons
3 spring onions (scallions), in long thin slices
a couple of handfuls coriander (cilantro) leaves
a couple of handfuls water mint leaves
carrot and daikon pickle (page 100), shaken out of their liquid

Preheat the oven to 180°C/350°F/Gas 4. Heat the baguettes until warm but not too crusty, 4–5 minutes.

Cut the baguettes open and drizzle a generous amount of sauce from the stove-top pork on both cut sides of each. Spread some pâté over one or both sides. Drizzle a little chilli sauce here and there on the bottom side and dab a few small blobs of mayonnaise on both sides.

Heap a couple of slices of pork, and/or a pork skewer and a pork patty, in each, and add a little extra sauce or squeeze in some lime. Pile in some cucumber and a small heap of spring onions, spreading them out along the length of the baguette.

Scatter in some coriander and water mint leaves and finish with a few pieces of pickle. Close up, lightly squash together and eat warm.

BAGUETTE WITH CONDENSED MILK

This is rather rich and delicious. Best eaten for breakfast or as a snack during the day when you need a boost of sugar.

Preheat the oven to 200°C/400°F/Gas 6. Slice a Vietnamese baguette or a 22cm (9in) piece of French baguette into 3 or 4 sections, but not all the way through. Loosely wrap the baguette in foil and warm in the oven until a bit crusty on the outside, but moist and warm inside.

In a bowl, whisk 125ml (½ cup) condensed milk with 1 tablespoon milk, then pour evenly into 2 shallow serving bowls or ramekins. The baguette can be torn into pieces and dipped into the bowl of sweet thick milk. (Don't eat too much.) A black coffee on the side, no sugar, would be perfect.

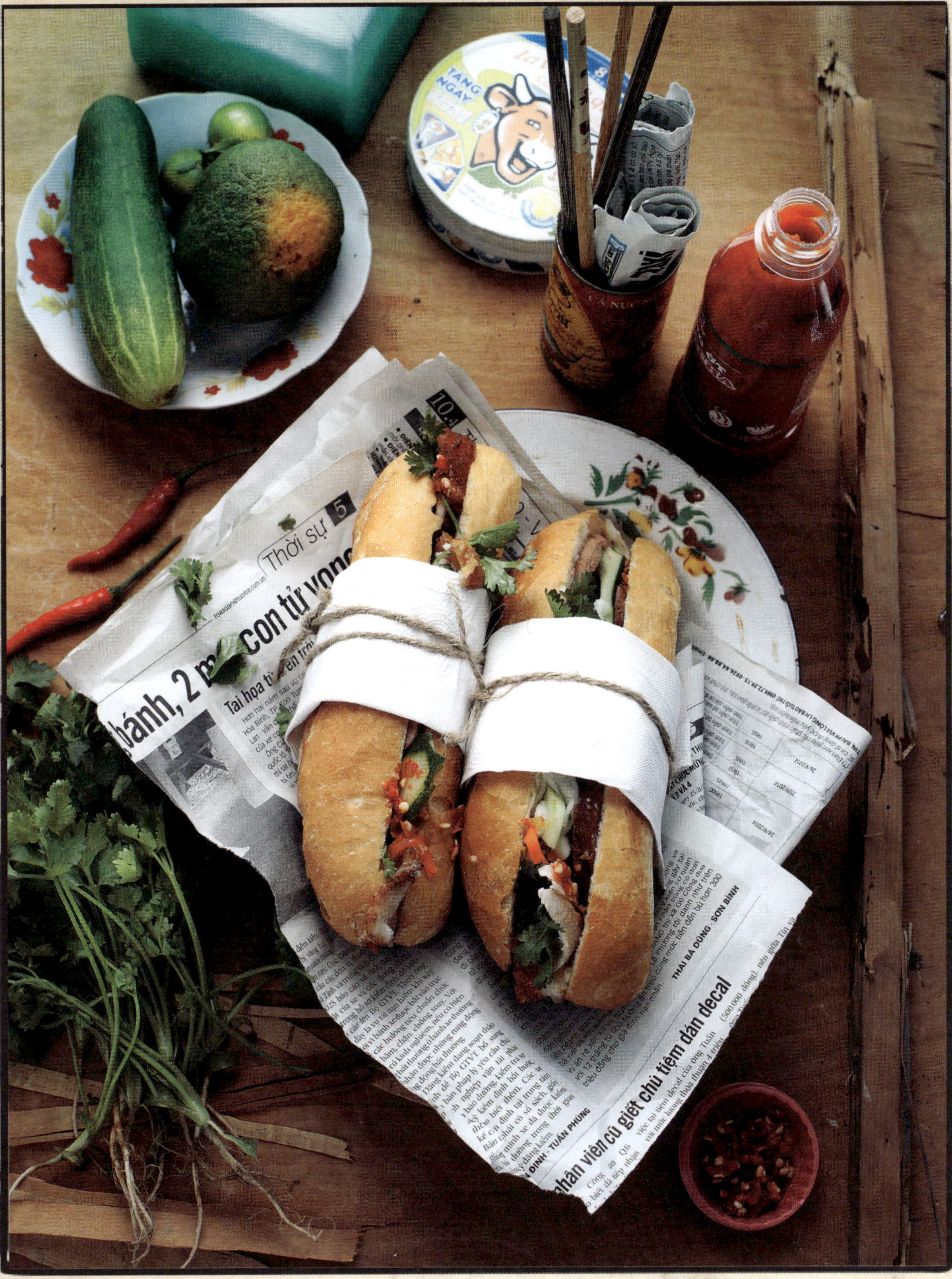

Thời sự 5
THÁI BÁ DŨNG - SƠN BÌNH

BARBECUED LEMONGRASS PORK

This very tasty dish is cooked on a barbecue. It is made with pork neck, which may look very fatty as you thread it raw onto skewers, but the fat will melt and char, giving you succulent meat with an amazing sweet flavour. I have used a couple of skewers for each piece of meat, to help keep it flat and facilitate turning. If you have a tight barbecue rack then you can use it here. These pork strips can be eaten on their own or used as a filling for banh mi (page 128).

Serves 4–5

800g (1¾lb) pork neck, in 1cm (⅜in) slices (about 6 slices)

For the marinade
2 garlic cloves, peeled and very finely chopped
2 tablespoons very finely chopped trimmed lemongrass, inner part only
2 small red chillies, deseeded and very finely chopped
2 tablespoons light brown sugar
3 tablespoons fish sauce
½ teaspoon salt
a scattering of freshly ground black pepper

For the marinade, combine all the ingredients in a dish (large enough to hold the pork) and mix together well. Cut each slice of pork into 3 or 4 strips, about 3cm (1¼in) wide. Bash these out with a meat mallet, to give strips about 20cm (8in) long and 4cm (1½in) wide, and less than 5mm (¼in) thick.

Lay the pork strips in the marinade, turning them over a couple of times to coat well. Cover and leave to marinate in a cool place for about 3 hours, or longer if more convenient, turning the strips over halfway through with a fork.

If using wooden skewers, soak them in water for an hour or so to avoid them burning on the barbecue. Heat up the barbecue.

Weaving the skewers in and out, thread the strips of meat onto 2 skewers, pushing one skewer through one side of the meat and one through the other, so the pork will lie flat. Place on the barbecue and cook until charred here and there and cooked through, but not so dark as to give a burnt taste.

Serve just as they are, or pull the skewers out for banh mi, along with the other waiting ingredients.

STOVE-TOP GARLIC AND SPICE PORK

Mrs Dong, a wonderful cook who taught me how to make this, says she likes to prepare it for banh mi (page 128). They especially like to eat it over the Vietnamese New Year, she said, as this pork keeps so well that they then don't have to cook over the holiday. The sauce is great for adding moisture and flavour to the insides of baguette, even with another meat instead, such as the pork patties on page 110. You can always serve this with a bowl of rice, or a vegetable dish, rather than in a baguette.

Serves quite a few, with enough for leftovers

1½ teaspoons Chinese five-spice powder
¾ teaspoon salt
3 teaspoons brown sugar
1 tablespoon chopped garlic
freshly ground black pepper
1.2kg (2¾lb) pork loin or flat piece of pork leg, with some fat on
4 tablespoons soya bean or vegetable oil
2 tablespoons soy sauce
½ teaspoon Vietnamese black peppercorns

In a bowl, mix 1 teaspoon of the five-spice powder with the salt, 1 teaspoon of the sugar, half the garlic and a good grind of pepper. Rub well all over the meat then leave for 10 minutes or so.

Heat the oil in a non-stick pan which has a lid and which will hold the meat compactly. When hot, fry the meat until nicely golden on all sides, taking care not to burn the garlic.

In the same bowl as the marinade was in, mix the soy sauce and peppercorns with the remaining five-spice powder, sugar and garlic. Add 185ml (¾ cup) water and swish it all around. Pour into the pan with the meat, cover the pan and simmer for 30–35 minutes, depending on the thickness of the meat.

Take off the heat and leave the pork to cool in the pan for a little while (you can skim off any fat from the sauce if it forms).

Remove the pork from the sauce and cut into slices. If eating it in banh mi, drizzle some of the hot sauce over both cut sides of a baguette, before stuffing it with warm slices of meat and other fillings of your choice.

ICED COCONUT COFFEE

Vietnamese drip coffee was introduced by the French and is something wonderful that has lingered on and become a big part of Vietnamese culture. Hot. Iced. Milky. With condensed milk. With whipped egg. With yogurt. You can use plain yogurt instead of the coconut cream here – you may just need a little extra swizzle of condensed milk. This is truly lovely in the summer heat.

Makes 2 large coffees

1½ cups crushed ice
200ml (7fl oz) coconut cream
6 tablespoons condensed milk
100ml (3½fl oz) cold strong, filtered Vietnamese coffee

Put the ice, coconut cream and condensed milk into a sturdy jug and blend using a hand-held blender until smooth.

Put the jug into the freezer until the mixture is just frozen but not completely set like ice cream, turning through once or twice with a fork.

Shake the coffee well in a sealed bottle then divide between 2 quite wide glasses. Gently spoon the coconut mixture over the coffee so it doesn't mix in.

Serve at once, with a long spoon and a straw.

I have eaten young rice and broken rice and sailed on the perfume river. Dreamed of eating duck with kumquats. Watched people drinking snake blood and swallowing the heart, eating live-fried silkworms and duck embryos. Coffee with frozen yogurt and coconut. Mung bean cakes with tea. And all the time I kept thinking it was a dream.

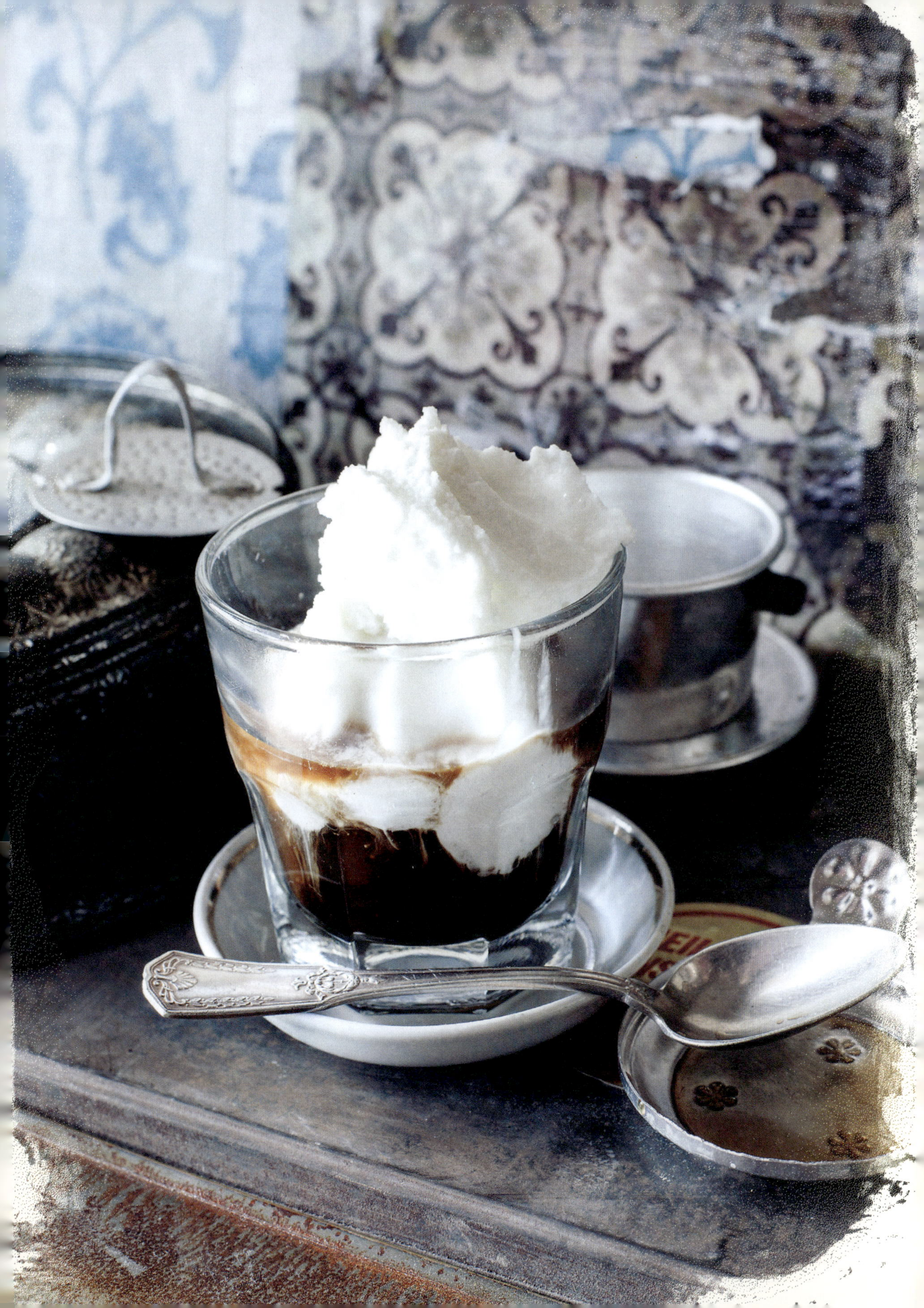

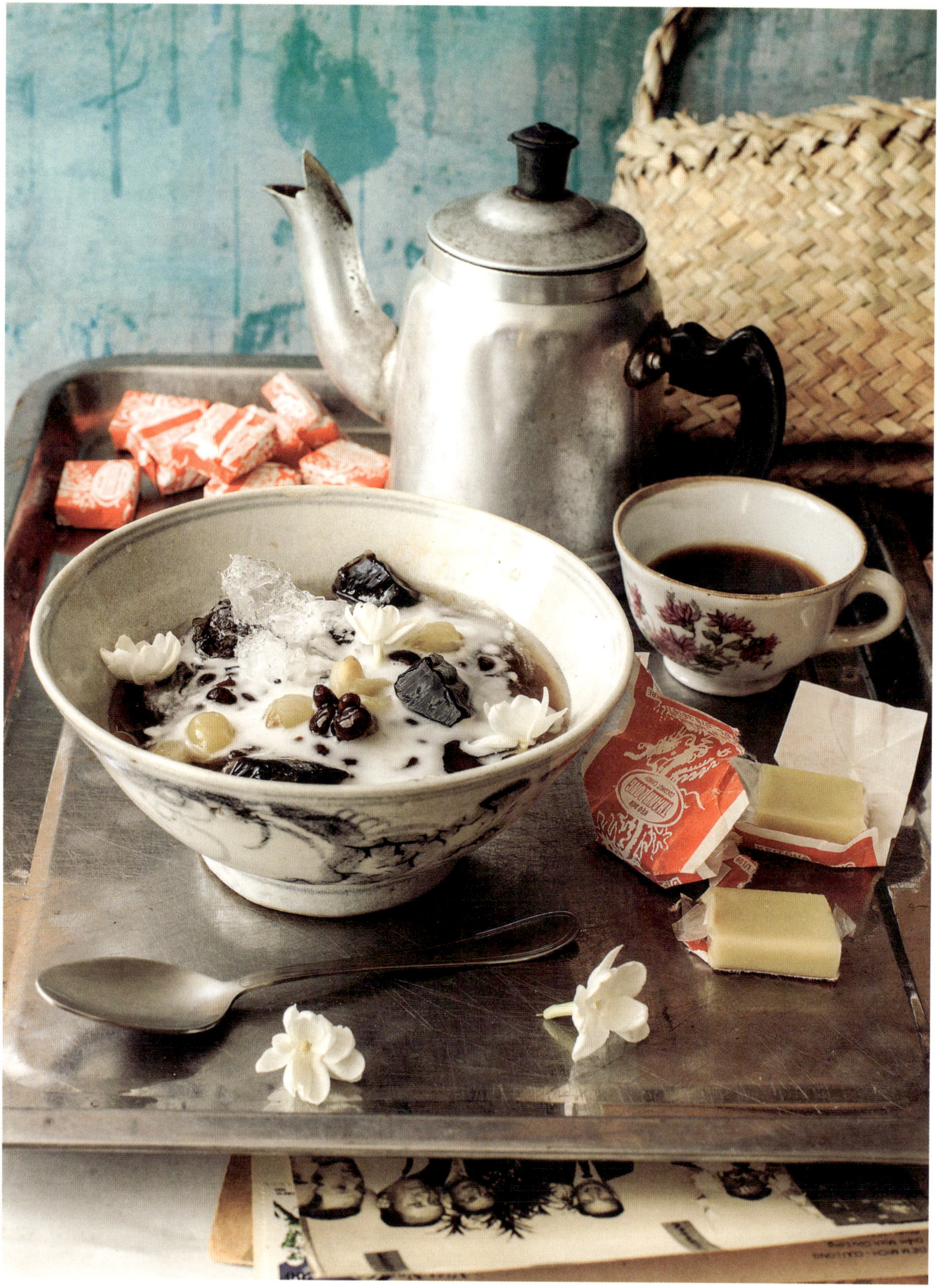

CHE

This sweet, chilled, dark bean soup is a beauty, like jewellery with its shiny gems of jelly, tapioca pearls and lotus seeds glinting up from the bowl. Taste-wise it is unique, interesting and refreshing, and the texture combination is incredible. Serve it either as a dessert or a drink.

Serves 6

For the black beans
230g (scant 1½ cups) small black beans
230g (heaped 1 cup) white sugar

For the lotus seeds
150g (5¼oz) dried lotus seeds
150g (¾ cup) white sugar

For the tapioca pearls
40g (⅓ cup) fine tapioca flour
a piece of fresh coconut, cut into 24 peppercorn-sized nibs

To serve
about 125ml (½ cup) coconut cream
a large handful shredded fresh coconut
about 1½ cups cubed grass jelly (available ready-made in cans or powdered in sachets, from Vietnamese stores)
about 1½ cups crushed ice
a handful edible jasmine (or other) flowers

Rinse the black beans in a fine colander then put into a pan and cover with cold water. Bring to the boil, then drain in the colander and rinse again. Return to the pan, cover with 2 litres (8 cups) cold water and bring to the boil. Cover and simmer until tender but not overcooked, 1–1½ hours, stirring through the sugar after 1 hour. Leave to cool completely in the pan, then transfer to a bowl, cover and refrigerate to chill.

Using the tip of a small, sharp knife, split each lotus seed in half; discard any inside pith.

Put the lotus seed halves in a bowl, cover with boiling water and leave for 2–3 minutes. Drain and put into a saucepan with 1 litre (4 cups) boiling water. Cover and simmer gently for 10 minutes, then add the sugar and stir until it dissolves. Simmer until the seeds are tender, 4–5 minutes more. Leave to cool.

Meanwhile, make the tapioca balls. Put the flour into a small bowl, add about 3 tablespoons hot water and mix to a thick, smooth paste. Leave for about 10 minutes to thicken, then break off bits the size of a soya bean and roll them between your palms. Push a coconut nib into the centre of each and roll into a smooth ball. You will need about 24. It is a lovely surprise to find these inside when biting into them, so persevere – you can become quite quick at it.

Bring a saucepan of water to the boil and add the tapioca balls. They will first seem to stick to the bottom but then they'll bob up. They are ready when transparent, after about 15 minutes. Remove with a slotted spoon and drop them into cold water. If not serving immediately, keep them in a little cold water with some of the lotus syrup splashed over them.

To serve, spoon a ladleful of beans and their syrup into each of 6 serving bowls or glasses. Drop in a few tapioca pearls and scatter some lotus seeds on top with a little of their syrup too. Drizzle in some coconut cream, scatter on some shredded coconut, add a few cubes of grass jelly and finish with some crushed ice and a few jasmine flowers for their perfume. Serve at once.

VIETNAM

LEMONGRASS CRÈME CARAMEL

In Vietnam these are usually steamed. Refreshing on a hot summer's night, they are particularly good served with coconut cream cool from the fridge. Often served with crushed ice over them.

Serves 8

240g (1 heaped cup) sugar
700ml (scant 3 cups) milk
2 lemongrass stalks, chopped into big pieces
5 eggs
5 or 6 tablespoons chilled coconut cream, to serve

Preheat the oven to 160°C/325°F/Gas 2½. Have eight 150ml (5oz) ramekin dishes or other moulds ready.

For the caramel, put 150g (¾ cup) of the sugar with 3 tablespoons water in a small, heavy-based saucepan over a high heat. You can stir initially, but once the caramel starts to colour around the edges stop stirring, and swirl the pan to move the caramel around. Lower the heat and keep an eye on it until it turns into a lovely deep golden caramel colour. Take care not to get it too dark – it can burn in a second.

Pour the caramel quickly but carefully into the base of the ramekins. Holding each ramekin with a cloth, as the caramel will be extremely hot, tip from side to side to coat the bases as well as slightly up the sides.

Meanwhile, put the milk and lemongrass in a saucepan over a medium heat and heat to just below boiling. Remove from the heat and leave to infuse.

Break the eggs into a bowl, add the remaining 90g (scant ½ cup) sugar and whisk until creamy but not too frothy. Reheat the lemongrass milk, then whisk this into the egg mixture a little at a time initially, then pour it all in and whisk gently to combine. Try to avoid froth.

Let the custard rest for 5 minutes or so for the flavours to mingle, then strain into a jug, discarding the lemongrass.

Carefully pour the custard over the caramel in the ramekins, dividing it equally.

Stand the ramekins in a roasting tin and pour warm water into the tin come halfway up the sides of the ramekins. Bake for 30–35 minutes, or until the custards are set on the top. They will still wobble slightly when shaken but will set in the fridge.

Take the ramekins out of the baking tin and leave to cool. Cover each with plastic wrap and put in the fridge to chill for a few hours, or overnight.

To serve, gently press the outer edges of the custards away from the sides of the ramekins, using your fingers. Invert each onto a small plate and wait for the caramels to slip upside down onto the plate.

Serve the crème caramels with a drizzle of coconut cream over the top.

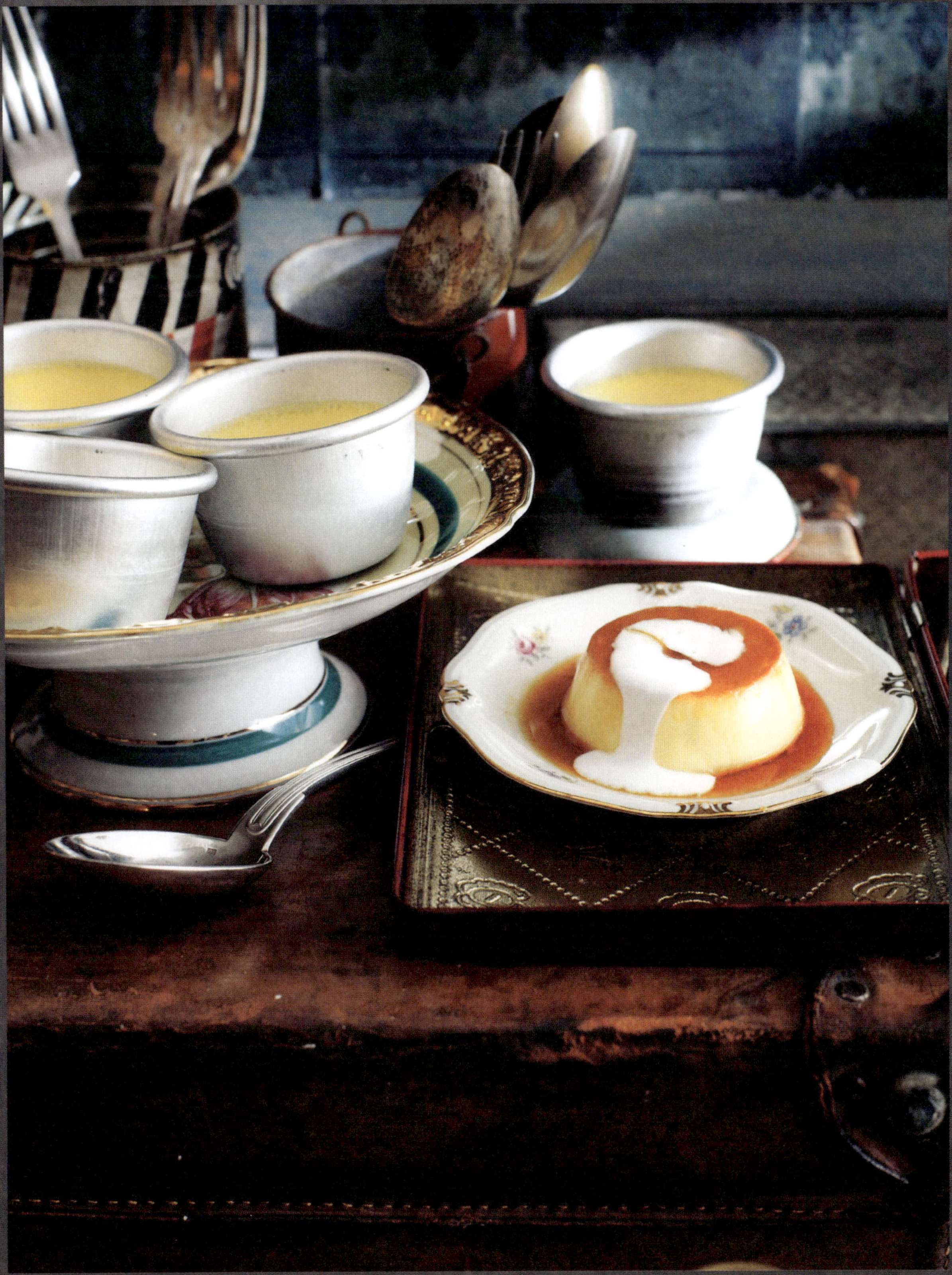

STICKY RICE WITH COCONUT AND GINGER

This rice has a great consistency. I love the plainness and smooth texture here of just rice and coconut, but if you like, you could add some chopped nuts or fruit in as a variation. If you have a simmer mat, use it here so the rice doesn't catch at the bottom of the pot.

Serves 6

350g (¾lb) sticky (glutinous) rice
50g (2oz) chunk of ginger, peeled and cut in 4 or 5 pieces
3 tablespoons white sugar
375ml (1½ cups) coconut cream, at room temperature
sea salt
6 heaped teaspoons light brown sugar, to serve

Soak the rice in cold water for 3–4 hours. Tip into a small-holed colander or large sieve and rinse well under the cold tap.

Put the rice into a pan with the ginger. Add 750ml (3 cups) water and bring to the boil. Lower the heat and simmer, covered, for about 10 minutes, stirring often to make sure the rice is not catching. When the water has been absorbed and it looks quite porridge-y, stir in the white sugar and a couple of pinches of salt.

Add the coconut milk, mixing through well, and simmer, uncovered now, for a few minutes to heat it through and finish cooking the rice.

Serve warm, scattering each portion with a heaped teaspoonful of sugar.

FRUIT WITH SALT AND CHILLI

Use a lovely mix of fruit here, such as dragonfruit, lychees, rose apples, pineapple, pears, green apples, mango…

a selection of fruit
fine salt
chilli powder

Cut the fruit into slices or halves. Put some salt into a bowl and stir in some chilli powder, a very little at a time, until it reaches the level of heat you prefer.

Either sprinkle the fruit and chilli salt over the fruit slices before serving, or serve it separately for everyone to add the amount they would like.

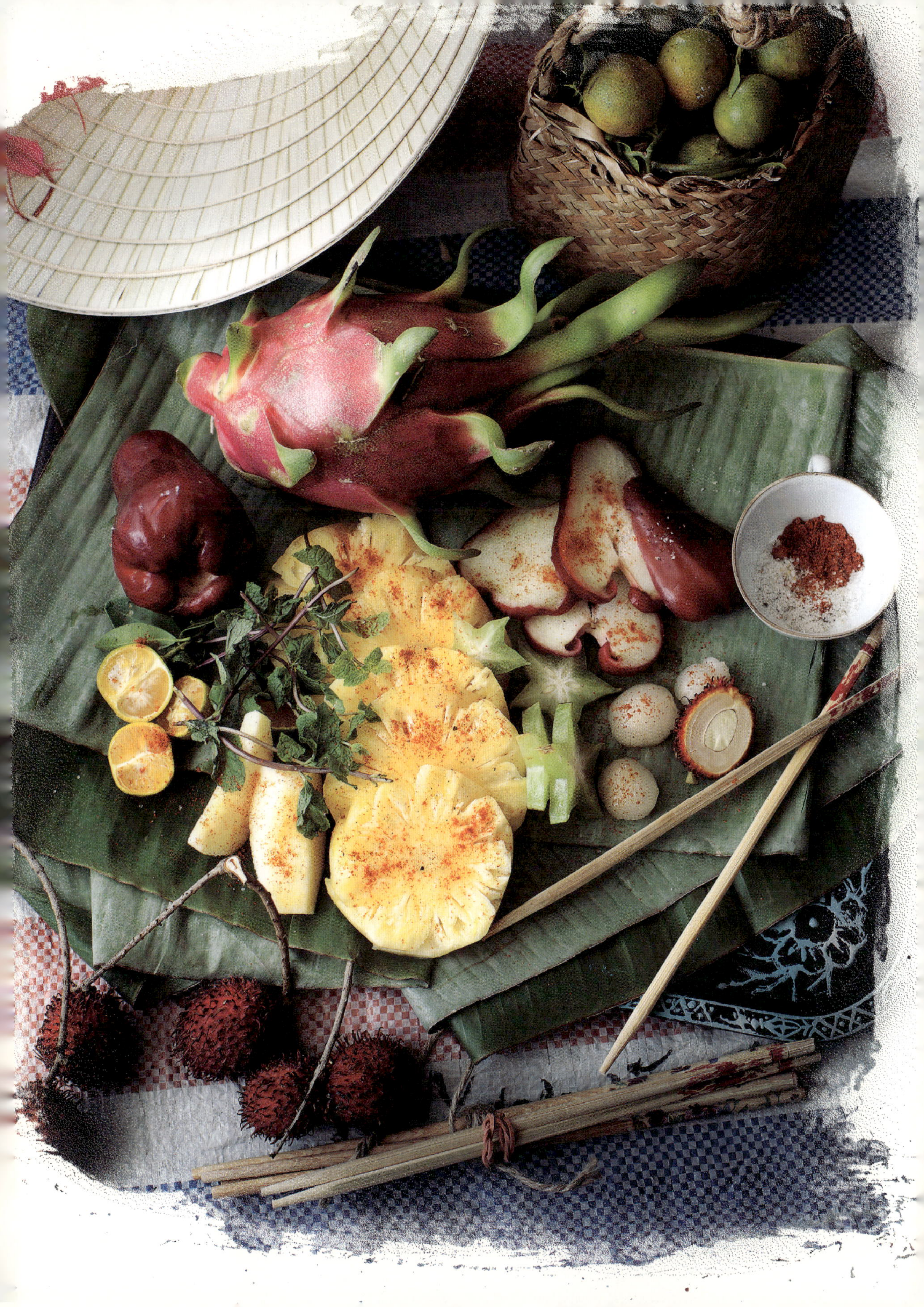

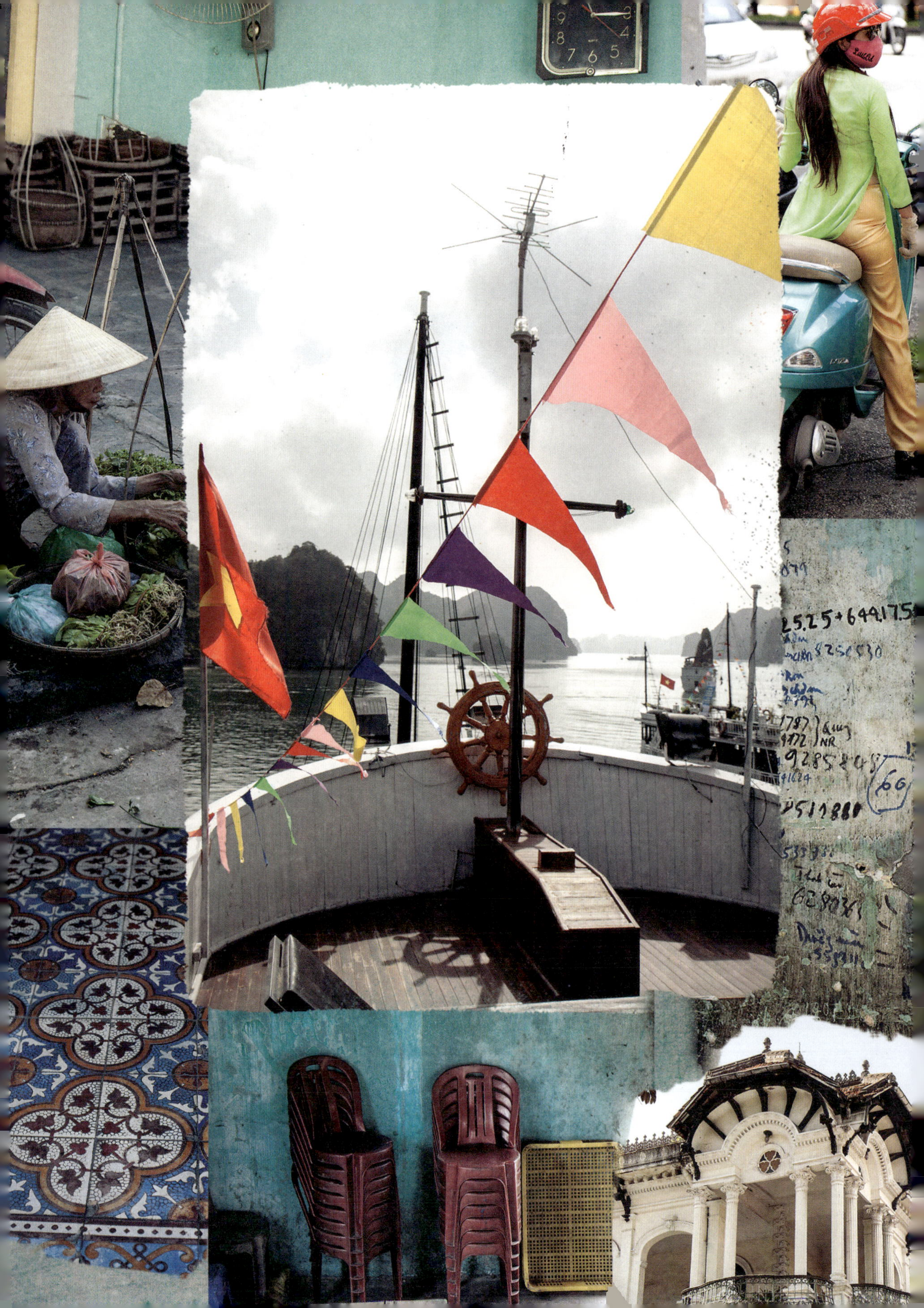

BÚN CHẢ HÀ NỘI

PONDICHERRY PUDUCHERRY PONDICHERY PONDY	SOUTHEASTERN INDIAN STATE OF TAMIL NADU, ON THE COROMANDEL COAST
FRENCH RIVIERA OF THE EAST	LA COMPAGNIE DES INDES FRANÇAISE
TREES: MANGO, BANYAN, NEEM, TAMARIND, CASHEW, EUCALYPTUS, BANANA, COCONUT, JACARANDA	
TROPICAL, WARM & HUMID. MODERATE MONSOON RAIN OCTOBER–DECEMBER	SEA: BAY OF BENGAL

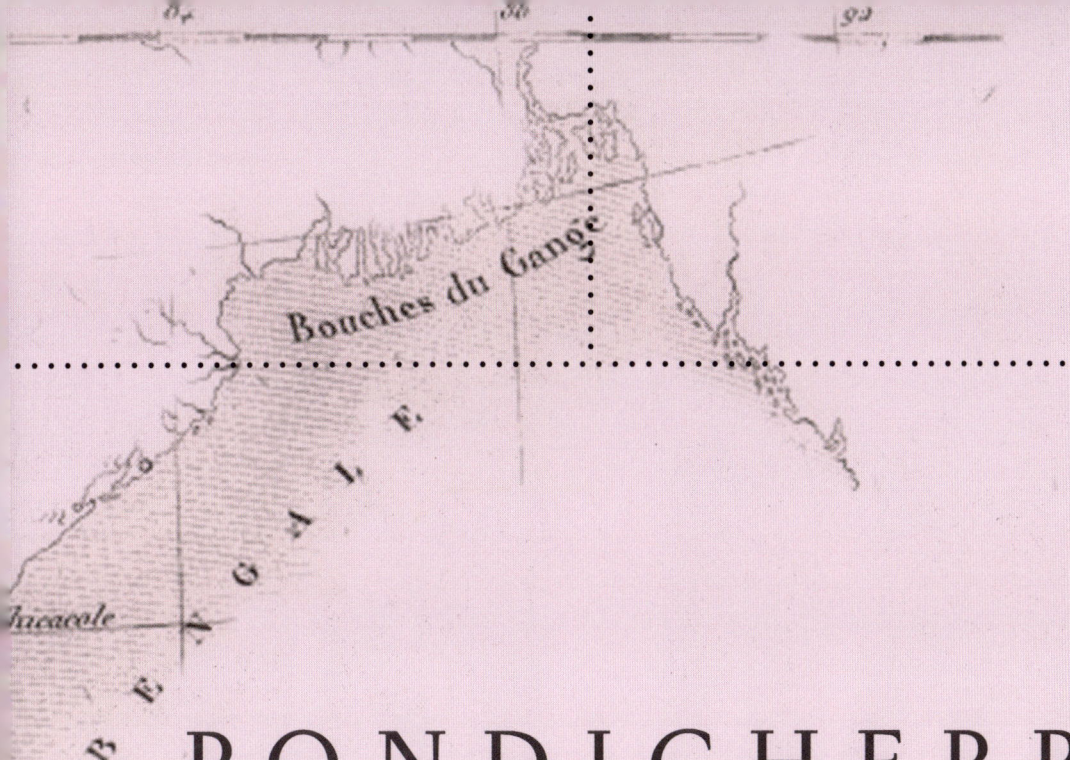

PONDICHERRY

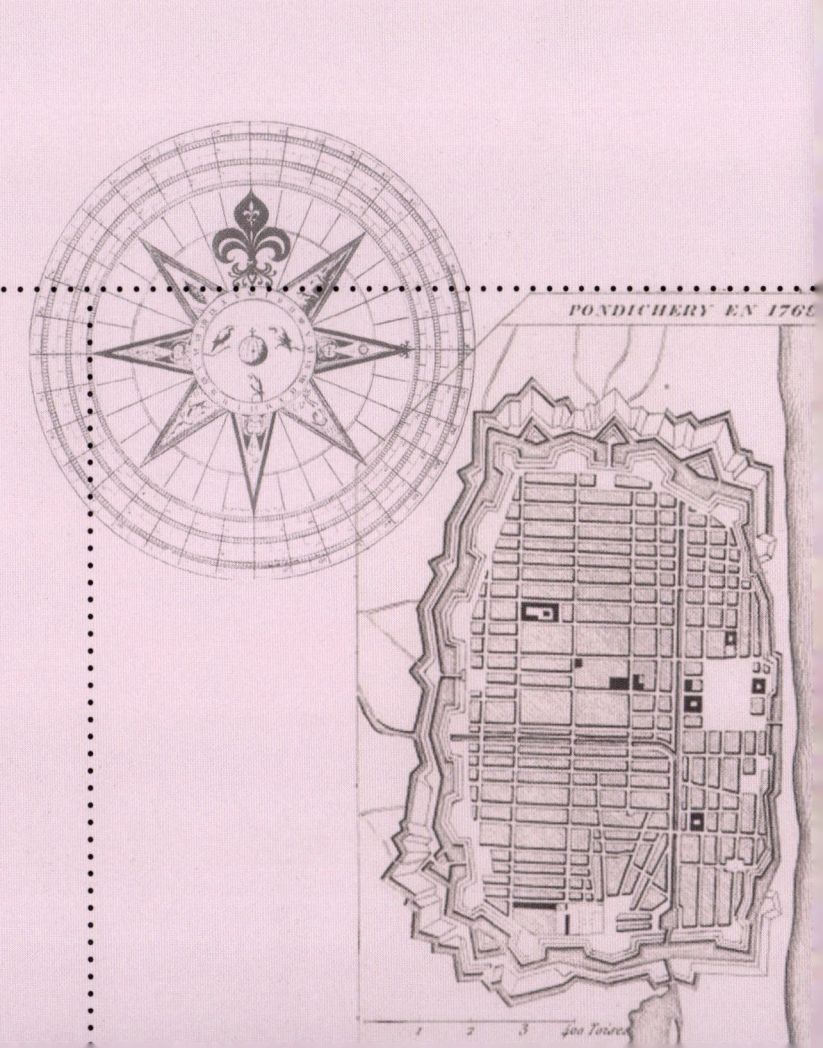

TRADITIONAL FLOOR: CEMENT WITH RED OXIDE FOR COLOUR. IT IS RUBBED WITH SCRAPED COCONUT TO POLISH IT

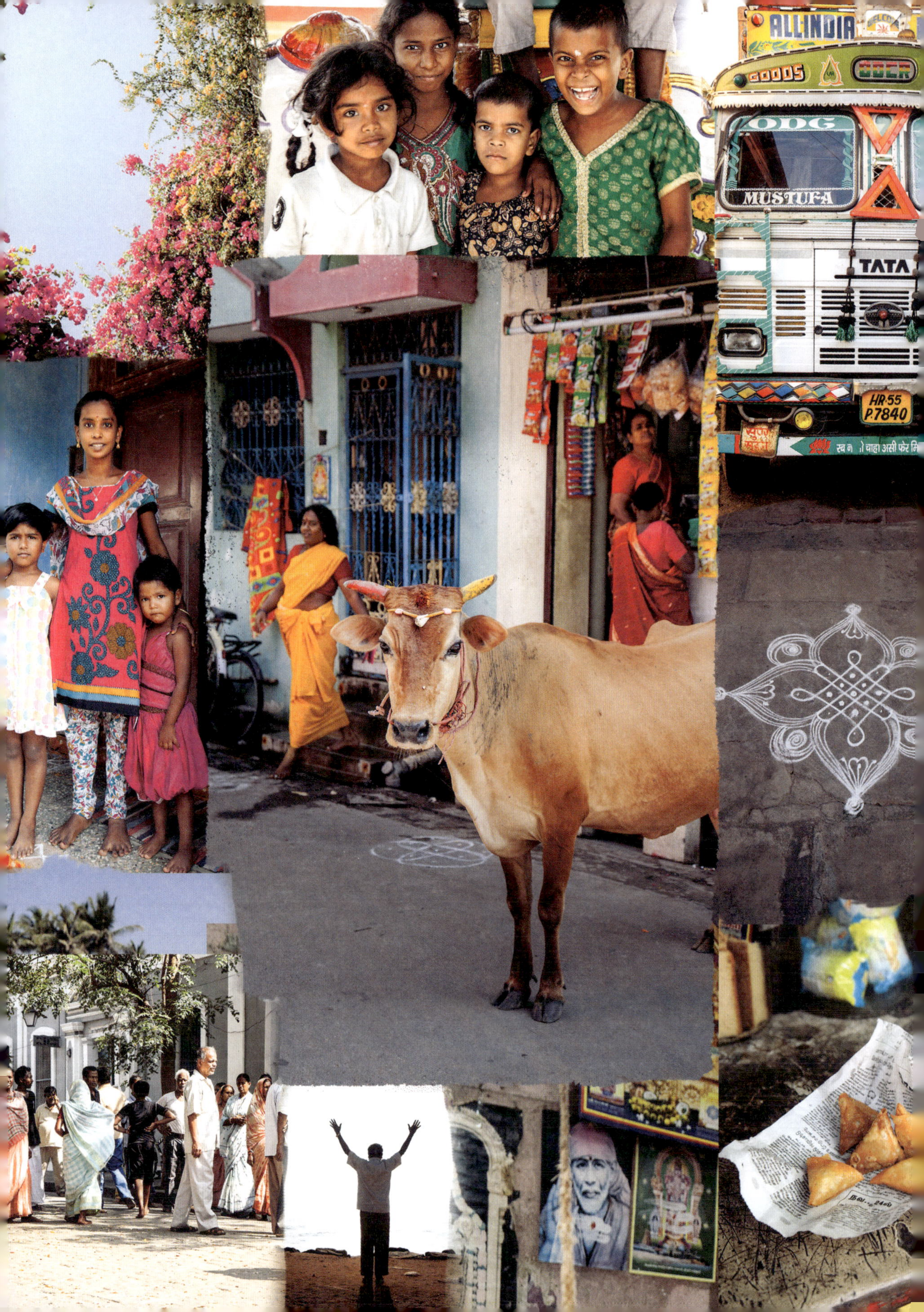
ALL INDIA
GOODS
MUSTUFA
TATA
HR 55
P.7840

PONDICHERRY

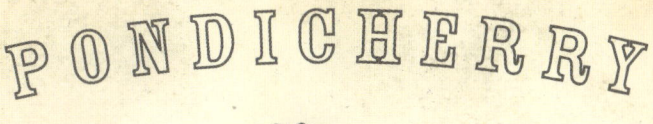

I WAS TOLD YOU HAVE TO VISIT INDIA AT LEAST THREE TIMES – **TO LET IT ALL SEEP INTO YOUR SOUL AND BREW PROPERLY, BEFORE YOU CAN FULLY APPRECIATE IT.**

I had been once before, to the north, and was intrigued to travel south now, to explore the palm-lined boulevards and kitchens of the old French colonial settlement of Pondicherry.

French presence in India was established in 1673, when the newly-formed French East India Company took over the small, strategically placed fishing village of Puducherry (since 2006 the town's official name once again). It became the administrative and cultural centre, and main port, for all French territories on the east coast. At the height of the colonial era the exotic and expensive spices, cottons, silks and precious stones of Pondicherry brought wealth to the French traders.

When the area was turned into a port town by the first French governor, Pondicherry was designed on the French grid system, with a freshwater canal running through, that became the dividing line between the Tamil quarter (ville noire) and French quarter (ville blanche).

The French influence is noticeable here on the streets, in the way of life and culture, in the schools. The architecture. There is a dusty shine still, and the atmosphere of a time gone by. I can picture the French here. Under the shade of these beautiful trees drinking chai, showing the locals their favourite dishes. At first glance, it is hard to see any influence left by the French on the food of Pondicherry. After a while though, some distinctions are noticeable: a more subtle combination of spices and chilli, and the use of certain French cooking techniques that lean towards a more delicate plate – loosely labelled as Creole and based on the cooking of South India.

I am told that in the colonial days, the canal was stocked with crocodiles, as a safety measure to prevent anyone from the Tamil side crossing over to the French, with just one wooden drawbridge at the time linking the two. It is hardly surprising, then, that there was not much overt mingling between the casseroles and kadais. However, many Tamil servants were employed in the French quarter, and they would have learned to deliver a lighter hand to satisfy the appetites of their employers. I can imagine the scene. The French pleading for a little respite, longing for a chicken roasted with thyme and white wine. And the local cooks, basting with extra masala and sliding a few chillies and mustard seeds in where they felt necessary. (I am sure they couldn't help it.) Because I watched them in the kitchen, and I thought how these people must truly be the kings at this. No one can throw that amount of spice and chilli into a pot so naturally.

Many Tamil people who I asked whether they liked French food or not, told me they didn't mind it – but no more than once a week! They need their heat and spices. French food would probably have been bowled out in the first round by the cinnamons and cardamoms. A combination of cuisines might have been frustrating for the locals, like a lukewarm lassi. When the French came to dinner, the dishes were spiced down. Less hot, more aromatic. In the typical Pondicherry fish curry with tamarind for example, I am told that the coconut milk was added for the French as it was just too spicy.

In many of the restaurants here, I found a dividing line on the menu, just like the canal. On one side were the southern Indian dishes, abundant in seafood and rich in spices. And on the other side were soupe a l'oignon and tarte au citron. As different as the French quarter is from the Tamil quarter.

Over time, as more mixed marriages came about, the food in the homes would have started blending into each other more. At dinner one night I watched a family at the table next to me. French father, Tamil mother. Beautiful children – speaking French with papa and wiping the plates with their dosas, and scooping up the sambar and coconut chutney. What a lovely place to live – surrounded by their mother and father tongues and meals.

They say this is a milder corner of India. The French quarter – maybe. But the rest is a full, rounded version, heaving with life. Nowhere to stop and take a breath, no break from the sights and sounds and smells. It is hyperbole and surprise all the way. Everyone holding hands, pressing through tailors, animals and flowers to get on with routine things. Drivers announcing their arrival on every corner with the horn.

Two women in saris on a building site, carrying bricks in baskets on their heads to the builders perched on fragile-looking bamboo scaffolding. Such a different set of rules.

The Indian women are incredible. It is as though a certain amount was allotted to the nation for decoration, and they collected all of the dockets and put them for the ladies. They are majestic, glittery and beautiful, with natural strong features and coconut-enriched hair. And wrapped in cottons and silks of every colour.

When you think of India, you imagine elephants, jewels and spices. In Pondicherry, you will find them all. But the elephant, Lakshmi, will be outside the temple, on the corner of Rue de Lauriston. And you can be blessed by the elephant giving you a good tap on your head.

The people of Pondicherry I found open, fun and easy to mingle with. While I have been here, I have been laughed at every day for something different. By children for not eating with my hands. For carrying an empty wooden mango box through the street. For crossing the road in a haphazard way. But – I have been blessed by an elephant and taught to cook by a local, Ashok. And I decided I just have to keep up with it all to understand the laddoos from the jangiris. To try to work out if a dish needed more turmeric or tamarind. And to take part in this continuous parade. To collect information at the washbasins in restaurants and the small happenings that the place and the people deliver to you with a thud and no warning. To join in the good humour of the people and be a part of this human collectivity.

ESSENTIAL FLAVOURINGS

The following recipes are traditional starting points in the cuisine of Pondicherry. Like all Indian cooking, the many spices and ingredients used add characteristic depth of flavour.

KUZHAMBU THOOL

A mixture of spices like this is regularly used in Pondicherry cooking, and here is my friend Ashok's recipe – a nice, hot version that adds a lovely layer to a dish. It is called a thool in powdered form, but can be called a masala also. You will need a spice or coffee grinder to grind it finely. Traditionally, these spices are put in the strong sun to roast before grinding.

Makes about ¾ cup

3 tablespoons coriander seeds
1 tablespoon cumin seeds
1 tablespoon black peppercorns
2½ teaspoons fenugreek seeds
2½ teaspoons toor dal
2½ teaspoons peeled urad dal
10g (¼oz) large dried red chillies, broken up, seeds included
2½ teaspoons ground turmeric

Put everything except the chillies and turmeric into a frying pan and dry-roast over a low heat for a few minutes until aromatic, adding the chillies for the last 10 seconds or so as they have a tendency to burn. Stir the turmeric through.

Grind to a powder in a spice grinder, in batches if necessary. Store in an airtight container, away from heat or light.

MASALA MIX

Here is a basic masala, which you can make up very easily if you have a spice or coffee grinder. It is good to grind fresh, little and often, so it keeps its aroma.

Makes about ½ cup

2 teaspoons cardamom seeds (removed from pods)
3 tablespoons coriander seeds
2 tablespoons cumin seeds
1 teaspoon fennel seeds
10cm (4in) piece of cinnamon stick, broken up
2 teaspoons black peppercorns
5 cloves
a few allspice berries
1½ teaspoons ground nutmeg
2 small dried bay leaves

Put everything except the nutmeg and bay leaves into a dry frying pan and dry-roast for a few minutes, stirring, until aromatic. Grind to a powder in a spice grinder, in batches if necessary. Stir through the nutmeg, transfer to an airtight container or jar and tuck in the bay leaves. Store away from heat or light.

VADAVAM

A spicy paste mashed into balls with shallots and garlic and dried out so that it keeps for ages, this is a traditional flavouring in Pondicherry, crumbled into dishes for deep flavour. In strong sun, they can be put on a tray for 3–4 days until dried and dark in colour.

Makes 6–8 balls

25g urad dal (with black skins)
2 tablespoons cumin seeds
1 tablespoon black mustard seeds
2 tablespoons fennel seeds
250g (9oz) shallots, peeled and roughly chopped
125g (4½oz) garlic cloves, peeled
¼ teaspoon asafoetida
¼ teaspoon ground turmeric
3 tablespoons sesame oil

Grind the urad dal, cumin, mustard and fennel seeds finely using a spice grinder. Tip into a bowl.

Process the shallots and garlic in a blender or food processor until finely chopped but with some slightly chunkier bits. Add to the bowl along with the asafoetida, turmeric and oil. Mix together then spread on a baking sheet and leave in a very low oven for several hours (up to 10 hours) until dry.

Squeeze out any liquid then roll into balls by taking small handfuls and squeezing very hard. Leave them on a tray, covered with a piece of muslin, to dry. When completely dry, store in an airtight container, where they will keep for months.

GARLIC AND GINGER PASTE

An extremely handy thing to keep in the fridge, ready for spooning into your pans; I can guarantee you will be glad at having made the effort, especially if you are making many Indian meals over a few days.

Makes about 185ml (¾ cup)

150g (5½oz) garlic cloves (from about 3 heads of garlic), peeled
75g (2½oz) peeled ginger, coarsely chopped
½ teaspoon salt
sesame oil

Crush the garlic and ginger together with the salt, using a pestle and mortar, in batches if necessary. (Alternatively, pulse in a blender or small processor until smooth.)

Spoon into a jar and cover with a thin layer of sesame oil (which will help it keep longer). Put the lid on and store in the fridge for 2–3 weeks.

LEMON PICKLE

Lemon or lime pickle is readily available in shops, but try making this version. I love the strong and sour element that it adds to food. The amount of chilli powder you use here will depend on the type and also on your personal threshold, so judge the amount accordingly. You will need to prepare the lemons 2–3 weeks ahead of making the pickle.

Makes about 2 x 250g (9oz) jars

500g (18oz) small lemons
150g (¾ cup) coarse salt
250ml (1 cup) white wine vinegar

For the paste
1 teaspoon black mustard seeds
1 teaspoon fenugreek seeds
½ teaspoon fennel seeds
1 garlic clove, sliced

For the pickle
4 tablespoons sesame oil
½ teaspoon mustard seeds
1 tablespoon garlic and ginger paste (page 149)
1½ teaspoons ground turmeric
1 teaspoon chilli powder (or more if you like)
2 teaspoons paprika
4 tablespoons white wine vinegar
½ teaspoon salt
2 teaspoons sugar
a pinch of asafoetida

Scrub the lemons well and wash in warm water. Quarter them, leaving them still attached at the base. Settle them into a sterilized jar that is just big enough to take them comfortably. In a saucepan, bring 375ml (1½ cups) water and the salt to the boil. Let it cool for a few minutes before adding the vinegar then pouring over the lemons. If necessary, put a weight on the lemons so they are fully submerged. Leave in a cool, dark place for 2–3 weeks, until the skin has softened and lost much of its bitterness.

Remove the lemons from the jar and put into a colander to drain. Cut through the bases to separate the lemons into quarters, then cut each quarter into 3 or 4 chunks of 2–3cm (¾–1¼in), removing and discarding the pips as you go.

To make the paste, dry-roast all the ingredients in a small dry frying pan, taking care not to burn them. Grind to a paste.

To make the pickle, heat the oil in a heavy-based pan over a low heat. Add the mustard seeds, the garlic and ginger paste and the spice paste and sauté for a minute. Add the turmeric, chilli powder and paprika and sauté for half a minute. Add the lemon pieces, vinegar, salt, sugar, asafoetida and 1 tablespoon water, and stir through. Simmer over a very low heat for about 10 minutes, using a simmer mat if you have one.

Remove from the heat, spoon into sterilized jars and seal immediately. Once cooled, it can be eaten straight away, or will improve if left to mingle for 2–3 weeks. Store in a cool dark place and, once opened, keep in the fridge.

RAITA

Refreshing and delicious, you can serve raita with just about anything, even with just a chapati. If you want it spicier, add a pinch or two of chilli powder. This can be eaten almost immediately, or left to mingle for a couple of hours.

Serves 4–6

250g (1 cup) yogurt or curd
2 teaspoons ground cumin
1 small green chilli, finely chopped
1 small tomato (about 100g/3½oz), peeled, deseeded and diced
80g (3oz) cucumber, peeled, deseeded and diced
2 tablespoons finely diced red onion
a few torn coriander (cilantro) leaves
salt

Mix everything together in a bowl, adding salt to taste. Leave for 15 minutes or so for the flavours to mingle before serving. The texture will loosen a bit due to the water in the vegetables.

MINT RELISH

This makes a lovely, liquid sauce. Serve with papadums, over rice or just about anything (you can even drink it!). Using ice helps to maintain the green colour and to keep it cool.

Makes about 250ml (1 cup)

1 handful (½ cup tightly packed) mint leaves
1 or 2 small green chillies, deseeded
2cm (¾in) piece of peeled ginger
2 tablespoons lemon juice
¼ cup crushed ice
about ½ teaspoon salt
125g (½ cup) yogurt or curd

Put the mint, chillies, ginger, lemon juice, ice and salt into a blender and purée until smooth. Add the yogurt and pulse to combine. Scrape into a bowl, give it a stir and serve while still cool.

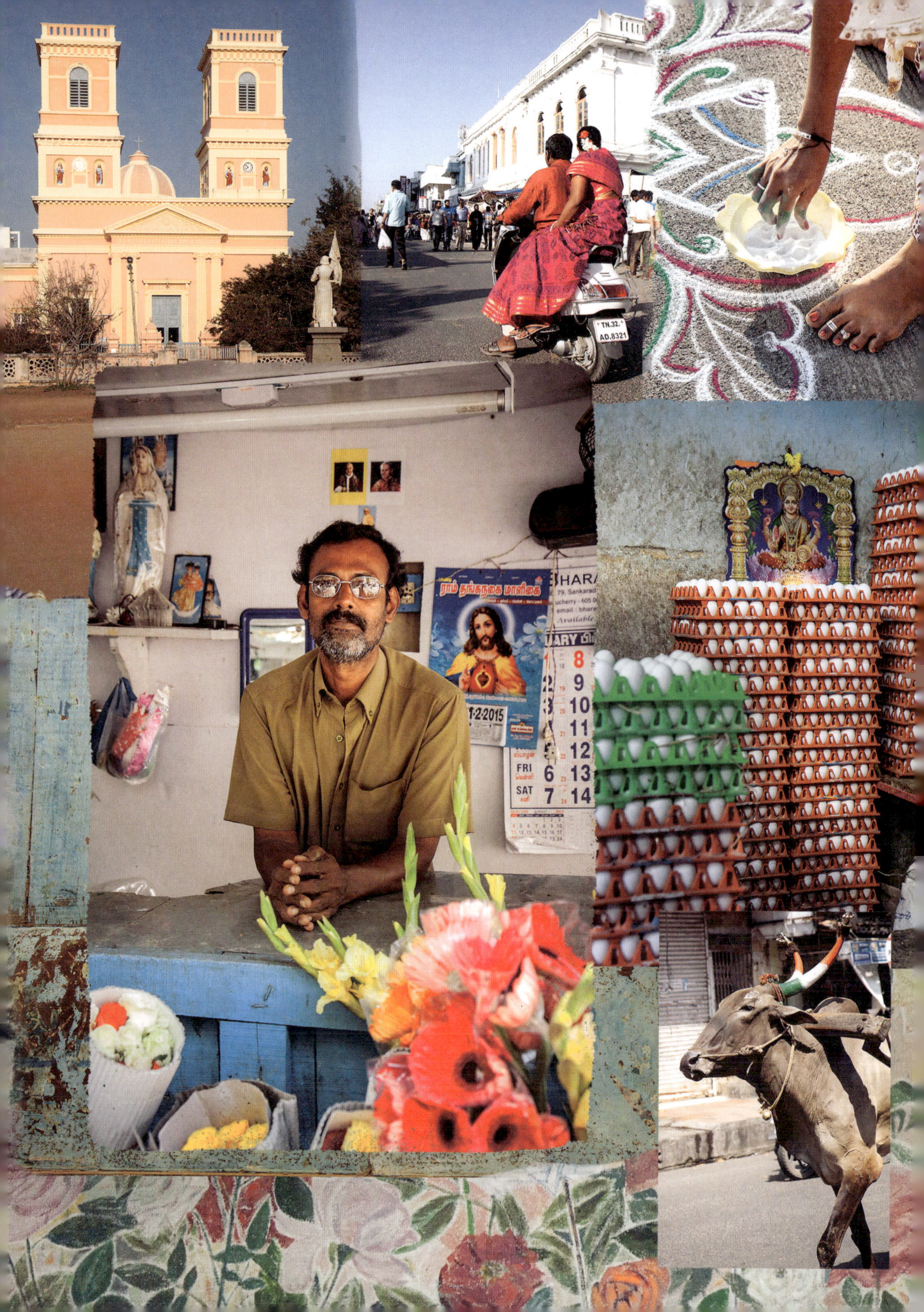
TN.32.
AD.8321
1-2-2015
FRI
SAT

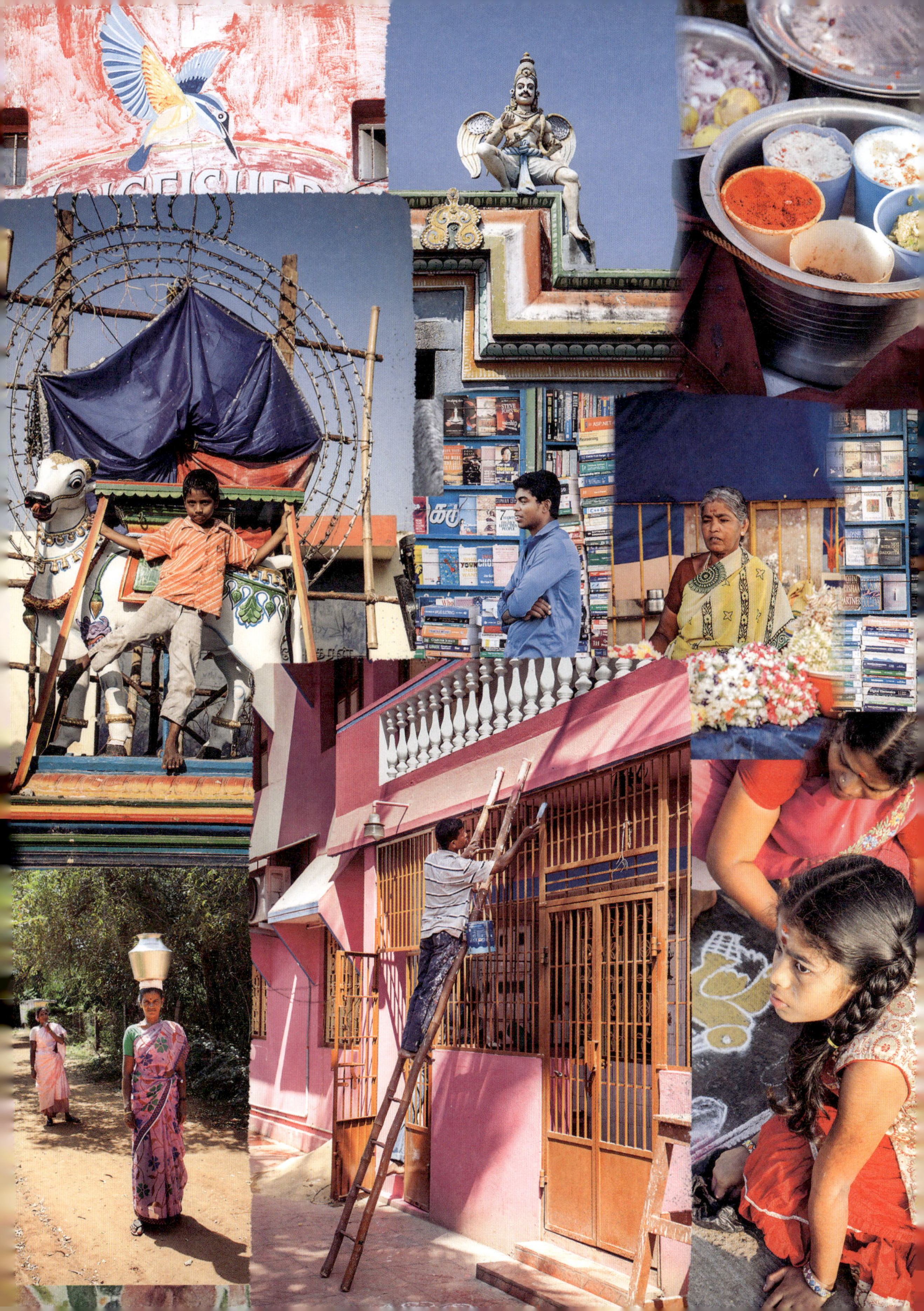

SPICED BUTTERMILK

I love the milk parlour kiosks selling buttermilk, lassi, curd, paneer, milk, ghee and more. You can even drink this, or drizzle over rice, for example. It's refreshing with a curry, or served with papadums and a few other chutneys and pickles. On a thali platter this could be served in place of a small dish of plain curd.

Makes 250ml (1 cup)

2 teaspoons ghee
¼ teaspoon black mustard seeds
¼ teaspoon cumin seeds
5 or 6 fresh curry leaves, torn
scant ¼ teaspoon ground fenugreek
¼ teaspoon pounded peeled ginger
1 small green chilli, finely chopped
250ml (1 cup) buttermilk
about ¼ teaspoon salt
1 tablespoon chopped coriander (cilantro)

Melt the ghee in a small saucepan over a medium heat. Add the mustard and cumin seeds and the curry leaves and sauté for a minute or so. Stir in the fenugreek, ginger and chilli and sauté together briefly. Remove from the heat.

Pour the buttermilk into a small bowl. Add the salt and stir in the coriander with the hot spices and ghee. Taste and adjust the seasoning. It is liquid so will need its own little bowl or cup for each serving.

CORIANDER CHUTNEY

This is lovely to serve with almost anything, even a spoonful with any curry is wonderfully uplifting. Some versions have mint and coriander, but I love it with just coriander.

Makes about 1 cup

4–5 large handfuls (4 cups tightly packed) coriander (cilantro) leaves
2 small green chillies, deseeded and finely chopped
2 teaspoons sesame seeds
2 teaspoons garlic and ginger paste (page 149)
3 tablespoons coarsely ground raw peanuts
3 tablespoons finely grated fresh coconut
4 tablespoons lemon juice
4 tablespoons vegetable oil
½ teaspoon salt

Put the coriander leaves, chillies, sesame seeds and garlic and ginger paste into a blender and process to a coarse paste, stopping to scrape down the sides and mix through so that the leaves all shred.

Add the ground peanuts and coconut and pulse a little to incorporate. Add the lemon juice, oil and salt and pulse quickly to mix through.

It will keep for a couple of days in the fridge in a covered container, and can also be frozen, in smaller portions.

TOMATO CHUTNEY

This is delicious served with egg dosa, or potato dosa, together with other chutneys. You can decide the amount of heat, by shaking out the chilli seeds or leaving them in.

Makes about 1 cup

4 tablespoons sesame oil
1 large red onion, chopped
1 tablespoon garlic and ginger paste (page 149)
1 large dried red chilli, torn in half
750g (26oz) ripe tomatoes, peeled and chopped
1 scant teaspoon salt
2 tablespoons sugar

For the tempering
1 tablespoon sesame oil
½ teaspoon black mustard seeds
½ teaspoon cumin seeds
5 or 6 fresh curry leaves
1 tablespoon torn coriander (cilantro) leaves

Heat the oil in a heavy-based pan. Add the onion and fry gently until it starts to get golden. Add the garlic and ginger paste, then the chilli, and sauté for a minute. Stir in the tomatoes and salt.

Cover and simmer for about 10 minutes to break the tomatoes down. Stir in the sugar and simmer, uncovered, for another 10 minutes or so, until most of the liquid has been absorbed, and it looks a bit jammy. Stir often, and crush any lumps with a potato masher.

For the tempering, heat the oil in a small pan and fry the mustard and cumin seeds with the curry leaves until they sizzle. Pour into the tomato mixture, add the coriander and stir through to mix the flavours. Store any leftover in the fridge in a jar.

COCONUT CHUTNEY

Best eaten freshly made, this will also keep for a couple of days in the fridge.

Makes about 1 cup

3 tablespoons coriander (cilantro) leaves
1 or 2 small green chillies, roughly sliced
¼ teaspoon salt
about 80g (3oz) finely grated fresh coconut
4 tablespoons yogurt or curd
1 tablespoon sesame oil
¼ teaspoon black mustard seeds
½ dried red chilli
2 or 3 fresh curry leaves
¼ teaspoon ground cumin
1 teaspoon garlic and ginger paste (page 149)
a pinch of asafoetida

Put the coriander, green chillies and 60ml (¼ cup) water into a blender and purée until smooth. Add the salt, scrape into a bowl, add the coconut and the yogurt and stir well to combine.

Heat the oil in a small saucepan and sauté the mustard seeds, dried chilli, curry leaves, cumin and garlic and ginger paste together until sizzling. Add the asafoetida and pour over the coconut, stirring in to combine. Taste for seasoning.

MUSSELS WITH MASALA

I like to make this with just a drop of cream to add a subtle richness to the spices. I love it with lemon pickle and chapati on the side. And to follow, a small bowl of fresh curd with a sprinkling of salt, just to calm the mouth a little.

Serves 3

1.5kg (3¼lb) mussels
2 tablespoons sesame oil
¼ teaspoon black mustard seeds
¼ teaspoon cumin seeds
2 teaspoons garlic and ginger paste (page 149)
2 small green chillies, finely chopped
5 or 6 fresh curry leaves
2 teaspoons masala mix (page 148)
200g (7oz) ripe tomatoes, peeled and chopped
1 tablespoon cream
2 tablespoons shredded coriander (cilantro) leaves

To serve
lemon pickle, homemade (page 150) or bought

De-beard the mussels, then scrub them with a brush under cold running water, discarding any that are open and don't close when tapped sharply on the work surface. Keep them in a bowl of cold water until you are ready to cook, but don't leave it too long.

Heat the oil in a wide pan large enough to hold all the mussels. Add the mustard and cumin seeds and, when they start to splutter, stir in the garlic and ginger paste and the green chillies. Tear in the curry leaves and sauté for a couple of minutes until it smells good, taking care that nothing burns.

Add the masala, stir through and then add the tomatoes with 125ml (½ cup) water. Bring to the boil then simmer over a low heat, covered, for about 5 minutes to break the tomatoes down. Stir in the cream (no seasoning needed) and let it bubble up for a moment before removing from the heat. Keep warm.

Drain the mussels and tip them into a large frying pan over a high heat. Put the lid on and steam until they open. Use a slotted spoon to transfer the opened ones to the sauce. Give any unopened ones a second chance over the heat, but if they still don't open, discard them.

Strain the mussel liquor in the frying pan into a jug, avoiding any sand or grit on the bottom. Add 185ml (¾ cup) to the mussels and sauce, increase the heat to high and turn the mussels through quickly so they all catch some of the sauce.

Scatter in the coriander and serve immediately, with lemon pickle.

PONDICHERRY

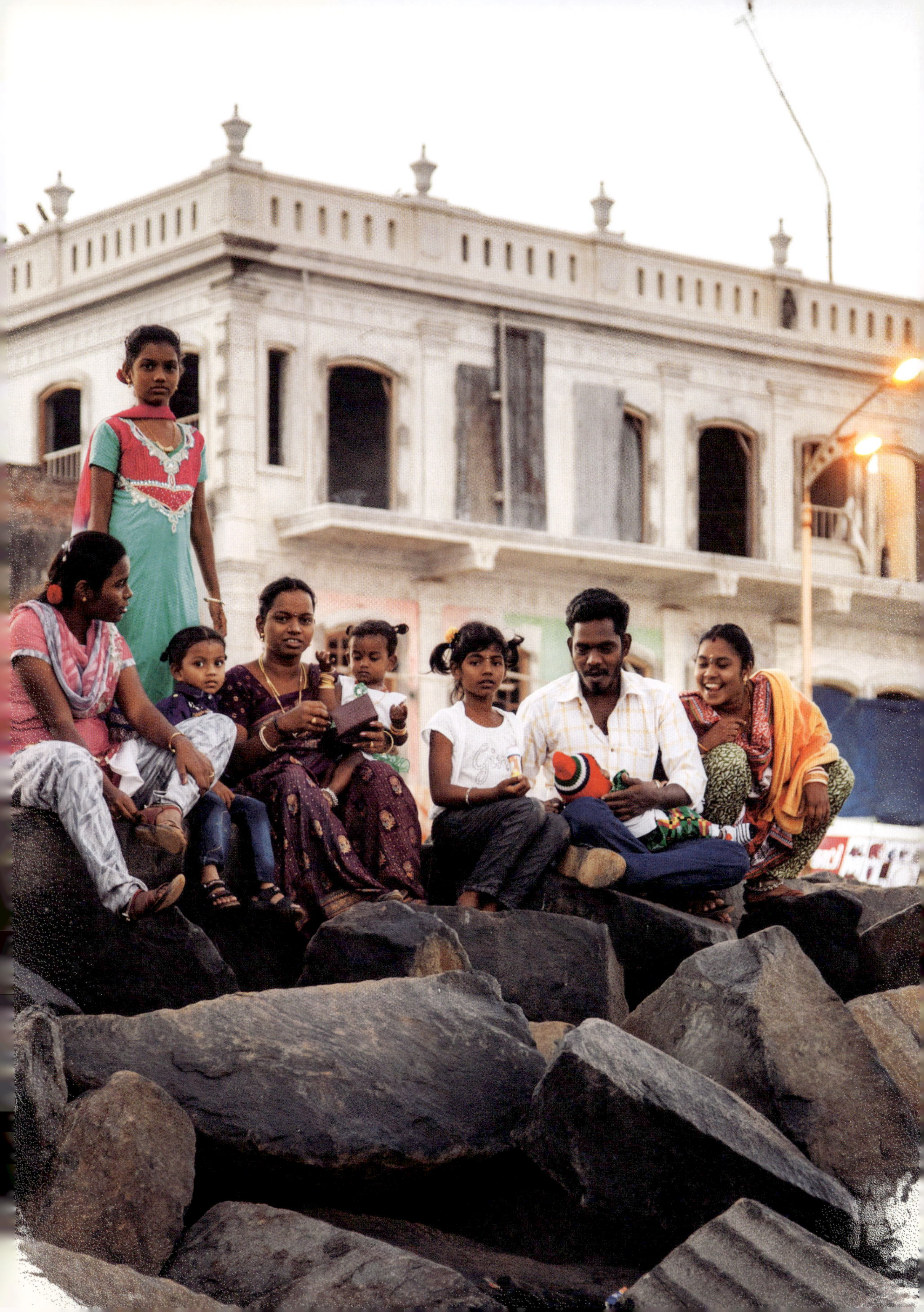

GHEE

Ghee is butter with the butterfats removed that can be heated to higher temperatures without burning. You can make as much of this as you like.

Makes about 185ml (¾ cup)

250g (9oz) butter, cut into pieces

Put the butter into a heavy-based saucepan and melt over a medium-low heat. When it starts to boil, leave it to simmer gently for about 10 minutes, depending on your butter and heat. Keep an eye on the fats accumulating on the bottom, as they will burn if the temperature is too high. Throughout cooking it will bubble and pop, then when it is ready it will go smooth and quiet, with scum having risen to the top.

Either scoop off the scum, or move it to one side before pouring the clear liquid ghee into a metal or warmed glass container. Allow to cool, then cover and keep in the fridge, for up to 3 months.

PANEER

Makes 120g (4½oz)

650ml (2¾ cups) full-fat (whole) milk
6 tablespoons lemon juice

Put the milk in a large saucepan and heat to just below boiling. Remove from the heat and stir in the lemon juice. Leave, covered, for 15 minutes, then strain through a muslin-lined strainer, pressing and squeezing the liquid through the muslin with the back of a wooden spoon.

This will give you paneer similar to cottage cheese. If you want it firm to cut into cubes, fold the muslin over to cover it and put a weight on top, still in the colander.

After 2–3 hours it will be solid enough to be sliced or broken up. Store in the fridge and use within 2 or 3 days.

CURD

To make a simple curd, slowly bring 1 litre (4 cups) full-fat (whole) milk to a gentle boil in a large saucepan. Let simmer over a very low heat for 10 minutes, ideally using a simmer mat. Remove from the heat and allow to cool to just warm, then stir in 2 teaspoons yogurt and ½ dried red chilli, deseeded and in one piece. (The chilli helps the curd to set without making it spicy.)

Cover with a cloth, then wrap in a thick towel or small blanket and leave in a warm, draught-free spot to let it thicken. It should be ready after 24 hours but can stay bundled like this for up to 4 days. Store the set curd in the fridge.

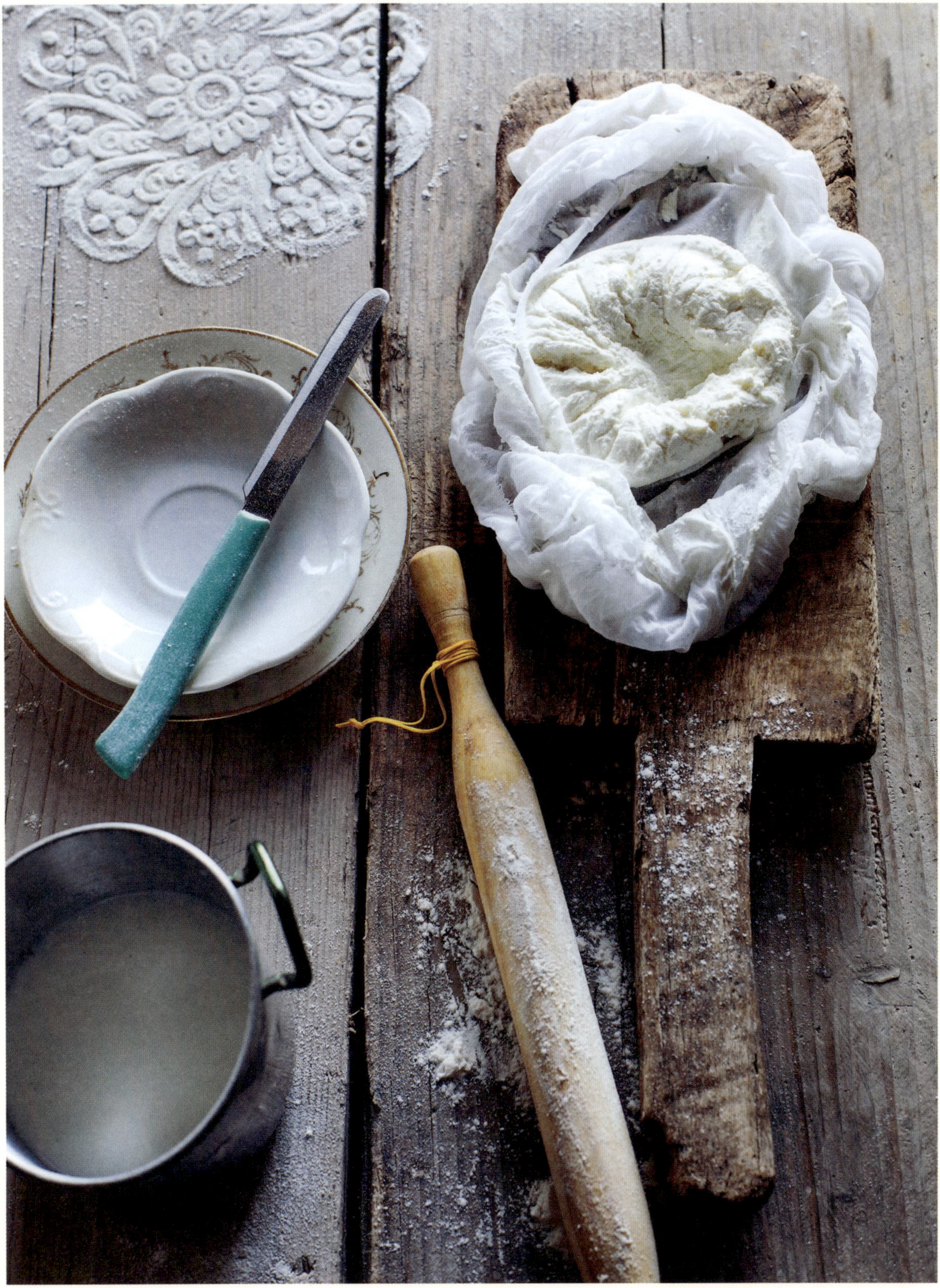

MANGO PATCHADI

This is often served for lunch with rice. I also love it with grilled fish. It doesn't keep well so you may as well finish it in one go.

Makes about 1½ cups

1 good, ripe mango, peeled and cut into small cubes
1 heaped tablespoon coarsely grated fresh coconut
1 small green chilli, finely chopped
1 tablespoon chopped fresh coriander (cilantro)
1 tablespoon lemon juice
salt

Mix the mango, coconut, chilli, coriander and lemon juice in a bowl. Scatter in a little salt and taste for chilli and lemon juice, adding more if necessary before serving.

WHITE RICE

This is a simple method for cooking rice whether to use in another dish or to serve plain. Check the cooking times on the package as they may vary.

Serves 4

250g (1¼ cups) basmati rice
½ teaspoon black mustard seeds
5 or 6 curry leaves
salt

Soak the rice in cold water for about 20 minutes then rinse well under cold water, in a colander.

Meanwhile, bring a large pan of water to the boil. Add the rice, mustard seeds, curry leaves and a little salt. When it comes back to the boil, lower the heat and simmer until the rice is tender, about 10 minutes. Take care not to overcook it.

Drain into a colander, shaking away all the water. (If you fear the rice is overcooked give it a quick rinse in the colander with cool water.)

If you will be serving it plain, return the drained rice to the saucepan with a few flicks of water. Cover with a cloth and leave to steam over the lowest possible heat (ideally on a simmer mat) for a few minutes. Fluff up to serve.

PONDICHERRY

LEMON RICE

This can be served on its own, or with a curry. It was one of my favourites of the various rice dishes I ate in Pondicherry.

Serves 4

2 tablespoons sesame oil
½ teaspoon black mustard seeds
½ teaspoon cumin seeds
½ teaspoon ground turmeric
½ large dried red chilli
8 fresh curry leaves
1 small green chilli, chopped
4 tablespoons lemon juice
a pinch of chilli powder
1 quantity cooked white rice (page 160)
a few coriander (cilantro) leaves
salt

Heat the oil in a frying pan over a medium heat. Add the mustard seeds, then the cumin seeds, then stir in the turmeric. Break in the dried chilli and sauté briefly.

Next, tear in the curry leaves and add the green chilli. Sauté for a moment, then add the lemon juice and a little chilli powder if you like things hot. Add a good couple of pinches of salt. Let it simmer for a couple of minutes then remove from the heat.

Add about half the rice and tear in the coriander. Stir through to distribute the flavours then tip in the remaining rice. Mix well to incorporate, taste for salt and serve.

CORIANDER RICE

Serve with a curry, or just with a small bowl of plain curd sprinkled with salt for lunch.

Serves 5

300g (1½ cups) basmati rice
3 tablespoons ghee
2 dried bay leaves
a piece of cinnamon stick
2 cardamom pods, cracked
1 teaspoon cumin seeds
1 medium red onion, chopped
2 teaspoons garlic and ginger paste (page 149)
1 or 2 small green chillies, finely chopped
3 large handfuls (2 cups) shredded coriander (cilantro) leaves
about 1 teaspoon salt
ground cumin, lightly toasted in a pan, to serve

Soak the rice in cold water for 20–30 minutes, then rinse under cold running water.

Heat the ghee in a large pan with the bay leaves, cinnamon, cardamom and cumin. Stir in the onion and cook gently until golden and sticky. Add the garlic and ginger paste and green chillies and sauté until it smells good. Stir through the coriander.

Add 750ml (3 cups) water and the salt. Bring to a fast boil, stir the rice in, then simmer, uncovered, until holes appear on the surface. Cover with a tight-fitting lid and simmer over a very low heat for about 5 minutes or until tender.

Take off the heat, remove the lid and fluff up the rice with a fork. Put a clean cloth over the pan and let stand for about 5 minutes. Fluff up again to serve and scatter with toasted cumin.

CURD RICE WITH LEMON PICKLE

Pomegranates and spicy lemon pickle served on the side is a wonderful, refreshing combination. As well as being served on its own, this is sometimes served after a curry. Best eaten freshly made as it doesn't keep very well.

Serves 5

2 teaspoons pounded peeled ginger
1 quantity cooked white rice (page 160), at room temperature
4 tablespoons chopped red onion
1 small green chilli, chopped
500g (2 cups) curd or yogurt
2 tablespoons sesame oil
1 teaspoon cumin seeds
¼ teaspoon black mustard seeds
½ large dried red chilli
5 or 6 fresh curry leaves
a pinch of asafoetida
3 tablespoons shredded coriander (cilantro) leaves, plus a few leaves to serve
salt

To serve
pomegranate seeds
lemon pickle, homemade (page 150) or bought

Put the ginger into a wide bowl. Cover with the rice and tip in the onion and green chilli. Mash with a potato masher a few times, to soften, but not mashing completely. Mix in the curd and season well with salt.

Heat the oil in a small frying pan. Add the cumin and mustard seeds and the dried chilli, and tear in the curry leaves. When it is sizzling, stir in the asafoetida. Add to the rice along with the coriander leaves, mixing together well. Taste and adjust any seasonings.

Serve the rice scattered with pomegranate seeds and coriander leaves, with a bowl of lemon pickle on the side.

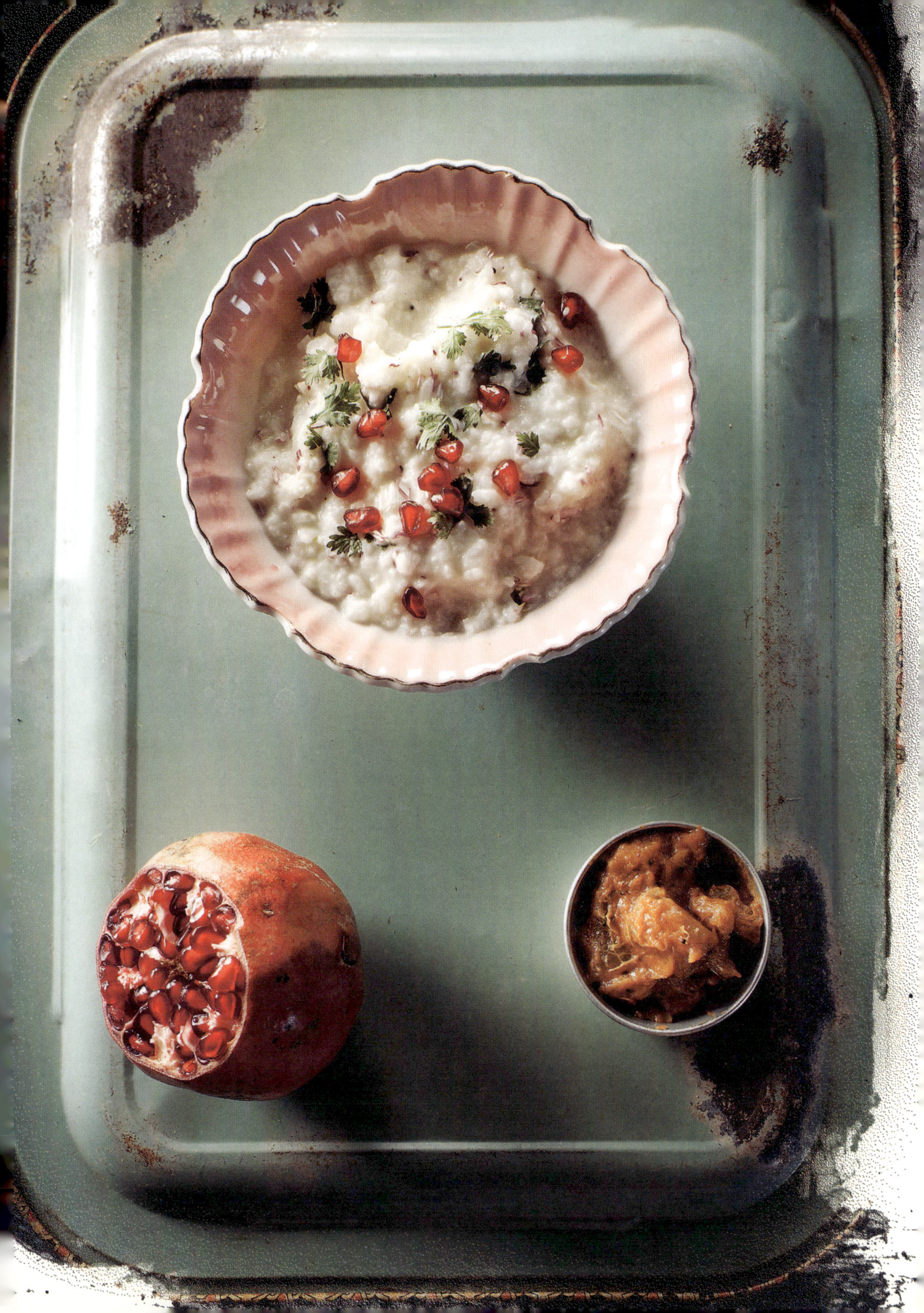

CHAPATI

These are so easy to make and can be turned out in a few minutes. I love them brushed with ghee and served with almost anything. The lovely coffee coloured dough will keep for a day or so in the fridge, covered (so you can make a few over a couple of days). I use a dosa or a crêpe pan, but any heavy-based flattish frying pan will do.

Makes 10

250g (heaped 2 cups) fine wholegrain flour, plus extra for dusting
½ teaspoon salt
2 tablespoons milk
2 teaspoons vegetable oil
about 150ml (⅔ cup) tepid water
a few tablespoons melted ghee

Mix the flour, salt, milk and oil together in a bowl, add the water and mix to a soft dough, adding a little more water or flour if necessary.

Transfer to a work surface and knead until smooth and spongy, about 5 minutes. Wrap in plastic wrap and leave to rest in the fridge for an hour or so (or up to 48 hours).

Divide the dough into 10 balls. Dust your work surface with a little flour. Roll out one ball to a round of about 15cm (6in). Heat a non-stick, heavy-based flat pan. Add a chapati round, flattening out any folds that might have formed. Using tongs, check the underside, and when deep golden spots appear, and the bread puffs a bit, flip over and cook the underside.

When the chapati is almost done, brush the top with ghee. Wrap in foil or a cloth to keep warm while you roll and cook the rest.

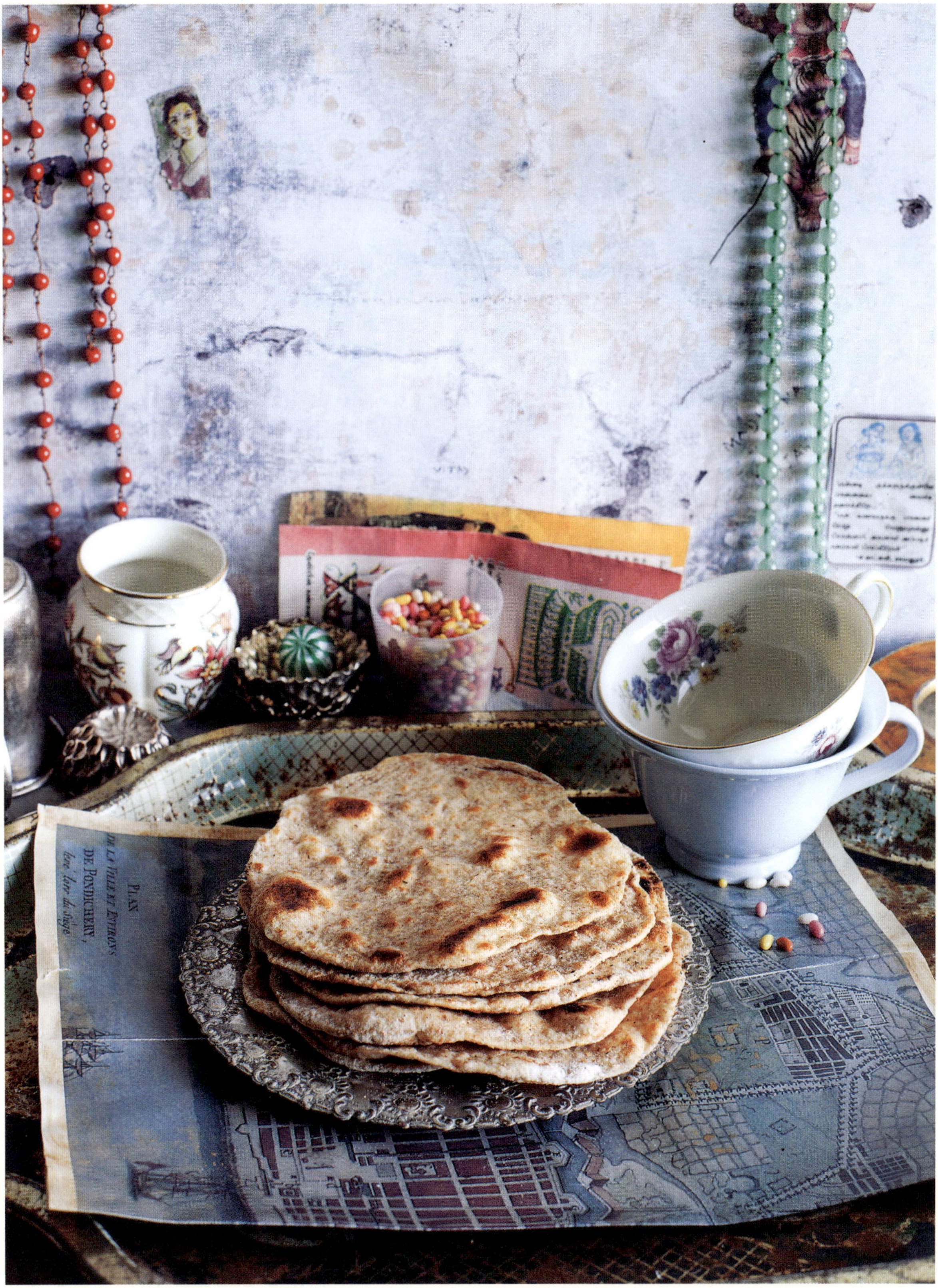
PLAN
DE LA VILLE ET ENVIRONS
DE PONDICHERY,

THALI

Very often in Southern India (where this is referred to as ilai sappadu), food is served on banana leaves. After being washed, they are laid onto a surface and a sprinkle of water is customary. On the top section the various dishes, pickles, chutneys, and sweet are arranged. Rice and papadums are generally served on the lower part of the leaf. If you go to a typical Indian eatery, rather than an elegant restaurant, generally they will not bring you cutlery. Follow your fellow diners and use your hands.

The thali collection

dal
spinach curry
sambar
vegetable curry with coconut milk
poriyal
brinjal curry
spiced buttermilk
rasam
coconut payasam

The recipes given on the following pages (for the spiced buttermilk see page 154) make up a vegetarian thali, but can of course also be served individually or with other dishes.

Traditionally, they are served with lemon pickle, coriander (cilantro) chutney, chapati and papadums. Dal is generally eaten first and the rasam last, often followed by a small sweet dish.

PONDICHERRY

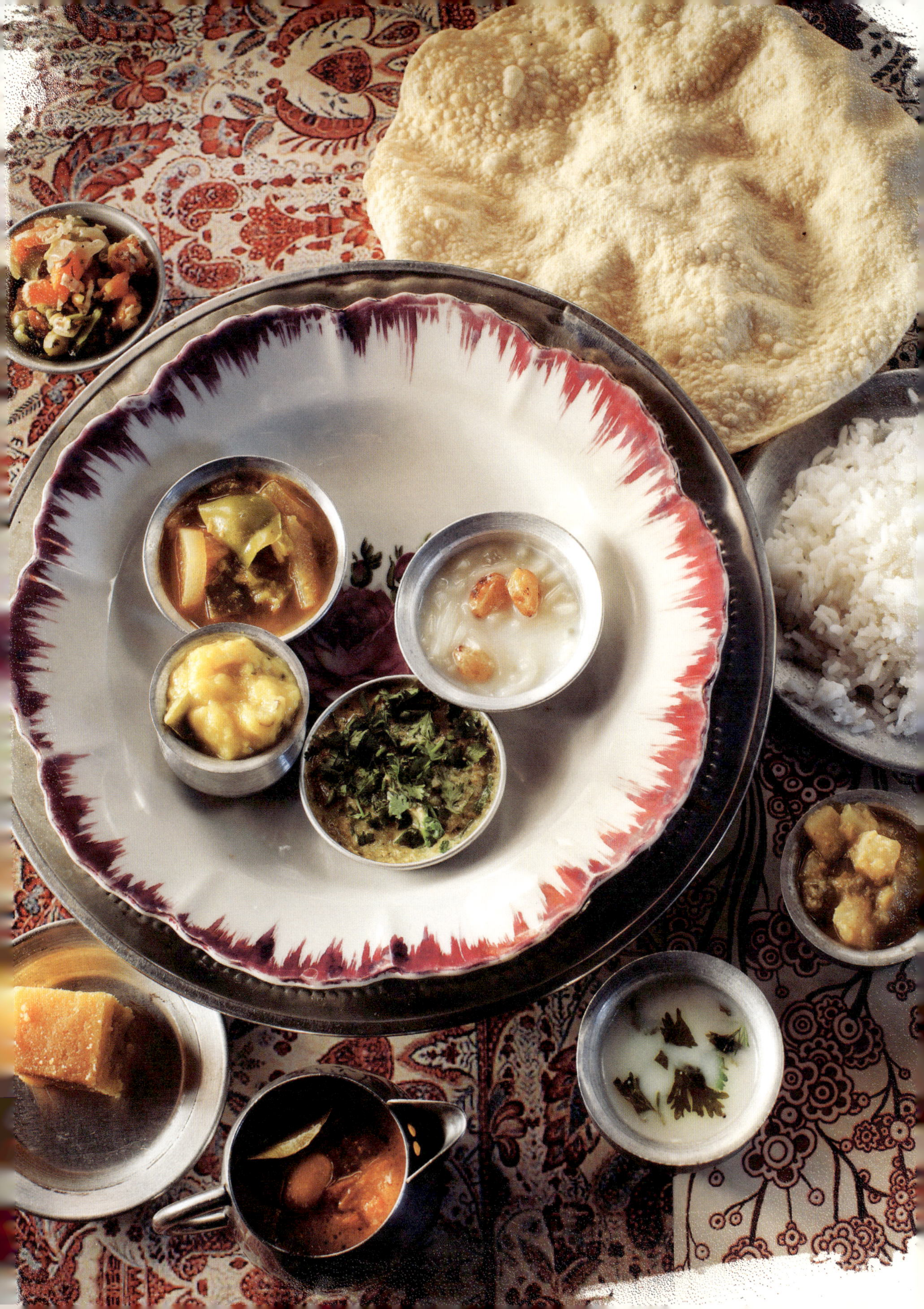

DAL

The southern Indian word for dal is paruppu. If you are not serving this immediately, you may need to add a little water when you reheat it.

Serves 4 as part of a meal, or 8–10 on a thali platter

250g (scant 1½ cups) toor dal
a pinch of chilli powder
1 teaspoon salt

For the tempering
2 tablespoons ghee
¼ teaspoon black mustard seeds
¼ teaspoon cumin seeds
½ large dried red chilli
4 or 5 curry leaves
½ red onion, chopped
1 small green chilli, finely chopped
1 teaspoon garlic and ginger paste (page 149)
¼ teaspoon ground turmeric
1 small ripe tomato, peeled and chopped
½ teaspoon masala mix (page 148)
a couple of pinches of asafoetida
1 tablespoon shredded coriander (cilantro) leaves
a few dried fenugreek leaves (methi), if available

Soak the toor dal in cold water for 30 minutes, then drain and rinse.

Put the dal into a pan with 1.25 litres (5 cups) cold water and bring to the boil. Skim the surface of any scum. Lower the heat and simmer, uncovered, until tender and most of the water has been absorbed, about 40 minutes, stirring often to prevent sticking, particularly towards the end. Halfway through, add the chilli powder, and the salt once the dal is softened. It will probably have collapsed on its own, if not, beat well with a wooden spoon to mash it up. Add a little more water if it seems too thick, or simmer for a little longer if too thin, stirring regularly.

For the tempering, heat the ghee in a small pan and add the mustard and cumin seeds and dried chilli. Tear in the curry leaves and sauté until they sizzle, then add the onion. Cook until golden and sticky, stirring. Add the green chilli, garlic and ginger paste and turmeric and sauté for a little longer until it smells good. Add the tomato and sauté until the tomato has broken down and is soft. Stir in the masala mix and asafoetida, then remove from the heat.

Stir into the dal and simmer for a few minutes to combine the flavours. Taste for seasoning and stir in the coriander leaves, and the fenugreek leaves.

Remove from the heat and leave to stand with the lid on for about 10 minutes before serving. Serve hot or at room temperature.

PONDICHERRY

SPINACH CURRY

This is a great addition to any meal. Fresh curry leaves can be kept in a plastic bag in the freezer where they won't dry out.

Serves 4 as part of a meal, or 6–8 on a thali platter

3 tablespoons sesame oil
½ teaspoon cumin seeds
1 red onion, chopped
2 teaspoons kuzhambu thool (page 148)
2 teaspoons garlic and ginger paste (page 149)
300g (10½oz) ripe tomatoes, peeled and chopped
1kg (2¼lb) spinach leaves, coarsely chopped
½ teaspoon tamarind paste
salt

For the tempering
1 tablespoon sesame oil
½ teaspoon cumin seeds
½ dried red chilli
4 fresh curry leaves

Heat the oil in a large, wide pan and sauté the cumin seeds over a medium heat until they sizzle. Add the onion and sauté until deep gold and sticky. Add the thool and the garlic and ginger paste and sauté until it smells good.

Add the tomatoes and cook for a few minutes to soften and break them down. Mash out any lumps with a potato masher.

Add the spinach, in two batches if necessary, with 250ml (1 cup) water and a small sprinkling of salt. Put the lid on and cook to wilt, turning it all through with tongs once or twice.

Stir in the tamarind and simmer over a high heat, uncovered, so that the liquid reduces and there is hardly any left, stirring a couple of times. Taste for salt and add a little more tamarind if you think it needs it.

Heat the oil for the tempering in a small pan. Add the cumin seeds, and tear in the chilli and the curry leaves. Fry until they start to splutter then pour the contents of the pan over the spinach. Stir through and serve hot.

SAMBAR

This is rather like a loose, spicy sauce and is served as part of a thali platter, or as an accompaniment to idli (page 178). A mix of a few different vegetables is good here. If you can find drumstick (the green, fresh pods of the moringa tree), this is a good recipe to use it in.

Serves 4 as part of a meal or 8–10 on a thali platter

2 tablespoons sesame oil
¼ teaspoon black mustard seeds
¼ teaspoon cumin seeds
1 small onion, sliced
1 teaspoon garlic and ginger paste (page 149)
1 tablespoon kuzhambu thool (page 148)
1 ripe tomato, peeled and chopped
2 small carrots, cut in small chunks
100g (3½oz) snake gourd or thin courgette (zucchini), cut in small chunks
1 drumstick, peeled, or ½ green (bell) pepper, cut into chunks
½ teaspoon sugar
½ teaspoon tamarind paste
250ml (1 cup) cooked toor dal (page 168)
salt

For the tempering
2 tablespoons ghee
½ tablespoon vadavam (page 149)
5 or 6 fresh curry leaves
about 2 tablespoons coriander (cilantro) leaves

Heat the oil in a non-stick pan and add the mustard and cumin seeds. Sauté until they start to splutter, then add the onion. Sauté gently until golden. Add the garlic and ginger paste along with the thool and sauté briefly.

Stir in the tomato, crushing it on the bottom of the pan with a wooden spoon. Add the carrots, snake gourd and drumstick, and continue to sauté until lightly golden.

Add 375ml (1½ cups) water, the sugar and tamarind paste, and season with salt. Bring to the boil then gently simmer, covered, for about 10 minutes, or until the vegetables are tender. Add the dal and simmer together for a few minutes more. Taste for seasoning.

Heat the ghee in a small pan. Crumble in the vadavam and tear in the curry leaves. Sizzle for a moment, stirring well. Remove from the heat and swirl into the sambar. Tear in the coriander and serve warm.

VEGETABLE CURRY WITH COCONUT MILK

As part of a thali platter, it is more convenient to cut the vegetables up into smaller bits to fit into little bowls, but if serving as a dish on its own then you can chunk the vegetables as large you like. You don't have to stick rigidly to this combination of vegetables.

Serves 4 as part of a meal, or 8–10 on a thali platter

3 tablespoons sesame oil
1 teaspoon black mustard seeds
1 teaspoon cumin seeds
½ large dried red chilli
1 medium red onion, chopped
2 teaspoons garlic and ginger paste (page 149)
5 or 6 fresh curry leaves
1 teaspoon ground turmeric
1 tablespoon kuzhambu thool (page 148)
250g (9oz) snake gourd or courgette (zucchini), cut into chunks
1 celery stick, in thick slices
400g (14oz) sweet potato (or regular potato), cut into cubes
1 carrot, chopped
100g (3½oz) green beans, topped
½ green (bell) pepper, cut in small chunks
125ml (½ cup) coconut cream
a small handful (¼ cup) coriander (cilantro) leaves, torn
salt

Heat the oil in a large, wide pan. Add the mustard and cumin seeds and the dried chilli and cook until the mustard seeds pop. Add the onion and sauté until golden. Add the garlic and ginger paste and tear in the curry leaves. Simmer for another minute before stirring in the turmeric and thool.

Add all the vegetables. Season with salt and pour in about 500ml (2 cups) water, or just enough to cover the vegetables. Bring to the boil, lower the heat and simmer, uncovered, for about 20 minutes, until the vegetables are tender and the sauce thickened, stirring a few times.

Add the coconut cream, cover and simmer for another few minutes. Taste for salt, remove from the heat and stir through the coriander.

PORIYAL

This is a dry curry – a mixture of several vegetables, seasoned with spices and served as part of a thali platter or as a vegetable dish to accompany a curry. The vegetables are lovely cut small here, so they fit well into little dishes around the platter.

Serves 4 as part of a meal, or 8–10 on a thali platter

4 tablespoons sesame oil
1 teaspoon black mustard seeds
1 teaspoon cumin seeds
1 large dried red chilli
5 or 6 fresh curry leaves
120g (1 cup) diced red onion
2 teaspoons garlic and ginger paste (page 149)
2 small green chillies, finely chopped
200g (7oz) carrots, diced
100g (⅔ cup) peas
100g (3½oz) green beans, topped and chopped
300g (10½oz) trimmed cauliflower in tiny florets
5 tablespoons finely grated fresh coconut
about 2 tablespoons coriander (cilantro) leaves
salt

Heat the oil in a wide heavy-based pan. Add the mustard and cumin seeds and let them sizzle for a minute. Tear the dried chilli and the curry leaves in half, and add them to the pan. Sauté for a minute.

Now add the onion and sauté until golden. Stir in the garlic and ginger paste and the green chillies and continue sautéeing for a little longer, just until you can smell them.

Add all of the vegetables, and season with some salt. Stir in 3 tablespoons water, put the lid on and simmer for about 15 minutes or until the vegetables are tender. Stir now and then to make sure nothing is sticking, especially at the end, but this is a dry curry and is lovely when the vegetables are golden in parts and a little sticky.

Stir the grated coconut through and simmer for a minute longer. Remove from the heat and tear in the coriander leaves.

Leave to stand, covered, for the vegetables to steam for a few minutes more before serving.

BRINJAL CURRY

If you can find drumsticks (green moringa pods) then add in a couple – I love their texture. The shallots used here are quite tiny so add a few more or less depending on the size you can get. The brinjals (aubergines) used here are also the smaller ones, so you may not need four.

Serves 4 as part of a meal or 8–10 on a thali platter

4 tablespoons sesame oil
1 teaspoon black mustard seeds
1 teaspoon ground coriander
2 teaspoons masala mix (page 148)
5 or 6 fresh curry leaves
1 small red onion, chopped
2 teaspoons garlic and ginger paste (page 149)
1 small green chilli, finely chopped
15–20 tiny shallots (madras onions), peeled and left whole
400g (14oz) aubergines (eggplants), about 4 small, cut into chunks
2 drumsticks, peeled and sliced into chunks
185g (¾ cup) tinned chopped tomatoes
2 teaspoons tamarind paste
125ml (½ cup) coconut milk
2 tablespoons torn coriander (cilantro) leaves
salt

For the tempering
1 tablespoon sesame oil
4 or 5 fresh curry leaves
a pinch of black mustard seeds
½ large dried red chilli

Heat the oil in a deep frying pan and add the mustard seeds, ground coriander and masala mix. Tear in the curry leaves and fry until the mustard seeds start to pop.

Now add the onion and sauté until golden. Add the garlic and ginger paste, green chilli and shallots and sauté for another minute. Add the aubergine and drumstick, season with salt and sauté until they have taken on a bit of colour.

Add the tomatoes and about 750ml (3 cups) water, rinsing out the empty tomato tin with some of it as you do so. Stir in along with the tamarind paste. Cover and simmer for about 30 minutes, removing the lid halfway through, until the aubergine is tender and the sauce thick, but there is still a nice amount.

Stir in the coconut milk and cook for another couple of minutes.

For the tempering, heat the oil in a small pan and stir in the curry leaves, mustard seeds and dried chilli. Sauté for a moment then pour into the curry and stir through. Add the coriander and turn through before serving.

TOMATO RASAM

Rasam is used to aid digestion and so is most often served at the end of the meal. There are several types, with some using coconut milk rather than water. This one has more tomato in.

Serves 4 as part of a meal, or 8–10 on a thali platter

2 teaspoons black peppercorns
2 large ripe tomatoes, 300g (10½oz) in total, peeled and chopped
5 garlic cloves, roughly chopped
1 small green chilli, chopped
1 teaspoon cumin seeds
½ red onion, roughly chopped
3 slices of peeled ginger
a small handful coriander (cilantro) leaves
½ teaspoon ground turmeric
1 teaspoon tamarind paste
1 tablespoon chopped coriander (cilantro) leaves
salt

For the tempering
1 tablespoon sesame oil
¼ teaspoon black mustard seeds
½ dried red chilli
3 or 4 fresh curry leaves, torn
½ teaspoon masala mix (page 148)
a pinch of asafoetida

Pound the peppercorns a little with a pestle and mortar, just to crack them.

Set aside about a third of the chopped tomato. Put the rest with the pepper, ½ teaspoon salt and the remaining ingredients, except the chopped coriander, into a pan. Add 500ml (2 cups) water and simmer gently over a low heat for a few minutes (it should not come to the boil). Press down gently on the ingredients with a potato masher, then remove from the heat, cover and set aside for 10 minutes or so. Strain through a fine sieve, pressing down with a wooden spoon to extract the flavour.

For the tempering, heat the oil in a small, non-stick frying pan with the mustard seeds, chilli, curry leaves and masala. When they start to sizzle, add the remaining tomatoes and a small sprinkling of salt. Sauté until the tomatoes break down, helping them with a wooden spoon and turning them through. Add the asafoetida then remove from the heat. Pour into the rasam, mixing through. Heat gently. Taste for salt, add the chopped coriander and serve hot, in small cups or bowls.

COCONUT PAYASAM

*In south India a sweet dish is often offered, sometimes even at the start of a meal.
A piece of jaggery or a little sugar makes everyone happy.*

Serves 3 as part of a meal, or 6 on a thali platter

60g (1 heaped cup) vermicelli
250ml (1 cup) coconut milk
2½ tablespoons grated jaggery (or brown sugar)
¼ teaspoon ground cardamom
2 teaspoons sultanas (golden raisins)
2 tablespoons coarsely grated fresh coconut
2 teaspoons rose water
2 teaspoons ghee
30g (¼ cup) cashew nuts, in chunky pieces

Rinse the vermicelli. Bring a small pan of water to the boil and add the vermicelli. Cook for a couple of minutes until tender, then drain in a colander. Rinse with cold water.

Meanwhile, simmer the coconut milk, jaggery, cardamom and sultanas together in a pan, letting it bubble gently for a couple of minutes. Stir in the grated coconut and rose water. Remove from the heat and leave to cool.

Heat the ghee in a small pan, add the cashew nuts and sauté until a little golden. Leave to cool.

Stir the cooled vermicelli and cashew nuts into the cooled coconut milk and serve. If serving later, add a little extra coconut milk.

PONDICHERRY

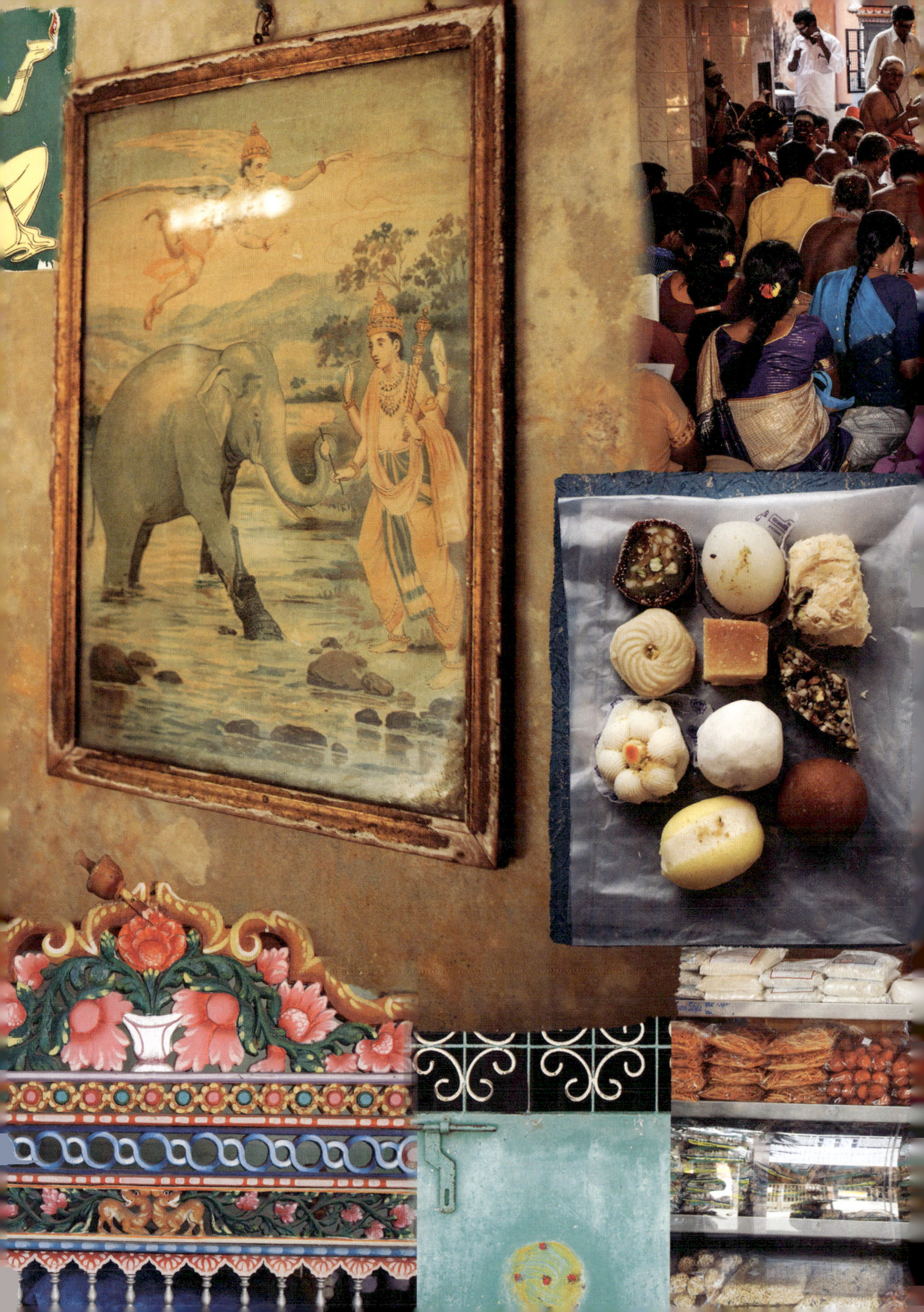

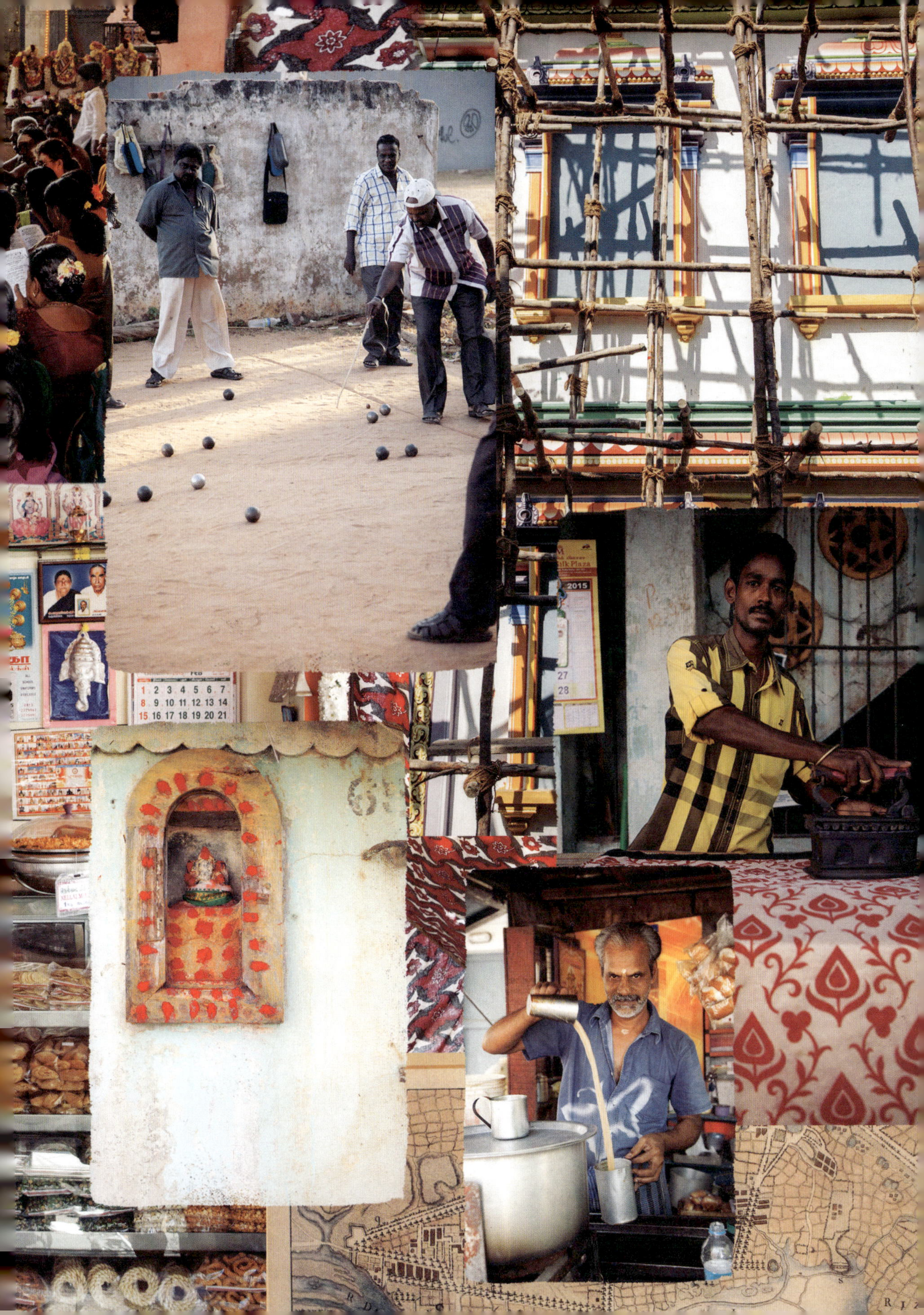

2015
27
28
1 2 3 4 5 6 7
8 9 10 11 12 13 14
15 16 17 18 19 20 21

IDLI

Breakfast in Pondicherry. Steamed rice cakes with coconut chutney and sambar. Ideally, you need idli moulds, but an egg poaching rack, or small bowls (about 7cm/2¾in diameter) that sit on a rack in the pan, can be used instead.

Makes 8–10

250g (9oz) idli rice
50g (heaped ¼ cup) urad dal (skinned)
¼ teaspoon fenugreek seeds
½ teaspoon salt
melted ghee, for brushing

To serve
coconut chutney (page 155)
sambar (page 170)

Put the rice in a bowl of cold water and the dal and fenugreek together in a separate bowl of cold water. Soak both for about 4 hours.

Drain the rice, saving some of the water. Pulse in a blender to as smooth as you can (it will become flour-like with a few little bits). Add enough of the reserved water (about 125ml/½ cup) to give a thickish batter. Transfer to a bowl.

Drain the dal and fenugreek, again saving some of the water, and pulse in the blender to as fine as possible, adding a little of their reserved water to give a crêpe-like batter. Pour into the rice batter and add the salt. Stir together well. Cover with a cloth (not plastic wrap) and leave until the batter ferments, about 8 hours or overnight.

The next day, choose a deep frying pan large enough to take the idli moulds. Put the moulds into the pan and pour enough water into the pan to reach the rounded bases of the moulds. Bring to a low simmer.

Brush the individual moulds with a little melted ghee, then fill each with batter almost to the brim. Put the lid on and steam over a very low heat for 8–10 minutes or until risen and set. Turn them out of the moulds and keep them warm. Brush and repeat. Serve the idli warm.

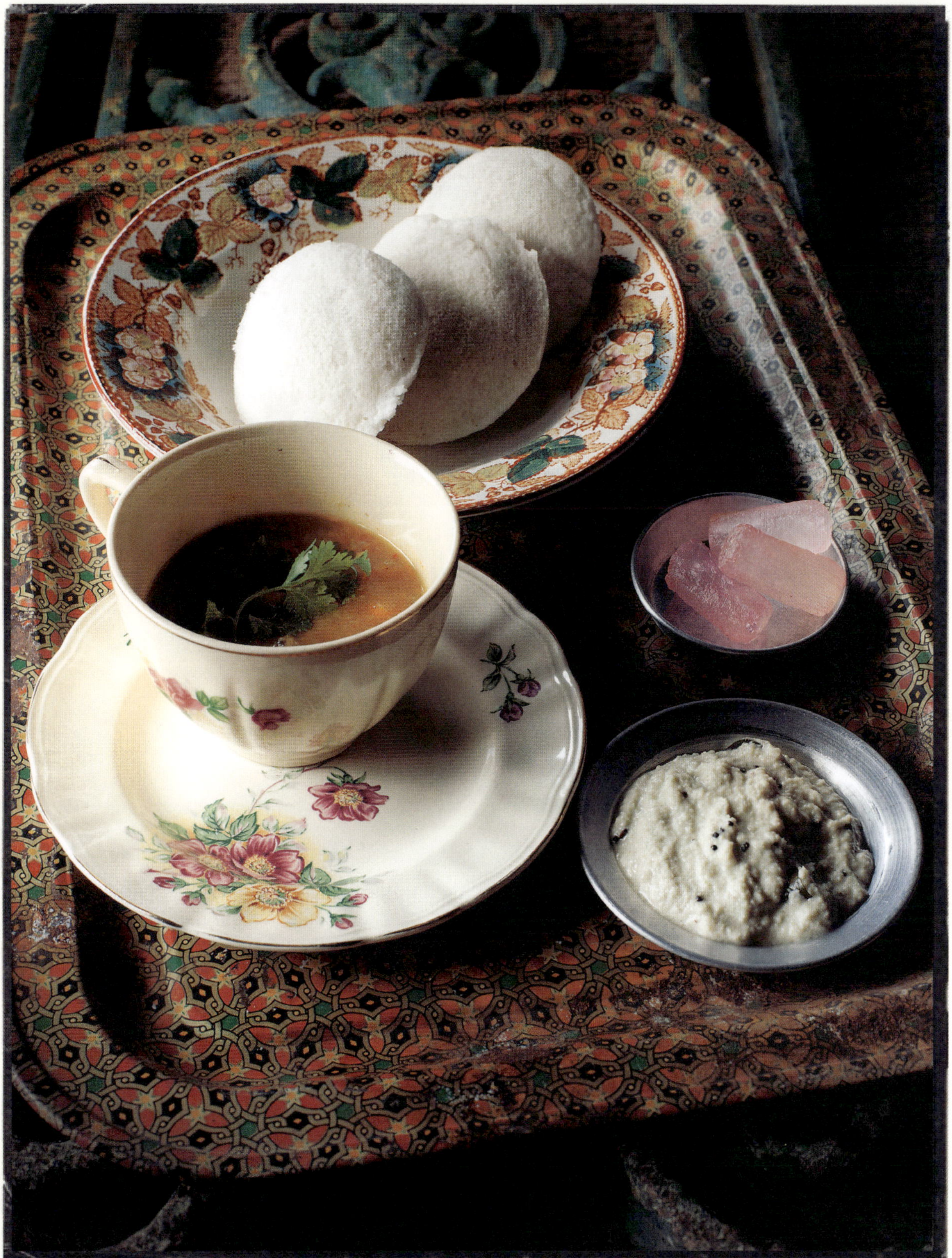

POTATO DOSA

Lovely for breakfast with large cups of sweet, milky tea. These are like large crêpes made from the same batter as idli. Here they are filled with potato curry and served with chutneys – coconut, tomato and coriander are all very good here.

Makes about 5

1 quantity idli batter (page 178)
1 quantity warm potato and onion curry (page 183)
To serve
a small handful coriander (cilantro) leaves
chutneys (pages 154 and 155)

Heat a dosa pan or other large, flat frying pan over a medium-high heat. Fill a large ladle with batter (about 125ml/½ cup) and pour into the dry pan, spreading it thinly then using the back of the ladle and rotating outwards (as you would make a crêpe). It should be very thin and about 20–22cm (8–9in) in diameter. (If the pan is too hot it can cause it to tear so lower the heat if necessary.)

When small bubbles start to appear over the surface, and the edges start to go crispy, turn the dosa over with a spatula. It is ready when the edges turn golden, but check that the underside is golden and browned in places before removing from the pan. Keep warm and repeat with the rest of the batter.

Put a warm dosa on each plate and spoon about 3 heaped tablespoons of potato curry along one side of the dosa. Tear over some coriander leaves and roll up. Serve with chutneys.

EGG DOSA

To make an egg dosa: when you see the surface bubbles appearing on the dosa, break an egg into the centre and shuffle it using a wooden spatula, dragging the egg to the edges here and there so you make a type of omelette (you could beat each egg lightly before adding if you prefer). Drizzle just a few drops of sesame oil around the sides and top, season the egg with a little salt and pepper. Flip when it is already set a bit to very briefly set the top side before removing it to a plate. Serve with a selection of chutneys.

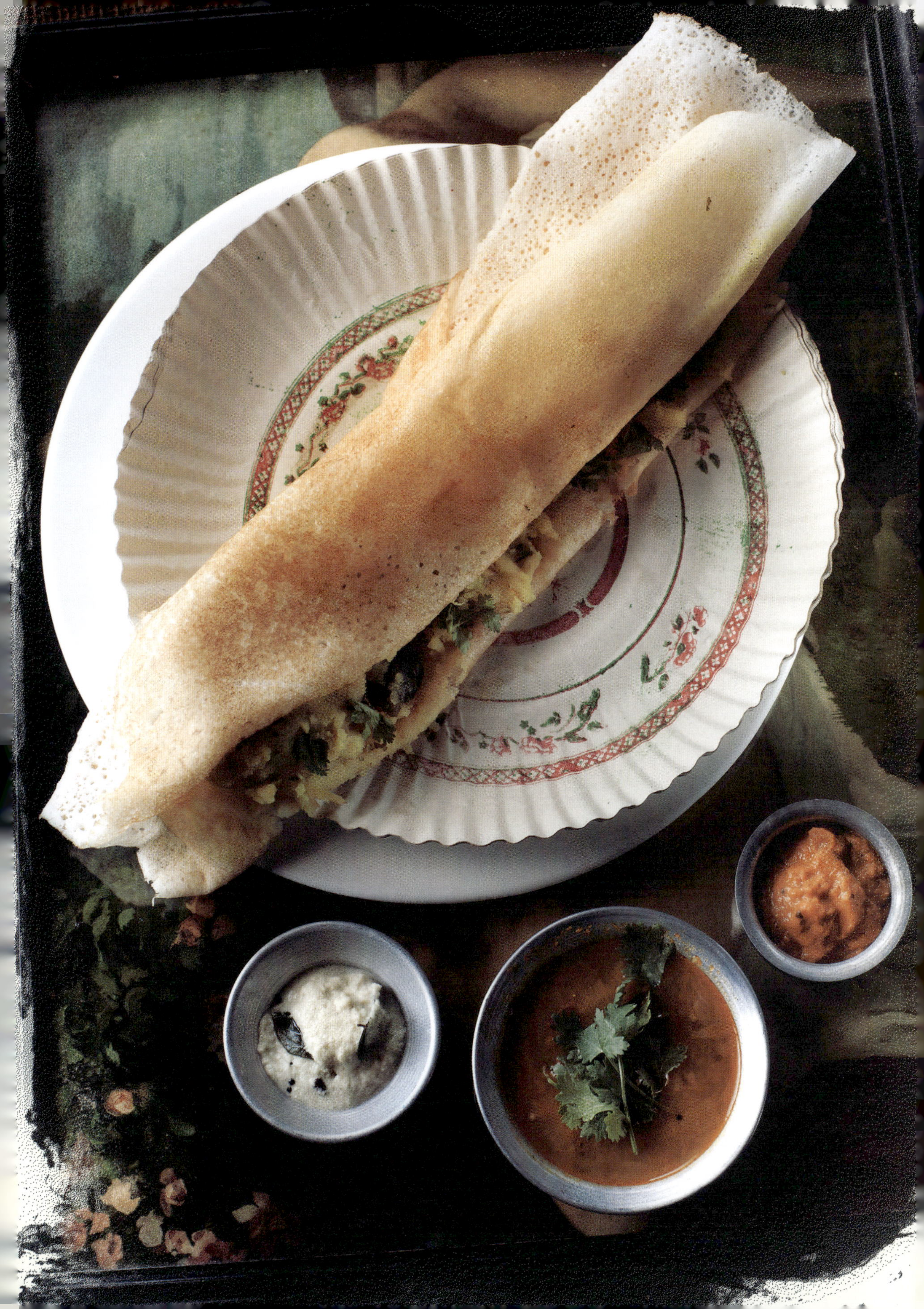

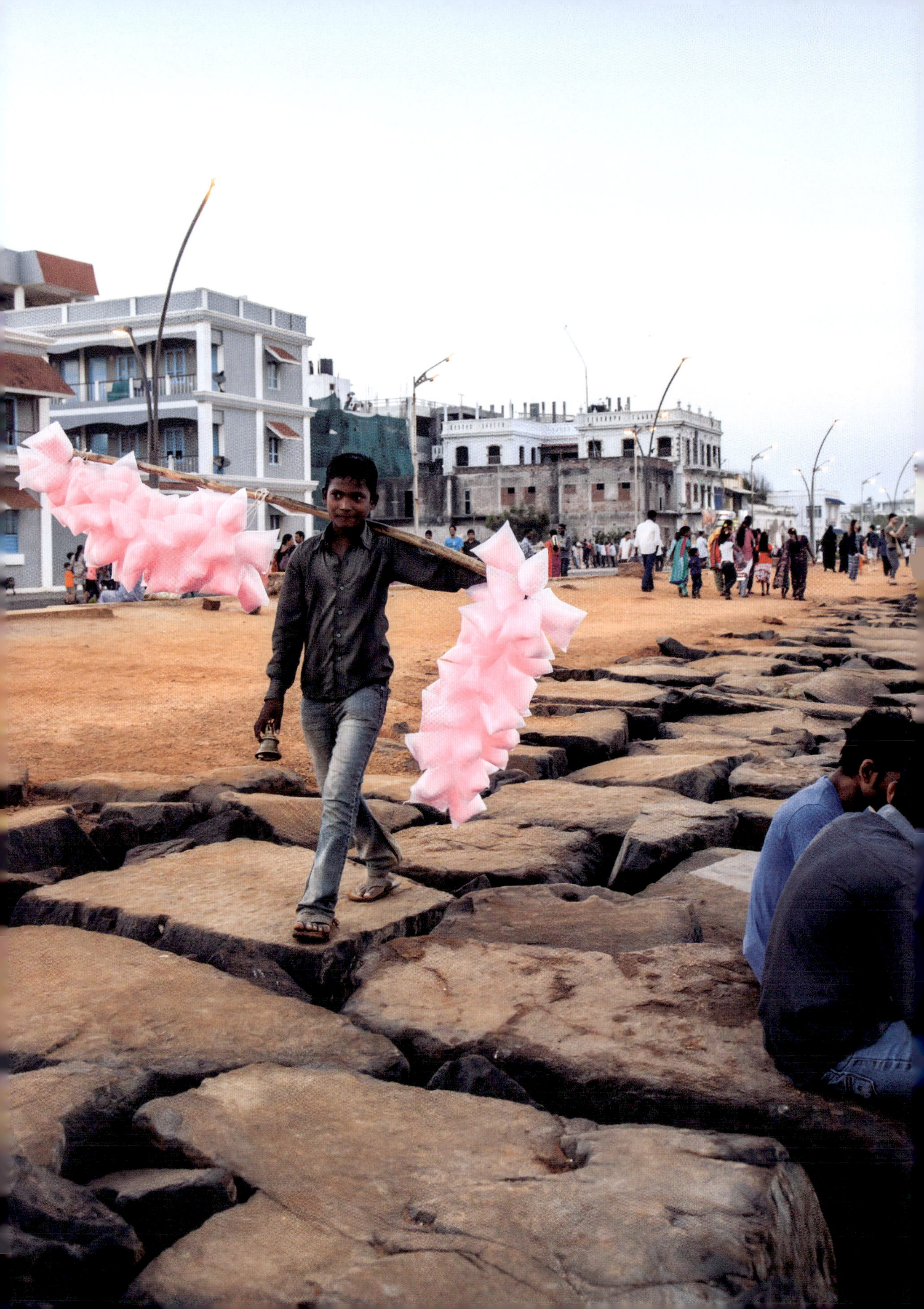

POTATO AND ONION CURRY

This is great eaten when just cooked, but if you make it in advance, add a little water when reheating it. I like the chunks of potato here, but if you will be filling dosas with it, then cut them into smaller cubes.

Serves 3–4 as part of a meal, or enough to fill 5 dosas

4 tablespoons sesame oil
2 teaspoons black mustard seeds
300g (10½oz/2 medium) onions, chopped
2 teaspoons garlic and ginger paste (page 149)
2 small green chillies, deseeded and finely chopped
5 or 6 fresh curry leaves
1kg (2¼lb) potatoes, peeled and cut into chunks
½ teaspoon sugar
a handful coriander (cilantro) leaves, shredded
salt

Heat the oil in a wide, heavy-based pan. Sauté the mustard seeds until they start to pop, then add the onions. Fry gently until golden. Stir in the garlic and ginger paste and chillies, tear in the curry leaves and sauté for a couple of minutes.

Add the potatoes, turning them through with a wooden spoon. Scatter in the sugar and about 1 teaspoon salt, then pour in about 375ml (1½ cups) water. Put the lid on, bring to the boil and simmer for about 10 minutes.

Remove the lid, lower the heat and simmer for another 10 minutes or so, turning often to make sure that nothing is sticking. The curry is ready when the potatoes are soft and much of the liquid has been absorbed.

Add the coriander leaves, take off the heat, cover and leave for 5 minutes or so. Taste for seasonings before serving.

PONDICHERRY FISH CURRY

For this traditional curry, use fillets of fish that will not break up during cooking. The fish is spiced and fried separately for extra flavour. Lovely with lemon rice and chapati.

Serves 4

1 teaspoon ground turmeric
1 teaspoon masala mix (page 148)
1 teaspoon kuzhambu thool (page 148)
500g (18oz) firm-fleshed fish fillets, such as snapper, cod or bream, cut into pieces about 3 x 8cm (1¼ x 3¼in)
3–4 tablespoons vegetable oil

For the sauce
3 tablespoons sesame oil
½ teaspoon black mustard seeds
½ teaspoon cumin seeds
2 red onions, chopped
1 small green chilli, deseeded and chopped
2 teaspoons garlic and ginger paste (page 149)
2 teaspoons kuzhambu thool (page 148)
2 ripe tomatoes, peeled and chopped
125ml (½ cup) coconut milk
2 teaspoons tamarind paste mixed with 60ml (¼ cup) hot water
salt

For the tempering
1 tablespoon sesame oil
4 or 5 fresh curry leaves, torn
½ large dried red chilli
1 teaspoon vadavam (page 149)

To serve
1 tablespoon shredded coriander (cilantro) leaves

Combine the turmeric, masala and thool in a bowl. Add the fish pieces and toss to coat well. Leave for about 20 minutes.

To make the sauce, heat the sesame oil in a wide pan and fry the mustard and cumin seeds until they sizzle. Add the onions and cook until golden and sticky. Add the green chilli and the garlic and ginger paste, and sauté until it smells good. Stir in the thool, then the tomatoes. and sauté for a minute.

Add 250ml (1 cup) water and season with salt. Simmer, uncovered, for 5 minutes, squashing down on the tomatoes with a potato masher to break up any lumps. Add the coconut milk and simmer, uncovered, for another 5 minutes.

Meanwhile, fry the fish. Heat enough oil in a non-stick frying pan to just cover the bottom over a medium-high heat. When hot, add the fish pieces and fry briefly until golden on both sides. Remove with a slotted spoon to the sauce.

Add the tamarind water and simmer, uncovered, over a low heat for about 8 minutes, rocking the pot to gently to shake things around without breaking up the fish.

For the tempering, heat the oil in a small pan and add the curry leaves, dried chilli and vadavam. Fry until it sizzles then pour the lot into the sauce. Add the coriander and fold through with a wooden spoon. Serve hot, with rice.

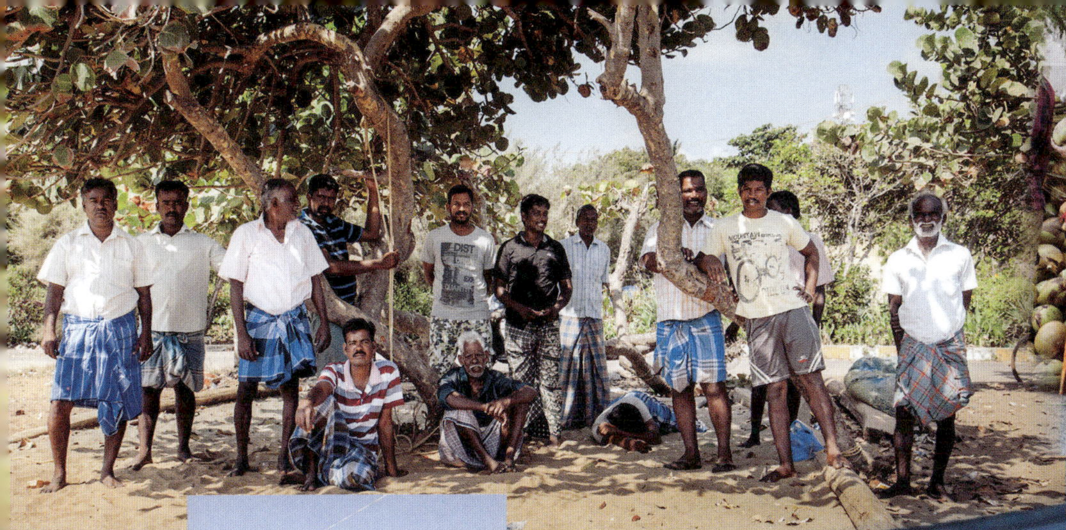
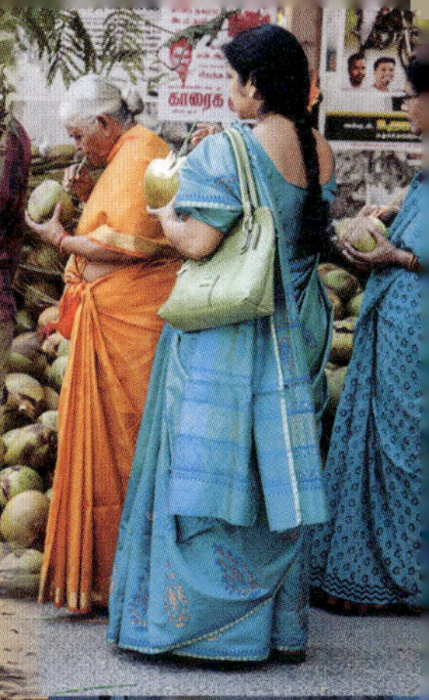
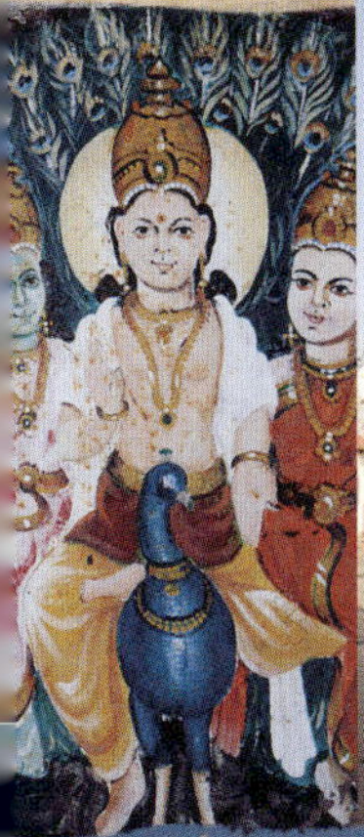
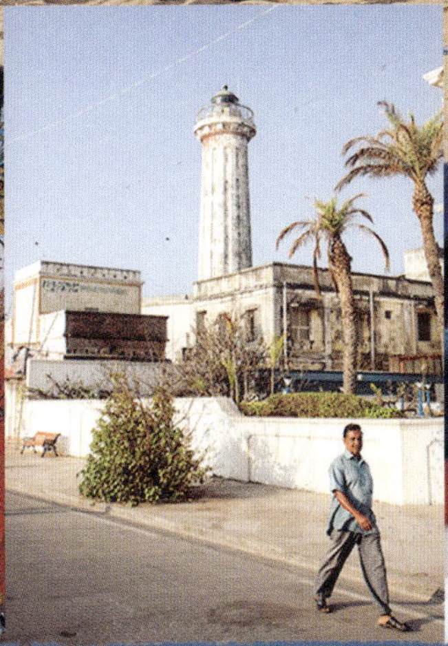
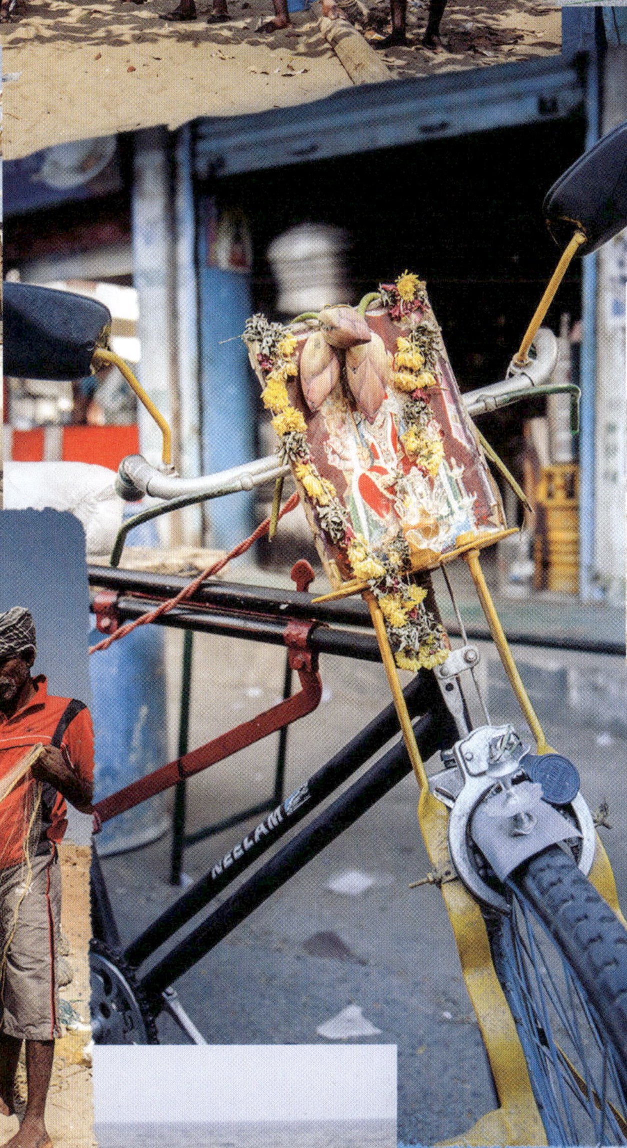
NEELAM
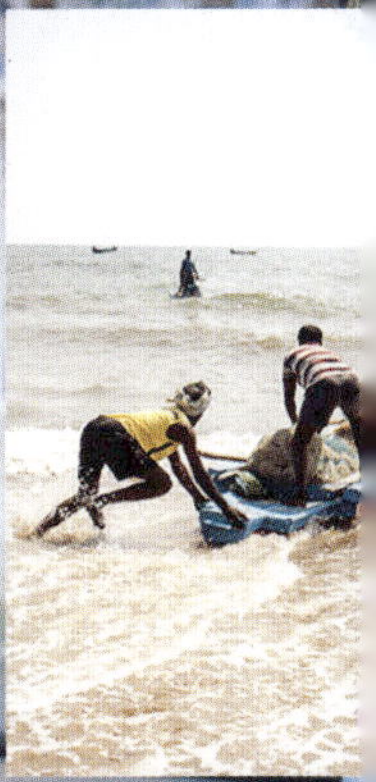
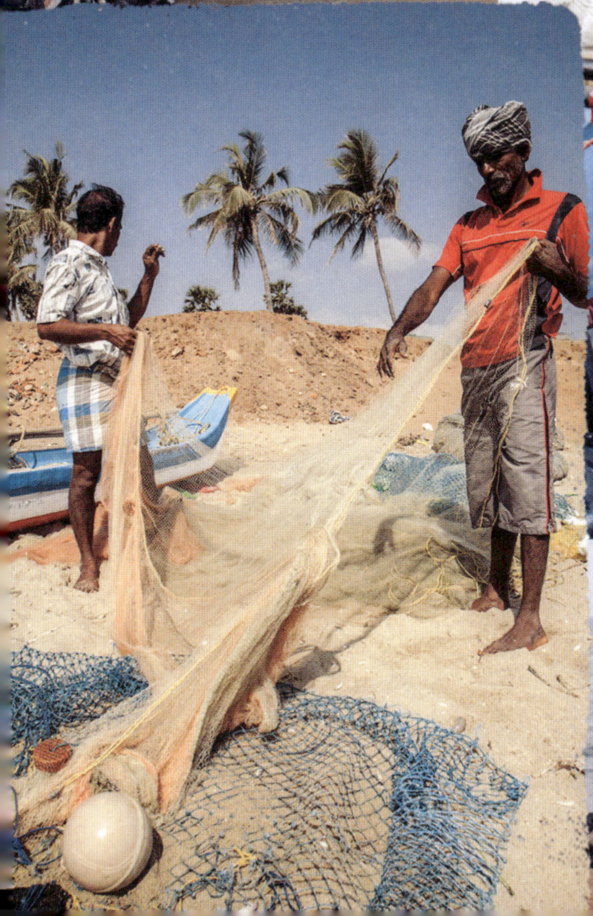
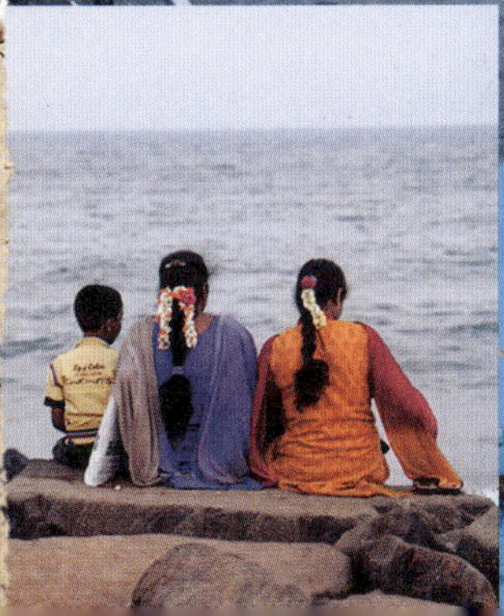
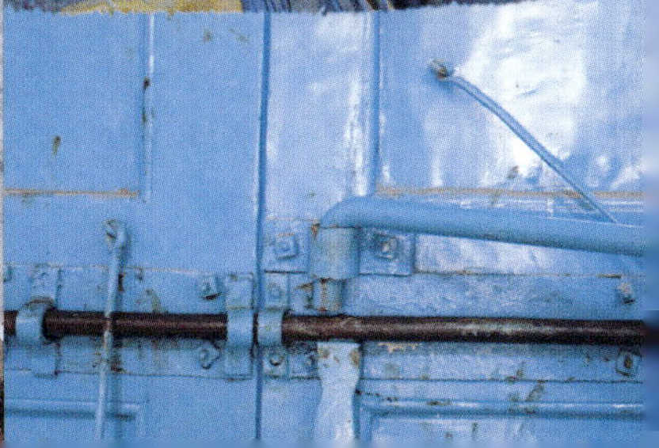

ASHOK'S MASALA PRAWNS

Ashok is an amazing cook from Pondicherry who taught me to make many things. He served this with raita, chapati and a small salad of finely shredded white and red cabbage, lettuce and carrot, with a lime for squeezing. I loved this combination.

Serves 3–4

800g (1¾lb/about 18) shell-on medium prawns (shrimp), heads removed
2 tablespoons sesame oil
¼ teaspoon black mustard seeds
¼ teaspoon cumin seeds
1 small green chilli, finely chopped
2 teaspoons garlic and ginger paste (page 149)
2 teaspoons masala mix (page 148)
125g (½ cup) tinned chopped tomatoes
2 tablespoons chopped coriander (cilantro) leaves
salt

To serve
raita (page 151)

Peel away the shells from the prawns, leaving the tail on. Devein them.

Heat the oil in a wide pan, add the mustard and cumin seeds and fry until the mustard seeds start to pop. Add the chilli and the garlic and ginger paste and sauté until it smells good. Stir the masala through and cook for another 10 seconds or so to toast it quickly.

Now add the tomatoes and 125ml (½ cup) water. Lower the heat and simmer, uncovered, for about 5 minutes to thicken. Add the prawns, season with salt, then turn them through the sauce. Cover and simmer for 5–6 minutes, until cooked through and opaque. Check that nothing is sticking.

Scatter in the coriander, cover and leave to stand for a few minutes before serving.

Accompany with raita, chapati, salad and lime wedges (and small dishes of lemon pickle and coriander chutney, if you like).

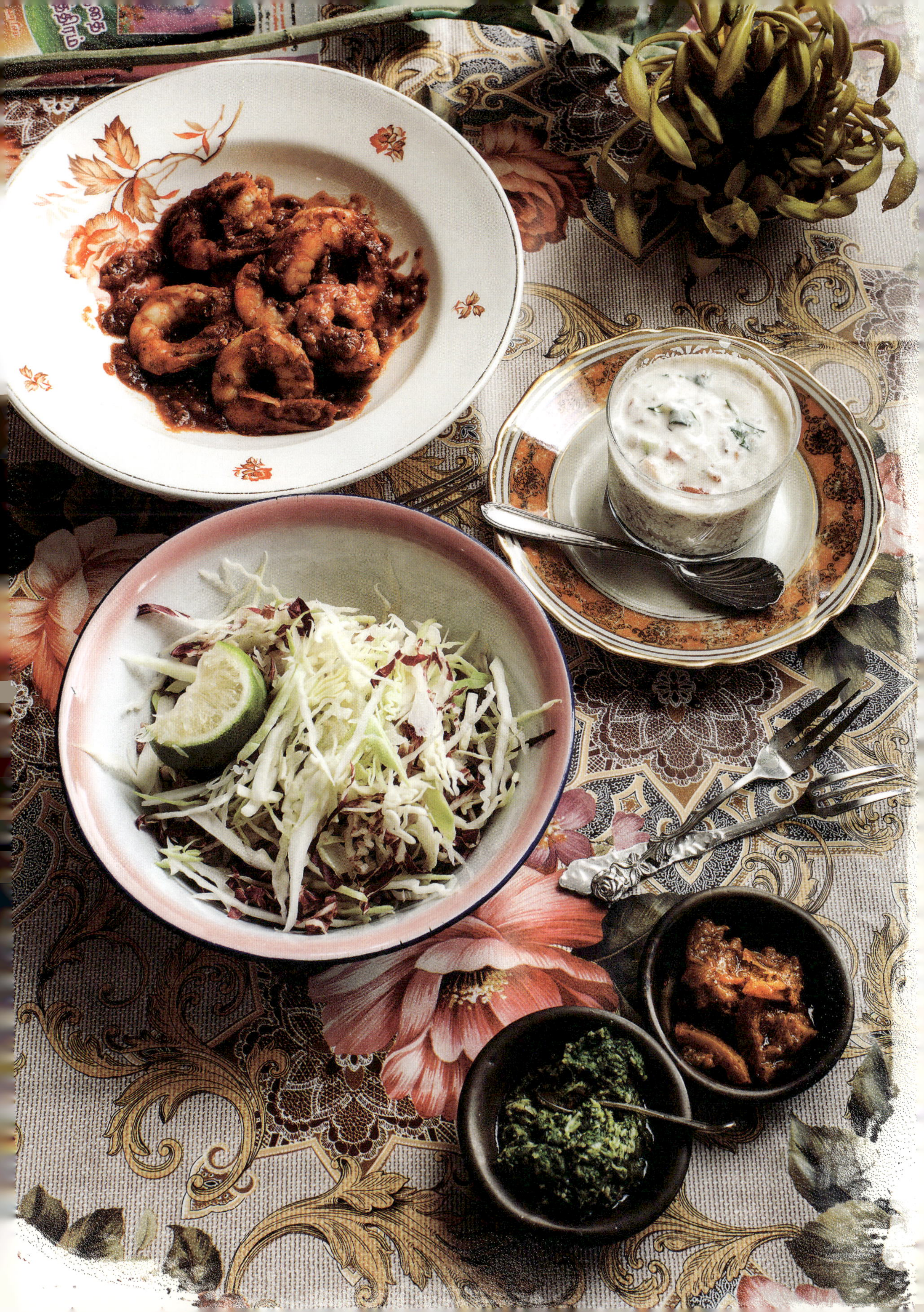

APPAMS

These are crisp rice flour pancakes cooked in a kadai (a circular, deep cast-iron pot like a wok) with handles and so come out bowl-shaped with thinner, crispy edges and thicker towards the centre. A small wok and a saucepan lid which fits snugly just inside the top of the wok will work. Serve with Pondicherry chicken curry (page 190) or with a vegetable coconut curry (page 171), accompanied by the coconut cream. It may seem a lot of coconut – but it is truly delicious.

Makes about 8

½ teaspoon dried yeast
1 teaspoon sugar
185ml (¾ cup) warm water
½ lightly beaten egg
435ml (1¾ cups) coconut milk
250g (heaped 2 cups) rice flour
1 teaspoon salt
sesame oil, for brushing

Put the yeast, sugar and all but 2 tablespoons of the water in a bowl and stir until the yeast has completely dissolved. Leave in a warm spot until foaming, 10–15 minutes. Gradually stir in the egg and coconut milk, then the rice flour and salt.

Cover the bowl loosely with plastic wrap, then a cloth and put in a warm, draught-free spot. Leave for at least 5 hours (or even overnight), until the batter ferments and bubbles.

Add the reserved 2 tablespoons water to the batter and stir until smooth.

Very lightly brush the kadai or small wok with a little oil. Put over a medium heat then ladle in 125ml (½ cup) batter. Holding both handles of the wok, quickly tilt it, swirl the batter around so it goes up the sides of the wok in a thin coating, graduating to a thicker centre at the bottom.

Put the lid on and cook, still over a medium heat, for about 5 minutes, until the centre is white and set and the edges light brown, crisp and lacy, and lifting away from the sides. The bottom too should be crisp and hold its shape. Turn the heat up a little if necessary. Gently lift out using a spatula and rest on a fine wire rack or a bamboo mat while you make the rest. Serve hot, as soon as they are all cooked.

CARDAMOM COCONUT CREAM

This is lovely and cooling. In a small bowl, mix 185ml (¾ cup) coconut cream with 2 scant teaspoons sugar and 2 good pinches of ground cardamom. Cover and chill before serving.

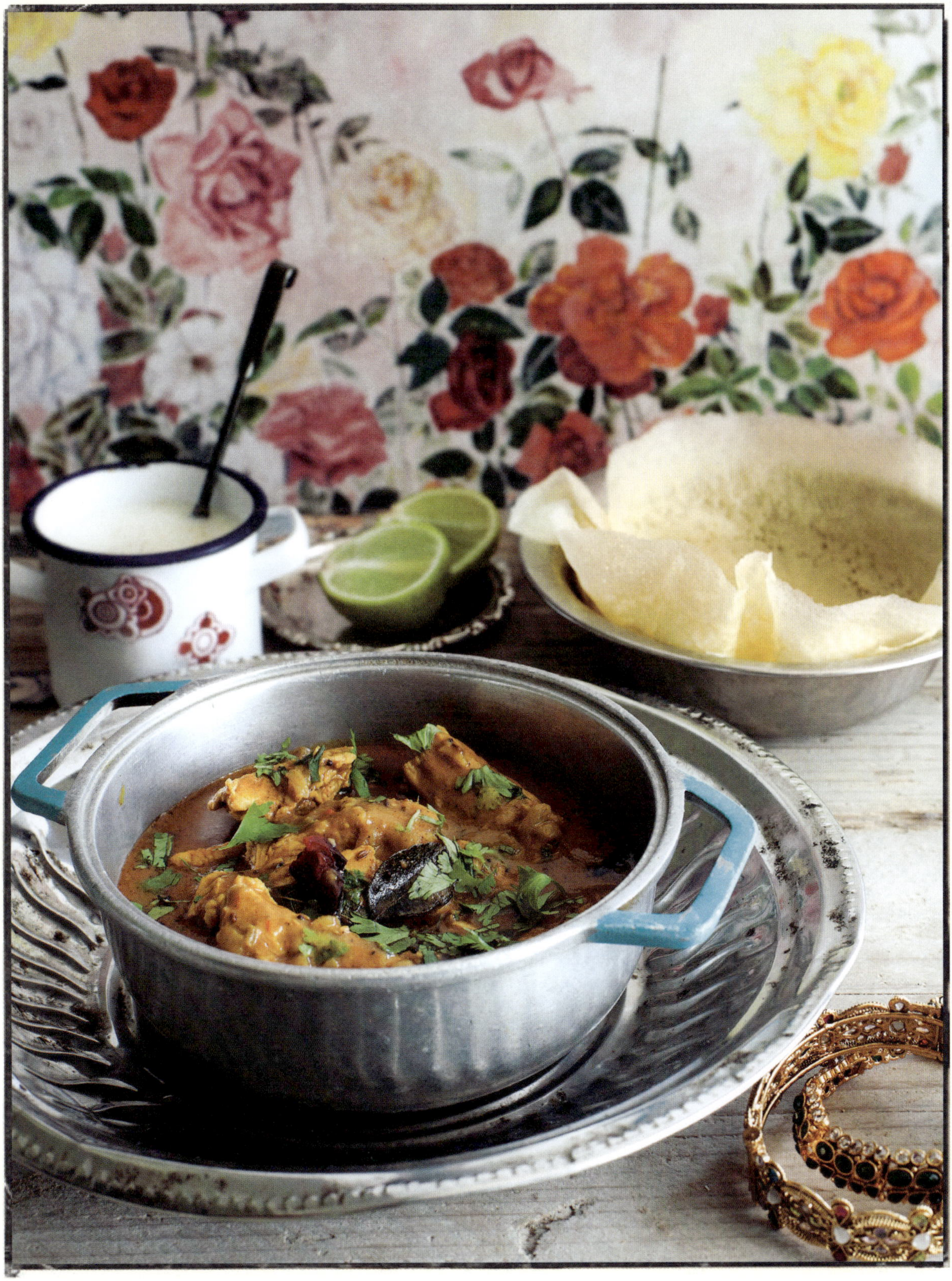

PONDICHERRY CHICKEN

This fairly mild curry is very quick and easy to make. If you want to make it hotter, then leave the seeds in the chillies, or just add more.

Serves 4

3 tablespoons sesame oil
¼ teaspoon black mustard seeds
¼ teaspoon cumin seeds
1 onion, chopped
2 teaspoons garlic and ginger paste (page 149)
2 green chillies, deseeded and finely chopped
2 teaspoons masala mix (page 148)
1 teaspoon ground turmeric
125g (½ cup) tinned chopped tomatoes
500g (18oz) skinless chicken breasts, cut in 2–4cm (¾–1½in) wide strips
250ml (1 cup) coconut milk
salt

For the tempering
1 tablespoon sesame oil
¼ teaspoon black mustard seeds
¼ teaspoon cumin seeds
½ large dried red chilli
3 or 4 fresh curry leaves, torn
1 tablespoon chopped coriander (cilantro)

To serve
chopped coriander (cilantro)
lime quarters
appams (page 188)
cardamom coconut cream (page 188)

Heat the oil in a wide, heavy-based pan and add the mustard and cumin seeds. Fry until they sizzle, then add the onion. Sauté until golden and softened. Add the garlic and ginger paste, the green chillies, masala and turmeric and sauté until it smells good.

Add the tomatoes, stirring and scraping up the spices from the bottom of the pan with a wooden spoon. Add 125ml (½ cup) water and simmer, uncovered, for a few minutes, until it reduces and thickens.

Add the chicken, season with salt and turn through. Pour in the coconut milk, lower the heat and simmer, covered, for about 15 minutes, stirring a few times to be sure that nothing is sticking. The sauce should be lovely and thick and the chicken tender.

For the tempering, heat the oil in a small pan and add the mustard and cumin seeds. Fry until they sizzle, then add the dried chilli and curry leaves. Fry for a little longer, then remove from the heat and pour over the chicken. Add the coriander and stir through.

Serve hot, scattered with extra chopped coriander. Accompany with the coconut cream, lime wedges and appams.

LAMB WITH CORIANDER AND MINT

One of the many dishes that Ashok, a Pondicherry cook, taught me, this is lovely and tender and goes well with rice on the side, or appams (page 188) and a couple of chutneys. You can use goat instead of lamb if you like.

Serves 4

4 tablespoons sesame oil
800g (1¾lb) boned lamb leg or shoulder, trimmed and cut into chunks
½ teaspoon black mustard seeds
½ teaspoon cumin seeds
1 red onion, chopped
2 teaspoons garlic and ginger paste (page 149)
1 tablespoon kuzhambu thool (page 148)
1 ripe tomato, peeled and chopped
1 very large handful (1 cup) shredded coriander (cilantro) leaves
1 very large handful (1 cup) shredded mint leaves
185ml (¾ cup) coconut milk
salt

For the tempering
1 tablespoon sesame oil
a pinch of black mustard seeds
½ large dried red chilli
4 or 5 fresh curry leaves, torn
½ teaspoon masala mix (page 148)

Heat the oil in a large pan over a high heat. Brown the lamb well on all sides, in a couple of batches. As each batch is done, scoop it from the pan and keep in a bowl.

Add the mustard and cumin seeds and the onion to the pan. Sauté until golden, then stir in the garlic and ginger paste and sauté for a moment before stirring in the thool.

Add the tomato and cook until pulpy. Return the lamb and season with salt. Add 500ml (2 cups) water, then cover and simmer for about 30 minutes, stirring a couple of times.

Add the shredded herbs and coconut milk and stir through. Cover and simmer for a further 15 minutes, checking that it is not too dry towards the end. The lamb should be very tender with a fairly thick sauce. Taste for seasonings and adjust if necessary. Take off the heat and leave to stand, covered, for a few minutes.

For the tempering, heat the oil in a small pan and add the mustard seeds, dried chilli and curry leaves. Add the masala and, when it is sizzling, swirl and pour the mixture over the lamb. Mix through and serve.

ROSE MILK KULFI

Hot, or cold, rose milk is wonderful, so this mixture might not even make it to the freezer. If you don't have a simmer mat, you will have to watch the milk like a hawk. I add a few drops of red food colouring, as I think rose milk does need to be a pale shade of pink. If you have some edible red flowers (for example, certain species of hibiscus or rose), then use those. Serve plain or with chopped pistachios.

Serves 4–6

625ml (2½ cups cups) full-fat (whole) milk, plus 1 tablespoon
125ml (½ cup) condensed milk
1 tablespoon rice flour
2 teaspoons rose water
3 tablespoons cream
a few drops of red food colouring (or a few dried flowers)

Put the milk into a large heavy-based saucepan and bring to a gentle boil. Have the heat very low, and the pan on a simmer mat if you have one, so that the milk is rippling rather than bubbling, to avoid the bottom catching. Cook for 30 minutes until the milk has thickened and reduced by about a third, stirring regularly to stop it catching on the bottom of the pan and burning.

Add the condensed milk and bring back to a low simmer. Mix the rice flour with the 1 tablespoon milk to dissolve it, then add to the pan. Simmer for a few minutes so that the rice flour cooks through, then stir in the rose water.

Take off the heat and stir in the cream and food colouring (or flowers). Leave to cool completely.

Strain to remove the flowers, if using, then pour into a freezer container and place in the freezer until just set but still soft. Whizz with a hand-held blender until smooth. Return to the freezer and repeat this step once more. Freeze until set firm, or spoon into small individual moulds before freezing for the final time.

RANJIT'S CHETTINAD WALL PLASTER:

egg white

limestone

for colour, add flowers

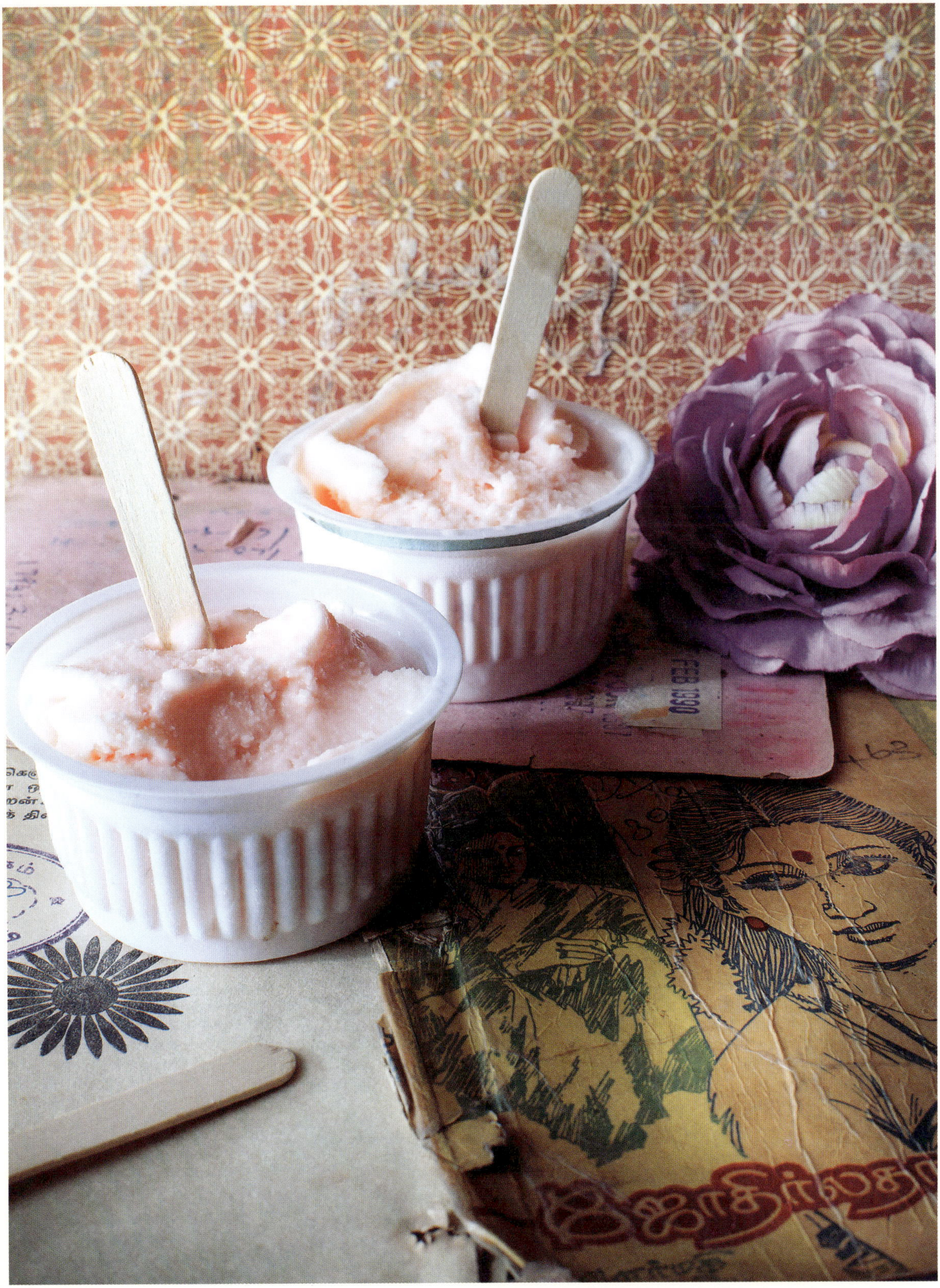

LASSI

A salty lassi is more common in the south of India, where it is called 'more'. It is refreshing on a steaming hot day.

Makes 1 large or 2 smaller glasses

250g (1 cup) plain yogurt, or curd
125ml (½ cup) cold water
a handful mint leaves
½ teaspoon salt
crushed ice

Mix everything except the ice together in a jug and put in the fridge to chill and mingle.

Pour into glasses, spoon as much ice as you want on top and serve icy cold.

SWEET MANGO LASSI

Here is a sweet version. Use a lovely small, sweet ripe mango.

Makes 1 large or 2 smaller glasses

1 small ripe mango, peeled and
    cut into pieces
about 2 teaspoons jaggery or light brown
    cane sugar
½ cup crushed ice, plus extra for serving
125g (½ cup) plain yogurt, or curd

Put the mango flesh, jaggery and crushed ice into a blender and blend to a smooth purée. Add the yogurt and blend briefly to combine, adjust sweetness to taste. Serve icy cold.

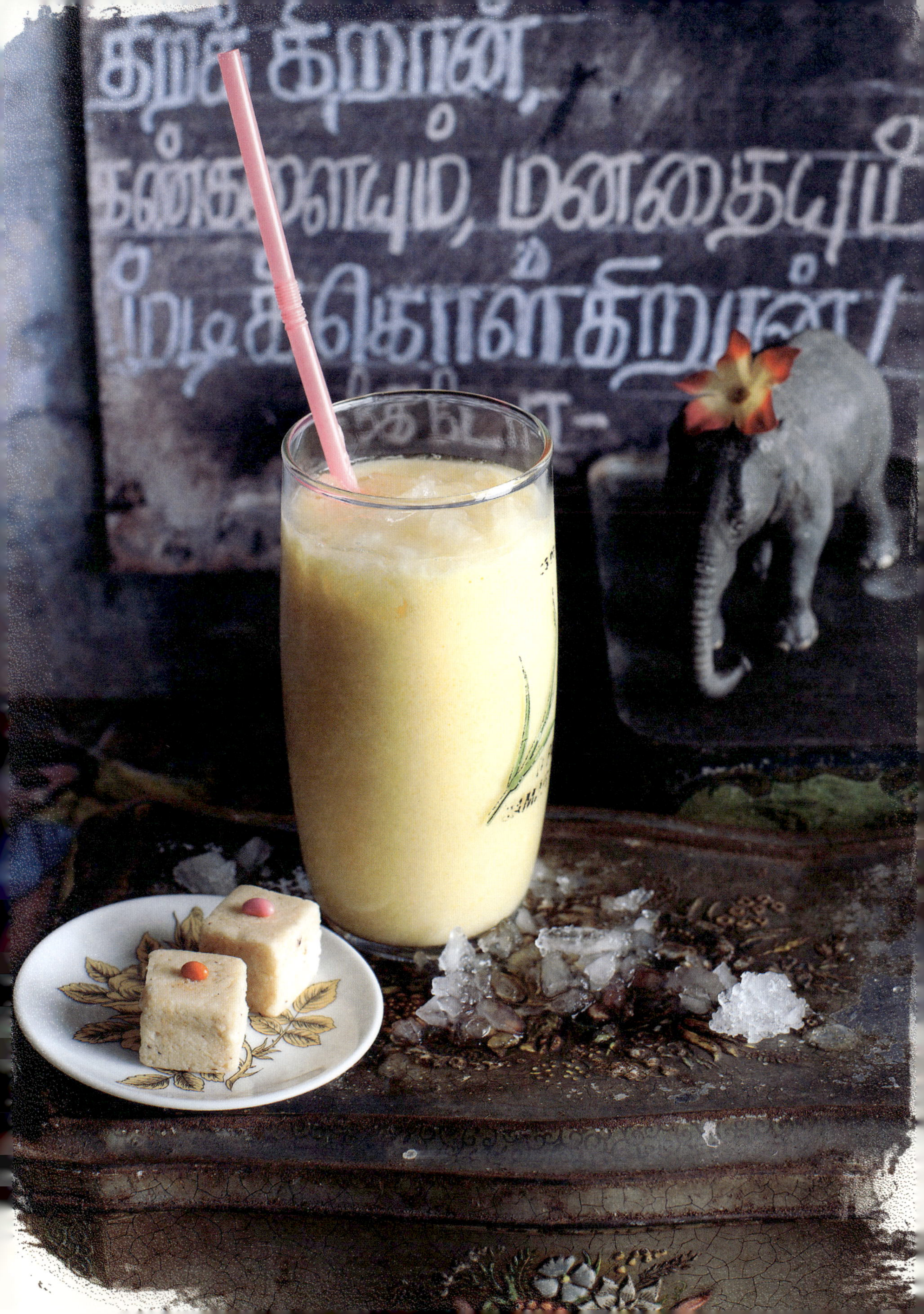

CARDAMOM RICE PUDDING

This is rich and simple. You can scatter over some cinnamon as well as cardamom to serve, if you like. If you have a simmer mat, then use it here towards the end of cooking to prevent the rice from sticking and burning.

Serves 4

200g (heaped 1 cup) basmati rice
1 litre (4 cups) milk
100g (½ cup) sugar
10 cardamom pods, cracked
125ml (½ cup) cream
ground cardamom

Soak the rice in cold water for 20–30 minutes, then rinse and drain.

Put the rice into a saucepan with 200ml (7fl oz) water and bring to the boil over quite a high heat. Once the water has been absorbed, stir in the milk, sugar and cardamom pods.

Bring to the boil, then lower the heat to a minimum and simmer, stirring often, until nearly all the milk has been absorbed, about 20 minutes. Towards the end of this time, stir continuously or move the pan to a simmer mat to prevent the rice sticking. It should be soft and porridgey, with a little thickened liquid. Stir in the cream and remove from the heat.

Spoon into individual bowls, scatter with cardamom and serve warm or at room temperature. Even from the fridge is good.

MASALA TEA (CHAI)

I always look forward to these milky cups of tea, and love it when it is served already sugared, often ultra sweet. Use a loose-leaf tea here, such as Assam.

Serves 4

600ml (scant 2½ cups) milk
12 green cardamom pods, cracked
1 teaspoon black peppercorns
3 cloves
7cm (2¾in) piece of cinnamon stick
5cm (2in) chunk (15g/½oz) of ginger, peeled
1½ tablespoons black tea leaves
at least 4 teaspoons sugar

Put the milk, cardamom, peppercorns, cloves, cinnamon and ginger in a saucepan and bring to a gentle boil. Remove from the heat and leave to infuse for 20 minutes or so.

Return to the heat and bring almost to the boil, removing from the heat as the milk starts to rise up the side of the pan. Repeat this once more, so that the milk has been heated 3 times.

Meanwhile, bring 300ml (1¼ cups) water to the boil in a saucepan. Take off the heat. Add the tea leaves and leave to steep for a few minutes, so it is quite strong.

Strain the just-boiled milk and the hot tea into a jug together. Stir in the sugar.

Pour into glasses or warm cups from a dizzying height, so it froths up. Add a cardamom pod to each glass, if you like.

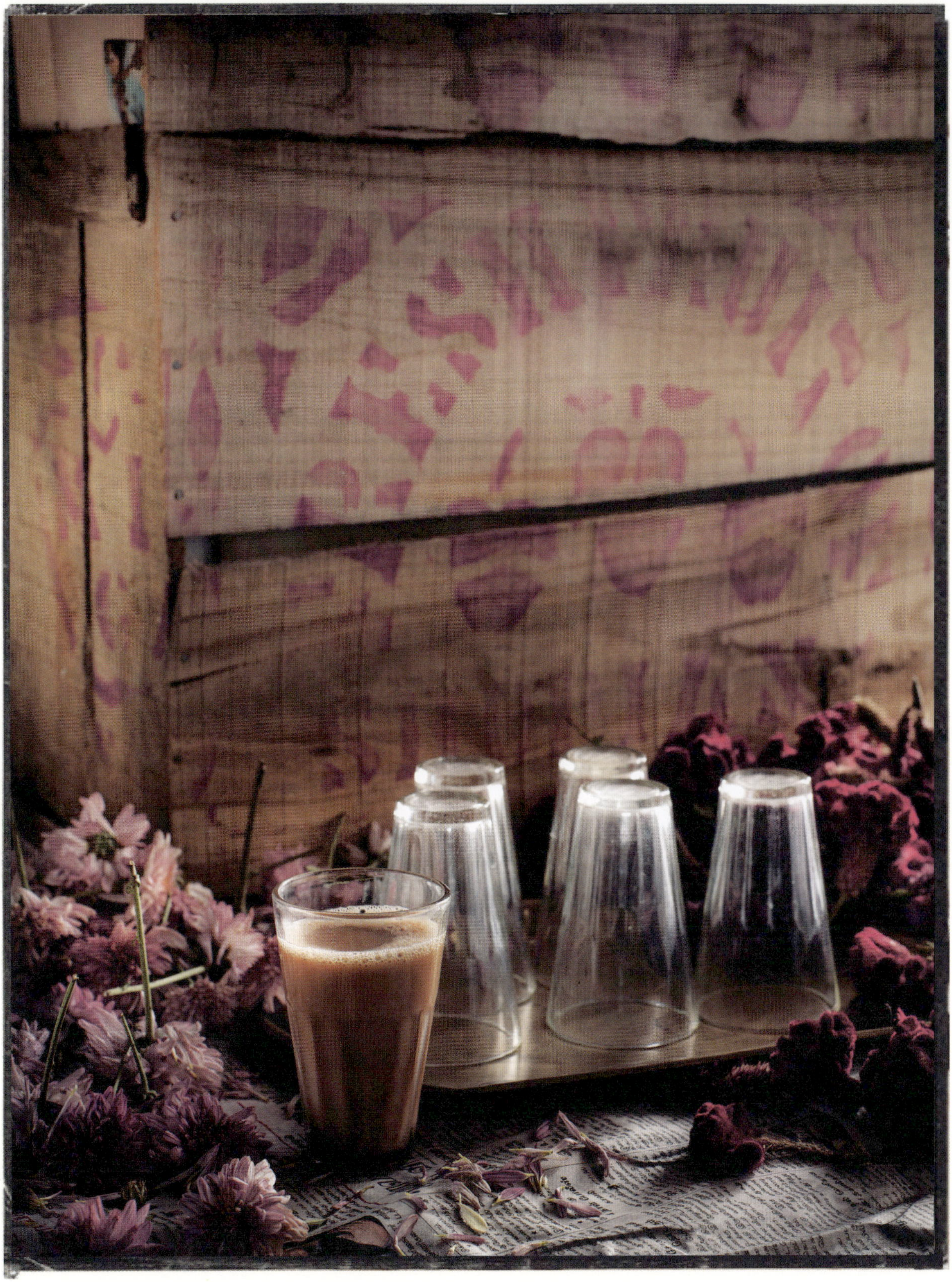

LA RÉUNION
ILE DE LA RÉUNION
ILE BOURBON

LOCATION: EAST OF MADAGASCAR, SOUTHWEST OF MAURITIUS

THE FRANCE OF THE INDIAN OCEAN

LANGUAGE: FRENCH & RÉUNION CREOLE

PRODUCES: SUGAR CANE, RUM, VANILLA, LENTILS, FLOWERS, VETIVER

ACTIVE VOLCANO: PITON DE LA FOURNAISE

*FRENCH OVERSEAS
DEPARTMENT &
REGION*

LA RÉUNION

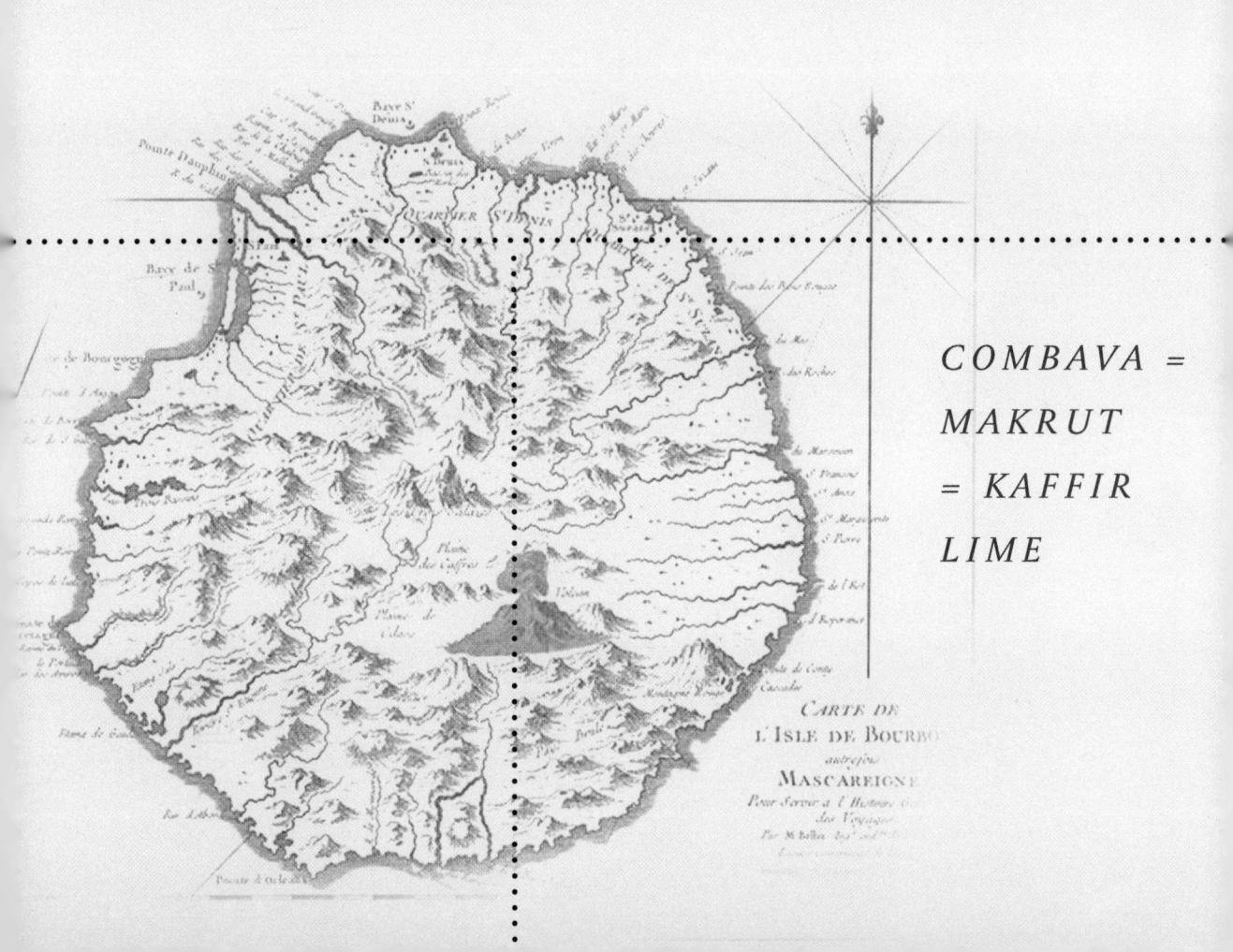

*COMBAVA =
MAKRUT
= KAFFIR
LIME*

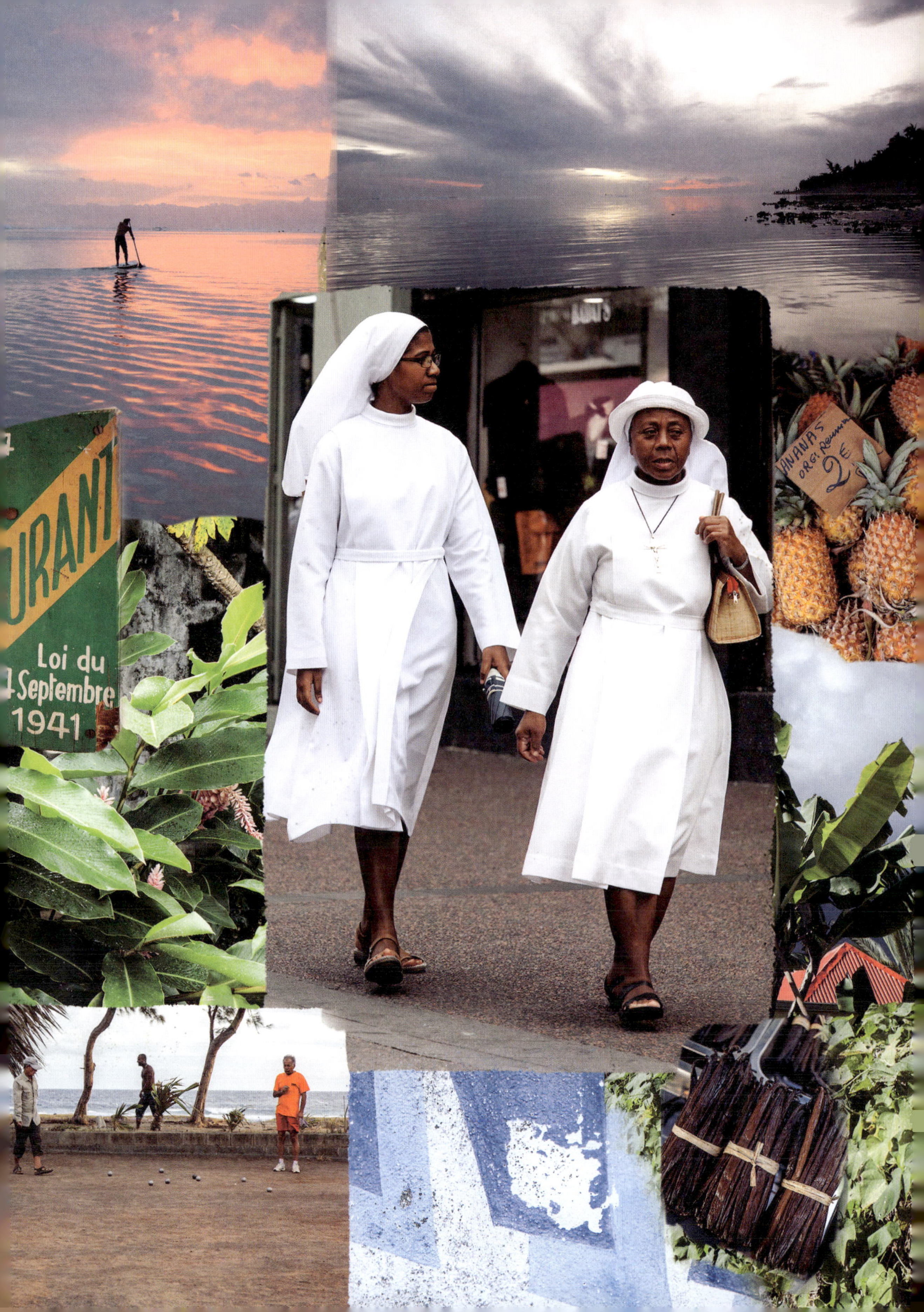
URANT
Loi du
Septembre
1941
ANANAS
2€

LA RÉUNION

I AM WOKEN BY THE BIRDS IN LA RÉUNION.

THE DAYS HAVE MOMENTS OF DRIZZLE AND SUN BEATING DOWN ON OUR BACKS, EVEN IN THESE COOLER MONTHS.

EACH DAY ENDS WITH AN EXTRAORDINARY SUNSET.

I had heard about this natural paradise, places nestled between dramatic mountain peaks, with volcanoes and oceans all around. Scatterings of diverse people descended from the days of slavery and colonialism, mixed in with exotic fruits and trees. A beautiful melange of African, Indian, Malagasy, European, French, Chinese and more.

The French claimed this previously uninhabited island in the Indian Ocean in 1642 and named it Île Bourbon. Colonization began a couple of decades later, when the French East India Company sent a small group of settlers to the island.

At first it was little more than a trading post, but with the first coffee plantations and the growing demand for coffee in Europe, full colonial life was firmly established. The planting of grains, cottons and spices followed with workers for the plantations brought in from Africa, India and China.

In 1810, during the Napoleonic Wars, the British claimed Réunion as well as neighbouring Mauritius, Rodrigues and the Seychelles, but five years later Réunion was returned to the French. Under the brief occupation of the British, sugarcane was introduced to the island, soon becoming its main source of wealth. Vanilla plantations followed and began flourishing.

. . . .

We drive up through mountain roads, almost into the clouds. I don't think we can get much higher than this. The landscape flattens out, and then we see the jaggedy tops again, draped with cloud. From the very top of the mountain, not even Mauritius is visible – it is too far away.

This is a blend of exotic Alps and King Kong. We swirl on towards the ancient, extinct volcano with its open crater in the middle – like a switched-off oven on the moon. There must be a million species of flowers and trees out here amongst the gorges, valleys and waterfalls, many of them seemingly untouched by a human hand.

We stop at a local fruit market. Bibasse, zatte, jackfruit, mangoes, sapate, lychees, small and sweet Victoria pineapples, passion fruit, palm hearts and papayas – along with chillies, cloves, pink peppercorns and rum.

Driving down from the heights we pass joggers, bikers and hikers through undulating fields of swaying sugarcane, vanilla plantations and temples. We stop at a lookout point and climb onto the lava rocks to see the souffleur – holes like Swiss cheese created in the rocks, where waves flush in, gain momentum and flush out again with an impressive splash. We had a real spectacle that day with a rainbow arching all the way through and a storm brewing in the gentle jungle all around. A couple of surfers waited and I watched the rain tumbling wildly into the Indian Ocean, then turn into a calm understated drizzle.

This is Réunion. A union of people from everywhere, blended with vanilla, sugar and rum. I had many questions. Then I met Michel who said he could introduce me to a few ladies who would have the answers. We walked into a small room and I looked around. Like many of the people from La Réunion it is impossible to pinpoint their exact origins. Fatma is Indian with an Australian grandfather. Tahera is of mixed Indian heritage. Catherine, from the metropole, has been here forever, she said. Marie, dark and dressed in turquoise from head to toe, and Micheline, a singer. They say that when the Indians were brought in, they came for the work, but also for the gout d'aventure. Many of them stayed – and here are all these people now.

One by one, Fatma was calling more people in, to describe their speciality to me. Bonbons piment, rougail de saucisse, morue, coco punch, samosas and tamarind chutney. Before long, the room was jammed with a collection of ladies and origins.

A small and sudden festival of women exchanging recipes and details. Tahera sat, like a wise judge, listening hard, offering nods of encouragement at regular intervals as the size of tomatoes was described and the details of ginger, garlic and piment to be crushed in a mortar with a little salt dispensed.

I was almost expecting a fire to be lit outside at any minute and a few chickens put to grill as we carried on. This was a splendid opportunity for me to see the Creoles at work. I could only imagine the outcome, had they been called to contribute to a picnic with family or friends – the kind of casseroles they would arrive with and the amounts of enthusiasm.

When it was time to go, I left with scatterings of papers, advice and a basket of combava that Michel had raked down from a tree in his garden. And recipes that are such a wonderful mixture of things. The cuisine here is like one of those parties where everyone brings a pot to put on the table. And all of it stayed – together becoming the traditional cuisine of the island.

I left Réunion, my suitcase filled with vanilla, Michel's combava, vetiver, goyavier, dark and intense sugars, caramels, tamarind. Never mind the flowers and fruits that I had to leave behind. When I opened my suitcase at home – no-one would have known if I was a cook or a parfumeur.

MOULES AU COMBAVA

The combava (makrut) has such an incredible flavour. Serve with baguette or fries.

Serves 3

1.5kg (3¼lb) mussels
1 tablespoon vegetable oil
50g (2oz) sliced spring onion (scallion), white and green part
250ml (1 cup) cream
a pinch of finely chopped hot green chilli
1 generous teaspoon finely grated makrut lime zest
freshly ground black pepper

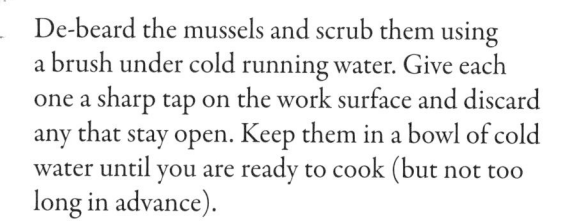

De-beard the mussels and scrub them using a brush under cold running water. Give each one a sharp tap on the work surface and discard any that stay open. Keep them in a bowl of cold water until you are ready to cook (but not too long in advance).

Heat the oil in a small pan. Add the spring onion and sauté gently for a couple of minutes until softened. Add the cream and let it bubble up for a moment. Add the chilli and lime zest and simmer gently for a minute, but don't let it thicken. Take off the heat and set aside to infuse.

Put the mussels into a large cooking pot, cover with a tight-fitting lid and cook over a high heat until they all open up. Give those that are closed a second chance, but then discard them if they don't open.

Pour the mussel juices from the pot into a jug, holding the mussels back with the lid. Add the cream sauce to the mussels with just a couple of tablespoons of the mussel broth and heat through quickly, mixing through to mingle the flavours as it heats.

Add a good grinding of black pepper, and serve at once, with a spoon for the sauce.

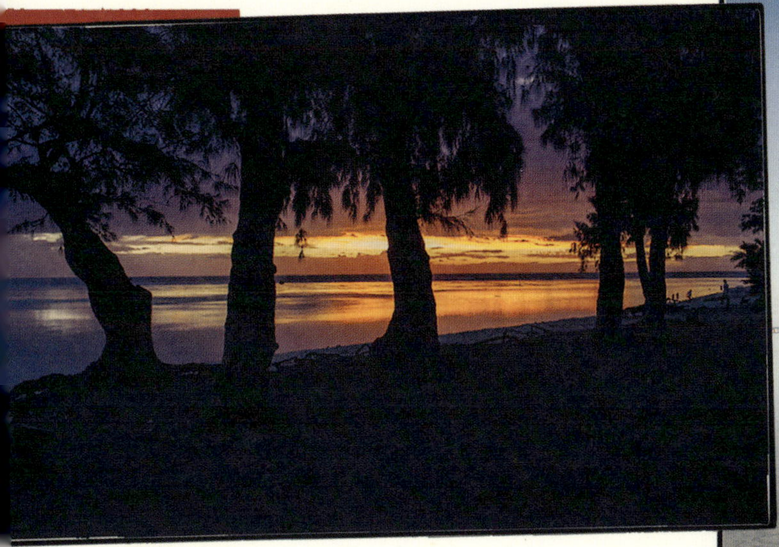

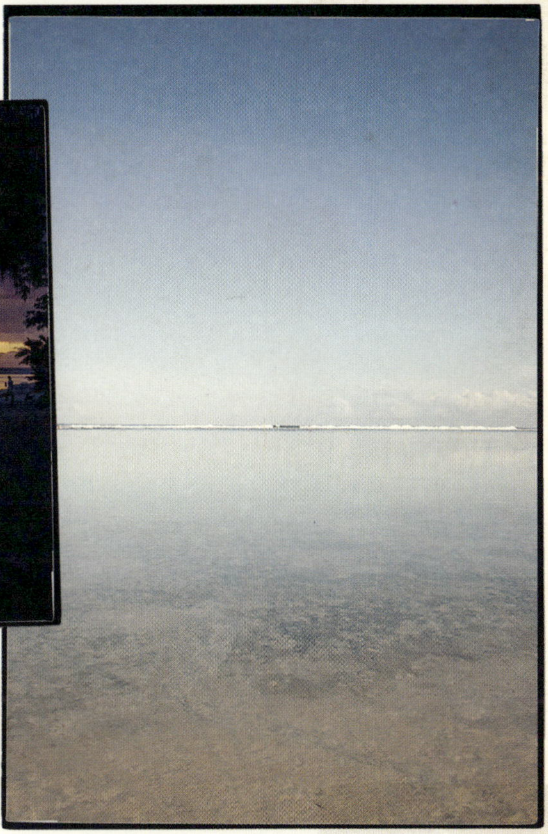

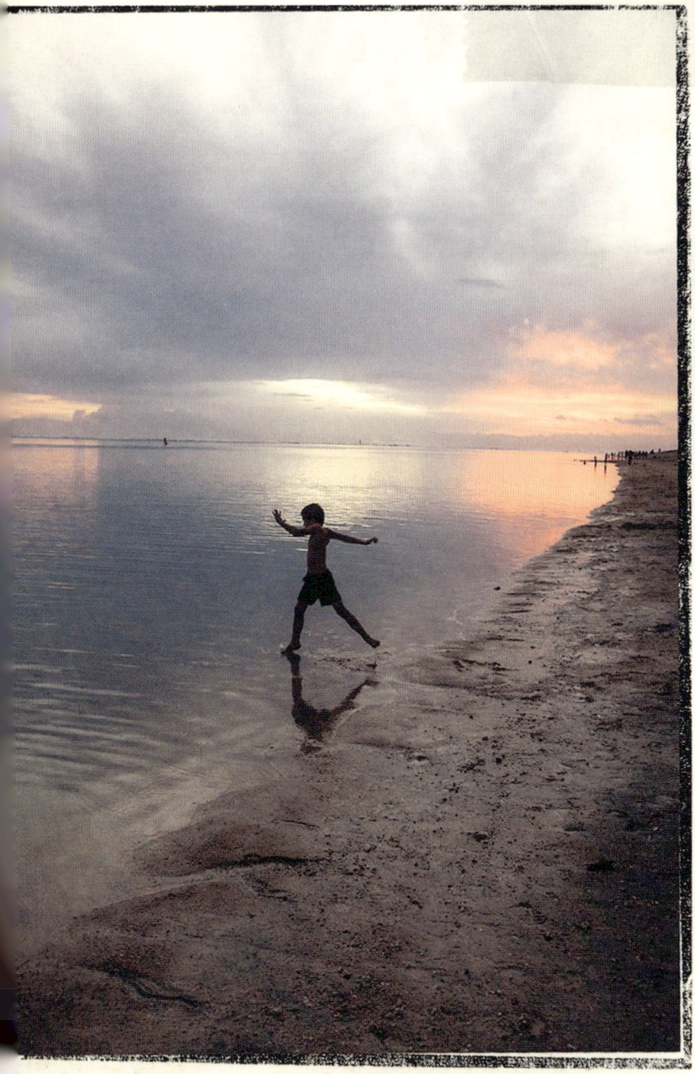

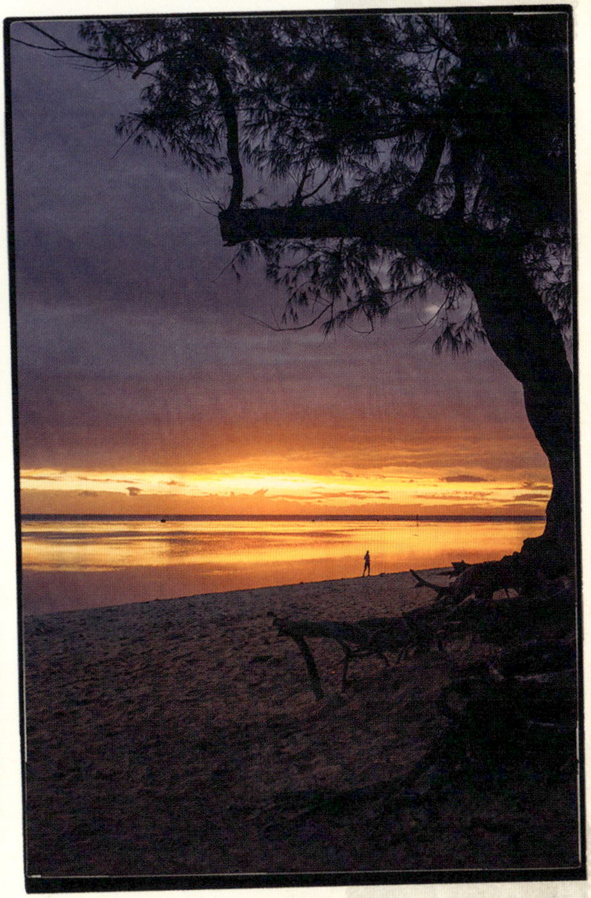

BONBONS PIMENT

These are generally served as an apéritif or snack. You can use other types of bean, or chickpeas, in place of the dried butter beans (called pois du Cap in Réunion). Add as much fresh chilli as you like, for heat. Good with pâte de tamarin vert (page 210) or a squeeze of lime juice.

Makes about 40

500g (18oz) dried butter (lima) beans, soaked overnight in cold water
100g (3½oz) spring onions (scallions), white and green part, chopped
a large handful coriander (cilantro) leaves, chopped
a large handful parsley leaves, chopped
1 teaspoon ground turmeric
1 teaspoon ground cumin
1 teaspoon salt
2 or 3 (or according to taste) small fresh chillies, roughly chopped
4cm (1½in) piece of peeled ginger, roughly chopped
vegetable oil, for frying
coarse salt and freshly ground black pepper

Drain the beans in a colander, slip off their skins and discard. Put the beans in a food processor and pulse to a smooth paste. Transfer to a bowl and add the spring onions, coriander, parsley, turmeric, cumin, salt and pepper.

With a pestle and mortar, pound the chillies and ginger with a pinch of coarse salt until pulpy. Add to the beans and mix well to combine.

Wet your hands or rub them with a little oil. Take a chunk of the mixture (just under 30g/1oz), roll into a ball and flatten slightly to a patty about 5cm (2in) in diameter. (To follow tradition, you can make a hole in the centre with your finger.) Repeat with the rest of the mixture.

Pour about a 1cm (⅜in) depth of oil into a frying pan and place over a medium heat. Line a couple of plates with paper towels. Fry the bonbons in batches until golden on all sides. As each batch is cooked, remove to the lined plate to drain.

Best eaten warm, with a cocktail, on the beach.

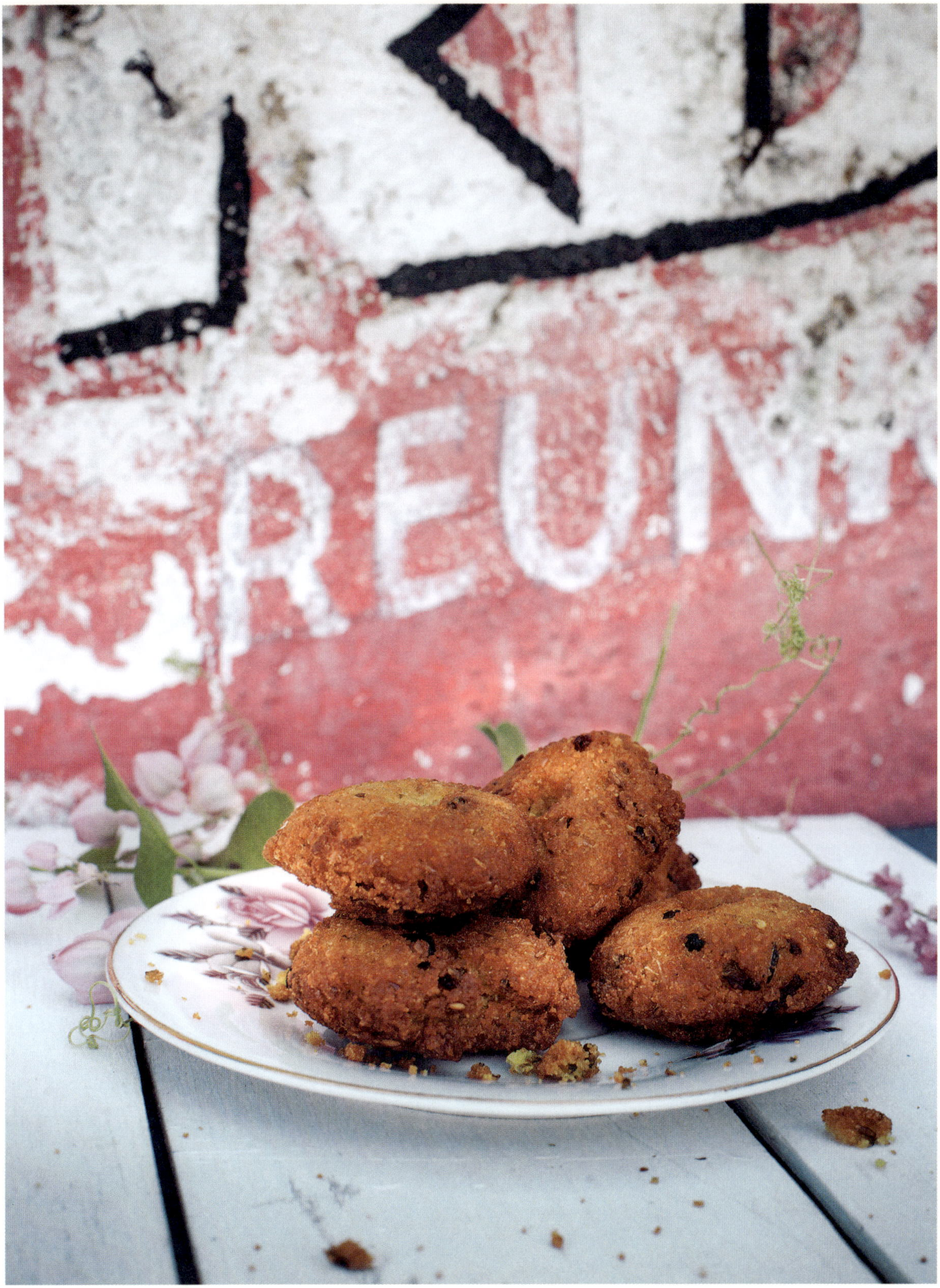
REUN

SAMOSAS AU THON

These are everywhere, served as an apéritif or snack with a variety of savoury fillings and even sweet ones like pineapple. This recipe comes from Tahera – a lovely cook, originally from India, who likes to serve them with a tamarind chutney. She often makes her own pastry but using ready-made, as in this recipe, makes it very easy. You can freeze these samosas once they are shaped, in a single layer without touching each other. Once frozen, transfer them to freezer bags.

Makes over 50

225g (8oz) drained tinned tuna in brine
125g (4½oz) spring onions (scallions), white and green part, finely chopped
a handful coriander (cilantro) leaves, chopped
2 garlic cloves, roughly chopped
5cm (2in) piece of peeled ginger, roughly chopped
2 small green chillies, finely chopped
1 teaspoon finely grated makrut lime zest
½ teaspoon ground turmeric
½ teaspoon salt
2½ tablespoons plain (all-purpose) flour
about 15 sheets of spring roll pastry, 20cm (8in) square
vegetable oil, for frying
tamarind chutney (page 210), to serve

Put the tuna in a bowl and mash it with a potato masher. Add the spring onions and coriander.

With a pestle and mortar, pound the garlic, ginger and chillies to a pulp and add to the bowl. Add the lime zest, turmeric and salt. Mix well using the potato masher or your hands to combine into a compact mix.

Mix the flour to a paste with about 2½ tablespoons water. Work with one spring roll pastry sheet at a time, keeping the others covered with a slightly damp cloth to prevent them drying out. Cut the sheet into 5cm (2in) strips.

Starting at one end of a strip, fold the end over to make a triangle. Fold this up to make a second layer of triangle. Then fold across again to make a third triangle layer, keeping the open side loosely open. Fill this pocket with a scant teaspoon of filling (or 2 big pinches as it will be easier with your fingers). Continue folding the triangle to seal in the filling, making sure the edges are sealed (your technique will improve as you go). Using a pastry brush, dab a little flour paste on the last flap of pastry to seal the samosa closed.

Place the samosas on a tray as they are shaped. They can be kept in the fridge for an hour or two at this stage, covered with plastic wrap or frozen.

Heat about a 1cm (⅜in) depth of oil in a deep frying pan. When hot, add as many samosas as will fit in one layer and fry until golden on both sides. Remove with tongs or a slotted spoon to a plate lined with paper towels; keep warm. Repeat to cook the rest of the samosas. Serve warm, as they are or with tamarind chutney.

BOUCHONS

These pork dumplings stem from the Chinese influence in La Réunion. They are good served with a hot sweet chilli sauce and soy sauce. You can steam, boil or deep-fry them to serve.

Makes about 40

For the bouchon (won ton) pastry
250g (2 cups) plain (all-purpose) flour
about ½ teaspoon sea salt
1 egg
cornflour (cornstarch), for dusting

For the filling
2 teaspoons sesame oil
500g (18oz) finely minced (ground) pork
1 heaped teaspoon pounded ginger
2 garlic cloves, peeled and crushed
1 teaspoon grated makrut lime zest
2 tablespoons soy sauce
1 tablespoon chopped coriander (cilantro)
20g (¾oz) trimmed spring onion (scallion), finely chopped

To serve
sweet chilli sauce
soy sauce

To make the pastry, combine the flour and salt in a bowl. In a cup, beat the egg with 125ml (½ cup) water, then gradually mix into the flour, using a fork. Work to a loose dough that holds together.

Tip onto a surface lightly dusted with cornflour and knead well until very smooth and elastic, about 7–8 minutes. Shape into a ball, dust with cornflour and cover with a damp cloth. Set aside to rest for 30–45 minutes.

Divide the dough into 4 pieces. Roll out each piece to a 25cm (10in) square, about 1mm (¹⁄₁₆in) thick. Leave to settle for 5 or so minutes, then using a ruler and a sharp knife, slice into 9 squares, each 8cm (3¼in). Trim the edges. Gather the trimmings and roll a tenth square. Stack the squares in piles, dusting in between each wrapper with cornflour to prevent them sticking. You can use them straight away, or wrap well in plastic wrap and refrigerate for up to 24 hours, or freeze for up to 3 months.

For the filling, put all the ingredients into a bowl and mix well. Take teaspoonfuls of the mix (each about 15g/½oz) and roll into small balls. Refrigerate, covered, for a few hours.

To shape the bouchons, put a ball of filling in the centre of a wrapper, then bring the 4 corners up and crimp together over the filling, pressing lightly to seal. If there is a lot of excess at the top, trim it away. Repeat to shape the rest.

Cook the bouchons in a steamer for about 15 minutes, or simmer in plenty of salted water for 4–5 minutes (or deep-fry in hot oil, in batches, for a few minutes until golden). Serve the bouchons hot, with sweet chilli sauce and a soy sauce for dipping.

SWEET CHILLI SAUCE

Put about 3 tablespoons chilli powder, 400g (2 cups) sugar, 500ml (2 cups) rice wine vinegar, 6 crushed garlic cloves, 1 teaspoon grated ginger and 2 teaspoons salt in a pan and bring to a gentle boil. Simmer for 15 minutes or until thickened slightly. Let cool, then pass through a sieve (keep the solids in a jar and use as a jam) and pour into a sterilized jar or bottle. Seal and store in a cool dark place or in the fridge.

LA REUNION

CHUTNEY DE TAMARIN

I love the sourness of tamarind. This chutney can be served on the side of any meal, and is perfect with samosas. Depending on how hot your chilli is, and how hot you like things, add just a little here, as the food you serve it with is likely to be spicy.

Makes about 250ml (1 cup)

125g (4½oz) tamarind pulp
2cm (¾in) piece of peeled ginger, roughly chopped
about ½ small hot green chilli, roughly chopped
juice of ½ lemon
3 tablespoons light brown cane sugar
coarse salt

Put the tamarind pulp into a pan with 375ml (1½ cups) water, bring to the boil and simmer for a few minutes, mashing into the tamarind with a wooden spoon to soften it. Strain into a clean pan, pressing the pulp through the sieve with the spoon to force as much through as possible. Discard the fibres and seeds left in the sieve.

Using a pestle and mortar, pound the ginger and chilli to a pulp with a little coarse salt. Add to the tamarind along with the lemon juice and sugar. Simmer for a few minutes. It may seem liquid but will thicken slightly as it cools, but if you like it thicker then leave it on the heat for a little longer.

Taste and adjust the seasoning if necessary. Keep in a sealed jar in the fridge.

PÂTE DE TAMARIN VERT

If you are able to find some young, green tamarind then you should make this, as it is delicious. You can add a little chopped chilli and crushed ginger, or simply leave it plain. It adds a wonderful sourness to your plate.

Peel and roughly slice some fresh green tamarind, put into a food processor and pulse until it is in small bits. Scrape into a bowl and mix in a little vegetable oil and some salt to taste. If you won't be eating it immediately, cover the paste with a layer of oil and store in the fridge.

PÂTE DE PIMENTS

This is on every table in Réunion, always served on the side so you can add more heat to your plate. Remove the seeds or leave them in for more fiery heat, as you prefer. I like to use a mix of half red and half green chillies.

equal quantities of small red and green chillies
salt
vegetable oil
crushed ginger, grated makrut lime zest,
    chopped garlic (if you like)

Finely chop the chillies, or pound with a pestle and mortar. Transfer to a sealable jar, add a little salt, and ginger, lime zest and garlic, if using. Cover the surface with a thin layer of oil. Put the lid on and store in the fridge. Make sure it is always covered with oil for storing.

PUNCH DE COCO

This is Micheline's wonderful cooling rum punch. Adjust the quantities to suit your own taste.

Put 250ml (1 cup) coconut milk into a small jug. Split ¼ vanilla pod lengthways and scrape out the seeds using the tip of a teaspoon into the jug. Toss in the piece of vanilla pod too. Add about 1½ tablespoons light cane sugar, stirring well to dissolve. Cover and chill.

When ready to serve, stir in about 75ml (⅓ cup) rum. Now taste. You may need a little more sugar or rum. Put plenty of crushed ice into 2 large cocktail glasses and pour on the punch.

LA REUNION

RHUM ARRANGÉ MAISON

In Réunion, everyone seems to have their own recipe for this. I was offered it at various times during the day, so it seems any hour is good, as long as you don't visit too many people in a day. This is served as an apéritif or digestif. It is also very nice sprinkled over fruit salad, ice cream, or in a cake. Here are a few ideas.

750ml (25fl oz) white rum bottles

Passion fruit
pulp of 5 passion fruits
about 2 tablespoons cane sugar

Lychee
about 10 peeled, fresh lychees, stoned
about 1½ tablespoons cane sugar
1 vanilla pod, split lengthways

Rum and Raisin
a large handful raisins
about 2 tablespoons cane sugar
1 vanilla pod, split lengthways
a pared strip of makrut (or regular lime) zest

Jean Hugue Lebeau's Orange
2–3 sliced oranges
about 3 tablespoons cane sugar or honey
1 vanilla pod, split lengthways

Goyavier
a handful each whole and halved goyaviers (strawberry guavas)
2–3 tablespoons cane sugar
1 vanilla pod, split lengthways

Strawberry and Vanilla
300g (10½oz) strawberries, some halved
1 vanilla pod, split lengthways
2 tablespoons brown sugar

Combava (makrut)
3 small makrut limes, well rinsed
2 makrut lime leaves
1 vanilla pod, split lengthways
3 tablespoons brown sugar

Spiced
3cm (1¼in) piece of peeled ginger
2 tablespoons cane sugar
1 vanilla pod, split lengthways
1 lemongrass stalk, halved
1 cinnamon stick
1 star anise
4 makrut lime leaves
a long, pared strip of makrut lime zest

For each flavour, add the ingredients to a separate bottle of white rum (you may have to remove some to make room), or in a sealable bottle with a wide opening. The amount of sugar you add is a matter of personal taste, and you can add more once you have tasted it.

Some ingredients will sink, so turn the bottle upside down regularly, and shake from time to time to dissolve any sugar crystals. Make sure the ingredients remain covered. Leave in a cool, dark place to mature for a few months. Either leave the ingredients in, or strain and keep as a clear, syrupy liquid.

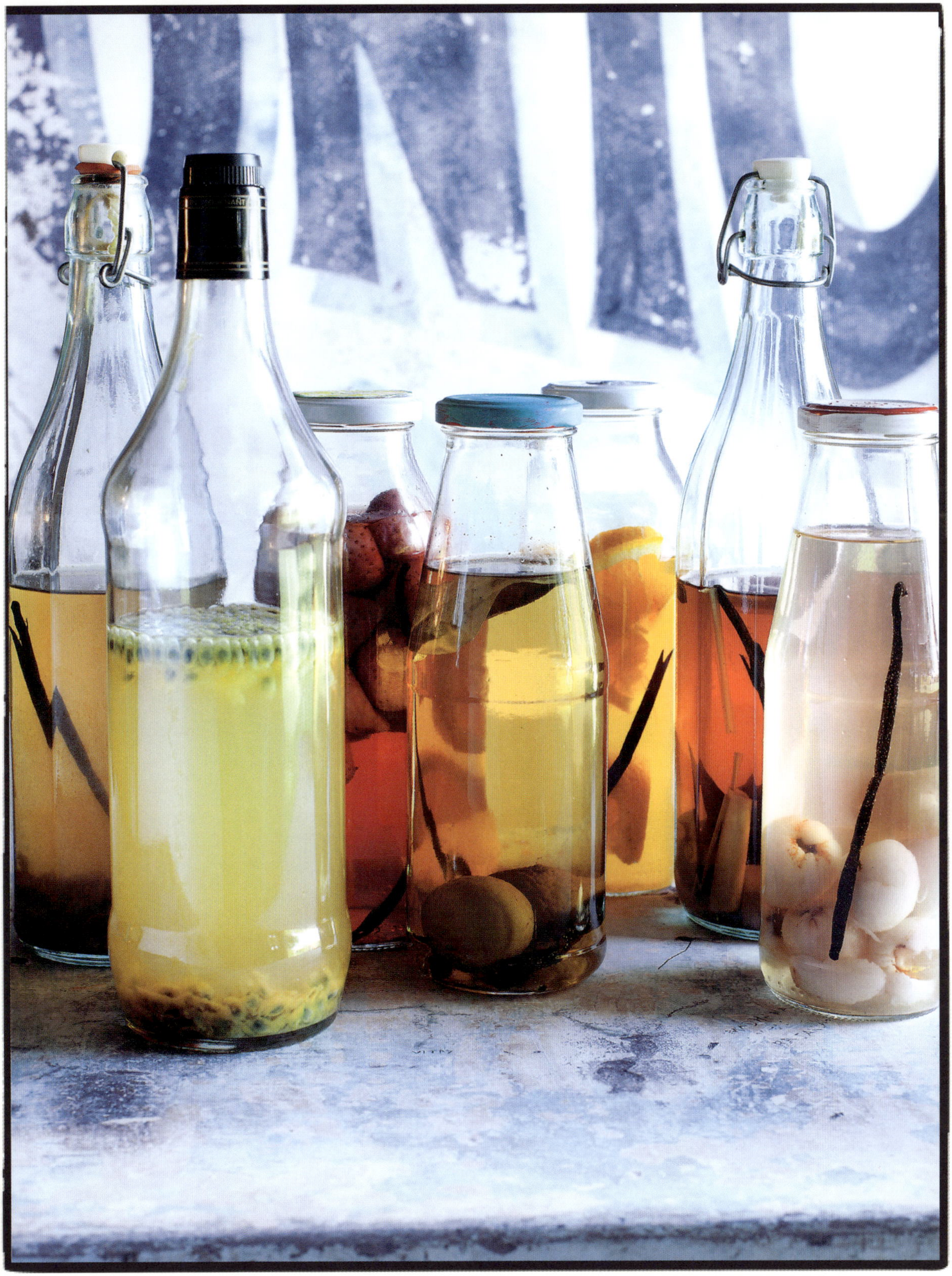

ROUGAIL

Rougail can either refer to a main dish or just to spicy side accompaniments or relishes, such as cucumber, tomato, crushed peanut or green mango – often served together. Often very hot! Make your rougail as hot as you like, but on a Réunion table there is almost always a dish of pâte de piments (page 211) so you can add heat to suit your personal taste. Choose a selection of these relishes to serve, to suit the dish.

ROUGAIL TOMATE

Many cooks add a little oil and vinegar to their rougail, but I like this one plain to keep it fresh.

Makes about 1½ cups

300g (10½oz) ripe tomatoes, cut into small chunks
½ small (60g/2oz) red onion, chopped
½ teaspoon finely grated makrut lime zest
2cm (¾in) piece of peeled ginger, roughly chopped
2 small, hot green chillies, deseeded and roughly chopped
coarse salt

Put the tomatoes, onion and lime zest in a small bowl. With a pestle and mortar, pound the ginger and chillies to a paste with a little coarse salt. Add to the tomatoes, season with salt and turn through well to mix the flavours. Serve freshly made, with any cari or grilled dish.

ROUGAIL CITRON

Lemon is a wonderful relish to serve with many dishes. Make it as fiery as you like: in Réunion, 5 or 6 chillies would be normal.

Makes about 1½ cups

3 lemons, well scrubbed
2cm (¾in) piece of peeled ginger, roughly chopped
2 small hot red chillies, or to taste, finely chopped
3 pinches of ground turmeric
2 teaspoons chopped spring onion (scallion), green part only
½ teaspoon salt
2–3 teaspoons vegetable oil

Cut the lemons into 2–3mm (⅛in) slices. Halve each, then cut each half into 3 triangles, removing the pips. With a pestle and mortar, pound the ginger to a pulp.

Put lemon slices and pulped ginger into a bowl and add the remaining ingredients. Turn through to combine.

Cover with plastic wrap and leave for the lemon skin to soften for at least 2–3 hours.

ROUGAIL MANGUE VERTE

Makes about 2½ cups

2 small, firm green mangoes, 300g (10½oz) each
1 small red onion, chopped
2 small green hot chillies, finely chopped
40g (1½oz) *gros piments* (small sweet green peppers), deseeded and chopped
about 2 tablespoons vegetable oil
salt

Peel the mangoes and cut the flesh into chunks, removing the stone. Pulse in a food processor until very fine. Transfer to a bowl and add the onion, chilli, gros piments and oil, to moisten. Add some salt and stir through well. Taste and adjust the seasonings before serving.

ROUGAIL CONCOMBRE

Makes about 1 heaped cup

1 large cucumber, about 300g (10½oz)
1 heaped tablespoon chopped spring onion (scallion), green part only
1 heaped tablespoon chopped coriander (cilantro)
2 small hot red chillies, or to taste, finely chopped
¼ lemon, thinly sliced
1 teaspoon lemon juice
2 teaspoons oil
salt and freshly ground black pepper

Peel the cucumber, halve lengthways and scoop out the seeds with a teaspoon. Finely slice the cucumber halves and put into a bowl. Add the spring onion, coriander and chillies. Cut the lemon slices into triangles, removing the pips. Add to the bowl with the lemon juice and oil, season with salt and pepper and mix well.

ROUGAIL GROS PIMENTS

Gros piments are the small sweet green peppers found on the island. Add as many hot chillies as you like.

Makes about 1½ cups

200g (7oz) *gros piments*
½ small red onion, chopped
1 or 2 small hot red chillies, or to taste, finely chopped
¼ lemon
1 tablespoon oil
salt

Cut the peppers in half lengthways and remove the seeds. Slice into chunks. Put into a bowl with the onion and chillies. Finely slice the lemon quarter, then cut each slice into triangles, removing the pips. Add to the bowl with the oil, and season with salt. Leave to mingle for a while before serving.

ROUGAIL OIGNON

Makes about 2 cups

2 small red onions (about 250g/9oz in total), chopped
2 tablespoons chopped parsley
2 tablespoons chopped coriander (cilantro)
2 small red chillies, finely chopped
2 tablespoons oil
juice of ½ lime
salt

Mix all the ingredients together in a bowl, adding salt to taste.

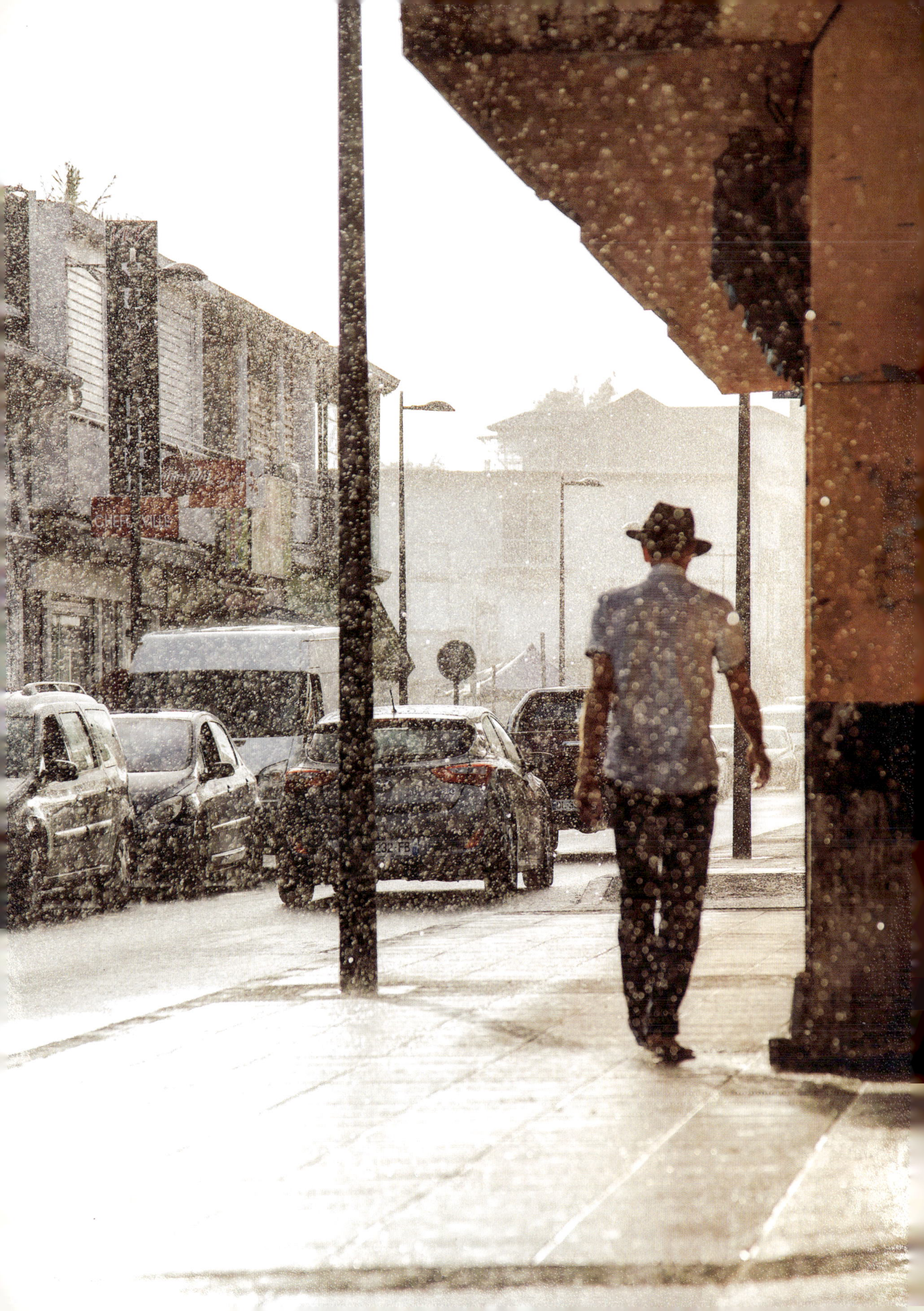

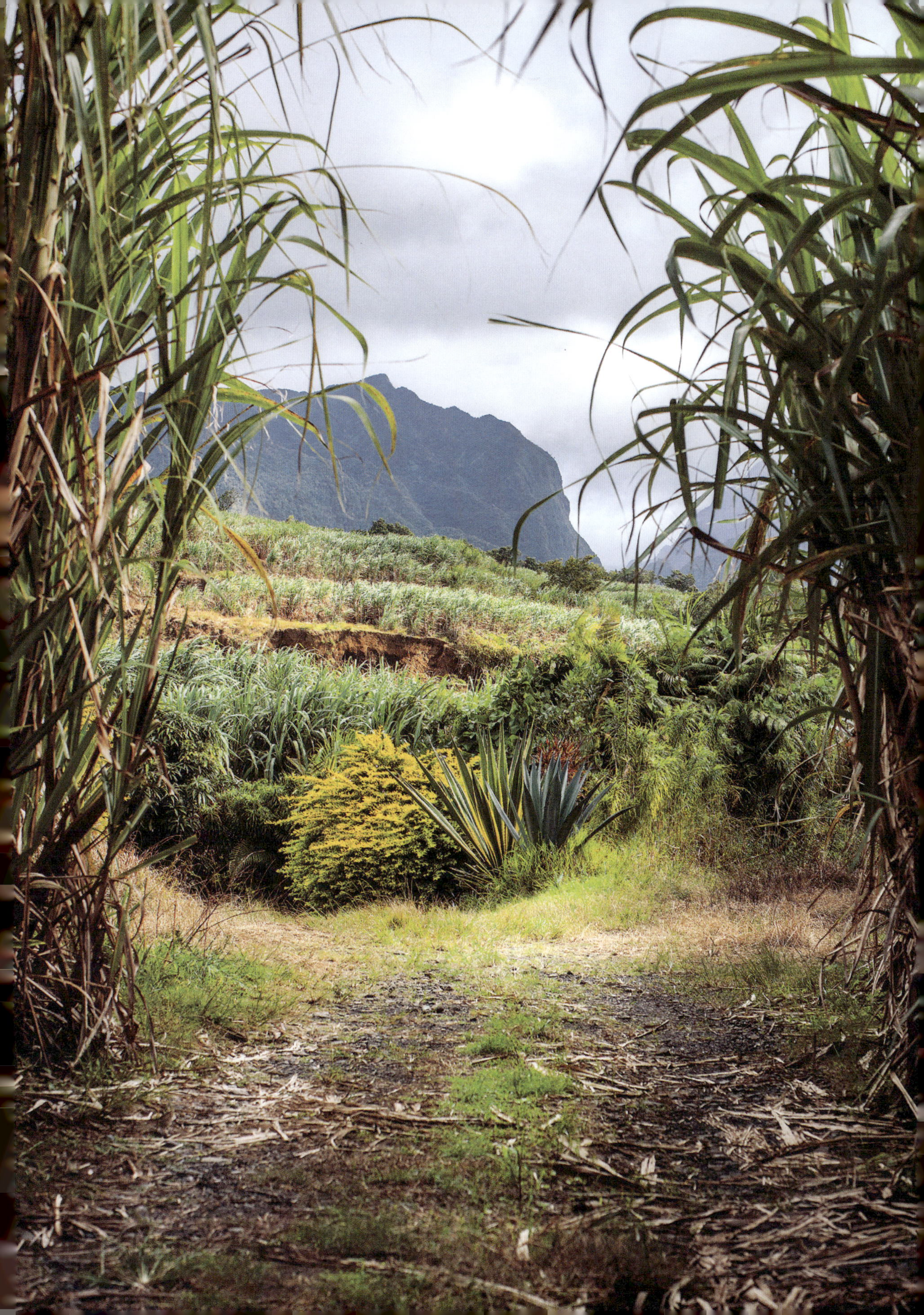

CARI DE THON AU COMBAVA

This Creole curry is best served with rice, beans and a tomato rougail (page 214).
And pâte de piments (page 211) on the side, so you can add extra heat.

Serves 4–5

3 tablespoons oil
1 red onion, chopped
4 garlic cloves, roughly chopped
5cm (2in) piece of peeled ginger, roughly chopped
2 small green chillies, finely chopped
½ teaspoon ground turmeric
4–5 thyme sprigs
a grating of fresh nutmeg
700g (25oz) ripe tomatoes, chopped
700g (1½lb) fresh tuna, in 2.5cm (1in) slice
1 teaspoon finely grated makrut lime zest
2 tablespoons chopped spring onion (scallion), green part only
salt and freshly ground black pepper

Heat the oil in a non-stick wide pan and sauté the onion until softened and golden. Meanwhile, with a pestle and mortar, pound the garlic and ginger to a pulp with a little coarse salt. Add to the onion along with the chillies, turmeric, thyme and nutmeg. Sauté until it smells good. Add the tomatoes and a little salt. Stir in 125ml (½ cup) water, cover and cook for 12–15 minutes until the tomatoes have collapsed into a thick sauce.

Cut the tuna into blocks of about 5cm (2in). Add to the pan, seasoning the pieces with a little salt and pepper, then add the lime zest. Spoon some of the tomato over the fish, cover and simmer for 5 minutes. Remove the lid and cook for another 5 minutes, or until the tuna is just cooked through and the sauce reduced and thick. Remove from the heat, scatter over the spring onion and leave covered for 5 minutes or so before serving.

LA REUNION

LENTILLES DE CILAOS

A dish of butter beans, haricot beans, coco beans, chickpeas or lentils are always present on the Réunion table. All cooked until soft and creamy. The lentils from Cilaos are really special, due to the volcanic soil. If you are not using Cilaos lentils, you could add about 3 tablespoons cream towards the end of cooking, to soften. Adjust cooking time and liquid according to your lentils.

Serves 6

250g (9oz) small brown lentils
3 tablespoons vegetable oil
2 red onions, chopped
4 garlic cloves, roughly chopped
2 pinches of finely chopped red chilli
2 or 3 pinches of ground cloves
2 or 3 pinches of ground turmeric
a few thyme sprigs
salt and freshly ground black pepper

Soak the lentils in a bowl of cold water for 2–3 hours. Drain then rinse. Put them in a pan with about 1 litre (4 cups) cold water and bring to the boil. Lower the heat, cover and simmer for 15 minutes.

Meanwhile, heat the oil in a non-stick frying pan and sauté the onions until they are nicely golden and sticky. Mash the garlic with a little coarse salt and add to the onions with the chilli, cloves, turmeric and thyme, sautéing for a minute or so more. Scrape into the lentils and add another 125ml (½ cup) water if it seems to need it (this will depend on your lentils).

Simmer, partly covered, for another 15 minutes, or longer if necessary, until the lentils are soft and creamy with just a little liquid left, keeping an eye on it and adding a little more water if needed. Season with salt and pepper towards the end of cooking.

ÎLE DE LA RÉUNION
Les Poissons Pélagiques

POISSON MASSALE EN POÊLE

I serve this lovely, spiced pan-fried fish with vanilla mash (page 222), lentils (page 219), greens and a lemon rougail (page 214).

Serves 4

4 fillets of cod, red snapper or sea bream (each about 180g/6½oz) with skin
2 garlic cloves, roughly chopped
5cm (2in) piece of peeled ginger, roughly chopped
½ teaspoon ground turmeric
2 pinches of ground cloves
1 teaspoon ground coriander
1 teaspoon ground cumin
½ teaspoon ground cardamom
½ teaspoon ground cinnamon
a grating of nutmeg
2 tablespoons vegetable oil
salt and freshly ground black pepper

Put the fish fillets into a dish in a single layer. With a pestle and mortar, pound the garlic and ginger to a pulp with a little coarse salt. Sprinkle over the fish.

Mix all the spices together and scatter over the fish with some salt and pepper. Add the oil and rub everything all over the fish to evenly coat. Cover with plastic wrap and leave in the fridge to marinate for an hour or two.

Heat a wide, non-stick frying pan to very hot. Add the fish skin side down and cook over a medium-high heat until the skin is crusty and golden. Reduce the heat to medium, gently turn the fillets over and cook the other side.

Check that they are cooked through. If not, put the lid on the pan, reduce the heat to low and cook for a minute or so more.

Serve each fillet with a pile of lentils and mash on the side, a dish of greens and lemon rougail.

PURÉE DE PATATE À LA VANILLE BOURBON

Bourbon vanilla pods are wonderfully plump and full of flavour. This mash is lovely served with the fish on page 221 or the sausage rougail on page 228.

Serves 6

310ml (1¼ cups) milk
1½ plump, top quality vanilla pods, halved lengthways
1.3kg (3lb) potatoes
80g (3oz) butter, cubed
salt and freshly ground black pepper

Put the milk and 2 of the vanilla pod halves in a pan and bring to the boil. Simmer gently for a couple of minutes then remove from the heat. Cover and leave to infuse for 30 minutes or so.

Peel the potatoes and put them into a pan of boiling, salted water with the remaining half vanilla pod. Cook until tender then drain well. Pass through a potato mill into a wide bowl, add the butter and beat through until melted.

Using the tip of a pointed teaspoon, scrape the seeds from the vanilla pods into the milk. Toss the pods back in too and heat the milk again until just about boiling. Pour into the potatoes. Add some pepper and check for salt. Beat together well and serve hot.

The vanilla pod was brought from Mexico to Île Bourbon (Réunion) and Mauritius by the French. The bee required for pollination was missing in La Réunion and a young boy developed a method for hand pollination – still used to this day. Vanilla grown on La Réunion is excellent. The pods should always be supple, plump and a deep brown – almost black.

BRÈDES

This is a general term covering the large and impressive pans of greenery served in Réunion. I love the interesting and jungly amounts of green possibilities available at the markets. They sit well next to any dish, a cari, grill, rougail or just about anything. They should be briefly cooked and remain a bit crisp. A very simple dish to make.

Serves 6

800g (1¾lb) green leafy foliage such as from taro or sweet potato, pumpkin leaves, manioc, chouchou, watercress, mafane, mourounque, morelle, parietaria, Chinese cabbage, lastron, soutine, dastron, water spinach
3 tablespoons vegetable oil
100g (3½oz) shallots, chopped
3 garlic cloves, roughly chopped
5cm (2in) piece of peeled ginger, roughly chopped
a small amount of finely chopped red chilli
salt and freshly ground black pepper

Clean and trim the greens according to their type. Cut those with stems into 3–4cm (1¼–1½in) chunks and tear the leaves. Rinse, then drain in a colander.

Heat the oil in a wide pan. Add the shallots and sauté over a medium heat until pale golden. Using a pestle and mortar, pound the garlic and ginger to a pulp with a little coarse salt. Add to the pan along with the chopped chilli, and sauté until it smells good.

Add the greenery (if necessary turning a batch through to wilt before adding the rest). They will have water from their rinse so you shouldn't need extra. Add a dash of salt and some pepper, and mix through. Cook quickly, uncovered, until wilted and tender, but still with some crunch (the cooking time will depend on the type of greens). If they need more cooking then put the lid on. If there is water in the bottom of the pan, sauté a little longer so it evaporates. Adjust the seasoning and serve hot.

LA REUNION

POULET AU MANGUE

I love the flavours of this mango chicken. It's good with a dish of greens, and both tomato and onion rougails (pages 214 and 215).

Serves 4

3 tablespoons oil
1 chicken, cut into 8 pieces
1 large red onion, chopped
2 garlic cloves, roughly chopped
6cm (2½in) piece of peeled ginger, roughly chopped
2 small chillies, finely chopped
nutmeg for grating
3 pinches of ground cloves
2 large ripe tomatoes, peeled and chopped
1 ripe mango, peeled, stone removed, flesh cut into big chunks
2 tablespoons chopped coriander (cilantro)
salt and freshly ground black pepper

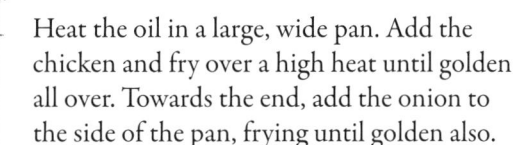

Heat the oil in a large, wide pan. Add the chicken and fry over a high heat until golden all over. Towards the end, add the onion to the side of the pan, frying until golden also.

With a pestle and a mortar, pound the garlic, ginger and chillies to a pulp, then add to the onion in the pan. Season the chicken on all sides with salt and pepper and a good grating of nutmeg. Add the cloves to the onions.

Add the tomatoes to the pan and stir, pushing them down around the chicken so they are touching the bottom of the pan. Cover, lower the heat and simmer gently for about 30 minutes. Check regularly as there is no extra liquid here; I like that the chicken gets a roasty kind of look. Turn the chicken pieces over once or twice.

Add the mango to the pan, gently mixing some through the sauce and also dolloping some here and there over the chicken pieces. Cover and cook over a low heat for 15 minutes, until the chicken is deep golden and tender and the mango is very soft and broken down. If necessary add just a few drops of water to stop anything from sticking and burning, and to make a little sauce. Scatter in the coriander and remove from the heat.

Leave to stand with the lid on for 10 minutes or so before serving warm, or at room temperature.

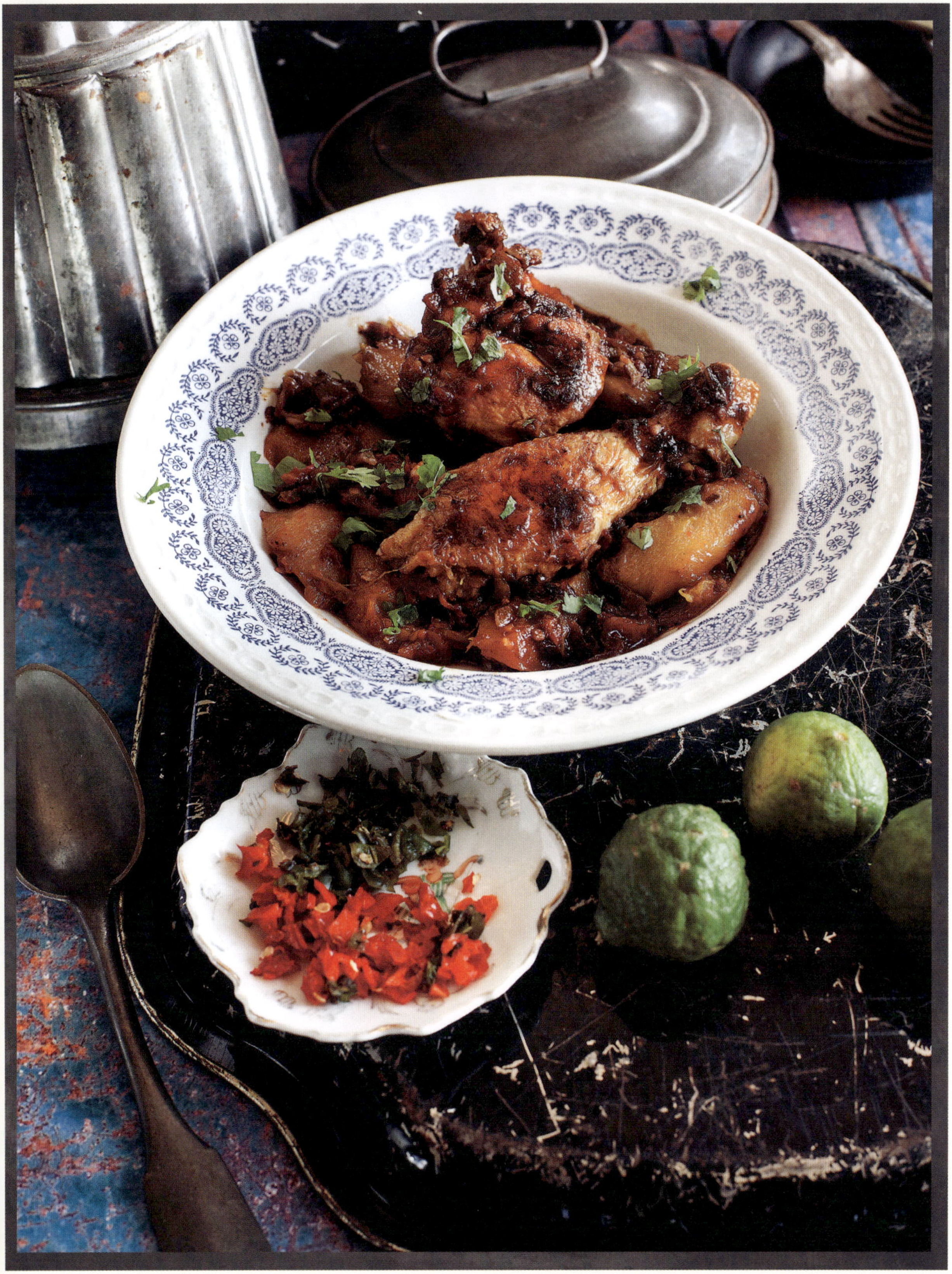

CANARD À LA VANILLE

This is enjoyed with sosso, a semolina-like grain, or rice. Tomato and green mango rougails (pages 214 and 215) go very well here, as do lentils and greens.

Serves 4–6

1 duck, about 1.8kg (4lb)
2–3cm (¾–1¼in) piece of fresh peeled ginger, cut into chunks
4 garlic cloves, peeled and cut into chunks
2 tablespoons vegetable oil
1 red onion, roughly chopped
about ¼ teaspoon grated nutmeg
a few thyme sprigs
2 vanilla pods, split lengthways
½ teaspoon vanilla extract
salt and freshly ground black pepper

Pat the duck dry with paper towels. Using kitchen shears, cut off the neck and fatty tail and discard. Cut off the end section from each wing. Cut the duck from top to bottom through the breast then cut down both sides of the backbone and remove it. You now have 2 halves. Trim away excess fat. Divide each half into 4 pieces; the wing/shoulder, breast, leg and thigh. You may need to use a cleaver to get through the joints. (Or ask your butcher to do all this.) Pierce the skin here and there with the tines of a fork or a sharp, pointed knife, to enable fat to seep out during browning.

With a pestle and mortar, pound the ginger and garlic to a pulp with a little coarse salt. Heat half the oil in a large non-stick pan. Brown the duck pieces well on both sides, making sure that most of the fat under the skin has melted and collected in the pan.

Scatter salt and pepper over the browned pieces and remove to a plate. Pour the fat from the pan (save it for future use).

Add the remaining oil to the pan and sauté the onion over a low heat until a little golden. Add the garlic and ginger pulp and the nutmeg, and stir until it smells good.

Return the duck to the pan and add the thyme, vanilla pods and 250ml (1 cup) water. Lower the heat, cover and simmer for 45 minutes. The liquid will have almost all evaporated and started to look caramelized. Let the duck brown now, turning over so that both sides get well browned, taking care that they don't burn (they will take on a lovely burnished look later on).

Add another 125ml (½ cup) water, cover and cook for another 1–1¼ hours, until the duck is very tender and pulls away from the bone. Keep an eye on the amount of sauce and add more water as needed, about 60ml (¼ cup) at a time, just enough to stop the sauce from sticking and burning. Add the vanilla extract 10 minutes before the end of cooking, turning the duck through the sauce to mix together well.

Remove the duck to a serving plate and keep warm. Add another 60ml (¼ cup) or so of water to the pan and simmer for a couple of minutes, scraping up all the flavourings from the bottom.

Pour the sauce around the sides of the duck pieces and serve at once.

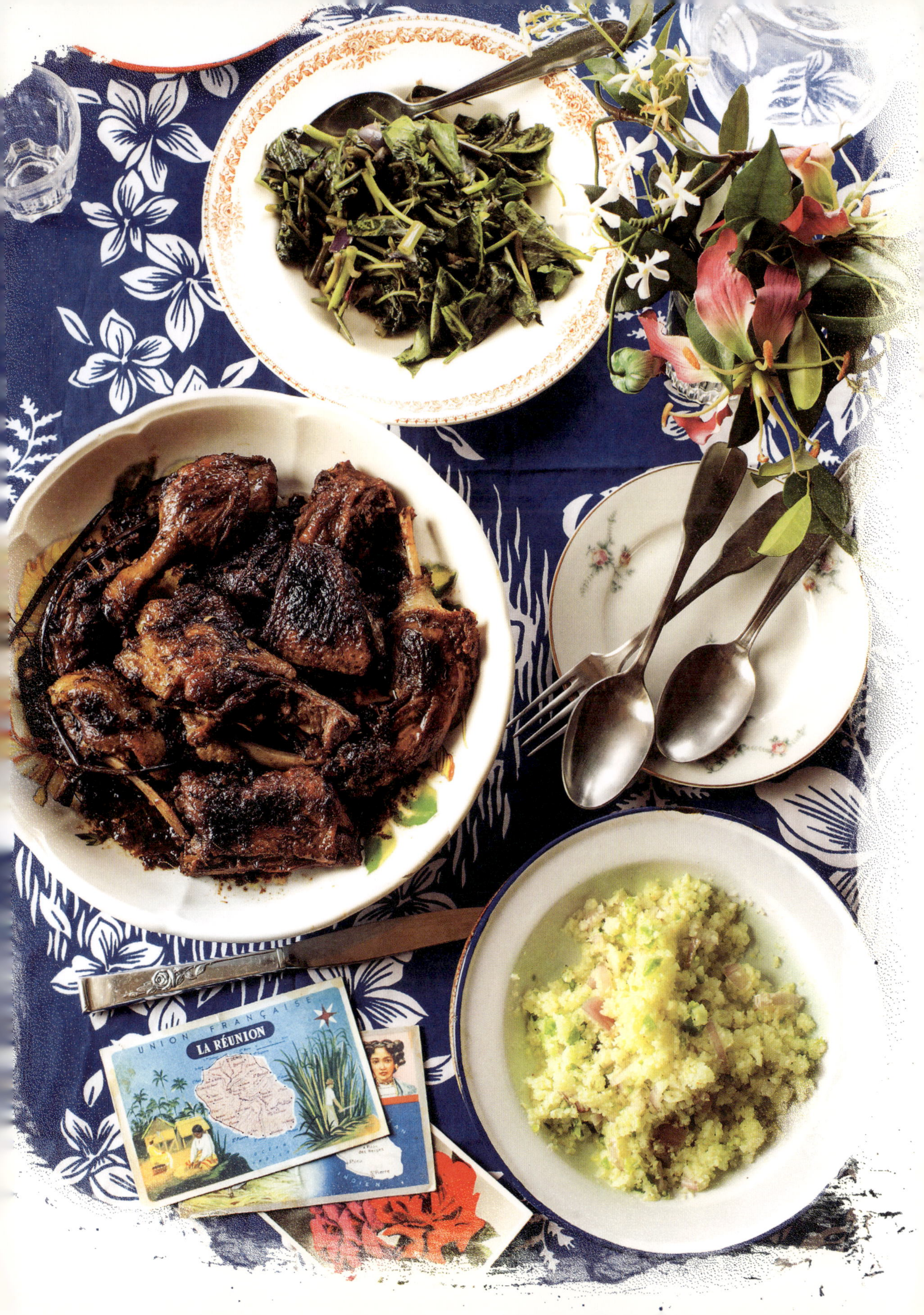
UNION FRANÇAISE
LA RÉUNION

CATHERINE'S ROUGAIL SAUCISSES

You can use smoked sausages, as many do, but Catherine prefers plain. Boudin noir is also sometimes used, but not boiled first. Catherine uses 4–6 chillies, but add them according to your taste. The tomatoes must be lovely and ripe, so use tinned if not. Serve with white rice and butter beans cooked until creamy and a side rougail of your choice. I also like this warm, stuffed into baguette.

Serves 4

8 large pork sausages
2 tablespoons vegetable oil
2 red onions, coarsely chopped
4cm (1½in) piece of peeled ginger, roughly chopped
2 or more small hot green chillies, roughly chopped
about 600g (1¼lb) ripe tomatoes, chopped into chunks
5 or 6 thyme sprigs
3 (about 80g/3oz total) small sweet green peppers, deseeded and cut into chunks
salt and freshly ground black pepper
a handful onion, garlic or chive flowers, to serve

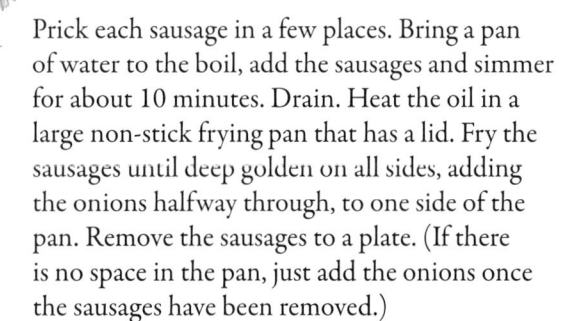

Prick each sausage in a few places. Bring a pan of water to the boil, add the sausages and simmer for about 10 minutes. Drain. Heat the oil in a large non-stick frying pan that has a lid. Fry the sausages until deep golden on all sides, adding the onions halfway through, to one side of the pan. Remove the sausages to a plate. (If there is no space in the pan, just add the onions once the sausages have been removed.)

With a pestle and mortar, pound the ginger and chillies to a pulp with a little coarse salt. When the onions are golden, add the pounded ginger mix to the pan and stir through. Add the tomatoes with a little salt and pepper (your sausages may already be well-seasoned, so not too much). Add the thyme, cover and simmer for 12–15 minutes, until the tomatoes have broken down into a chunky sauce.

Return the browned sausages to the pan and add the green peppers, stirring through. Cover and simmer for another 5 minutes or so, adding just a little water to the pan if it seems dry.

Remove from the heat and leave, covered, for about 10 minutes before serving, scattered with the flowers.

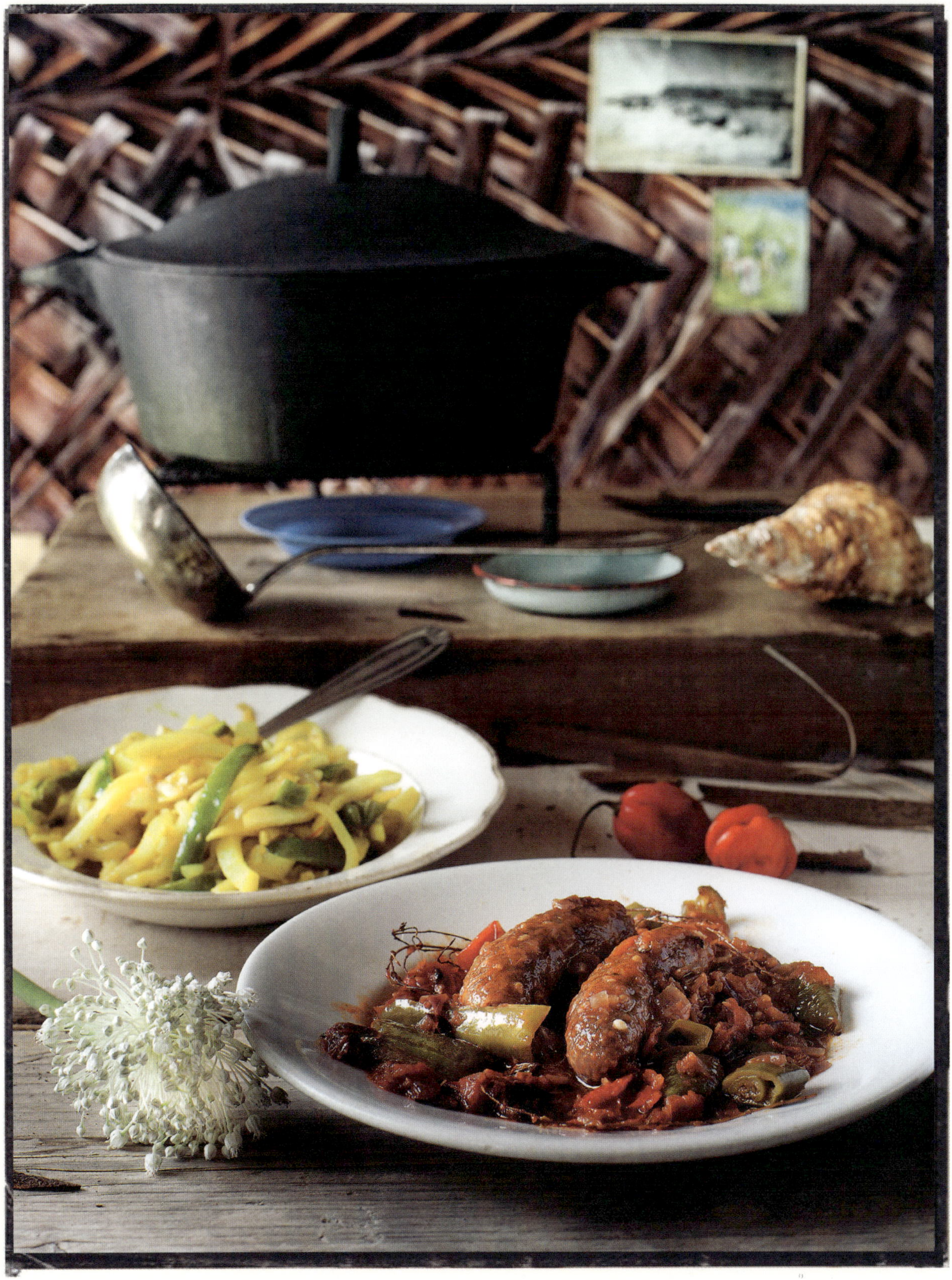

GRATIN DE PAPAYE VERT

You can use any vegetable for this dish. In Réunion I also ate it with palm hearts, which was exceptionally good; pumpkin is often used too.

Serves 6

2 green papayas (about 1kg/2¼lb in total)
1 tablespoon coarse salt
1 tablespoon white vinegar
2 tablespoons oil
1 small purple onion, chopped
2 garlic cloves, roughly chopped
4cm (1½in) piece of peeled ginger, roughly chopped
a small amount of finely chopped red chilli
a few thyme sprigs
salt and freshly ground black pepper

For the béchamel
50g (2oz) butter
40g (heaped ¼ cup) plain (all-purpose) flour
500ml (2 cups) milk
a little nutmeg for grating
about 80g (3oz) Gruyère, grated
1 heaped tablespoon dried breadcrumbs

Peel the papayas, halve them and scoop out the seeds. Cut the flesh into small chunks. Put the papaya into a bowl with the salt and vinegar and add enough cold water to cover. Leave to soak for about an hour.

Heat the oil in a wide pan, add the onion and sauté gently until golden. Using a pestle and mortar, pound the garlic, ginger and chilli to a pulp. Add to the onions and sauté for a minute.

Drain the papaya and add to the pan, turning the chunks through the spices. Add the thyme, season with salt and pepper and pour in 125ml (½ cup) water. Cover and simmer for 25–30 minutes, until tender but not collapsed. Add a little more water if it seems to be dry, but at the end most of the liquid should have been absorbed. Taste for seasoning and remove the thyme. Transfer to a wide gratin dish.

Preheat the oven to 200°C/400°F/Gas 6. Meanwhile, make the béchamel. Melt the butter in a small heavy-based saucepan. Stir the flour in and cook for a minute or so. Gradually add the milk, whisking well. Add salt, pepper and a grating of nutmeg. Cook, stirring, over a low heat until smooth and thickened.

Dollop the sauce evenly over the papaya – it will spread as it bakes. Scatter the cheese evenly over the top, and then sprinkle on the breadcrumbs. Bake for about 20 minutes, until the cheese is melted and golden in places.

ACHARDS DE CHOUCHOU

This is of Indian origin. It is often made from a mixture of carrots, peppers, cabbage, onions and green beans, but I liked this simple chouchou version. Generally, it is served at room temperature as an accompaniment to a meal.

Serves 6

2 chouchou (chayote/christophines/chokos)
3 tablespoons vegetable oil
1 purple onion, chopped
2 garlic cloves, roughly sliced
5cm (2in) piece of ginger, roughly sliced
1–2 small green chillies, finely chopped
¼ teaspoon ground turmeric
2 tablespoons red wine vinegar
60g (2oz) *gros piments* (small sweet green peppers), cut in long strips

Rinse, quarter and peel the chouchou, and cut out the pip. Slice the flesh thinly, then cut the slices into thin strips.

Heat the oil in a large pan and sauté the onions until golden. Using a pestle and mortar, crush the garlic and ginger with a little coarse salt to a pulp. Add to the onions with the chillies and turmeric, and sauté for another minute.

Add the vinegar, let it bubble up then add the chouchou. Season with salt and pepper. Turn through and let it cook for a few minutes until it wilts, but is still a little crisp.

Add the peppers and cook for a minute more, turning everything through. Taste for seasoning before serving.

SALADE DE PALMISTE

Palm hearts must be the artichokes of the tropics. Such a great flavour. I like the luxurious simplicity of this salad as a starter, which is how it was served to me in Réunion, before a meal with spices and several accompaniments. If you cannot get fresh palm hearts, then use tinned, draining them well.

Serves 2–3

250g (9oz) tender inner palm hearts
2 tablespoons vegetable oil
2 tablespoons lemon juice
½ teaspoon Dijon mustard
1 teaspoon chopped shallot
sea salt and freshly ground black pepper

Shave the palm hearts into long thin slices with a vegetable peeler, or slice very thinly. Put into a serving bowl.

In a small bowl, whisk the oil, lemon juice and mustard with a little salt and pepper. Whisk in the shallot. Pour over the palm hearts and taste for seasoning.

GÂTEAU DE PATATE DOUCE

I like this sweet potato cake on its own, but if you want you can dress it up with a fruit coulis, such as papaya on the side, and some whipped cream. This is also very good the next day.

Serves 8–10

1 vanilla pod, split lengthways
750g (26oz) white sweet potatoes, unpeeled
120g (½ cup) butter, cubed, plus extra for greasing
½ teaspoon vanilla extract
120g (½ cup) light brown cane sugar
3 eggs
2 tablespoons rum
60g (½ cup) plain (all-purpose) flour, plus extra for dusting
2 pinches of salt

Using the tip of a pointed teaspoon, scrape the seeds from the vanilla pod into a large bowl.

Put the sweet potatoes in a pan with plenty of water to cover, throw in the scraped out vanilla pod and bring to the boil. Simmer for about 30 minutes, until tender when poked with a skewer. Drain in a colander. Peel when cool enough to handle.

Either cut the sweet potatoes into smaller pieces and mash thoroughly in the bowl with the vanilla, or pass through a potato mill into the bowl. Add the butter and stir through until fully melted. Put the bowl in the fridge and leave uncovered until completely cold.

Preheat the oven to 180°C/350°F/Gas 4. Butter and flour a 22cm (9in) pie dish.

Add the vanilla extract and sugar to the sweet potato and stir to mix. Whisk the eggs in a small bowl until creamy, then remove 2 tablespoons to a cup and keep. Add the rest of the egg with the rum to the sweet potato mixture, and whisk in well. Whisk in the flour and salt, then spoon into the prepared dish, levelling the surface.

Gently brush or dab the surface all over with the reserved beaten egg. Make criss-cross ridges with the tines of a fork on top. Bake for about 1 hour, until set and the surface is golden and glossy. If necessary, cover the top with a piece of foil towards the end so it doesn't get too dark before it is set, and take care so that it doesn't get too dry and ruin the lovely texture.

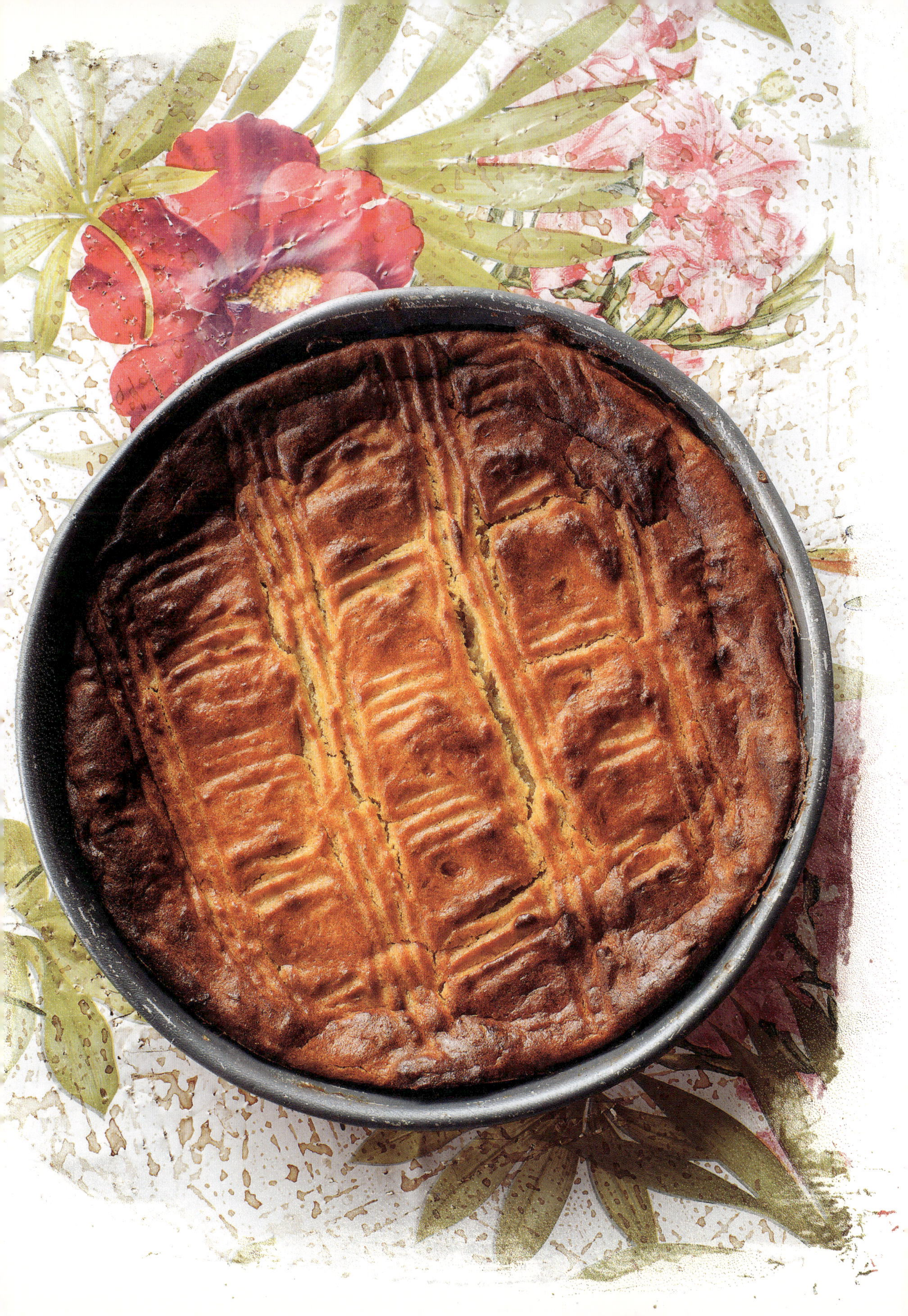

SORBET DE GOYAVIERS

The taste and colour of this sorbet is fresh and beautiful. Nice on its own, or with cream poured over.

Serves 6

570g (1¼lb) ripe goyaviers (strawberry guavas), cut into chunks
120g (scant ⅔ cup) light brown cane sugar

In a food processor, purée the fruit with 250ml (1 cup) water, then strain through a sieve into a saucepan. Stir in the sugar and heat gently to dissolve. Take off the heat and leave to cool, then refrigerate until chilled.

Pour the mixture into an ice-cream machine and churn until set, according to the manufacturer's instructions. Transfer to a suitable container and store in the freezer.

SORBET DE TAMARIN

I love the sharp surprise of tamarind. This sorbet is good served on its own after a spicy meal. Pour over a little cream, if you like.

Serves 4

150g (5oz) tamarind pulp
140g (scant ¾ cup) light brown cane sugar

Put the tamarind in a saucepan and pour on 500ml (2 cups) water. Break it up with a wooden spoon then put over a medium heat and bring to the boil. Simmer for a few minutes, mashing the tamarind with the spoon or a potato masher. Remove from the heat, cover and leave to cool.

Pass the cooled mixture through a fine sieve into a bowl, pressing it to extract as much liquid as possible from the pulp. Put the pulp back into the pan, add 250ml (2 cups) water and bring to the boil. Simmer for a few minutes, again mashing it down with the spoon or potato masher.

Strain into the bowl with the other tamarind liquid and discard the pulp. Pour the contents of the bowl back into the pan and stir in the sugar. Bring up to the boil then simmer for 8–10 minutes, until thickened. Remove from the heat, leave to cool, then chill.

Pour into an ice-cream machine and churn until set, according to the manufacturer's instructions. Transfer to a suitable container and store in the freezer.

FRUIT et léaumes

Gilaos Dégustation
presque Toute gratn
variété le Goût Tradition

CRÈME BRÛLÉE PASSION ET VANILLE

You can make meringues with the egg whites, or freeze them for later use. A kitchen blowtorch is best for the caramelized tops, then you can serve them immediately after browning the sugar.

Serves 6

500ml (2 cups) cream
1 vanilla pod, split lengthways
4 egg yolks
65g (⅓ cup) white sugar
pulp of 2 passion fruits
soft light brown cane sugar, for the tops

Put the cream into a saucepan. Using the tip of a teaspoon, scrape the vanilla seeds from the pod into the cream then add the pod too. Bring to a gentle simmer and cook for a couple of minutes to infuse the flavour. Remove from the heat and let it sit for a few minutes longer.

Preheat the oven to 150°C/300°F/Gas 2. In a wide bowl, whisk the egg yolks and white sugar together until creamy. Gradually whisk in the warm cream, a little at a time to prevent it scrambling. Remove the vanilla pod.

Whisk in the passion fruit pulp and divide between 6 shallow dishes or ramekins. Sit the dishes in a roasting tin and add warm water to come halfway up the dishes. Cook in the oven for about 45–50 minutes, until set and pale golden, rotating the tin halfway through for even cooking. The brûlées will still wobble slightly when you shake them gently, and the cooking time will depend on the depth of the mixture/size of the dishes, so check often.

Remove from the oven and leave to cool, then put in the fridge to chill.

Spoon a little cane sugar over each and smooth it to an even, very thin layer using the back of a teaspoon. If you have one, use a kitchen blowtorch to caramelize the tops, then serve. Alternatively, put the ramekins on a baking sheet under a very hot grill (broiler) until the sugar on top is golden and caramelized, keeping an eye on them as they can suddenly burn. Replace in the fridge to set and cool before serving, as the time under the grill will have heated the custard.

LA RÉUNION

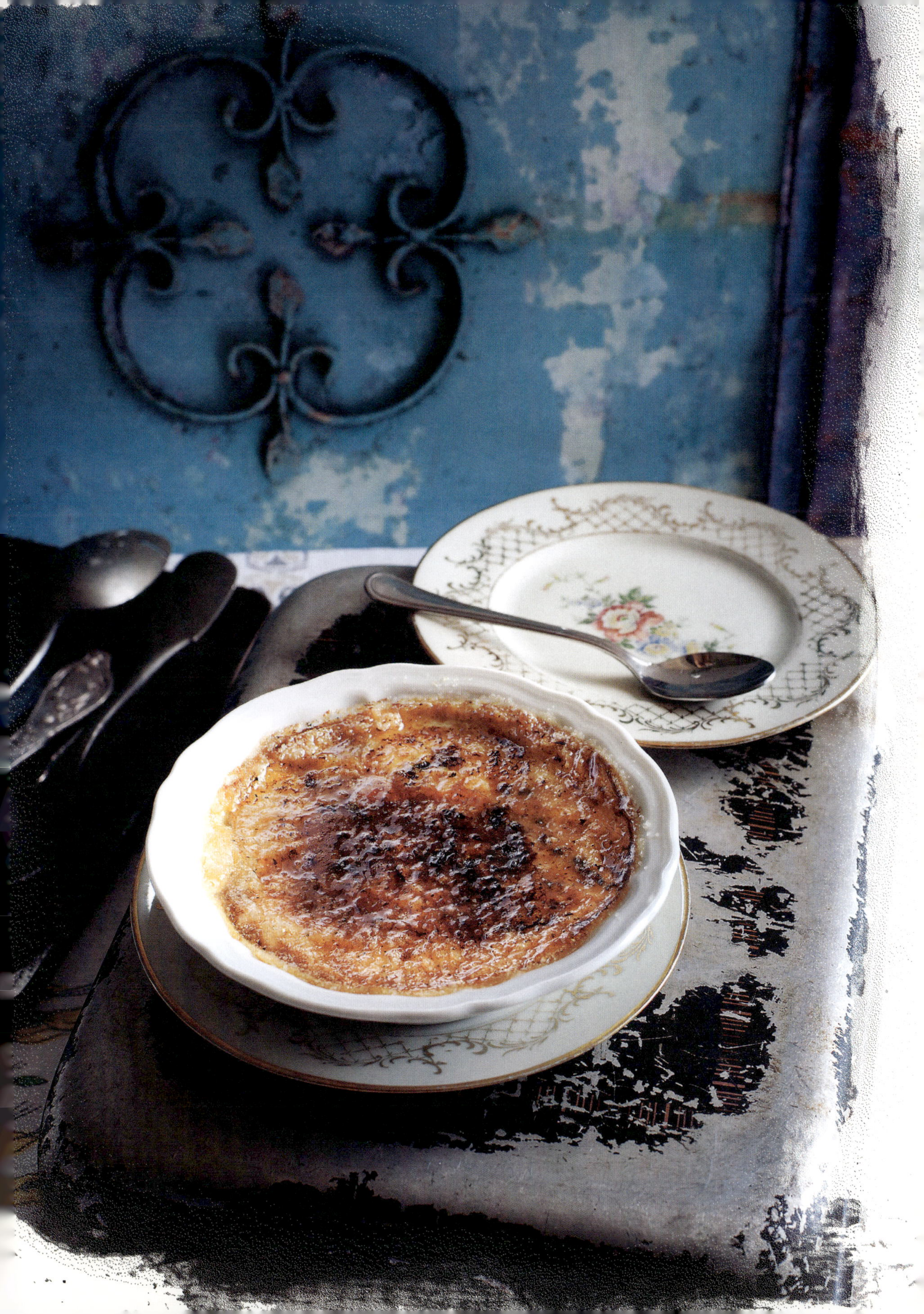

GRATIN DE FRUITS EXOTIQUES

The amounts here are very easy to adjust according to how much fruit you will be using and the type. Just use a good variety. Add more or less rum to suit your taste.

Serves 2

4 lychees, peeled, halved and stoned
1 guava, sliced
3 goyaviers (strawberry guavas)
2 pineapple slices, halved
4 good slices of mango
2 tablespoons cream
2 tablespoons rum, or to taste
4 small blobs of butter
3 tablespoons cane sugar
scant ½ teaspoon ground ginger

Lightly butter 2 shallow ramekin dishes, about 11cm (4¼in) diameter and 3cm (1¼in) deep. Divide the fruit between them.

Splash the cream and rum over each, followed by 2 blobs of butter each. Mix the sugar and ginger together and scatter evenly over the tops.

Preheat the grill (broiler) to hot. Grill until deep golden and charred here and there. Let it cool down just a little before serving.

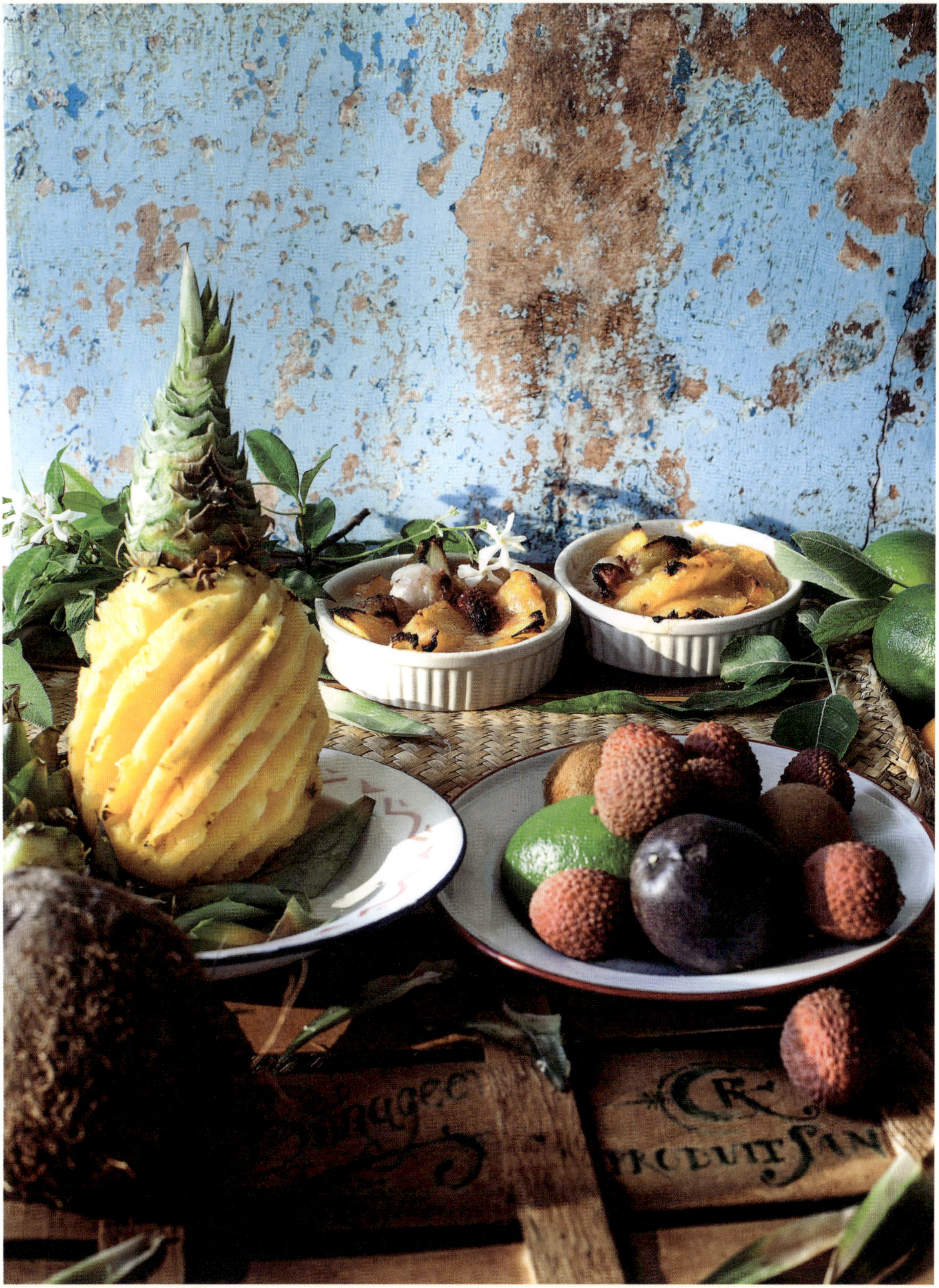

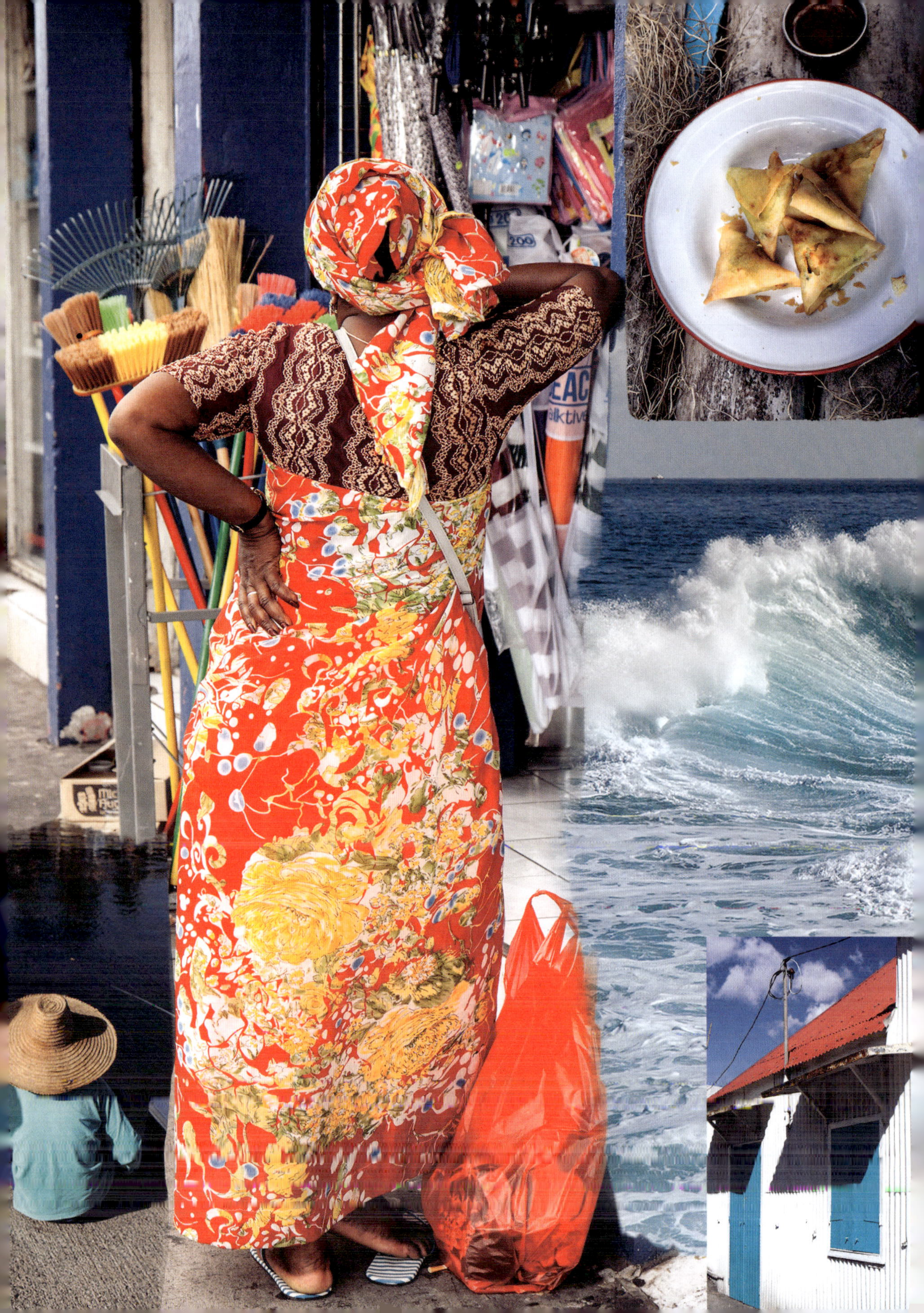

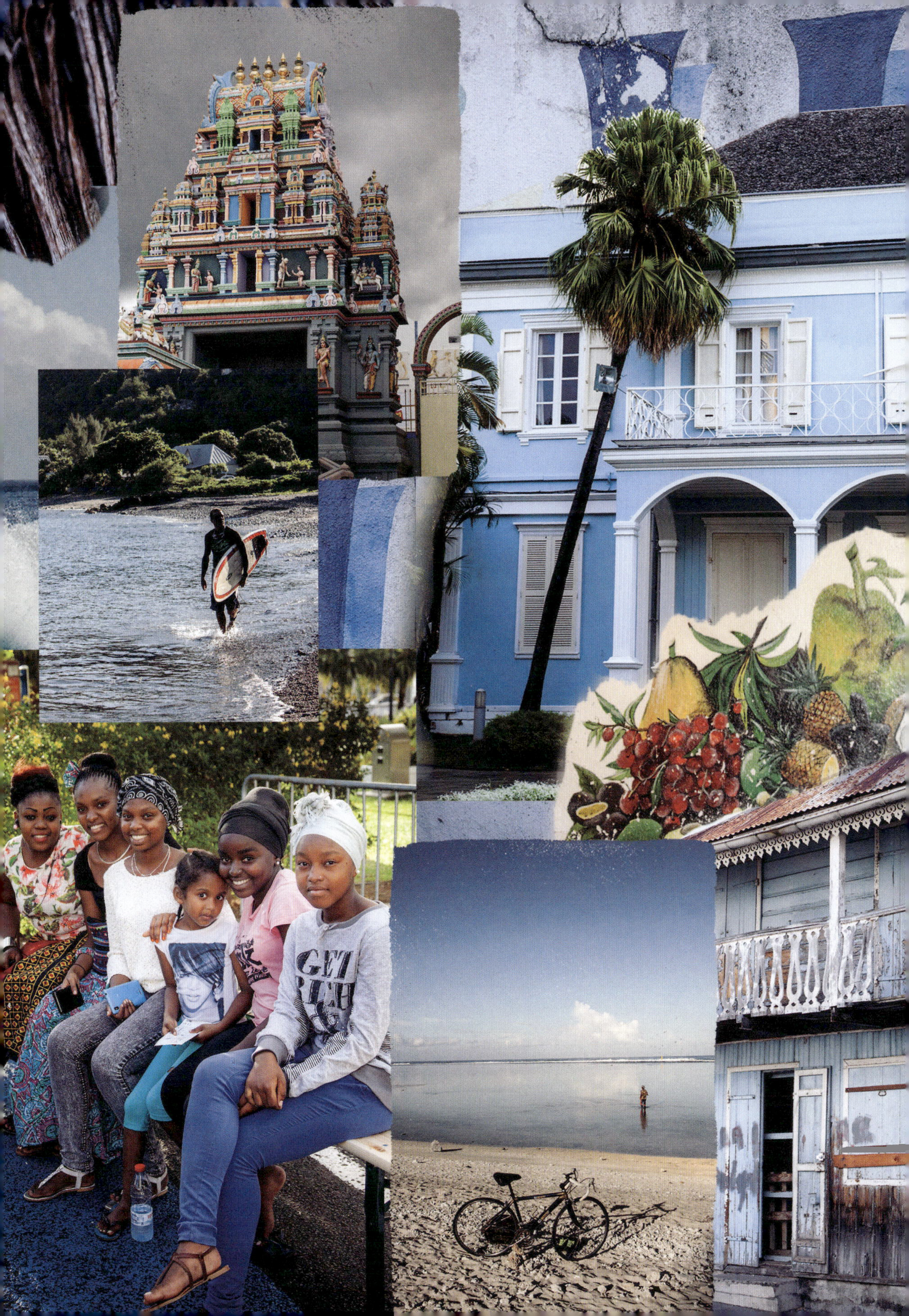

NORMANDY
NORMANDIE

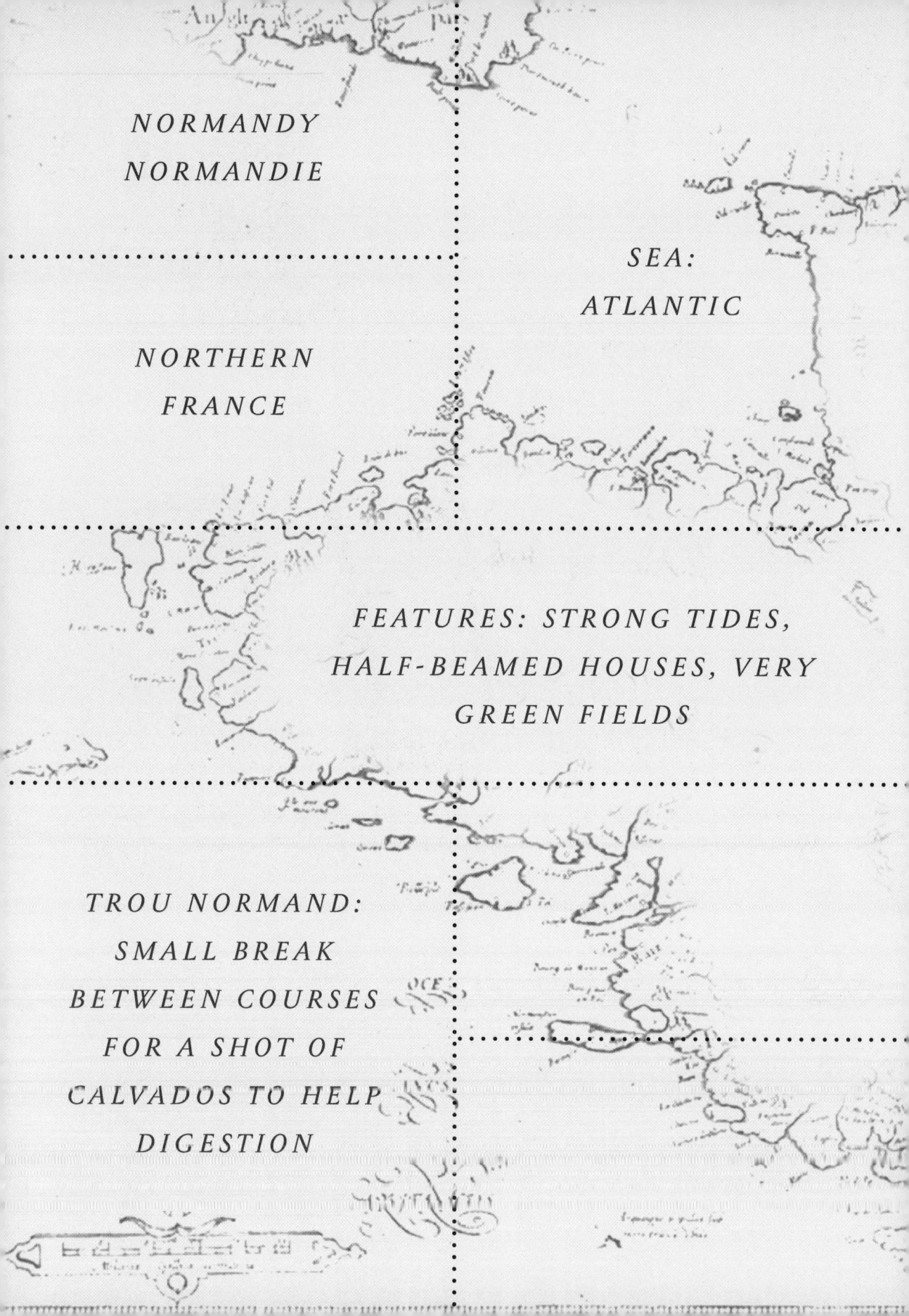

SEA:
ATLANTIC

NORTHERN
FRANCE

FEATURES: STRONG TIDES,
HALF-BEAMED HOUSES, VERY
GREEN FIELDS

TROU NORMAND:
SMALL BREAK
BETWEEN COURSES
FOR A SHOT OF
CALVADOS TO HELP
DIGESTION

NORMANDY

*PRODUCES:
APPLES, CIDER,
CIDER VINEGAR,
OYSTERS, MUSSELS,
BUTTER, CREAM,
CHEESE, BISCUITS,
CALVADOS*

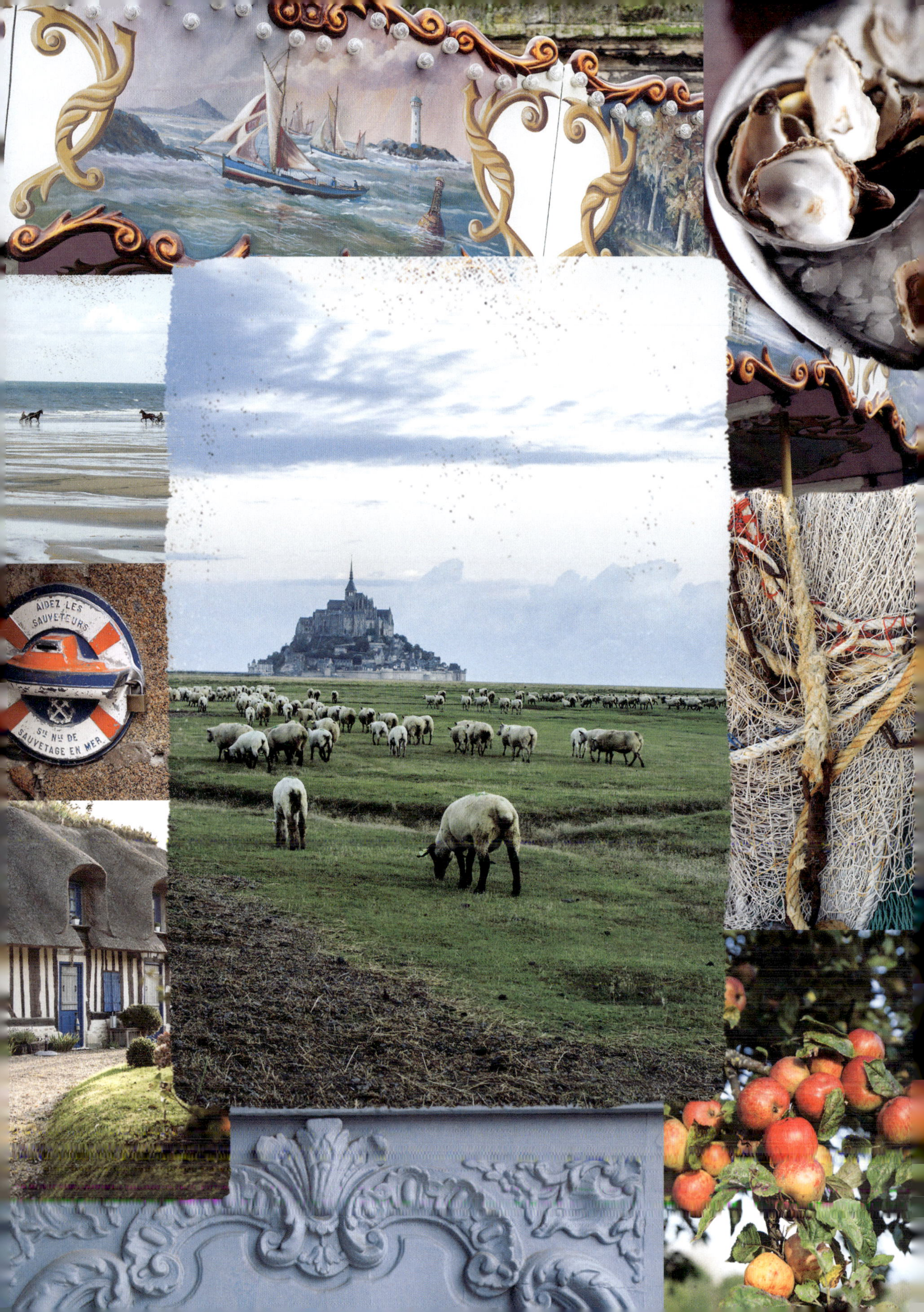
AIDEZ LES SAUVETEURS
Ste Nle DE SAUVETAGE EN MER

NORMANDY

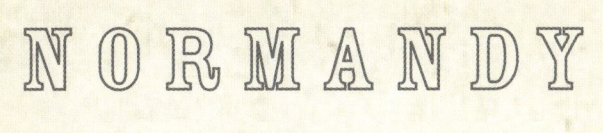

When I arrived in Normandy, the sun was just setting and hung behind the clouds, casting a spectacular light over the apple-green meadows and generally giving a fairy-tale feeling to the countryside and billowing hills.

I continued my journey through the winding country lanes towards the coast and its generous sea views. And the sky and beautiful light kept following – unusual and dramatic – sometimes clear blue and other times storm-cloud grey.

In the seventeenth century, in search of new lands, the French set up colonies across the New World, setting off in ships from the coastal provinces of France, including the Normandy ports of Le Havre and Dieppe. And so began a flourishing trade of sugar, spices, salt cod, furs and other exotic foods and resources – reciprocal influences that can still be seen in the cuisine today.

In 1635, it was Pierre Belain d'Esnambuc of Normandy who claimed Martinique in the West Indies for France; the colonization of Guadeloupe followed. These sugar colonies became a grand source of wealth for the French.

I am told that Normandy is the worldwide capital of boudin noir, which is especially good grilled with apple. It is interesting to see how popular boudin noir is in Guadeloupe – how something so seemingly out of place on a Caribbean island can make so much sense. The sometimes bold and other times more subtle crossing over of ingredients and customs in the places where the French unpacked their pots is lovely to see.

I am drawn to Normandy for its rich, earthy, essential ingredients, like butter, cider and fresh, thick cream. And for the beautiful choice of fresh seafood.

The scenery here is an open menu. Rich pastures studded with dappled cows, plump with milk, cream, butter, caramels and cheeses-to-be. There are goats and lambs grazing in salt meadows and blossoming apple and pear orchards everywhere.

Tacked all along one side is the vast ocean, with its store of luxurious seafood: oysters, mussels, scallops, sole… It is all there for us to see. No secret ingredients. I have never seen such an open book, of what will come from the surroundings to the table.

The hedgerows and carpeted hills give way suddenly to the broad open sea, stretching for miles. One moment you will be sidling past tractors through orchards and pastures, admiring the lush countryside, and the next moment you will find yourself looking out to the unending rippling ocean.

In the narrow cobbled streets, the houses in some of the villages seem perfectly modelled. Like dolls' houses in a theatre set that you could pass a toy train through. Perfect and detailed facades, timber-fronted with many windows and dominant chimneys. Sloping slate-grey roofs peaked with large attics that are, I imagine, filled with many treasures.

The country houses and barns seem much wider. Heavy-structured and sturdier looking. I was almost expecting a small and gentle giant to emerge from one of the farmhouses, rosy-cheeked and carrying a tray of rice pudding for two with cider.

I feel greedy in Normandy. The food is satisfying me on a deep level. Maybe it's the earthy roundedness of the ingredients that feel so well looked-after. The sometimes dramatic weather blows harsh winds through the markets, flapping makeshift awnings about and forcing the vendors to collect their cheeses and rooty vegetables, apples and seafood, and set up stall elsewhere.

I drove through many miles of luminous green, stopping for caramels and cider, all the way up the coast to the edge of the map. Then all along and down the other side, so that I could see it all and breathe in the immense beauty of Normandy and taste all the products that were being so generously offered around me. Wonderful lamb and beef dishes, chicken simmering in cream and apples, and more apples and pears slid into pastries and fermented into bubbly ciders and brandies. Tiers of fresh seafood, raw and poached, served with fluffy mayonnaise and shallot vinaigrettes. Pots of mussels in cidery sauce. There are omelettes, sweet and savoury, and lemon buttery cod and skate. Shallots, leeks, cabbages, cauliflowers and apples everywhere. Sablés, galettes and beignets. An abundant variety of mussels sold in litres. Beyond is a cheese market then rows of patisserie with apple and pear tarts of every size.

The seagulls are everywhere, in flocks circling together and calling each other. No doubt after the easy scraps to be had from the fishmongers and boats. I watched a seagull eating oysters. He took one from a box that had been collected along the pier. And then flew up with it to a good height before dropping the oyster down to shatter the shell a little on the rocks below. He swooped down then to collect his prize.

As I leave Normandy I am craving a mottled, cool, boskoop apple and a piece of creamy camembert. I must be addicted. So I stop at the Panier Vert to buy some apples. And a selection of cheeses to take home with me. And cider and calvados too. And I leave this flurry, this enchanting land behind me.

MOULES AU CIDRE

Small and sweet, mussels are everywhere in Normandy. Serve these with a spoon for the sauce and fries. The fries should be sprinkled with a little salt and dipped into the sauce at the bottom.

Serves 3

1.5kg (3¼lb) mussels
250ml (1 cup) cider
125ml (½ cup) cream
25g (scant 2 tablespoons) butter
50g (scant 1 cup) leeks, thinly sliced, rinsed
40g (1½oz) celery stalks, sliced into roughly 1cm (½in) chunks
1 tablespoon chopped parsley
freshly ground black pepper

De-beard the mussels and scrub them using a brush under cold running water. Give each one a sharp tap on the work surface and discard any that stay open. Keep them in a bowl of cold water until you are ready to cook (but not too long in advance).

Put the cider into a smallish heavy-based pan and simmer vigorously for about 10 minutes so that it reduces by half.

Add the cream to the pan and simmer for another 5 minutes or until it has reduced by about a third to a thick and glossy sauce (you should have about 170ml/⅔ cup).

Meanwhile, melt the butter over a medium heat in a wide, heavy-based pan that has a lid and will hold all your mussels. Add the leeks and celery and sauté for a few minutes, leaving the celery with some crunch.

Add the drained mussels, put the lid on and cook over a high heat until all the mussels have opened. Remove from the heat then discard those that have not opened.

Strain the mussel broth into a jug, holding the mussels back with the help of the saucepan lid and leaving them in the pan. Add about 125ml (½ cup) of the mussel broth to the cider and cream sauce and simmer for a minute.

Pour the sauce over the mussels, give a grind of black pepper, add the parsley and heat through together for a minute, turning through well to mix the mussels with the sauce.

Serve immediately with another grinding of black pepper and a bowl of fries on the side.

KIR NORMAND

A regional version of the classic kir royale that is usually made using white wine, or Champagne. Vary the proportions to suit your personal tastes.

Put 2 teaspoons of crème de cassis in a chilled glass, pour on 125ml (½ cup) dry pear or apple cider and mix with a cocktail spoon. Santé!

CN 260144

BOULANGERIE

LES HUÎTRES ET VINAIGRETTE D'ÉCHALOTE

The oysters in Normandy are truly wonderful. You can walk through a seafront market and eat "Les 6, 9 or la douzaine" oysters, served with shallot vinaigrette, a lemon wedge and black pepper, with brown bread and butter on the side. And a good glass of white wine. Very decent. They may be served as part of a mixed seafood platter with other raw and cooked shellfish and some mayonnaise.

Serves 1 or 2

1 shallot (30g/1oz)
60ml (¼ cup) red wine vinegar
2 tablespoons cider vinegar
50ml (scant ¼ cup) crisp white wine, such as a Muscadet
a dozen oysters, chilled
lemon wedges
salt and freshly ground black pepper

Peel the shallot and cut into tiny dice. Put into a bowl with the red wine vinegar, cider vinegar, white wine and add a little salt and black pepper.

When ready to serve, shuck the oysters: hold a folded cloth in one hand and put the oyster on it. With the other hand, insert the tip of an oyster shucking knife into the hinge of the oyster, between the two shells. Twist the knife firmly to lever the hinge open. Using the knife, remove the top shell and discard.

You can loosen the oyster from the lower shell or, better, let the diners do their own.

Arrange the oysters in their half-shells on a bed of crushed ice or seaweed. Serve with the shallot vinaigrette to spoon over, and lemon wedges and black pepper on the side.

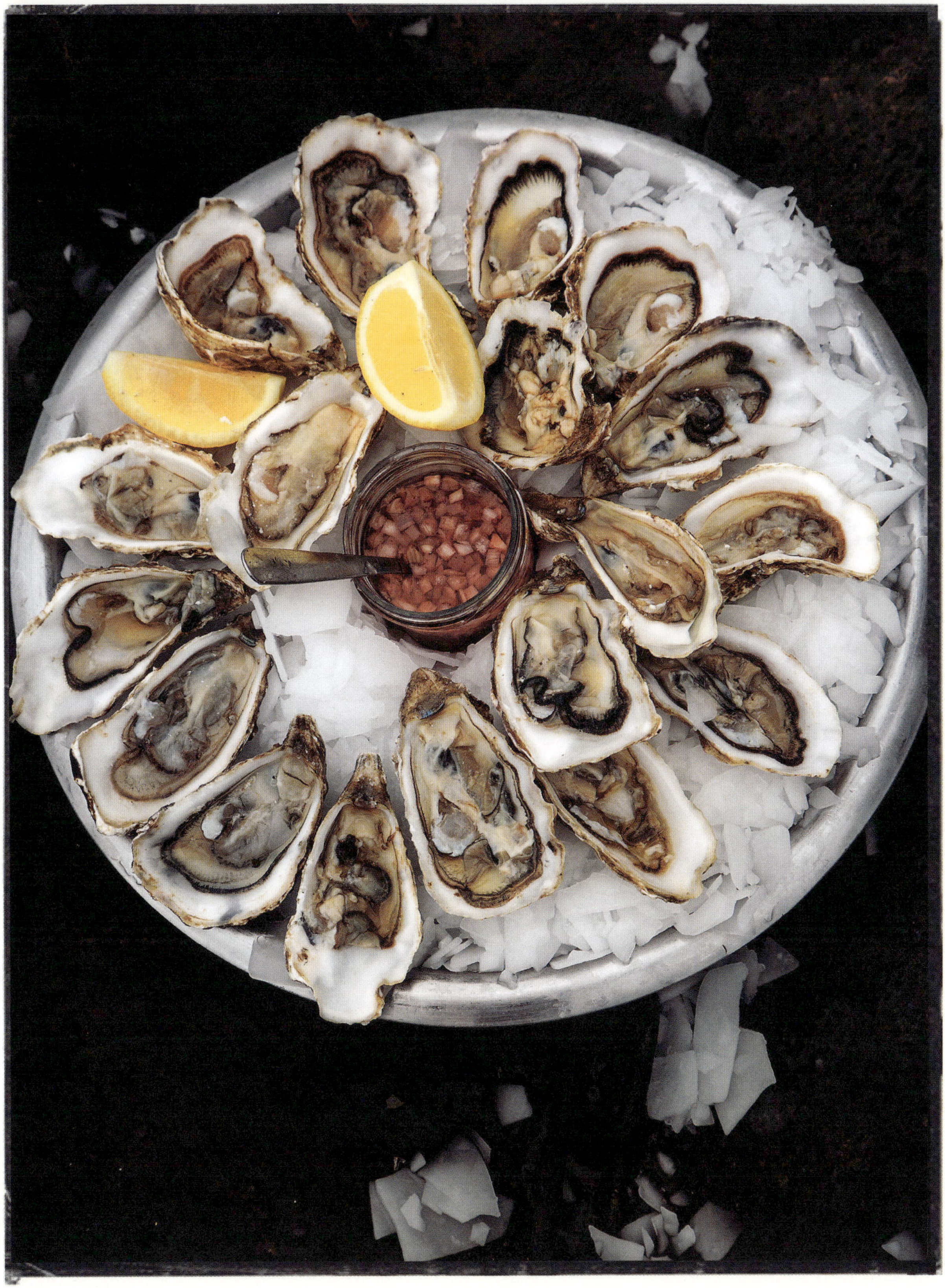

COQUILLAGE GRATINÉE

Normandy's excellent shellfish is presented in many ways: raw, boiled and served with mayonnaise, or gratinéed, as here. You can use whatever shellfish you like – it is nice to have a variety. This is lovely as a starter, served with baguette.

Serves 2

4 oysters, cleaned, in the half-shell
4 scallops, cleaned, in the half-shell
4 medium raw prawns (shrimp), no heads, peeled and deveined, tails left on
12 mussels, scrubbed and de-bearded
4 large clams, ideally Venus
4 tablespoons chopped parsley
1½ teaspoons finely chopped garlic
60g (4 tablespoons) butter
2 tablespoons cream
1 scant tablespoon dry breadcrumbs
salt and freshly ground black pepper

Preheat the oven to 200°C/400°F/Gas 6.

Take 2 oysters from their shells and add one to each of the remaining oysters so that you have 2 oysters in 2 half shells. Do the same with the scallops. Put 2 prawns each into the 2 empty oyster shells.

Put the mussels and clams into a saucepan with 3–4 tablespoons water, cover and cook over a high heat until they all open. Drain, then remove the mussel flesh from the shells.

Put 6 mussels into each of the 2 empty scallop shells. Pluck the clam flesh from their shells, then nestle it back in place.

Put the parsley, garlic and butter into a bowl and season well with salt and pepper. Mash with a wooden spoon. Add the cream and continue mashing until incorporated. Divide the butter mixture between the shells. Sprinkle some breadcrumbs with your fingertips over the tops of each.

Arrange all the shells in a large, shallow baking dish, making sure they are flat and the butter won't leak out. Put in the oven for 15 minutes, or until bubbling, golden and crusty here and there. Serve hot.

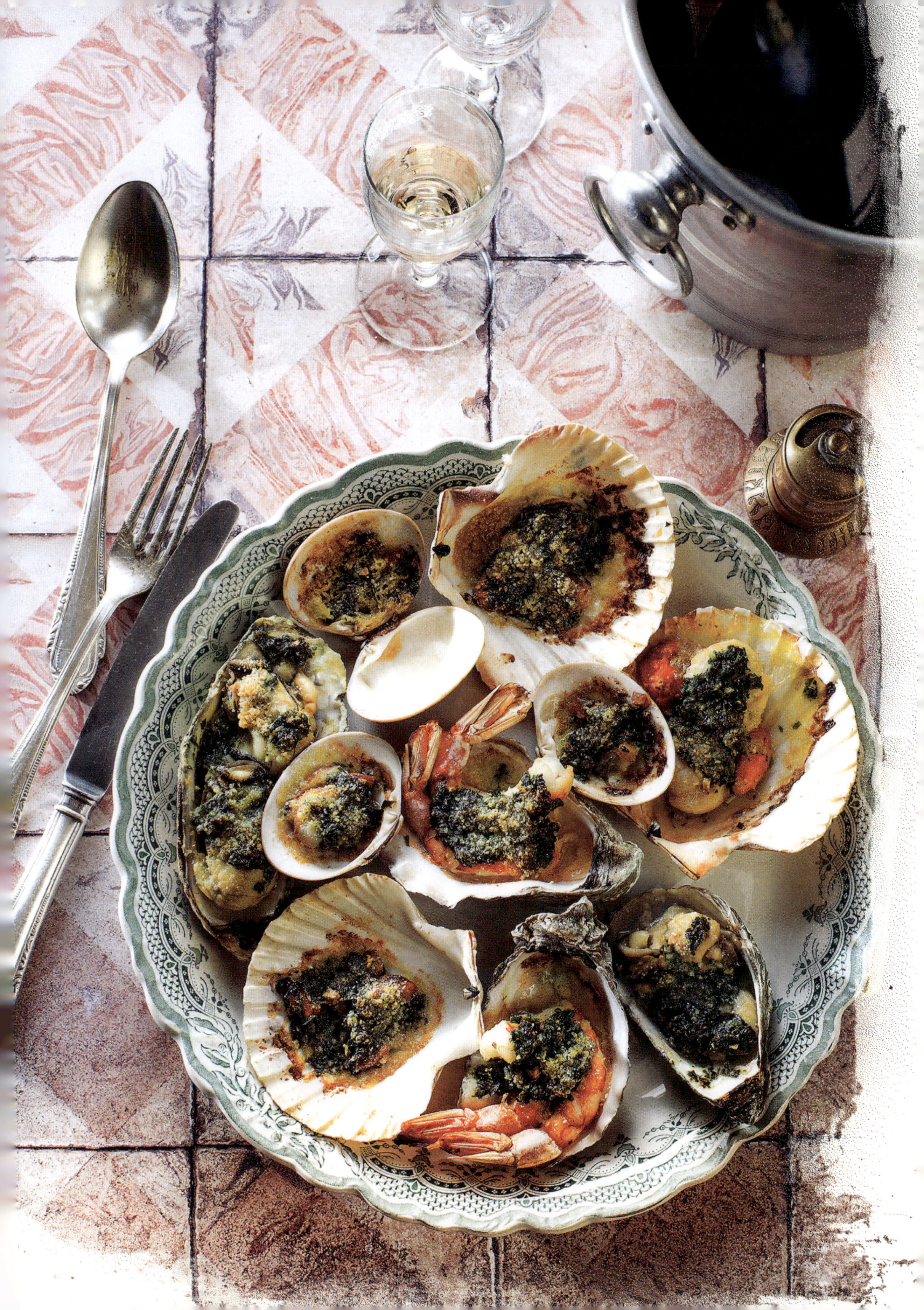

SAINT-JACQUES POÊLÉES

The scallops in Normandy are sweet and plump. Here they are sautéed with apples and cream and served with a celeriac mash. They must be seared quickly in a hot pan, to get a nice crust on the outside and just cook through, yet remain tender inside; take care to avoid overcooking.

Serves 4

For the apples
15g (1 tablespoon) butter
1 crisp apple, such as Boskoop, Reinette or Pink Lady, peeled, cored and cut into 4–5mm (¼in) slices
1 teaspoon sugar
1 tablespoon Calvados

For the scallops
about 12 scallops (depending on size), cleaned, corals retained, in the half shell
15g (1 tablespoon) butter
1 large celery stalk, de-stringed and cut into batons on the diagonal
2 tablespoons Calvados
4 tablespoons cream
salt and freshly ground black pepper
a little chopped parsley, to serve

To prepare the apples, heat the butter in a small non-stick frying pan and add the apple slices. Fry until deep golden on both sides. Scatter in the sugar and cook until the juices caramelize a little, then add the Calvados and simmer for a couple of minutes. Keep warm.

Meanwhile, to cook the scallops, heat a large non-stick frying pan over a high heat, then add the butter. When it is sizzling, add the scallops and celery. Cook the scallops for about 1 minute on each side until they turn opaque and golden crusty on the outside but are still tender inside, and the celery is a little golden but still crunchy. Season with salt and pepper.

Add the Calvados and immediately flambé, standing well back and using a long match (or just let it cook off). Once the flames have died down, transfer the scallops to a plate; keep warm.

Add the cream and 2 tablespoons water to the pan, lower the heat and simmer until the sauce thickens slightly.

Serve the scallops immediately, on a heap of celeriac mash, with a scattering of parsley and a few warm apple slices, a couple of pieces of celery each, and the sauce drizzled around.

PURÉE DE CÉLERI-RAVE

Peel and cube 300g (10½oz) celeriac and 250g (9oz) potatoes and cook in separate pans of boiling, salted water until tender. Drain. Mash the potatoes with 50g (2oz) butter, 2 tablespoons cream and 2 tablespoons milk. Purée the celeriac with a hand-held blender and add to the potato. Mix well, stir in 1 tablespoon lemon juice and check the seasoning, adding pepper to taste and scattering over some crunchy salt.

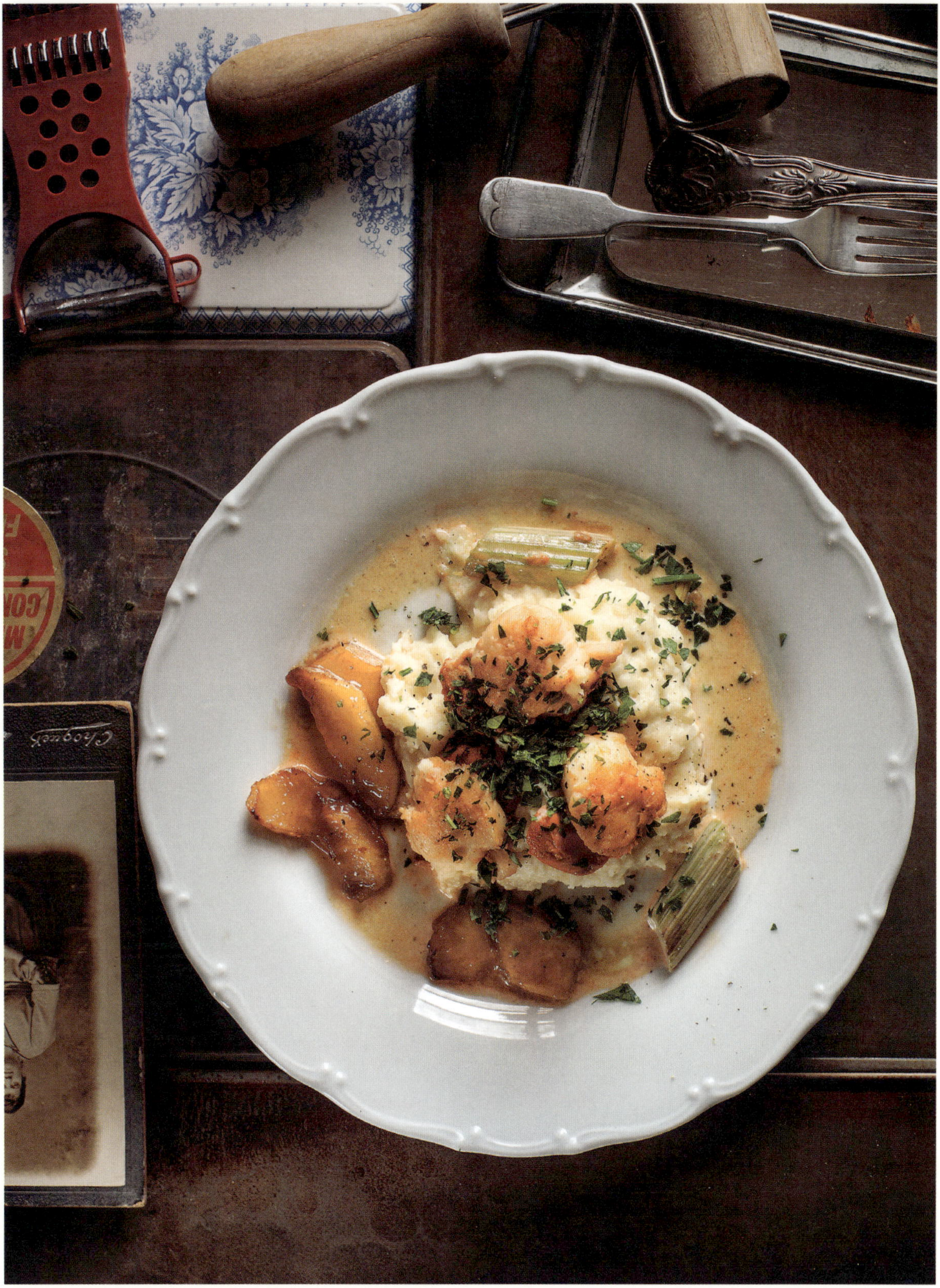

CROUSTILLANT DE CAMEMBERT, LIVAROT ET PONT L'ÉVÊQUE

These three classic Normandy cheeses are wonderful eaten on their own after a meal, but also fried and served with a salad, as here. Depending on what else you will be serving, this could be a starter, or a meal in itself with some baguette. You can use just one type of cheese if you prefer. Have the cheeses chilled in the fridge before you start, so there is less chance of it oozing out as it cooks.

Serves 4

For the dressing
4 tablespoons olive oil
2 tablespoons cider vinegar
1 teaspoon Dijon mustard
salt and freshly ground black pepper

For the salad
4 large handfuls mixed leaves, such as red chicory, curly cress, frisée or escarole
¼ red onion, thinly sliced
1 apple, such as Boskoop, Reinette or Pink Lady, peeled, quartered and fairly thinly sliced
40g (⅓ cup) toasted skinned hazelnuts, coarsely chopped

For the fried cheeses
about 4 tablespoons plain (all-purpose) flour
1 egg, lightly beaten
about 75g (2½oz) dry breadcrumbs
½ Camembert cheese (125g/4oz total weight), cut into 4 slices
½ Livarot cheese, cut into 4 slices
4 slices of Pont l'Évêque cheese, the same size as the other cheese slices
vegetable oil, for shallow-frying

To make the dressing, whisk the ingredients together in a cup or small bowl, seasoning to taste with salt and black pepper.

Divide the salad leaves between 4 plates. Add the onion slices, then the apple slices. Sprinkle the hazelnuts over the top.

Have the flour, breadcrumbs and egg ready in separate shallow bowls. Pat the cheese pieces in the flour first, then coat well with egg, then roll in the breadcrumbs to cover completely.

Over a medium-high heat, heat enough oil in a non-stick frying pan to half immerse the cheese pieces. When hot, add the cheese in small batches and fry until deep golden on all sides and soft on the inside, but without the inside running out. Remove to a plate lined with paper towels to absorb some of the oil.

Drizzle about a tablespoon of the dressing over each salad and put the rest aside for anyone wanting more.

Divide the hot cheeses between the plates so everyone gets a piece of each cheese type. Serve immediately, with good chunks of baguette.

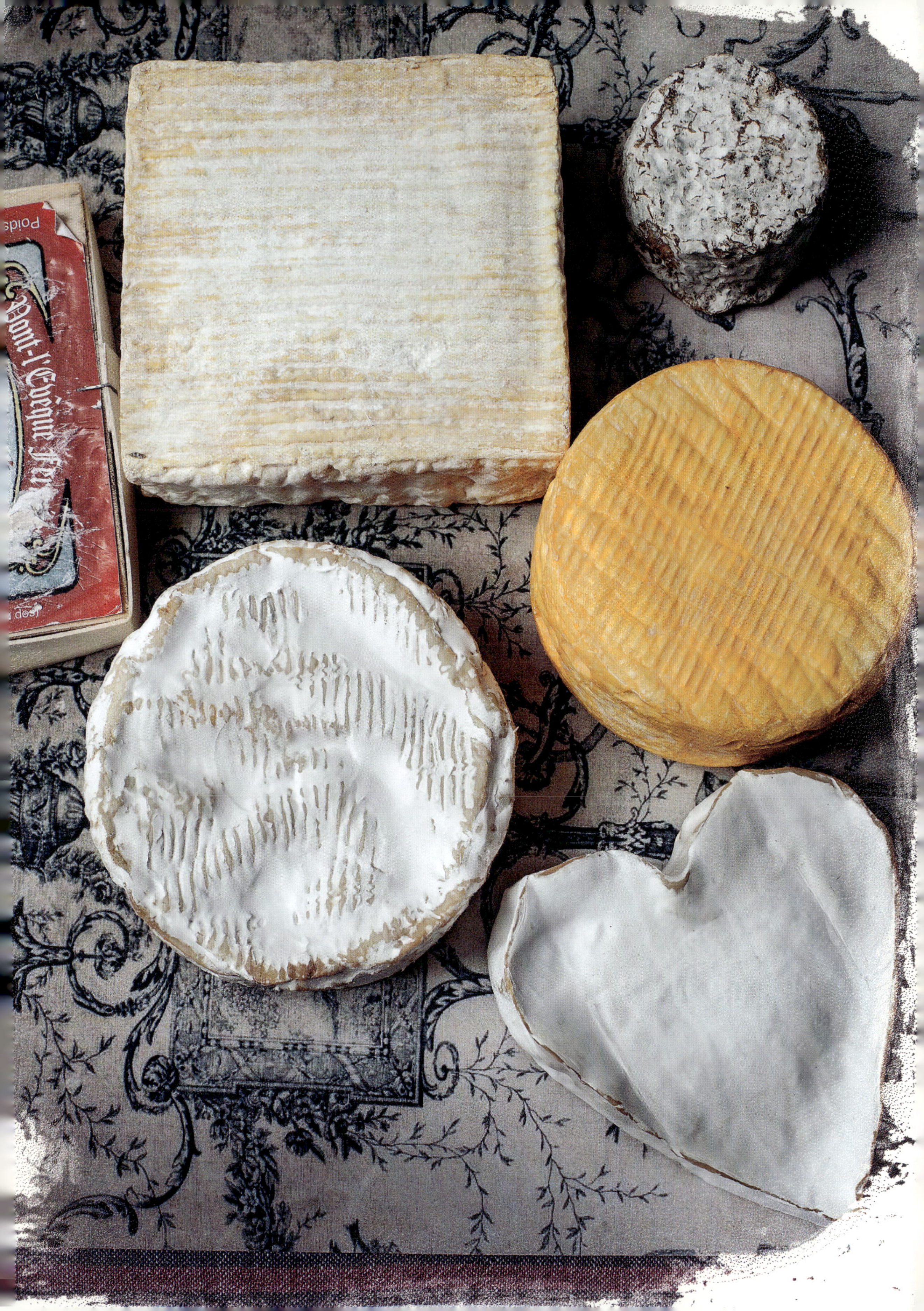
Poids

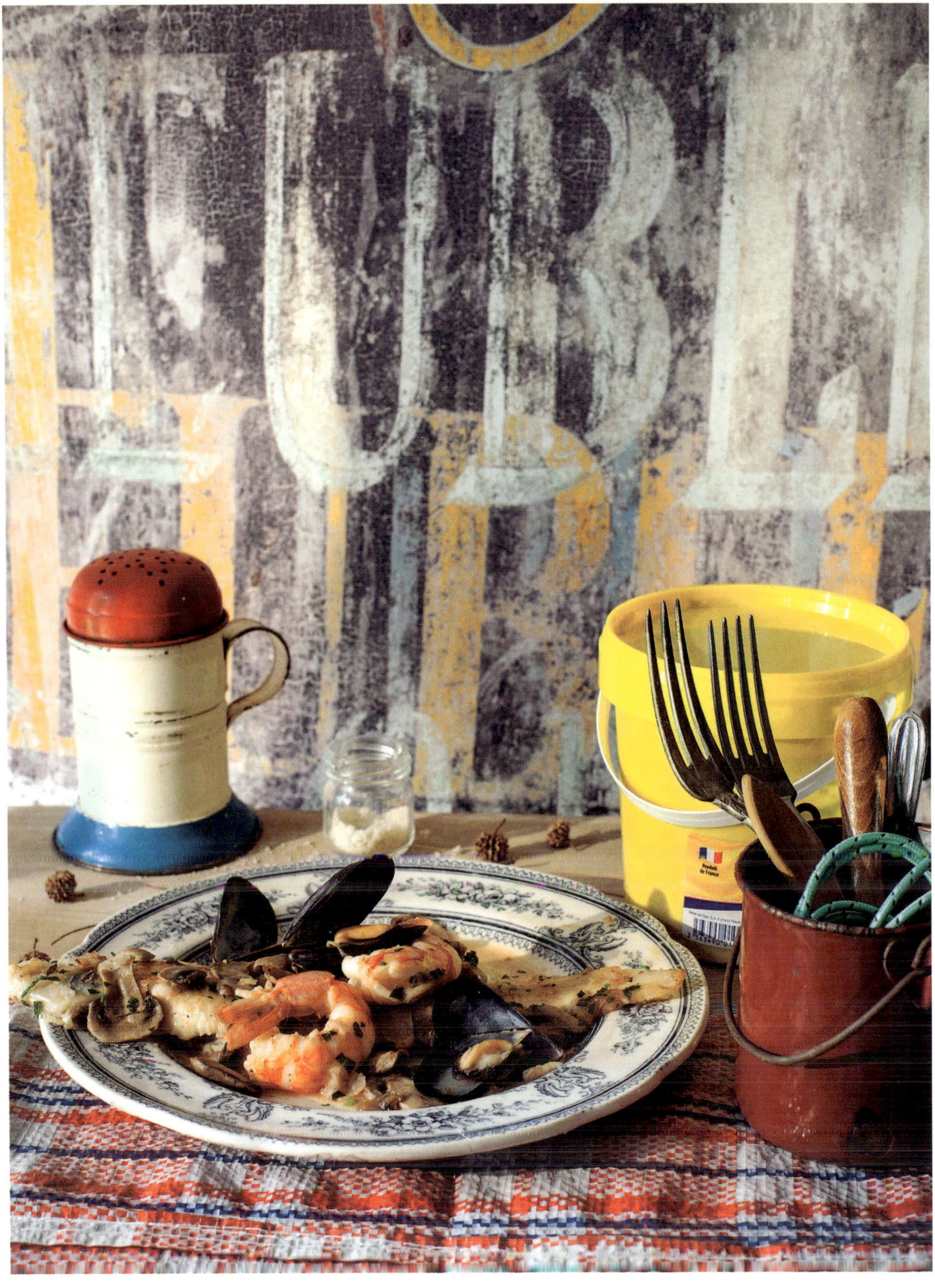

SOLE DIEPPOISE

Sole from Dieppe, and generally all along the coast of Normandy, is considered special. There are several versions of this dish, some more complicated than others, and while this may seem fiddly at a glance, it is actually straightforward. You can add a splash of cream to the sauce if you like, at the end. I like to serve the soles whole, and so cut away all the small fin bone parts along both sides of the soles before cooking, to avoid any stray bones on the plate mingling in the sauce. If you prefer, you can use fillets to start, or serve it filleted.

Serves 2

40g (1½oz) butter
1 small shallot, sliced
160g (1½ cups) button mushrooms, thinly sliced
a small handful plain (all-purpose) flour
2 soles, cleaned
1 tablespoon Calvados
about 125ml (½ cup) cider
a bouquet garni (a few parsley and thyme sprigs and a bay leaf, tied together with string)
4 raw prawns (shrimp), no heads, peeled and deveined, tails left on
10 small mussels, scrubbed and de-bearded
1 tablespoon chopped parsley
salt and freshly ground black pepper

Heat half the butter in a small, non-stick pan, add the shallot and sauté until softened. Add the mushrooms and season with salt and pepper. Cook until all the liquid has evaporated and the mushrooms are lightly golden. Remove from the heat and set aside.

Spread the flour out on a plate. Using kitchen scissors, trim away all the fins and other spiky bits from both sides of the soles. Pat them in the flour to coat both sides well, and shake off the excess.

Melt the remaining butter in a non-stick frying pan large enough to hold both fish, over a medium heat. Add the soles and cook just until pale golden on both sides (the fish will cook further once the other ingredients are added), scattering each side with salt and pepper.

Add the Calvados and let it almost cook out, then add the cider, along with the bouquet garni, and let it bubble up for a couple of minutes.

Tip the mushrooms and shallots over the soles. Add the prawns and mussels to the pan around the soles. Cover and cook over a medium heat for a couple of minutes until the mussels open and the prawns are opaque and cooked through. If it seems too dry add a few drops more cider to the pan.

Scatter over the chopped parsley, remove from the heat and leave to stand with the lid on for a couple of minutes so it all settles.

Divide the seafood between 2 warm plates and serve at once, with a little salt over the prawns, and baguette.

MARMITE DU PÊCHEUR ET BEURRE BLANC AU CIDRE

A marmite is traditionally a deep, pot-bellied casserole with handles, used for long, slow cooking. You can, as I have here, just use a low-sided wide pan and plate the fish to serve, which is how I ate this in Normandy. Use whatever fish you like, even a couple of langoustines, but a variety is good. If you worry that your clams may have sand in, then you can cook them separately in a small pan to open and then add them to the main fish pan just at the end.

Serves 4

500g (18oz) small new potatoes, well scrubbed
200g (7oz) green beans, topped
1 shallot, peeled
1 celery stalk
a bouquet garni (a few parsley and thyme sprigs and a bay leaf, tied together with string)
2 salmon fillets (each about 150g/5½oz)
2 scorpion fish (or cod) fillets (each about 125g/4½oz)
2 plaice (or sole or whiting) fillets (each about 110g/4oz)
2 sea bass (or snapper or John Dory) fillets (each about 150g/5½oz)
4 raw prawns (shrimp), no heads, peeled and deveined, tails left on
8 clams, soaked in cold water
8 mussels, scrubbed and de-bearded
1 tablespoon chopped parsley
salt and freshly ground black pepper
1 quantity beurre blanc au cidre (page 262), to serve

Bring a pan of salted water to the boil. Add the potatoes and cook for 7–8 minutes before adding the beans. Continue cooking until both are tender, then drain and keep warm.

Meanwhile put the shallot, celery and bouquet garni into a large, wide pan (about 32cm/12½in across) and add 250ml (1 cup) water and a good pinch of salt. Bring to the boil.

Add all the fish fillets to the pan in a single layer then sprinkle salt and pepper lightly over them. Cook gently until just opaque, about 4 minutes. Add the prawns, drained clams and the mussels. Put the lid on and cook until the mussels and clams open.

Remove from the heat and leave, covered, for a couple of minutes before serving.

Halve each salmon, scorpion fish, plaice and bass fillet and divide between 4 warmed deep plates. Add a prawn, 2 clams and 2 mussels to each plate. Arrange some potatoes and beans beside the seafood.

Add a scattering of parsley and pepper, with the beurre blanc served in a separate bowl, to dollop generously over the seafood. Serve at once.

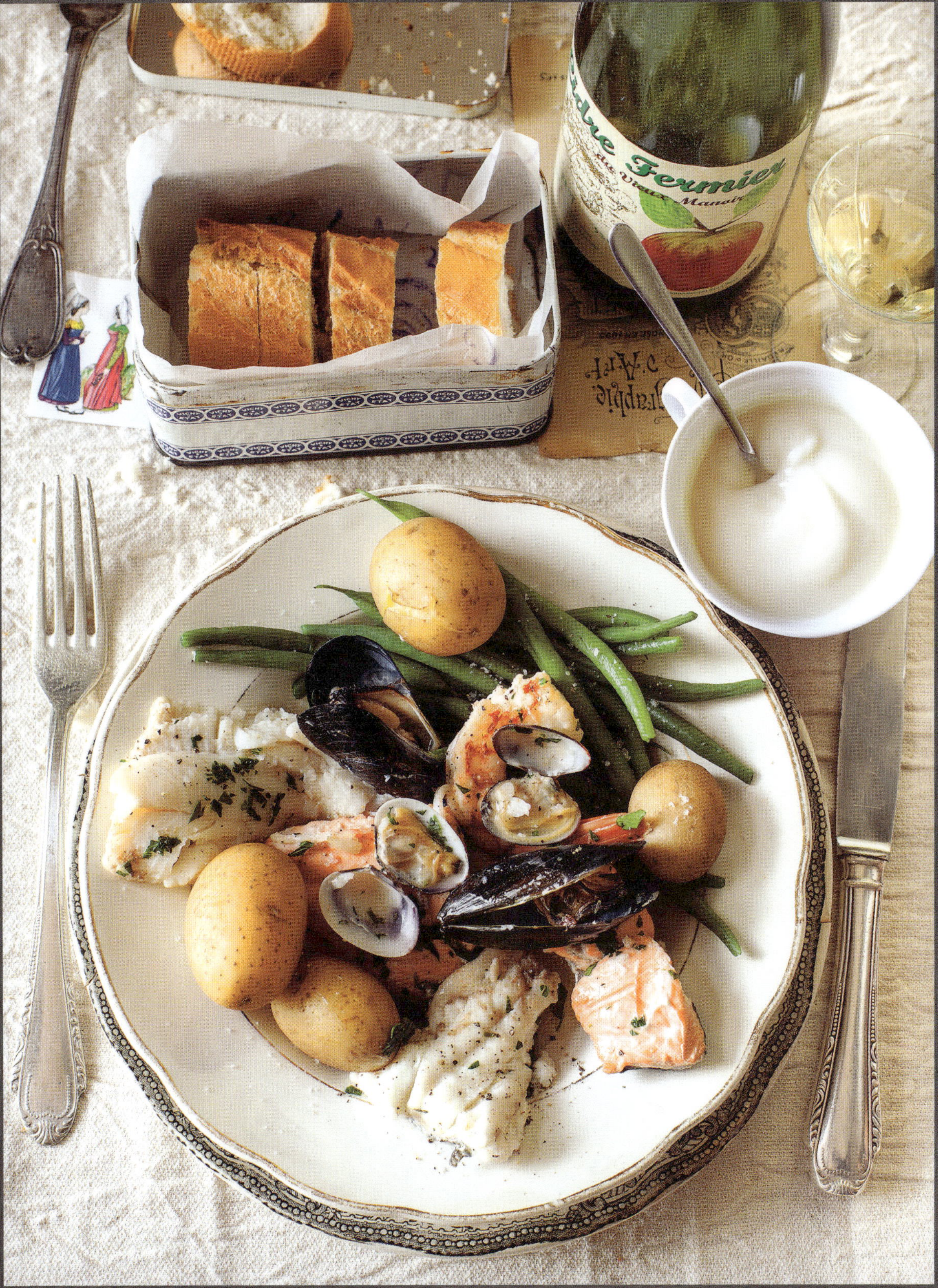
Fermier

BEURRE BLANC AU CIDRE

This typical sauce uses cider in place of white wine, and has cream added. On hot days, rest the plate of chilled butter cubes on a bed of ice cubes as you work – if the butter is allowed to come to room temperature it may melt too quickly and the sauce could split. You could use a bain marie instead of a saucepan on a simmer mat.

Makes about 185ml (¾ cup)

3 tablespoons cider vinegar
3 tablespoons dry cider
2 shallots (about 60g/2¼oz in total), finely chopped
6 black peppercorns
3 tablespoons cream
180g (6oz) unsalted butter, cut into small cubes and chilled
1 tablespoon lemon juice
salt

Put the vinegar, cider, shallots and peppercorns in a small saucepan and bring to the boil over a medium heat. Simmer, uncovered, until reduced by two thirds, so it is about 2 tablespoons. Strain through a fine sieve into a small, clean saucepan, pressing down firmly with a wooden spoon to extract the flavour, then discard the shallots and peppercorns.

Add the cream to the pan and simmer until reduced by about half. Put the pan on a simmer mat over a very low heat and, without letting it boil, start adding the butter, whisking constantly with a balloon whisk. Gradually add it cube by cube, only adding the next cube once the previous one has been totally incorporated. It will take 8–10 minutes for all the butter to be added and the sauce to be rich and smooth, like thick cream. If you feel the sauce is getting too hot and may split, (the cream will help to prevent this) take off the heat and continue whisking until it cools a little.

Remove from the heat and whisk in the lemon juice, then season to taste with salt.

Either serve now, spooned over seafood, or leave to cool down and thicken. Any leftover sauce can be stored in the fridge and is delicious over warm vegetables.

ESCALOPES DE POULET À LA SAUCE CAMEMBERT

This is good with fries, sautéed thinly sliced potatoes, or just a salad. What you decide to accompany it with (and what will come before and after) will determine how many the dish will serve. Leftover sauce is great with cooked vegetables.

Serves 2–4 (depending on accompaniments)

2 large chicken breast fillets (about 450–500g/1lb in total)
4 tablespoons plain (all-purpose) flour
50g (generous ½ cup) dry breadcrumbs
1 egg, lightly beaten
30g (2 tablespoons) butter
1 tablespoon olive oil
250ml (1 cup) cream
125g (4½oz) Camembert (about ½ large one), rind removed as best you can, cut into pieces
sea salt and freshly ground black pepper

Slice the chicken fillets in half horizontally to get 4 thinner escalopes. Trim away any fat, then pound gently to an even thickness.

Spread the flour and breadcrumbs out on separate plates. Season the flour with salt and pepper. Pour the egg into a shallow dish. Pat the escalopes in the flour on both sides to coat, then dip them in the egg, then finally pat in the breadcrumbs, turning to coat completely.

Heat the butter and olive oil in a non-stick frying pan over a medium heat. Add the escalopes and fry until deep golden on the underside, then turn them over and fry the other side until they are cooked through. Sprinkle a little salt on each side once cooked.

Meanwhile, heat the cream in a heavy-based saucepan. When it bubbles, add the Camembert. Simmer, stirring, for a few minutes until smooth and thickened. Purée if there are any lumpy bits.

Serve the escalopes on warmed plates. Spoon the sauce over and around them but don't cover the chicken completely, to retain some of the crispness. Add a grind of pepper and serve.

POULET VALLÉE D'AUGE

A traditional chicken dish made with Normandy's superb produce. It is lovely, sweet and caramelly in flavour. It is nice served with a pile of buttered wide fresh pasta ribbons or a gratin of endives or potatoes.

Serves 4

20g (¾oz) butter
1 chicken (about 1.2kg/2¾lb), cut into 8 pieces
2 apples, such as Boskoop, Reinette or Pink Lady, peeled, cored, each cut into 8 small wedges
3 tablespoons Calvados
500ml (2 cups) cider
4 tablespoons cream
salt and freshly ground black pepper

Melt the butter in a large, wide non-stick frying pan in which all the chicken pieces will fit in a single layer, and which has a lid. Add the chicken and brown until golden on all sides.

Season with salt and pepper and add the apple wedges. Fry them too, over a high heat, so they turn deep golden on both sides, but are still firm.

Add the Calvados to the pan and let it cook off. Gently remove the apples to a plate. Add half the cider to the pan, lower the heat a little, cover and simmer for about 45 minutes, turning the chicken pieces over during this time. Keep an eye on the sauce so that it doesn't burn, and when the liquid has reduced right down, add the rest of the cider. (Turn the heat up if it looks as though there is too much liquid and it hasn't reduced, as you want a lovely caramelly sauce.)

Return the apple wedges to the pan and continue cooking for another 5 minutes or so, still covered, watching that it doesn't caramelize too far – there should still be a nice amount of sauce in the bottom.

Add the cream, rock the pan to distribute then simmer, uncovered, for another 5 minutes.

Taste for seasoning, remove from the heat and leave to stand with the lid on for a few minutes before serving.

GRATIN D'ENDIVES

A lovely accompaniment to any main course, also delicious on its own.

Preheat the oven to 180°C/350°F/Gas 4. Drizzle 2 tablespoons olive oil over the base of an ovenproof dish about 22 x 30cm (9 x 12in). Halve about 6 chicory bulbs lengthways and arrange in the dish in a single layer. Scatter with salt and pepper and dot 40g (1½oz) butter over the top. Cover with foil and bake for 30 minutes.

Remove the foil and drizzle 4 tablespoons cream over the top. Rock the dish a little to distribute the cream, then spoon the juices from the bottom of the dish all over the chicory.

Bake, uncovered, for another 30 minutes, or until golden around the edges. Scatter about 70g (⅔ cup) grated Gruyère over the surface and bake for another 10 minutes, or until the cheese is melted and golden.

LAPIN À LA MOUTARDE ET AU CIDRE

This can also be made using skinned chicken instead of rabbit (it will need a shorter cooking time). It is very good with potato gratin, boiled parsley potatoes or with wide pasta ribbons on the side. Here I add most of the mustard at the start and a tablespoonful at the end, to keep the flavour intense.

Serves 3–4

a small handful plain (all-purpose) flour
1 rabbit (about 1.35kg/3lb), cut into 8 pieces
3 tablespoons olive oil
30g (2 tablespoons) butter
5 garlic cloves, peeled and left whole
a bouquet garni (a couple of bay leaves and a small bundle each of tarragon and parsley, tied together with string)
500ml (2 cups) cider
3 tablespoons Dijon mustard
salt and freshly ground black pepper

Scatter the flour on a plate. Pat the rabbit pieces dry with paper towels, then dust them lightly on all sides with the flour. Shake off the excess flour.

Heat the oil in a large non-stick frying pan, big enough to take all the rabbit pieces in a single layer, and which has a lid. Brown the rabbit over a high heat, seasoning the browned sides as you go. Take care that the flour doesn't burn.

Add the butter and garlic to the pan, cook for a minute or so, then add the bouquet garni and cider. Stir 2 tablespoons of the mustard into the cider. Once it bubbles up, put the lid on, lower the heat to a minimum and simmer for 1 hour, turning the rabbit 2 or 3 times. Towards the end the sauce will start reducing quite rapidly and you might need to add a few tablespoons of water to give a nice sauce consistency; not too runny and not too thick.

Stir the remaining 1 tablespoon of mustard into the sauce. Serve hot, with the sauce spooned over the rabbit.

RÔTI DE PORC AU CIDRE, POMMES ET PRUNEAUX

This is delicious and easier than it may seem. Ask your butcher to cut into the chine so that you are able to cut through the joint to serve individual pork chops. If you prefer, you could cut the meat away from the chine and ribs after roasting and serve in thinner slices (which you can also do the next day with any leftovers). Good with potato or endive gratin.

Serves 6

1 pork rib roast, with 6 chops
3 tablespoons olive oil
1 large onion, halved and fairly thickly sliced
3 apples, such as Boskoop, Reinette or Pink Lady, peeled, cored and each cut lengthways into 8 wedges
about 18 pitted prunes
3 sage sprigs
250ml (1 cup) cider
4 tablespoons cream
salt and freshly ground black pepper

Preheat the oven to 180°C/350°F/Gas 4. Score the pork skin in line with how you will carve, between each chop. Season the meat well with salt and pepper, and rub salt over the skin. You might have to tie it with string to keep it together, depending on how deep the chine cuts are.

Put the oil into a large roasting tin. Sit the pork in the tin, skin side up, and distribute the onion slices around it. Roast for 30 minutes.

Salt and pepper the apple slices. Take the roasting tin from the oven. Using tongs, lift the pork and push any onions already looking very golden underneath, then sit the pork back down over them.

Put the apples, prunes and sage around the pork. Baste the apples with some of the roasting oil. Increase the heat to 200°C/400°F/Gas 6 and roast for 30 minutes.

Remove the tin from the oven; the apples should be golden in places, and cooked. Spoon them onto a plate and keep warm.

Pour the cider around the sides of the pork and return to the oven. Cook for another 25–30 minutes, or until deep golden and crisp on the top. (This will depend on your oven and the size of the joint, so keep a close eye on it and make sure it doesn't get dry and overcooked.) Check that the pork is cooked through by inserting a skewer into the deepest part. The juices should run clear.

Remove the pork, onions and prunes to a plate and keep warm. Add the cream to the tin and put over a medium-high heat to bubble up and combine. If there doesn't seem to be enough sauce, add a little water, but it may not be necessary.

Carve the pork into single chops. Serve on warm plates with a few apple slices, some onions, a couple of prunes, some sauce spooned over the pork and some pepper ground on top.

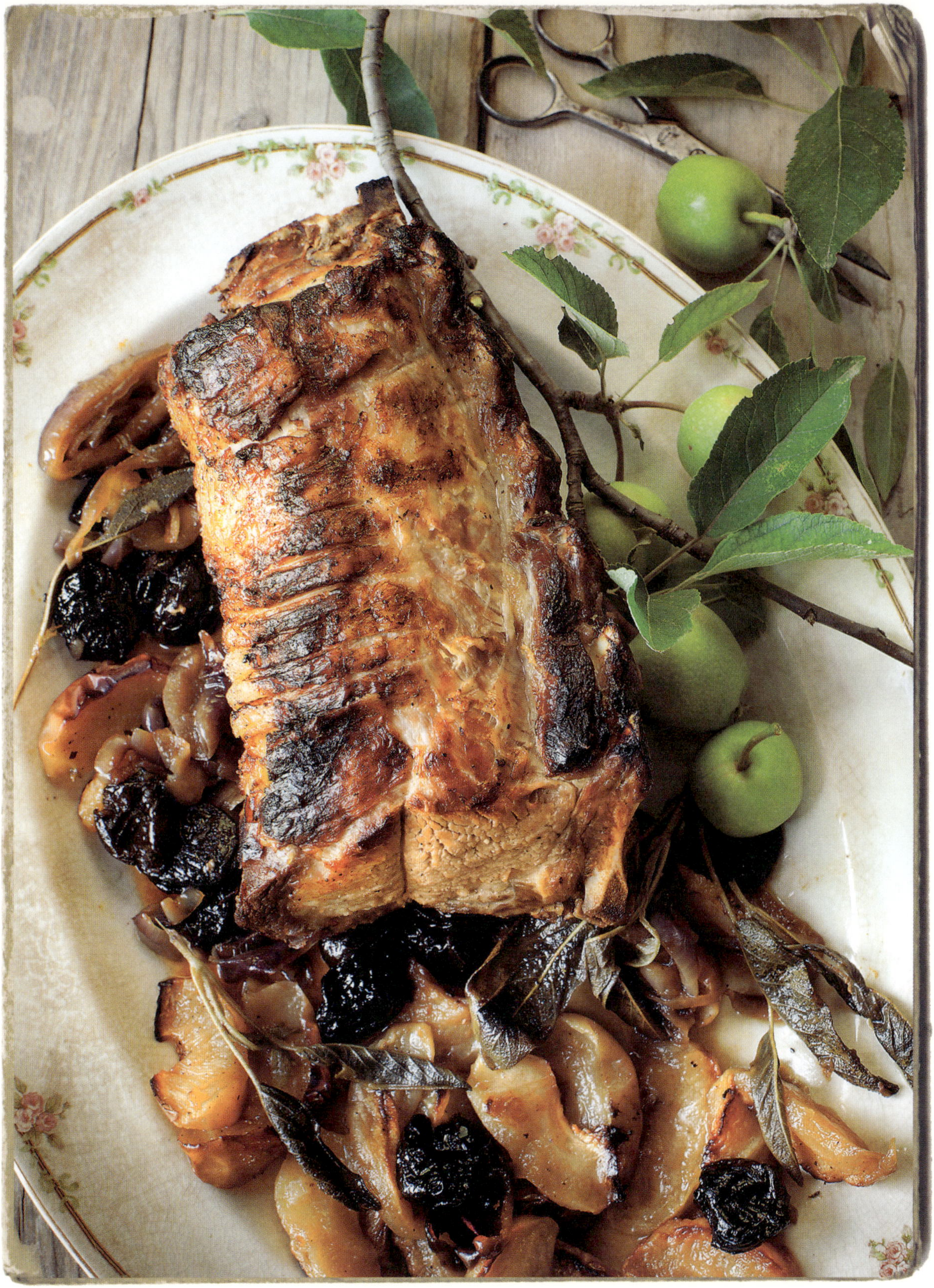

STEAK AU POIVRE ET CALVADOS

This is such a great meal. You need to get the timing of the fries and steak right as they need to be served together, both hot. Bring the steaks out of the fridge an hour or two before you cook them, so they are not cold. I like this with a green salad on the side.

Serves 2

French fries for 2
1 level teaspoon black peppercorns
1 level tablespoon green peppercorns in brine, quickly rinsed
30g (2 tablespoons) butter
2 entrecôte, rib-eye or sirloin steaks, each about 220g (8oz) with some fat
3 tablespoons Calvados
125ml (½ cup) cream
fleur de sel or sea salt flakes

Have the potatoes frying and a plate lined with paper towels to absorb the oil when they are done.

Crush the black peppercorns just a little with a pestle and mortar so they are still in chunky bits. Tip onto a plate. Do the same to the green peppercorns, to just crack most of them, then mix with the black peppercorns.

Heat a non-stick heavy-based frying pan over a high heat. When the pan is very hot (this is important to get a good searing and colour) add half the butter. When sizzling, add the steaks and cook until the undersides are deeply seared, about 2 minutes.

Turn the steaks over and add the remaining butter to the pan. Season the cooked sides with salt flakes and scatter the combined peppercorns over and around. Cook the steaks quickly for about 2 minutes, still over a high heat, until the other side is deep golden. If you prefer them well done, cook for a little longer on each side. Turn the steaks on their sides briefly using a pair of tongs, to sear the fat.

Shake the pan a little and add the Calvados. Standing well back and using a long match, flambé if you like, and allow the flames to subside. Otherwise, just let the alcohol cook out. Remove the steaks to warm plates and keep warm.

Add the cream to the pan. Lower the heat slightly and simmer the sauce for a couple of minutes, scraping the bottom and sides of the pan with a wooden spoon.

Serve the steaks with the sauce spooned over the top generously, and hot fries on the side.

POT AU FEU DE LAURENT

A pot au feu would normally be made with a couple of cuts of beef and marrow and other pieces. My friend Laurent cooked me this version using lamb. The lamb in Normandy is quite special, particularly from the area around Mont Saint-Michel where it feeds on the salty marsh. Serve in deep bowls with the broth, meat and vegetables all together. Or you could start with the broth and follow with the meat and vegetables. Boiled new potatoes in their skins go very well. And cornichons, coarse salt and Dijon mustard on the side.

Serves 4

4 large shallots (about 80g/3oz in total), peeled and left whole
2 or 3 cloves
3 carrots, peeled and halved lengthways
3 parsnips, peeled and halved lengthways
½ small Savoy cabbage, about 300g (10½oz), cut into 4 wedges but intact at the stem
2 celery stalks, halved
40g (1½oz) butter
a bouquet garni (a bay leaf and a few sprigs each of thyme, sage and tarragon, tied together with string)
3 tablespoons olive oil
about 1.3kg (3lb) lamb shoulder, in roughly 5 x 10cm (2 x 4in) chunks
500ml (2 cups) cider
salt and freshly ground black pepper, plus coarse salt or fleur de sel, to serve

Preheat the oven to 180°C/350°F/Gas 4. Stud a couple of the shallots with the cloves. Arrange the vegetables in a large cast-iron casserole dish that has a tight-fitting lid. Sprinkle with salt and pepper and add the butter and bouquet garni.

Heat the oil in a large, non-stick frying pan over a medium heat. Brown the lamb on all sides until nicely deep golden. Salt and pepper the browned sides as you go. Add the cider and let it bubble up.

Transfer to the casserole and gently turn the vegetables through. Put the lid on and bake for about 2 hours, until the lamb is tender and the vegetables golden. Turn through once or twice during cooking, swapping things from bottom to top so each gets a chance in and out of liquid.

Turn the oven off and leave the casserole in the oven for 30 minutes or so before serving.

Serve hot in warm bowls, with cornichons, coarse salt and Dijon mustard on the side.

LA TEURGOULE NORMANDE

This rice pudding is a speciality of the region. Traditionally it is baked in a large earthenware dish and cooked for ages so you can't feel the grains in the rice as they will have almost melted into a purée. Corinne puts butter in hers, and eats it warm. It is her favourite dessert. Here is her recipe.

Serves 6

1.25 litres (5 cups) full-cream (whole) milk
¼ teaspoon vanilla extract
120g (⅔ cup) short-grain (round) rice
80g (scant ½ cup) sugar
20g (¾oz) butter
2 pinches of salt
¼ teaspoon ground cinnamon

Preheat the oven to 150°C/300°F/Gas 2. Bring the milk to the boil in a saucepan with the vanilla. Put the rice (unrinsed) into a fairly deep oval earthenware or ceramic ovenproof dish, roughly 20 x 30cm (8 x 12in). Add the sugar, butter, salt and cinnamon, then pour in the hot milk and stir to combine.

Put the dish into the oven and bake for 30 minutes. Reduce the temperature to 120°C/250°F/Gas ½ and bake for a further 2½ hours. It will have bubbled up and formed a deep gold skin on top, which some people peel off and others eat. Leave to stand and cool a little, then serve warm.

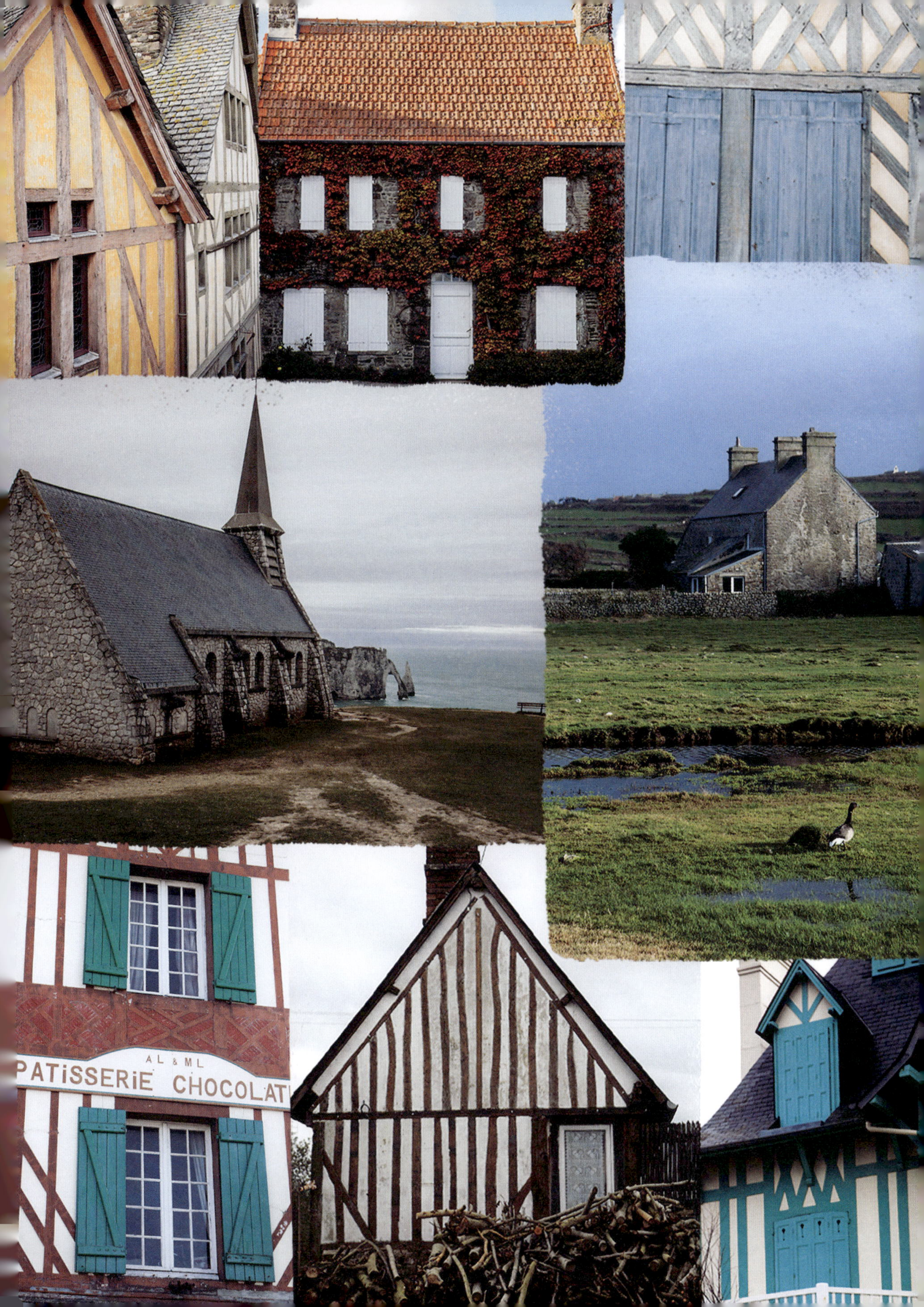
AL & ML
PATISSERIE CHOCOLAT

POTS DE CRÈME AU CARAMEL

Like most people, I think, I love anything with caramel in. You can make meringues with the egg whites, or freeze them for future use.

Serves 5

120g (scant ⅔ cup) sugar
170ml (⅔ cup) milk
330ml (1⅓ cups) cream
4 egg yolks
¼ teaspoon vanilla extract

Preheat the oven to 150°C/300°F/Gas 2. Put the sugar and 2 tablespoons water in a saucepan over a medium-high heat and cook until the sugar melts. Heat, without stirring, until it becomes a lovely golden caramel. Swirl the pan around to distribute the caramel that darkens around the edges first. Take care that the caramel doesn't burn, but it must turn a deep amber colour.

Meanwhile (but without taking your attention too far from the caramel), heat the milk and cream together in a separate saucepan and keep warm. Whisk the egg yolks in a medium-large bowl until pale and thick. Add the vanilla.

When the caramel is deep amber, lower the heat and whisk in a little of the hot milk mixture, being careful as it will splutter. Gradually add the rest and whisk until smooth.

Add this mixture a little at a time to the eggs, whisking continuously (but try not to make too much froth and bubbles).

Strain into a jug and then divide between 5 ramekin pots (125ml/½ cup capacity). Stand the pots in a roasting tin and pour warm water into the dish to come halfway up the sides.

Bake in the oven for 50–55 minutes until set, rotating the baking dish once during this time for even cooking, and covering the dish with foil for the last 10–15 minutes of cooking so they don't get too dark and sticky on top. When done, they will still wobble slightly if you gently shake them, and the tops should be golden brown.

Remove the ramekins from the roasting tin, leave to cool, then refrigerate for at least 2–3 hours before serving just as they are.

SORBET AU CIDRE AVEC SAUCE AU CARAMEL

This refreshing sorbet cuts through anything rich you may have eaten. The amount of sugar you need depends on the cider – I use a sparkling semi-sweet apple cider here. Once the mixture has cooled, taste it and add more sugar if necessary. The sorbet won't freeze too hard and it melts quickly, so have your serving bowls chilled and ready. You can serve it on its own, or with a drizzle of caramel sauce, and a sablé on the side.

Serves 6

For the sorbet
500ml (2 cups) cider
70g (2½oz) sugar
For the caramel sauce
125g (scant ⅔ cup) light brown sugar
2 tablespoons Calvados
150ml (⅔ cup) cream
a few drops of vanilla extract
2 pinches of sea salt flakes
3 tablespoons milk, plus a little extra if needed

To make the sorbet, put the cider and sugar into a saucepan and heat, stirring, just until the sugar dissolves. Remove from the heat and leave to cool, then chill.

Pour into an ice-cream machine and churn according to the manufacturer's instructions until you have a frozen apple snow. Store in the freezer.

If you don't have an ice-cream machine, pour the mixture into a bowl and freeze, beating with a fork every 20–30 minutes, until frozen.

To make the caramel sauce, put the sugar, Calvados and 1 tablespoon water into a heavy-based saucepan. Bring to a simmer over a medium heat and cook, without stirring, to a deep golden caramel. Once the edges start to turn deep golden, swirl the pan around to ensure even cooking. (Any sugar crystals forming on the side of the pan should be brushed away using a pastry brush dipped in hot water – to avoid crystalizing.)

Meanwhile, heat the cream with the vanilla in a small saucepan. When the caramel is an even deep golden colour, whisk in the hot cream bit by bit, taking care as it will initially splash up quite a bit. Simmer for a couple of minutes, then whisk in the salt, remove from the heat and stir in the milk. Allow to cool. If the sauce thickens a lot on cooling, add a little extra milk to thin it down. Give it a whisk before serving.

Serve the cider sorbet scooped into dishes with a drizzle of caramel sauce over and a biscuit on the side if you like. Eat quickly!

TARTE AUX POMMES

You find so many different apple tarts in Normandy and here is a lovely thin one. Boskoop is a good apple to use here if you can get them – they are not too sweet and hold their shape well. I love this tart just warm, on its own, or you could serve it with thick cream.

Makes 1 x 26cm (10in) tart

For the flaky pastry
125g (4 oz) chilled unsalted butter, cut into small cubes
125g (1 cup) plain (all-purpose) flour, plus extra for dusting
a pinch of salt
2 tablespoons chilled water
30g (2 tablespoons) butter, melted and still warm
3 not too big (about 550g/1¼lb total) apples, such as Boskoop, Reinette or Granny Smith
about 60g (2¼oz) sugar
3 tablespoons Calvados

To make the pastry, put the butter, flour and salt into a bowl and rub in the butter with your fingertips until the mixture resembles coarse crumbs. Add the water and mix it in until the pastry comes roughly together.

Roll out on a floured surface to a neat rectangle of about 20 x 30cm (8 x 12in). Fold one third over from the short end to cover the middle third, then fold the remaining third to cover that, as you would fold a letter. Now fold the block of pastry in half, wrap in plastic wrap and chill in the fridge for about 30 minutes. Roll out again to a 20 x 30cm (8 x 12in) rectangle and repeat the folds once more. It is now ready to use or can be kept in the fridge for a couple of days, or frozen.

Preheat the oven to 200°C/400°F/Gas 6.

Brush some of the melted butter over the base and sides of a 26cm (10in) pie or springform tin and sprinkle with flour. Roll out the pastry on a lightly floured surface to a circle a few centimetres (1 inch) larger than the tin diameter. Using your rolling pin to assist, lift the pastry into the tin, easing the sides down and pressing them gently against the sides of the tin. Neaten the edges of the pastry; the sides should be no more than 2cm (¾ in) high.

Peel, halve and core the apples. Slice the halves into 2mm (⅛in) half moons and arrange over the pastry elegantly in concentric circles, starting from the outside and overlapping the slices, working tightly in circles toward the middle. If necessary flatten the slices out with your palms and fill any spaces with leftover apple slices.

Gently brush the surface all over with the warm melted butter, taking care not to drag any of the apples away from their spot. Scatter the sugar evenly over the top. Bake (with a tray underneath if using a springform tin) for about 35 minutes, until golden and caramelized in some places.

Remove from the oven and splash the Calvados here and there over the top. Bake for a further 10 minutes or so, until burnished on the edges and glossy looking. Remove and gently loosen any sugary edges that may have stuck to the sides, using a knife.

Serve the tart warm, in slices. The pastry is fragile so take care when cutting and lifting the slices.

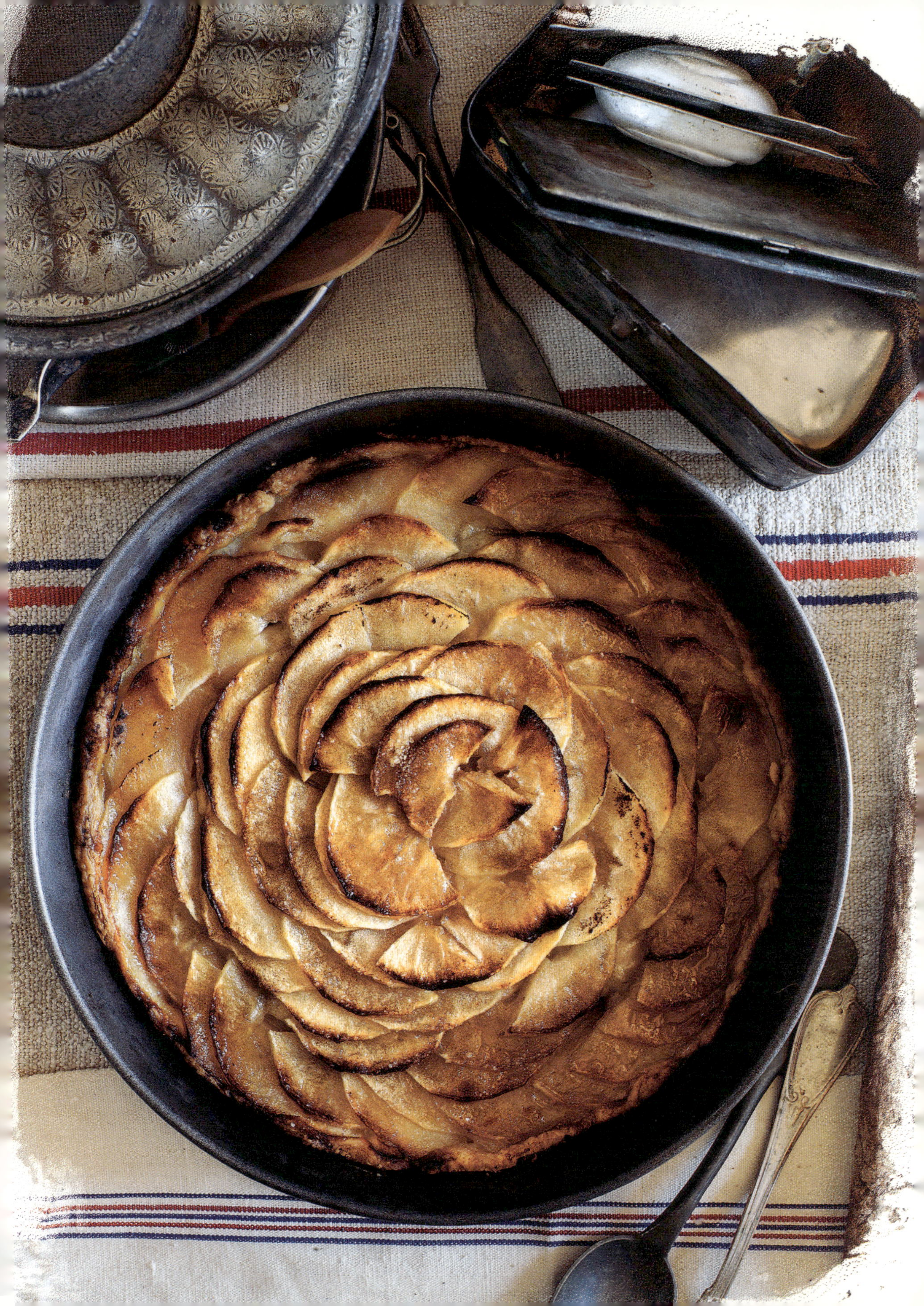

CROISSANTS

Use a top quality butter here (ideally a Normandy butter such as Isigny). Don't be put off by the long-seeming method; it is quite straightforward, but read through the recipe before you start. You will be rewarded with lovely, buttery homemade croissants. Your work space needs to be cool so the butter stays chilled and the pastry manageable. If the dough becomes too soft at any time, chill it for a while before proceeding. Once baked, the croissants can be frozen and then warmed directly in a hot oven to thaw and heat through.

Makes 12

310ml (1¼ cups) tepid milk
1 sachet (7g/1½ teaspoons) dried yeast
3 tablespoons sugar
230g (8oz) plain '00' flour
230g (8oz) strong white bread flour
1 teaspoon salt
250g (9oz) block of unsalted butter, at room temperature
1 egg, lightly beaten with 2 teaspoons water

Stir the milk, yeast and 1 tablespoon of the sugar together in a small bowl. Leave until it starts to foam and bubble on the surface, 15–20 minutes.

Put the remaining sugar, both flours and the salt in a large bowl. Add the yeast mixture and stir with a wooden spoon until a rough dough comes together. Turn out onto the work surface and knead until smooth and elastic, 8–10 minutes. Add a little more flour if needed (of either type), but the dough should be quite soft.

Put the dough back into the bowl. Cover with a cloth and leave for 1½ hours, or until the dough puffs and doubles in size.

Meanwhile, put the butter on a sheet of baking parchment and cover with a second sheet.

Use a rolling pin to bash it out to a 20 x 10cm (8 x 4in) rectangle. Cover with plastic wrap and refrigerate until firm.

Knock the dough down to release air. Knead it briefly to a smooth ball, then roll out to a rectangle 45 x 14cm (18 x 5½in). Place the butter on the lower half of the dough and fold over the top half to cover, so you now have a block roughly 22.5 x 14cm (9 x 5½in). Seal all around the edges to completely encase the butter, keeping the fold the furthest side from you. From top to bottom, gently and evenly (so you don't tear the dough but so the butter is evenly distributed) roll the dough out to 22cm (9in) wide and 45cm (18in) long.

Fold over the top third (short end) and fold up the bottom third to cover the first to give a block roughly 15 x 22cm (6 x 9in). Wrap in plastic wrap and refrigerate for 30 minutes.

Put the pastry block on the work surface with the folded side now to your right. Roll out as before, up and down, to a 45 x 22cm (18 x 9in) rectangle, then fold as before to a 15 x 22cm (6 x 9in) block. Wrap and chill for 30 minutes.

Repeat the process twice more (starting with the fold to your right each time and rolling up and down). By the end, it will have been rolled, folded and chilled 4 times.

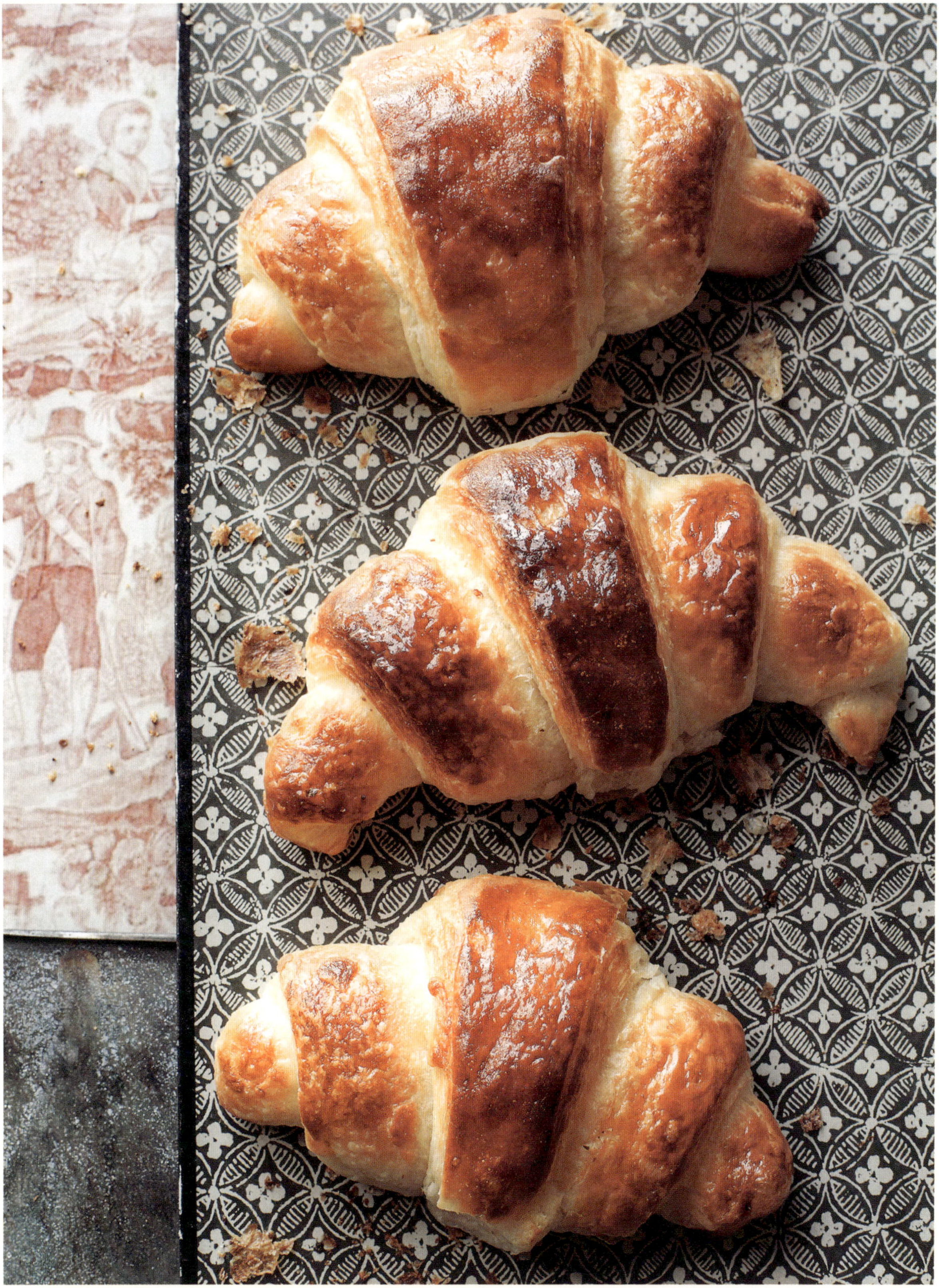

Line 2 baking sheets with baking parchment. It is important that the dough is firm now so chill it for longer if it is not.

Cut the dough in half, to give two blocks, each 15 x 11cm (6 x 4½in). Keep half in the fridge while you roll out the first one. Turn the dough so the cut side with exposed butter layers is facing to your left. Roll out to a rectangle of 40 x 20cm (16 x 8in) then trim so the sides are straight.

Using a sharp knife, divide into 3 rectangles (just over 13cm/5in each). Now cut each rectangle into 2 triangles, to give 6 long triangles in total.

Working quickly, stretch out all 3 points of a triangle to lengthen, particularly the 2 shorter points. Cut a small slit a few millimetres (1/16in) in the middle of the base.

Starting from the base, roll up gently in a fairly tight roll with one hand, with the other stretching the edges to lengthen. Tuck the central point underneath and place on one of the prepared sheets. Angle the ends in towards the point to form a crescent, or leave them straight if you prefer.

Repeat with the remaining triangles, placing them a few centimetres (1½ inches) apart on the tray. Cover loosely with plastic wrap and place in the fridge. Repeat with the second half of dough to shape 6 more croissants, then cover in plastic wrap and chill both sheets for at least 5 hours, or overnight if convenient.

Take the sheets from the fridge and leave covered very loosely with the plastic wrap. Leave in a warm, draught-free place until puffed to almost double their size, anything from 40–90 minutes, depending on the temperature of your kitchen.

At the appropriate time, preheat the oven to 190°C/375°F/Gas 5.

Brush the croissants very gently (so they don't deflate) with the egg glaze. Bake for 15–20 minutes, or until puffed, crisp and golden. Take care not to let them get too crisp and dark, as they will lose their lovely texture. Let the croissants cool for just a short while before eating.

NORMANDY

SABLÉ

You can find several wonderful biscuits made with the rich Normandy butter. You can add some crushed almonds or hazelnuts in here, or some grated lemon or orange zest to take them in a different direction. They are good to have stored in a tin for a snack, or for breakfast – with jam – or serve them with a dessert.

Makes about 28

185g (6½oz) unsalted butter, softened
60g (2¼oz) sugar
½ teaspoon vanilla extract
1 egg, lightly beaten
250g (2 cups) plain (all-purpose) flour, plus extra for dusting
a pinch of salt
¼ teaspoon baking powder

Using an electric mixer, beat the butter and sugar together until pale and glossy. Add the vanilla and half the beaten egg and beat until combined.

Add the flour, salt and baking powder and, by hand, work them in lightly until you have a smooth, soft dough. Don't overwork it. Pat into a disc, wrap in plastic wrap and refrigerate for at least 1 hour.

Preheat the oven to 180°C/350°F/Gas 4. Line 2 baking sheets with baking parchment. Divide the dough in half so it is easier to work.

On a lightly floured surface, roll out one half to a compact, even log 28cm (10½in) long. Using a sharp knife, cut 2cm (¾in) thick discs (you should get 14). Gently flatten them with the heel of your hand to rounds of about 5cm (2in) in diameter (don't worry if they are not all identical). If they lose their roundness, wheel them on their sides along your work surface and straighten out with your other hand.

Put the biscuits onto one of the prepared sheets, leaving a little space between each, and repeat with the remaining dough to shape more, putting them on the second sheet.

Drag the tines of a fork (or sharp knife edge) along the tops of the biscuits to make lines or a criss-cross pattern.

Brush the tops with the remaining beaten egg. (If you prefer more sugary biscuits, you can scatter the tops with a little extra sugar here.) Bake until golden, about 15 minutes.

Cool on wire racks and store in an airtight container.

CARAMELS AU BEURRE SALÉ

These salted caramels are good no matter what – if you cook them a little more or less, it is just a question of chewiness. They are delicious as is – or, once set, can be dipped in melted chocolate and left to set again. Use an authentic Normandy butter if you can. Take care not to burn yourself.

Makes about 25

300g (10½ oz) caster (superfine) sugar
4 tablespoons clear, light honey
250ml (1 cup) cream
70g (5 tablespoons) salted butter
¼ teaspoon fleur de sel, plus extra for sprinkling
1 vanilla pod, split lengthways

Before you cook, measure all the ingredients; you don't want to be distracted when you are keeping an eye on the temperature. Line a rectangular cake or baking tin, about 10 x 20cm (4 x 8in), with baking parchment.

Put 200g (7 oz) of the sugar in a medium, heavy-based pan. Cook over a medium heat, stirring continuously with a wooden spoon, until the sugar dissolves. After this point you may swirl the pot, but do not stir. Continue to cook until amber, allowing the syrup to smoke for a minute or two as the colour deepens, but make sure it doesn't burn.

Lower the heat to a minimum, then carefully stir in the remaining 100g (3½ oz) sugar, the honey and cream. Be careful as the caramel will bubble up. If some clumps form just take it off the heat and stir until they dissolve.

Bring back to the boil over a low heat then simmer for another minute or two. Take the pan off the heat and whisk in the butter and salt.

Add the vanilla pod and return to the heat, with a cooking thermometer. Let it bubble without stirring until just before it reaches 123°C/255°F, which will take up to 20 minutes (if you prefer a softer toffee, remove from the heat just after it reaches 121°C/250°F).

Immediately remove the pan from the heat and swirl it gently until the bubbles subside and the caramel becomes smooth.

Pour the mixture into the prepared tin and remove the vanilla pod with tongs. Leave for 20 minutes or so to cool and begin to set, then sprinkle over a little more fleur de sel if you wish.

It will take a few hours more to set completely, and possibly overnight in hot weather, but after a few hours wrap the tin tightly in plastic wrap and chill in the fridge.

Using the baking parchment to lift it out, put the caramel on a board and, using a large sharp knife, cut into little blocks of about 2 x 4cm (¾ x 1½in), or smaller as you prefer. Wrap individually in pieces of baking parchment.

The caramels will keep for a few days at room temperature if cool, or for up to 2 weeks stored in the fridge.

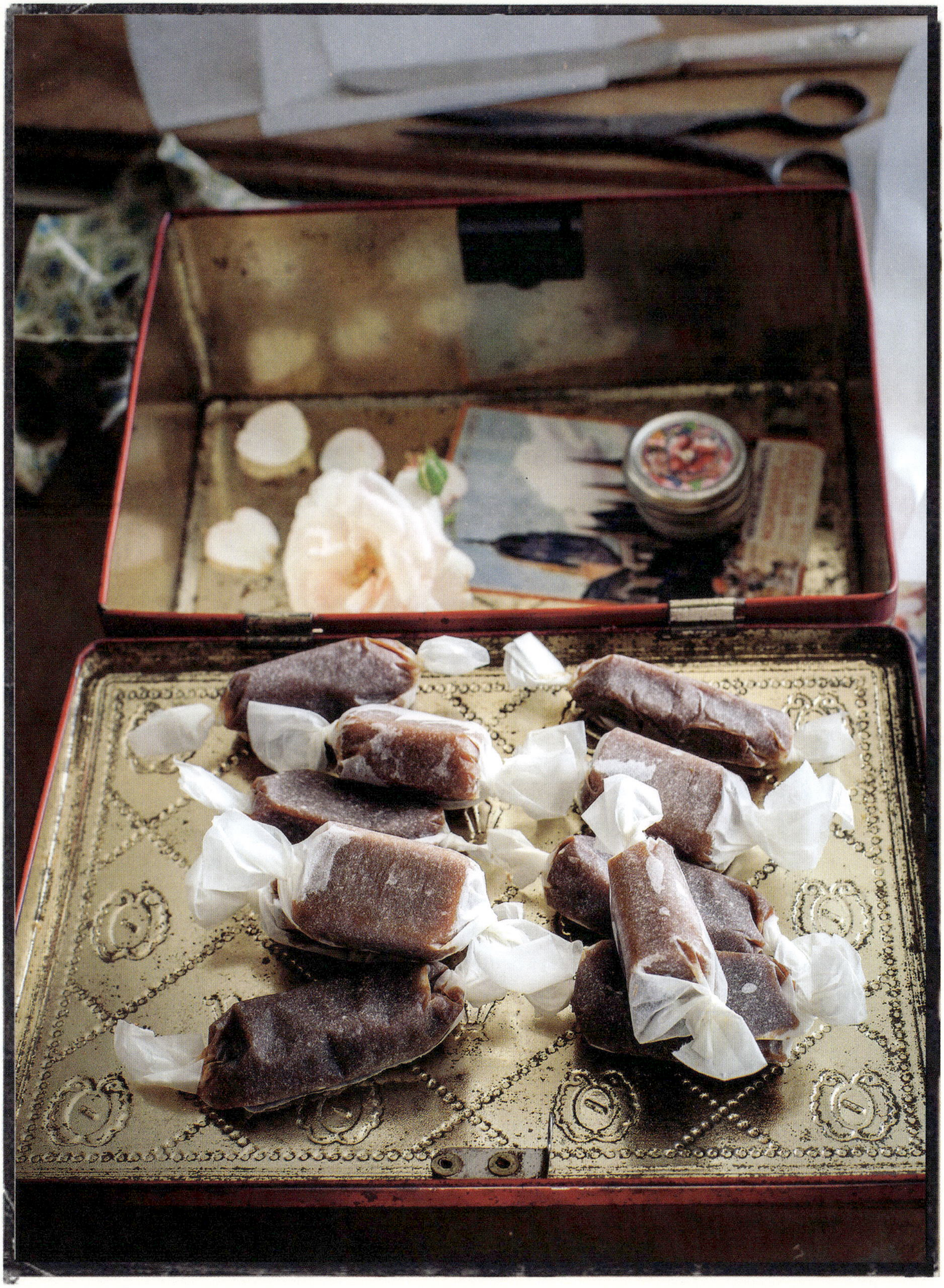

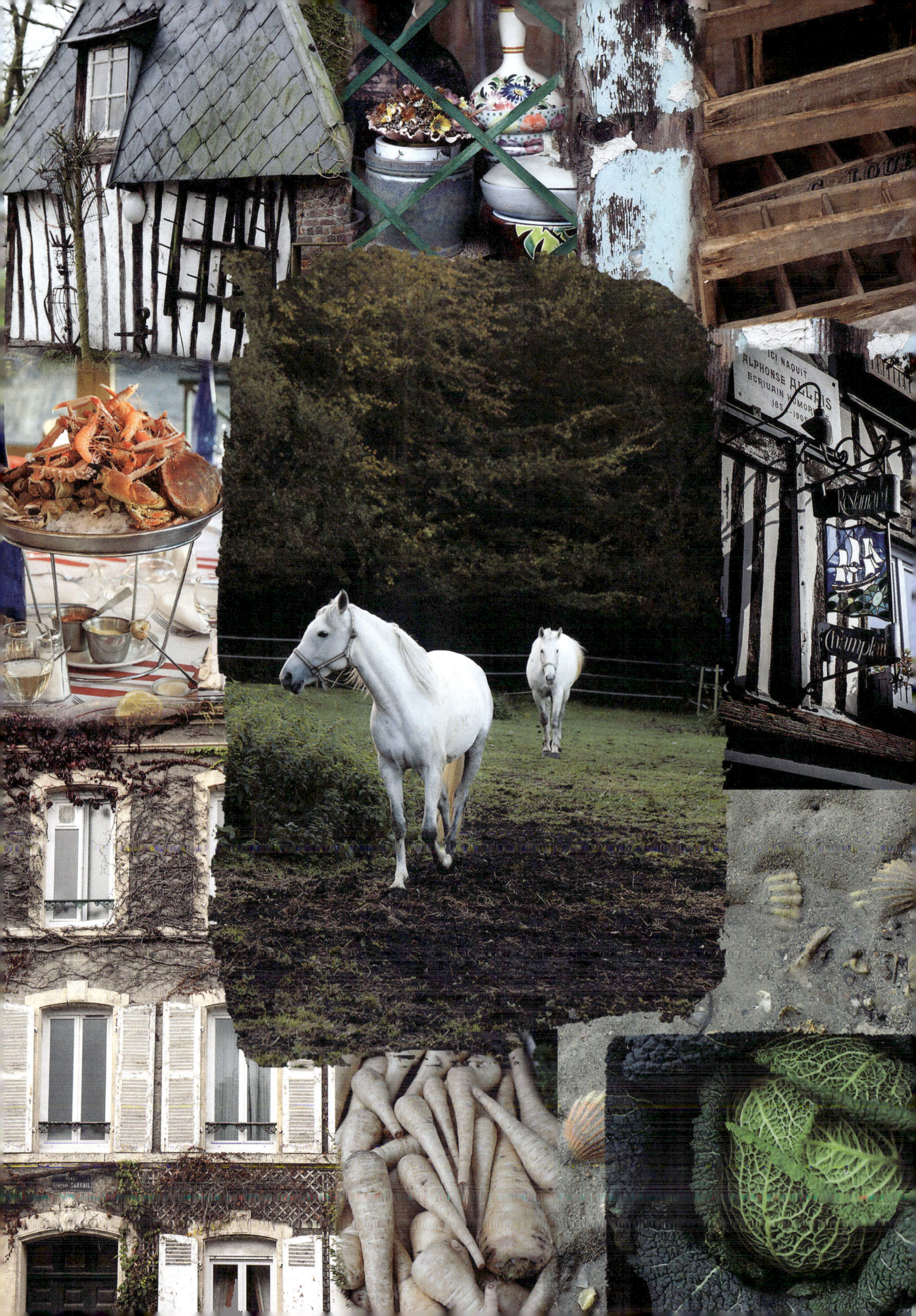
ICI NAQUIT
ALPHONSE ALLAIS
ECRIVAIN
Champlain

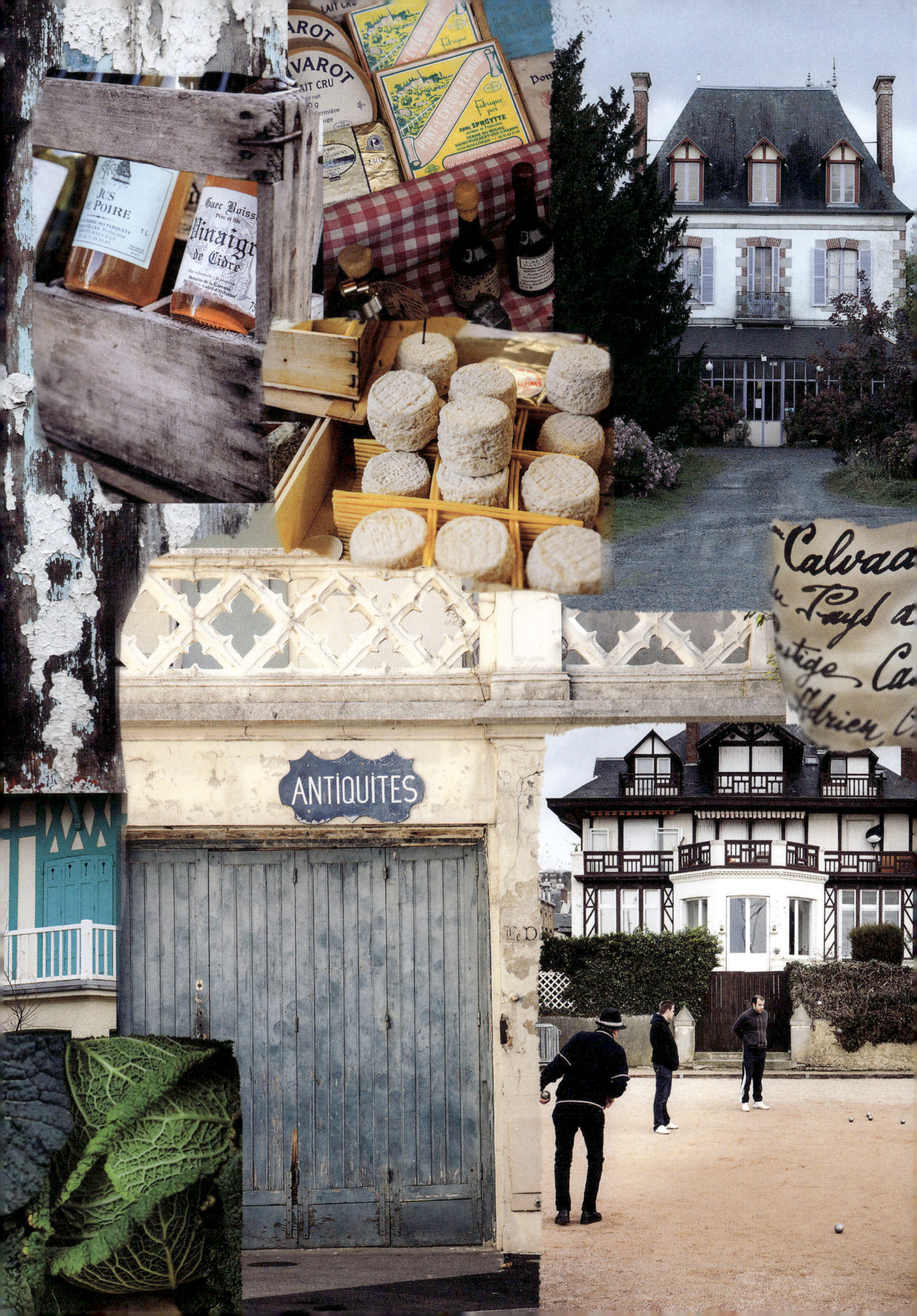
ANTIQUITES

INDEX

A
achards de chouchou 231
acras de morue 62
aïoli 29
almonds:
    sacristains 50–2
anchovies: entrecôte à l'anchoïade 44
    gigot d'agneau aux anchois 38
appams 188
apples: poulet Vallée d'Auge 264
    rôti de porc au cidre, pommes et pruneaux 266
    Saint-Jacques poêlées 254
    tarte aux pommes 274
artichokes: artichauts à la barigoule 40
Ashok's masala prawns 186
aubergines: brinjal curry 173
    ratatouille créole 82

B
baguette 126
    baguette with condensed milk 128
    banh mi 128
bananas: bananes flambée au rhum 88
    blaff de poisson 70
banh mi 128
bean sprouts: bun bo 108
beans: bonbons piment 206
    riz et haricots rouge 78
béchamel sauce 230
beef: bo bit tet 122
    bo sot vang 120
    bun bo 108
    daube de boeuf 41
    entrecôte à l'anchoïade 44
    Joelle's soupe des habitants 79
    morning glory and beef salad 116
    pho bo 104
    steak au poivre et Calvados 268
beurre blanc au cidre 262
beurre rouge 76
biscuits: sablé 279
black beans: che 135
blaff de poisson 70
blettes au gratin 35
bo bit tet 122
bo sot vang 120
bonbons piment 206
bouchons 209
bouillabaisse 25–6
brandade de morue 27
bread: baguette 126
    baguette with condensed milk 128
    banh mi 128
    chapati 164
    pan bagnat 17
breadfruit fries 60
brèdes 223
brinjal curry 173
bun bo 108
bun cha 110
butter: beurre blanc au cidre 262
    beurre rouge 76
    ghee 158
butter (lima) beans: bonbons piment 206
buttermilk, spiced 154

C
cakes: gâteau de patate douce 232
    plantation chocolate cake 91
canard à la vanille 226
caramel: caramel au beurre salé 280
    coconut caramels 88
    crème brûlée passion et vanille 236
    lemongrass crème caramel 136
    pots de crème au caramel 272
    sauce au caramel 273
cardamom pods:
    cardamom coconut cream 188
    cardamom rice pudding 196
    masala tea (chai) 196
cari de thon au combava 218
carrot and daikon pickle 100
Catherine's rougail saucisses 228
celeriac: purée de céleri-rave 254
chai 196
chanh muoi 102
chapati 164
che 135
cheese: croustillant de Camembert, Livarot et Pont L'Évêque 256
    escalopes de poulet à la sauce Camembert 263
    gratin d'endives 264
    gratin de papaye vert 230
    macaroni au gratin 34
    paneer 158
chicken: colombo de poulet 75
    escalopes de poulet à la sauce Camembert 263
    Pondicherry chicken 190
    poulet à l'ail 32
    poulet au mangue 224
    poulet au poivron, fenouil et olives 33
    poulet Vallée d'Auge 264
chicken liver and pork pâté 125
chicory: gratin d'endives 264
chilli: fruit with salt and chilli 138
    pâte de piments 211
    sweet chilli sauce 209
chocolate:
    plantation chocolate cake 91
    tarte au chocolat et passion 87
chouchous, achards de 231
chutney: chutney de tamarin 210
    coconut chutney 155
    coriander chutney 154
    tomato chutney 155
cider: beurre blanc au cidre 262
    kir normand 248
    lapin à la moutarde et au cidre 265
    moules au cidre 248
    poulet Vallée d'Auge 264
    rôti de porc au cidre, pommes et pruneaux 266
    sorbet au cidre 273
clementines, crispy duck with kumquats and 114
coconut: coconut caramels 88
    coconut chutney 155
    sorbet à la noix de coco 84

tarte à la noix
  de coco 86
coconut cream:
  cardamom coconut
    cream 188
  che 135
  iced coconut
    coffee 132
  sticky rice with
    coconut and
    ginger 138
coconut milk:
  appams 188
  coconut payasam 175
  punch de coco 211
cod: poisson massale
  en poêle 221
  see salt cod
coffee, iced coconut 132
colombo powder 76
  colombo de poulet 75
condensed milk,
  baguette with 128
coquillage gratinée 252
coriander leaves:
  coriander chutney 154
  coriander rice 161
  lamb with coriander
    and mint 191
coriander seeds: colombo
  powder 76
court-bouillon de
  poisson 66
crème brûlée, passion et
  vanille 236
crème caramel,
  lemongrass 136
crème de cassis: kir
  normand 248
crème Chantilly 48
crème glace nougat 48
croissants 276–8
croustillant de
  Camembert,
  Livarot et Pont
  L'Évêque 256
cucumber: raita 151
  ratatouille créole 82
  rougail
    concombre 215
cumin seeds: grains
  à roussir 76
curd 158

curd rice with lemon
  pickle 162
curry: brinjal curry 173
  cari de thon au
    combava 218
  Pondicherry
    chicken 190
  Pondicherry fish
    curry 184
  poriyal 172
  potato and onion
    curry 183
  spinach curry 169
  vegetable curry with
    coconut milk 171

D
daikon (white radish):
  carrot and daikon
    pickle 100
dal 168
daube de boeuf 41
dosas: egg dosa 180
  potato dosa 180
drinks: chanh muoi 102
  iced coconut
    coffee 132
  kir normand 248
  lassi 194
  masala tea (chai) 196
  punch de coco 211
  rhum arrangé
    maison 212
  spiced buttermilk 154
  sweet mango lassi 194
  ti'punch 64
duck: canard à la
  vanille 226
  crispy duck with
    clementines and
    kumquats 114
dumplings:
  bouchons 209

E
eggs: egg dosa 180
  Thuong's spring onion
    omelette 124
entrecôte à
  l'anchoïade 44
escalopes de poulet à la
  sauce Camembert 263

F
fennel: loup de mer au
  fenouil et pastis 30
  poulet au poivron,
    fenouil et olives 33
fish: bouillabaisse 25–6
  marmite du
    pêcheur 260
  Pondicherry fish
    curry 184
  see also red snapper,
    salt cod etc
fish sauce: nuoc cham 98
flaky pastry 86, 274
frangipane:
  sacristains 50–2
fritters: acras de
  morue 62
  bonbons piment 206
fruit: fruit with salt and
  chilli 138
  gratin de fruits
    exotiques 238
  see also apples;
    mangoes etc

G
garlic: aïoli 29
  garlic and ginger
    paste 149
  poulet à l'ail 32
  vadavam 149
gâteau de patate
  douce 232
ghee 158
gigot d'agneau aux
  anchois 38
ginger: garlic and
  ginger paste 149
  sticky rice with
    coconut and
    ginger 138
goyaviers: rhum arrangé
  maison 212
  sorbet de goyaviers 234
grains à roussir 76
gratin d'endives 264
gratin de fruits
  exotiques 238
gratin de papaye vert 230
gratin de pommes de
  terre 43

green leaves: brèdes 223
gros piments, rougail 215
guavas, strawberry see
  goyaviers

H
herbes de Provence 17
les huîtres et vinaigrette
  d'échalote 250

I
ice cream: crème glace
  nougat 48
  rose milk kulfi 192
iced coconut coffee 132
idli 178

J
Joelle's soupe des
  habitants 79

K
kaffir limes: rhum
  arrangé maison 212
kir normand 248
kulfi, rose milk 192
kumquats, crispy duck
  with clementines
  and 114
kuzhambu thool 148

L
lamb: gigot d'agneau
  aux anchois 38
  lamb with coriander
    and mint 191
  pot au feu de
    Laurent 269
langouste flambée au
  vieux rhum 64
lapin à la moutarde
  et au cidre 265
lapin au thym, ail et
  lardons 34
lassi 194
  sweet mango lassi 194
lemon: lemon pickle 150
  lemon rice 161
  rougail citron 214
  tarte au citron 46
lemongrass crème
  caramel 136

lentils: lentilles de Cilaos 219
limes: chanh muoi 102
  lime, salt and pepper dipping sauce 100
  rhum arrangé maison 212
liver: chicken liver and pork pâté 125
lotus seeds: che 135
loup de mer au fenouil et pastis 30
lychees: rhum arrangé maison 212

M
macaroni au gratin 34
Madame Clotilde's court-bouillon de poisson 66
mangoes: mango patchadi 160
  poulet au mangue 224
  rougail mangue verte 215
  sweet mango lassi 194
marmite du pêcheur 260
masala mix 148
  Ashok's masala prawns 186
  mussels with masala 156
masala tea (chai) 196
mayonnaise: aïoli 29
milk: curd 158
  masala tea (chai) 196
  paneer 158
  rose milk kulfi 192
  la tergoule normande 270
mint relish 151
morning glory and beef salad 116
moules au cidre 248
moules au combava 204
moules frites à fruit à pain 60
moules au pistou 16
mushrooms: sole Dieppoise 259
mussels: moules au cidre 248
  moules au combava 204
  moules frites à fruit à pain 60
  moules au pistou 16
  mussels with chilli, lime, lemongrass and coconut 102
  mussels with masala 156
  sole Dieppoise 259

N
noodles: bo sot vang 120
  bun bo 108
  bun cha 110
  crispy spring rolls 112
  pho bo 104
nougat: crème glace nougat 48
nuoc cham 98

O
olives: pistounade 19
  tapenade 19
omelette, Thuong's spring onion 124
onions: pissaladière 20
  potato and onion curry 183
  rougail oignon 215
oranges: rhum arrangé maison 212
oysters: les huîtres et vinaigrette d'échalote 250

P
palm hearts: salade de palmiste 231
pan bagnat 17
pancakes: appams 188
  egg dosa 180
  potato dosa 180
paneer 158
papayas: gratin de papaye vert 230
passion fruit: crème brûlée passion et vanille 236
  rhum arrangé maison 212
  tarte au chocolat et passion 87
pasta: macaroni au gratin 34
pastis 16
pastries:
  croissants 276–8
  sacristains 50–2
  samosas au thon 208
pastry 22, 46
  bouchon (won ton) pastry 209
  flaky pastry 86, 274
  pâte sablée 87
pâte de piments 211
pâte sablée 87
pâte de tamarin vert 210
pâtés: chicken liver and pork pâté 125
  warm pâté with sticky rice 125
peanuts, roasted crushed 98
peppers: Catherine's rougail saucisses 228
  ratatouille créole 82
  rougail gros piments 215
  rouille 25–6
pho bo 104
pickles: carrot and daikon pickle 100
  lemon pickle 150
pigeon peas: pois d'angole 78
pissaladière 20
pistou 16
pistounade 19
plantation chocolate cake 91
pois d'angole 78
poisson grillé et sauce créole 69
poisson massale en poêle 221
Pondicherry chicken 190
Pondicherry fish curry 184
poriyal 172
pork: banh mi 128
  barbecued lemongrass pork 130
  bouchons 209
  bun cha 110
  chicken liver and pork pâté 125
  crispy spring rolls 112
  ragoût de porc, yam et pois d'angole 77
  rôti de porc au cidre, pommes et pruneaux 266
  stove-top garlic and spice pork 131
pot au feu de Laurent 269
potatoes: bo bit tet 122
  brandade de morue 27
  gratin de pommes de terre 43
  potato and onion curry 183
  potato dosa 180
  purée de céleri-rave 254
  purée de patate à la vanille bourbon 222
pots de crème au caramel 272
poulet à l'ail 32
poulet au mangue 224
poulet au poivron, fenouil et olives 33
poulet Vallée d'Auge 264
prawns, Ashok's masala 186
prunes: rôti de porc au cidre, pommes et pruneaux 266
pumpkin: ratatouille créole 82
punch de coco 211
purée de céleri-rave 254
purée de patate à la vanille bourbon 222

Q
quail, chargrilled marinated 113

R
rabbit: lapin à la moutarde et au cidre 265

lapin au thym,
  ail et lardons 34
ragoût de porc, yam et
  pois d'angole 77
raita 151
rasam, tomato 174
raspberry coulis 48
ratatouille créole 82
red beans: riz et haricots
  rouge 78
red snapper: blaff de
  poisson 70
  Madame Clotilde's
    court-bouillon de
    poisson 66
  poisson grillé et sauce
    créole 69
relish, mint 151
rice: cardamom rice
  pudding 196
  colombo powder 76
  coriander rice 161
  curd rice with lemon
    pickle 162
  idli 178
  lemon rice 161
  riz et haricots rouge 78
  sticky rice with
    coconut and
    ginger 138
  la tergoule
    normande 270
  warm pâté with sticky
    rice 125
  white rice 160
rice flour: appams 188
riz et haricots rouge 78
rose milk kulfi 192
rôti de porc au cidre,
  pommes et
  pruneaux 266
rougail 214–15
rougail saucisses 228
rouille 25–6
rum: bananes flambée au
  rhum 88
  langouste flambée au
    vieux rhum 64
  punch de coco 211
  rhum arrangé
    maison 212
  ti'punch 64

S
sablé 279
sacristains 50–2
Saint-Jacques
  poêlées 254
salads: croustillant de
  Camembert, Livarot et
  Pont L'Évêque 256
  morning glory and
    beef salad 116
  pan bagnat 17
  salade de palmiste 231
salt, sesame 99
salt beef: Joelle's soupe
  des habitants 79
salt cod: acras de
  morue 62
  brandade de morue 27
sambar 170
samosas au thon 208
sausages: Catherine's
  rougail saucisses 228
scallops: Saint-Jacques
  poêlées 254
sea bass: loup de mer au
  fenouil et pastis 30
sesame salt 99
shallots: fried shallots 99
  vadavam 149
shellfish: coquillage
  gratinée 252
sole Dieppoise 259
sorbets: sorbet au
  cidre 273
  sorbet de goyaviers 234
  sorbet à la noix de
    coco 84
  sorbet de tamarin 234
soups: che 135
  Joelle's soupe des
    habitants 79
spices: colombo
  powder 76
  grains à roussir 76
  kuzhambu thool 148
  masala mix 148
  vadavam 149
spinach curry 169
spring onion
  omelette 124
spring rolls 112

squid with lime salt
  and pepper 103
steak au poivre et
  Calvados 268
sticky rice with coconut
  and ginger 138
stove-top garlic and
  spice pork 131
strawberries: rhum
  arrangé maison 212
strawberry guavas see
  goyaviers
sugar, vanilla 113
sweet potatoes: gâteau
  de patate douce 232
Swiss chard: blettes
  au gratin 35

T
tamarind: chutney
  de tamarin 210
  pâte de tamarin
    vert 210
  sorbet de tamarin 234
tapenade 19
tapioca: che 135
tarts: pissaladière 20
  tarte au chocolat et
    passion 87
  tarte au citron 46
  tarte à la noix de
    coco 86
  tarte aux pommes 274
  tarte à la tomate 22
tea: masala tea (chai) 196
la tergoule
  normande 270
thali 166
Thuong's spring onion
  omelette 124
tian de légumes 35
ti'punch 64
tomatoes: Catherine's
  rougail saucisses 228
  rougail tomate 214
  tarte à la tomate 22
  tomato chutney 155
  tomato rasam 174
toor dal: dal 168
  sambar 170
tuna: cari de thon au
  combava 218

pan bagnat 17
samosas au thon 208

V
vadavam 149
vanilla: canard à la
  vanille 226
  crème brûlée passion
    et vanille 236
  purée de patate à la
    vanille bourbon 222
vanilla sugar 113
vegetables: aïoli 29
  Joelle's soupe des
    habitants 79
  poriyal 172
  ratatouille créole 82
  tian de légumes 35
  vegetable curry with
    coconut milk 171
vermicelli: coconut
  payasam 175

W
won ton pastry 209

Y
yams: ragoût de porc,
  yam et pois d'angole 77
yogurt: lassi 194
  raita 151
  sweet mango lassi 194

Thank you to the many who helped create this book.

Manos and Michail, I am so grateful to you both for your vision and the fun. Jo Glynn, thank you for your patient recipe testing and extraordinary help. I have enjoyed all of it immensely.

Thank you Arielle – for your sensitivities and your breath of air. To all at Quadrille – thank you for your hard work – and to Helen and Simon for holding it all together. Jane, thank you for this opportunity. Felicity, thank you for your support, and Emma, for your help.

In Guadeloupe, thanks to Jeanne and Philippe, Moise, Joelle, Nicole, Almira. To Mme Evelyne Verge-Depre and Francieuse Charles (Pharmacie de la Plage Boulevard in Saint Anne). And to Madame Clotilde (Chez Tatie Clotilde in Sainte Anne) I am especially grateful for your openness, help and knowledge.

In Provence, thank you Jean-Marie, Francoise and Sebastien from Patisserie Bergèse in Saint-Remy-de-Provence for your kindness and help. Thank you Fanny and Moussa from Filles du Patissier in Saint-Remy. And Monsieur Miane Rogeur Coiffeur in Saint-Remy. Thank you also Vincent from Bistrot du Paradou in Paradou for advice.

Prior to my Vietnam journey, thank you Sharlee Gibb and Erica K, and Intrepid Tours for inviting me at that moment. I treasure these instances of serendipity.

In Vietnam, thanks to Tracey Lister, Ms Nguyen Dzoan Cam Van, chef Quang, Jessica, Thuy Do, Thuong, Mrs Dong and Loi with all recipe help and advice, and to Kanh Dinh for being a fantastic tour guide.

In Pondicherry, thank you to Ranjit Kumar and to chef D. Ashok at Hotel de l'Orient for your very valuable help. Thanks also to Rupesh Kumar, Shan Karan, Shandal, Jayanthi and to Mr Singh for inspiration.

In Réunion, thank you to Michel, Fatma, Tahera, Catherine, Marie, Micheline, Yolaine, chef Mattieu, Jean-Hugue and Reinne for your recipes, suggestions and enthusiastic help.

In Normandy, to Corinne, and to Laurent, thanks for your time and knowledge.

Thank you Luisa for your assistance – I very much appreciate it all. Thank you Rebecca – trusted patissier. Renato, Agnese and Luigi Casini, Sulla and Roberto, Lisa G, Artemis, Leontine, Peta, Laura, Claudia,

Anjalika, Bell, Mario, Wilma – thank you for all your various help and encouragement, and to Sue and to Richard Pflederer for your enthusiasm, advice and valuable historical wisdom. A grand thank you to Lisa McG for tirelessly reading all of it and for champagne and cheesecake encouragement all the way.

To my family Giovanni, Yasmine and Cassia, thanks for rolling with it always so well – I very much value your every word. Thank you Anais for your special help and to Ludi and Nin. Mom and dad, thanks for being there always, for your support and all that you do.

To all those who helped along the way with suggestions, recipes and information – I am extremely grateful for your precious gifts.

Publishing Consultant: Jane O'Shea
Creative Director: Helen Lewis
Designer: Arielle Gamble
Editors: Janet Illsley and Simon Davis
Photographer: Manos Chatzikonstantis
Stylist: Michail Touros
Food Editor: Jo Glynn
Production: Stephen Lang and Vincent Smith

First published in 2016 by
Quadrille Publishing
Pentagon House
52–54 Southwark Street
London SE1 1UN
www.quadrille.co.uk
www.quadrille.com

Quadrille is an imprint of Hardie Grant
www.hardiegrant.com.au

Text © Tessa Kiros 2016
Photography © Manos Chatzikonstantis 2016
Design and layout © Quadrille Publishing 2016

The rights of the author have been asserted. All rights reserved. No part of this book shall be reproduced, stored in a retrieval system, or transmitted by any means – electronic, mechanical, photocopying, recording, or otherwise – without written permission from the publisher.

Cataloguing in Publication Data: a catalogue record for this book is available from the British Library.

ISBN: 978 184949 723 7

Printed in China